French Films, 1945–1993

French Films, 1945–1993

A Critical Filmography of the
400 Most Important Releases

by MELISSA E. BIGGS

McFarland & Company, Inc., Publishers
Jefferson, North Carolina, and London

British Library Cataloguing-in-Publication data are available

Library of Congress Cataloguing-in-Publication Data

Biggs, Melissa E., 1967–
    French films, 1945–1993 : a critical filmography of the
400 most important releases / by Melissa E. Biggs.
      p. cm.
    Includes bibliographical references (p.).
    ISBN 0-7864-0024-2 (lib. bdg. : 50# alk. paper) ∞
    1. Motion pictures — France — Evaluation — Catalogs.
2. Motion pictures — France — Plots, themes, etc. I. Title.
PN1993.5.F7B52   1996
016.79143′75′094409045 — dc20   95-10539
                                        CIP

Manufactured in the United States of America

McFarland & Company, Inc., Publishers
  Box 611, Jefferson, North Carolina 28640

To my grandmother, from whom I get
my little bit of French ancestry,
and to my mother and father,
who have supported and encouraged
my love of France

Table of Contents

I believe in the possibility of entertaining friendship and in the difficulty of maintaining love. I believe in the value of effort. And I believe above all in Paris. In my work I do not want to prove anything except that life is stronger than everything else.

— JACQUES BECKER

Introduction

The first French film I saw was Albert Lamorisse's *The Red Balloon*. The first view I had of Paris was riding a barge up the Seine in the falling light of early June. Skirting the tip of Ile-Saint-Louis, we came upon Notre Dame from behind, its arches and gargoyles, at once somber and spirited, like the lesson of the red balloon. Would that all introductions to a culture were so seductive. From the first sight of the red balloon bobbing above the steep gray steps of Montmartre to the view of the Seine at dusk, France has always been to me an aesthetic wrapped inside a culture wrapped inside an aesthctic. The essence of the country, her art, and her cultural enthusiasm is nowhere better expressed than in her movies.

There is a French saying about how opinionated the French are, which applies particularly to French film — given a worthy subject, everyone and their butcher has an opinion. As film comment is a national pastime, the proverbial man on the street in Paris has more to say on the subject of the seventh art than most graduate film students in other countries. I say this in part to explain the passion from which the art springs, but also as a form of disclaimer.

I wanted this book to serve the dual purpose of a definitive reference work and as an all-purpose film guide. Not everyone would agree with all of my choices. Certainly any cinéphile worth his *Cahiers du Cinéma* subscription would complain that I have left out some national treasure and have included in its place an embarrassment, but I wanted to be representative, as well as inclusive. So I didn't put in every film by Godard, while I did include some commercial hits; they all make up part of the story of the past fifty years in French film.

From *Les Enfants du paradis* (*Children of Paradise*), which was made in the shadows of the Occupation and opened as Paris was liberated, just as Carné had wished, to *Les Nuits fauves* (*Savage Nights*), the first major cinematic exploration of AIDS, French history and French films cannot be separated. The social and cultural upheavals of the nation are reflected in her art, just as her art has reacted to World War II and the riots of 1968.

Since 1945, French films have risen to world dominance and faltered to a point where they now need government protection to compete against

1

Hollywood. At their best, French filmmakers have established cinéma-vérité, mastered literary filmmaking and film noir, invented the New Wave, flirted with thrillers, and produced such unique and unclassifiable geniuses as Truffaut and Tati. I have tried to reflect as a broad and complete a range of this legacy as possible.

In all of these films, I have glimpsed that flicker of France. In the tilt of Monsieur Hulot's pipe, in Catherine Deneuve's sly smile, in Jean-Paul Belmondo's tearing around Paris in a stolen car, there is that same somber spiritedness that, to me, is France.

—MELISSA E. BIGGS
December 1995

Selected Bibliography

Armes, Roy. *French Cinema*. New York: Oxford University Press, 1985.
_____. *French Cinema Since 1946. Volume One: The Great Tradition*. London: Zwemmer, 1966.
_____. *French Cinema Since 1946. Volume Two: The Personal Style*. London: Zwemmer, 1966.
Bessy, Maurice, and Raymond Chirat. *L'Histoire du cinéma français: Encyclopédie des films 1940–1950*. Paris: Éditions Pygmalion, 1986.
_____, _____, and André Bernard. *L'Histoire du cinéma français: Encyclopédie des films 1951–55*. Paris: Éditions Pygmalion, 1989.
_____, _____, _____. *L'Histoire du cinéma français: Encyclopédie des films 1956–60*. Paris: Éditions Pygmalion, 1990.
_____, _____, _____. *L'Histoire du cinéma français: Encyclopédie des films 1961–65*. Paris: Éditions Pygmalion, 1991.
_____, _____, _____. *L'Histoire du cinéma français: Encyclopédie des films 1966–70*. Paris: Éditions Pygmalion, 1992.
Blanchet, Christian. *Claude Chabrol*. Paris: Éditions Rivages, 1989.
Boiron, Pierre. *Pierre Kast*. Paris: Éditions Pierre Lherminier, 1985.
Bonnaffons, Elisabeth. *François Truffaut*. Lausanne: Éditions l'Âge d'Homme, 1981.
Braucourt, Guy. *Claude Chabrol*. Paris: Éditions Seghers, 1971.
Buache, Freddy. *Le Cinéma français des années 70*. (Bibliothèque du Cinéma.) Lausanne: Héliographia, 1990.
Cahiers du Cinéma, various issues.
Chardère, Bernard. *Claude Autant-Lara en 33 films: Une exposition*. Lyon: Institut Lumière, 1983.
Chirat, Raymond. *La Quatrième République et ses films*. (Bibliothèque du Cinéma.) Lausanne: Hatier, 1985.
Cinéma, various issues.
Collet, Jean. *François Truffaut*. Paris: Lerminier, 1985.
Dictionnaire des Films under the direction of Bernard Rapp and Jean-Claude Lamy. Paris: Larousse, 1990.
Dubois, Colette. *La Maman et la putain de Jean Eustache*. Crisnée, Belgium: Éditions Yellow Now, 1990.
Durgnat, Raymond. *Luis Buñuel*. Berkeley: University of California Press, 1967.
Écran, various issues.
Estève, Michel. *Agnès Varda*. Paris: Lettres Modernes: Études Cinématographiques, 1991.

Fanne, Dominique. *L'Univers de François Truffaut*. Paris: Éditions du Cerf, 1972.
Films and Filming, various issues.
Flot, Yonnick. *Les Producteurs: Les Risques d'un métier*. (Bibliothèque du Cinéma.) Lausanne: Hatier, 1986.
Frydland, Maurice. *Roger Vadim*. Paris: Éditions Seghers, 1963.
Guérif, François. *François Truffaut*. Paris: Edilig, 1988.
Guitry, Sacha. *Le Cinéma et moi*. Paris: Éditions Ramsay, 1977.
Higginbotham, Virginia. *Luis Buñuel*. Boston: Twayne, 1979.
Insdorf, Annette. *François Truffaut*. New York: Simon & Schuster, 1989.
Jeanclos, Jean-Pierre. *Le Cinéma des Français: La Cinquème République (1958–1978)*. Paris: Editions Stock, 1979.
Jeune Cinéma, Oct.–Nov. 1986.
Knapp, Bettina L. *Sacha Guitry*. Boston: Twayne Publishers, 1981.
Lefevre, Raymond. *Luis Buñuel*. Paris: Edilig, 1984.
Magny, Joël. *Claude Chabrol*. Paris: Cahiers du Cinéma Collections, 1987.
Michalczyk, John J. *The French Literary Filmmakers*. Cranbury, N.J.: Associated University Presses, 1980.
Mitry, Jean. *Filmographie universalle: L'École française, 1930–1960*. Volume 27. Bois d'Arcy: Publications du Service des Archives du Film du Centre National de la Cinématographie, 1986.
_____. *Filmographie universalle: L'École française, 1940–1970*. Volume 28. Bois d'Arcy: Publications du Service des Archives du Film du Centre National de la Cinématographie, 1986.
_____. *Filmographie universalle: L'École française, 1950–1980*. Volume 29. Bois d'Arcy: Publications du Service des Archives du Film du Centre National de la Cinématographie, 1986.
_____. *Filmographie universalle: L'École française, 1960–1980*. Volume 30. Bois d'Arcy: Publications du Service des Archives du Film du Centre National de la Cinématographie, 1986.
_____. *Filmographie universalle: L'École française, 1960–1980*. Volume 32. Bois d'Arcy: Publications du Service des Archives du Film du Centre National de la Cinématographie, 1986.
Monaco, James. *The New Wave: Truffaut, Godard, Chabrol, Rohmer, Rivette*. New York: Oxford University Press, 1976.
Paris, James Reid. *The Great French Films*. Secaucus, N.J.: Citadel, 1983.
Positif, various issues.
Philippon, Alain. *André Téchiné*. Paris: Cahiers du Cinéma Auteur Séries, 1988.
Prédal, René. *Le Cinéma français depuis 1945*. Paris: Éditions Nathan, 1991.
_____. *Jean-Pierre Mocky*. Paris: Éditions des Quatre-Vents, 1988.
La Revue du Cinéma, various issues.
Roud, Richard. *Cinema: A Critical Dictionary. The Major Filmmakers*. Volumes 1–2. London: Secker & Warburg, 1980.
Sabria, J.C., and J.P. Busca. *L'Index du film français*. Paris: Cinéma de France SARL, 1985.
Sadoul, Georges. *Chroniques du cinéma français 1939–1967*. Paris: Union Générale d'Éditions, 1979.
La Saison Cinématographique, 1957–1992.
Schulz Huffhines, Kathy, ed. *Foreign Affairs: The National Society of Film Critics' Video Guide to Foreign Films*. San Francisco: Mercury House, 1991.

Shale, Richard. *Academy Awards: An Ungar Reference Index*. 2d ed. Compiled and introduced by Richard Shale. New York: Frederick Ungar, 1982.

Truffaut, François. *Les Films de ma vie*. Paris: Flammarion, 1975.

Vialle, Gabriel. *Georges Franju*. Paris: Editions Seghers, 1968.

The Films

1 *À nos amours (To Our Loves)* 1983 Color *Director* Maurice Pialat; *Producer* FR3, Gaumont, Films du Livrdoir; *Screenplay* Arlette Langman and Maurice Pialat; *Photography* Jacques Loiseleux; *Music* Purcell; *Set* Outdoors; *Sound* Jean Umansky, François de Morant, Julien Cloquet, Thierry Jeandroz; *Costumes* Valérie Schlumberger, Martha de Villalonga; *Editing* Yann Dedet, Sophie Coussein, Valérie Condroyer, Corinne Lazare, Jean Gargonne, Nathalie Letrosne and Catherine Legault. Running time: 102 minutes.

Cast: Sandrine Bonnaire, Maurice Pialat, Evelyne Ker, Dominique Besnehard, Anne Sophie Maillé, Christophe Odent, Cyr Boitard, Maïté Maillé, Pierre Louis Rajoy, Cyril Collard, Nathalie Gureghian, Jacques Fieschi, Guénoté Pascal, Caroline Cibot, Valérie Schlumberger, Tom Stevens, Tsilka Théodorou, Vrangel Théodorou, Isabel Prades, Hervé Austen, Alexandre de Dardel, Alexis Quentin, Pierre Novion, Eric Vieillard.

Fifteen-year-old Suzanne (Bonnaire) hopes to find self-knowledge and self-esteem through a string of sexual encounters. Set against the disintegration of the girl's immigrant family, Suzanne's sexual escapades bring her some moments of sensual satisfaction and escape from her unhappy home life, but not the deeper self-knowledge and happiness that she seeks.

A fascinating look at adolescence, which uses a teenage girl's sexual appetites and abandon as a vehicle for a spiritual quest. The intensity of Pialat's direction reveals the violence of the homelife and the moral crisis Suzanne faces in such a way as to raise this film far above the soap-opera level of the plot. Pialat himself plays Suzanne's father in the film and presents the perfect mix of a kind and brutish boor.

American critic Henry Sheehan in *The Boston Phoenix* write: "It's a fierce film, brilliantly realistic and tough, and its reticence about right and wrong, its reluctance to judge rather than observe, make it the most wrenchingly honest film about sex to hit the screens since *Luna*." Other critics complained that Bonnaire's lackluster performance made the film a poor cousin to such coming-of-age films as *The 400 Blows*. It won the Prix Louis Delluc in 1983, Best Picture at Cannes in 1984, and Bonnaire won a César for Best Newcomer in 1984.

The Ace of Aces *see* **L'As des as**

2 *Adieu Philippine* 1962 B&W *Director* Jacques Rozier; *Producer* Unitec Films, Alpha Productions, Rome Paris Films, Euro-International Films; *Screenplay* Michèle O'Glor and Jacques Rozier with Renée Kammerscheit; *Photography* René Mathelin; *Music* Jacques Denjean, Paul Mattei, and Maxime

Saury; *Sound* Maurice Larouche, Jean-Michel Poud; *Editing* Marc Pavaux. Running time: 110 minutes.

Cast: Jean-Claude Aimini, Stafania Sabatini, Yveline Céry, Vittorio Caprioli, Daniel Descamps, David Tonelli, Annie Markhan, André Tarroux, Christian Longuet, Michel Soyet, Arlette Gilbert, Jeanne Perez, Maurice Garrel, Charles Lavialli, Patricia Andrieux, Olivia Clatienne, Couquette Deschamps, Edmond Ardisson, Albert Benamou, Pietro Cortini, Mitzi Hahn, Reine Marvanne, Marianne Padovani, Alain Douchin, Pierre-Charles Lucciard, Michèle Padovini, Nadine Staquet, Jean Lucchetti, Lulu, José Pantieri, Marco Perrin, Maxime Saury and his orchestra, Dominique Tozza, and the actors of the *Monserrat* television program.

A love story and coming-of-age film about Michel (Aimini), a young man who works in television. One day he picks up two teenage girls, Lilianne (Céry) and Juliette (Sabatini), whom he toys with on his days off. Then he takes them on a vacation to Corsica. Both girls fall madly in love with him, but Michel cannot choose between them. When he must join the army to fight in Algeria, he bids them both adieu.

This lovely film about the end of innocence was one of the most influential New Wave films. It was hailed by critics as bridging a monumental artistic impasse, in a way because it managed to say everything in its silences. Eric Rohmer and Jacques Rivette hailed it as a masterpiece that ingeniously joined the innovations of cinéma vérité with inspired fictional filmmaking. While this film introduced an incredible talent, unfortunately Rozier only made one more film in the next decade.

Adieu Philippine was not a commercial success when it came out, despite the critics' raves. It was not shown in the United States until 1973, and was never broadly distributed. *Le Cinéma en question* said: "*Adieu Philippine* is a certain number of moments caught in movement, autonomous instants. In the end it is a documentary on film language. Here is the entire story of *Adieu Philippine*, a boy between two girls; a cinéaste between two shots."

The Adolescent *see* **L'Adolescente**

3 *L'Adolescente (The Adolescent)* 1978 Color *Director* Jeanne Moreau; *Producer* Pierre Dussart, Tarak, Ben Ammar; *Screenplay* Henriette Jelinek and Jeanne Moreau; *Photography* Pierre Gautard; *Music* Philippe Sarde; *Set* Noël Galland; *Sound* Dominique Dalmasso, Jacques Maumont; *Editing* Albert Jurgenson and Colette Leloup. Running time: 90 minutes.

Cast: Laetitia Chaveau, Edith Clever, Simone Signoret, Francis Huster, Jacques Weber, Roger Blin, Hughes Quester, Jean-François Balmer, Hélène Vallier, Michel Blanc, Juliette Brac, Hughes Quester, Charles Millot, Isabelle Sadoyan, Bérangère Bonvoison, Frank Muth, Hélène Vallier, Michel Lesnoff, Pierre Forget, Jacques Rispal, Elisabeth Margony, Maurice Baquet, Nadine Basile, Françoise Bette, Anne Bernier, Marjorie Routaboul, Eric-André Vigroux, Eric Revel.

A tender coming-of-age story about a young Parisian girl (Chaveau) who spends what turns out to be her last summer of innocence in a village in the Auvergne region of France with her grandmother (Signoret). Set in 1939, the film explores the tender relations between the young woman and her grandmother and the turbulent emotions that she encounters as she falls in love with a young Jewish doctor, with whom her mother is actually having an affair.

Une Affaire de femmes (The Story of Women), 1988; directed by Claude Chabrol.

Moreau's finest film as director, *The Adolescent* is apparently somewhat auto-biographical, which may explain how Moreau manages to balance sweetness and sorrow, while avoiding the sentimental. The scene in which 12-year-old Marie announces her love to the doctor is so full of awkward innocence that the audience squirms for her. Moreau narrates.

Critics found this a surprisingly intelligent and sensitive girl's tale. Judy Stone of *The San Francisco Chronicle* declared: "The film is so richly resonant with warmth and understanding for all the varieties of human experience from childhood to old age that it generates a kind of glow of happiness rarely created in movies today."

The Adultress *see* **Thérèse Raquin**

4 *Une Affaire de femmes (The Story of Women)* 1988 Color *Director* Claude Chabrol; *Producer* MK2 Films, Films A2, Films du Camélia, La Sept, Sofinergie; *Screenplay* Claude Chabrol and Colo Tavernier O'Hagan, based on the novel by Francis Szpiner; *Photography* Jean Rabier; *Music* Mathieu Chabrol; *Set* Françoise Benoît-Fresco; *Sound* Jean-Berthieu Chabrol; *Costumes* Corinne Jorry; *Editing* Monique Fardoulis. Running time: 110 minutes.

Cast: Isabelle Huppert, François Cluzet, Nils Tavernier, Marie Trintignant, Dominique Blanc, Lolita Chammah, Aurore Gauvin, Guillaume Foutrier, Marie Bunel, Dani, François Maistre, Vincent Gauthier, Frank Lapersonne, Caroline Berg, Evelyne Didi, Myriam David, Jacques Brunet, Thomas Chabrol, Louis Ducreux, Michel Beaune.

During World War II in a provincial town, money and love are hard to come by. When Marie (Huppert) gives a neighbor an abortion because her husband is away at war, she discovers a way to make money and to escape the suffocation that she feels in being poor and dependent on a husband that she doesn't love. Her freedom and happiness abruptly end when she is turned in, and the Vichy government decides to make an example of her.

One of Chabrol's masterpieces, this film once again proves what a brilliant cinematic storyteller Chabrol is, as he continues to champion feminist points of view in mainstream French movies. By constantly revealing Marie from different characters' points of view, Chabrol creates a highly complicated portrait of a woman's actions during the war. One minute, the extreme measures to which Marie resorts seem justified and in the next, they are revealed to be horribly insensitive. Isabelle Huppert earns her title as one of France's best contemporary actresses.

Critics applauded Chabrol's subtlety, intelligence and restraint, all of which keep the picture free of didacticism and easy judgments. By recounting the plot in a seemingly straightforward fashion, he in no way simplifies complicated material. By presenting a portrait of a multi-faceted woman, he avoids fashioning her into a moral lesson.

5 *Alphaville, une étrange aventure de Lemmy Caution (Alphaville)*
1965 B&W   *Director* Jean-Luc Godard; *Producer* Chaumiane Productions, Filmstudio; *Screenplay* Jean-Luc Godard, based on Paul Eluard's *La Capitale de la douleur*; *Photography* Raoul Coutard; *Music* Paul Misraki; *Set* Pierre Guffroy; *Sound* René Levert; *Editing* Agnès Guillemot. Running time: 100 minutes.

Cast: Eddy Constantine, Anna Karina, Akim Tamiroff, Howard Vernon, Laszlo Szabo, Michel Delahaye, Jean-André Fieschi, Jean-Louis Comolli.

A blend of *série noire*, romance and science-fiction thriller, in which a secret agent, Lemmy Caution (Constantine), travels to the futuristic city of Alphaville on a mission to remove the totalitarian ruler/scientist Professor von Braun (Vernon). Among the trademark Constantine gun battles with robots, love blossoms between Lemmy Caution and von Braun's daughter (Karina), which, of course, complicates his escape from Alphaville.

This film has been called the most influential of science-fiction movies, along with Kubrick's *2001*. It is also one of Godard's most accessible films. It is futuristic and yet heavy with literary allusions to myths, poetry and American detective novels. Much of the horror Godard represented in *Alphaville*, the sterility and inhumanity, is not so far from what we know today, which was undoubtedly one of his aims, since he used his native Paris' modern office buildings as *Alphaville's* set. And yet in the end, love still exists in this barren, cold world.

Many French critics hailed the movie as further proof of Godard's genius. For the most part, foreign critics found things to applaud and to criticize. *Film Quarterly* called *Alphaville* "the ultimate Message Movie" and "the ultimate Meaningless Movie." *The New Yorker* summed up critical sentiment saying the film was "impressive, irritating, boring, and worth seeing."

6 *L'Amant (The Lover)* 1992 Color   *Director* Jean-Jacques Annaud; *Producer* Renn Productions, Burrill Productions, Films A2; *Screenplay* Jean-Jacques Annaud and Gérard Brach, based on the novel by Marguerite Duras; *Photography* Robert Fraisse; *Music* Gabriel Yared; *Set* Thanh At Hoang; *Sound*

Laurent Quaglio; *Costumes* Yvonne Sassinto de Nesle; *Editing* Noëlle Boisson. Running time: 92 minutes.

Cast: Jane March, Tony Leung, Frédérique Meininger, Arnaud Giovaninetti, Melvil Poupaud, Lisa Faulkner, Xiem Mang, Raymonde Heudeline, Philippe Le Dem, Anne Schaufuss, Quach Van An, Tania Torrens, Yvonne Wingerter, Hélène Patarot, Do Minh Vien, Nguyen Thi Hoa, Frédéric Auburtin, Nguyen Van Lam, Minh Trang, Truong Thu, Ly Nguyen Phat, Lam Thanh, Vu Kim Trong, Vu Dinh Thi, Lu Van Trang, Nguyen Thi Cam Thuy, Tieu Nu, Thai Giang, Chau Sieu, Alido H. Gaudencio, and the voice of Jeanne Moreau.

Set in colonial Vietnam in the 1920s, this is a love story about a poor French schoolgirl (March) and her wealthy Chinese lover (Leung). The tale is narrated by the woman who is looking back fifty years. She remembers their meeting on a ferry crossing the Mekong River. They were separated by age, class, race and economics, but a steamy love affair ensued.

Based on Duras' autobiographical novel, this film is a beautiful, erotic film that encompasses issues of love, lust, colonialism, and much more. The film is amazingly sensual, in tone and setting. It was the first Western film to be shot in Vietnam in decades, and Annaud overcame great difficulties to shoot his exterior shots there. He chose to make it in English, with the model Jane March making her cinematic debut. She and Leung are both wonderful. Their sex scenes were so steamy, in fact, that a scandal arose over the question of whether or not they really had had sex in some of the scenes. When the film opened in Britain, March was hounded and harassed over the explicit scenes. Duras' prose is narrated by the rich, husky voice of Jeanne Moreau.

Though some critics faulted the film for not living up to their idea of the book and others complained it was all sex, no substance, *The Lover* was a great critical and commercial success internationally.

7 *Les Amants (The Lovers)* 1958 B&W   *Director* Louis Malle; *Producer* Nouvelles Editions de Films; *Screenplay* Louis Malle and Louise de Vilmorin; *Photography* Henri Decaë; *Music* Brahms; *Set* Jacques Saulnier and Bernard Evein; *Sound* Pierre Bertrand; *Editing* Léonide Azar. Running time: 89 minutes.

Cast: Jeanne Moreau, Jean-Marc Bory, Alain Cuny, José Luis de Villalonga, Judith Magre, Gaston Modot, Claude Mansard, Jean-Claude Brialy, Michèle Giradon, Georgette Lobre, Pierre Frag, Gib Grossac.

Jeanne Tournier (Moreau) is the wealthy wife of a newspaper man. Bored with her provincial life in Dijon, she tries to keep occupied with visits to her best friend in Paris and her polo-player lover. On the way to a dinner she has organized for her husband to meet her Parisian friends, her car breaks down. A young archaeologist, Bernard (Bory), picks her up, and she invites him to dinner. Her husband insists he stays the night. Jeanne and Bernard come across each other in the middle of the night in the park outside the house and make love beneath the moon. The next day the two drive off together.

A wonderful love story that broke cinematic ground, caused a scandal when it came out, and made Moreau and Malle famous worldwide. In France a newspaper called for a boycott of the film. The Vatican's newspaper declared it obscene. The manager of a movie theater in an Ohio suburb was prosecuted and sent to jail for showing the "obscene" film, though the case was dismissed by the Supreme Court. The immoral content of the film was not the problem so much as

Les Amants (*The Lovers*), 1958; directed by Louis Malle.

the sexual realism, in particular, the love scenes in which Jeanne Moreau's pleasure is expressed as no other actress had dared to express it before.

While the love scenes seem tame now, François Truffaut hailed Louis Malle's second feature film as "the cinema's first night of love." It was a great commercial success. It won the Special Jury Prize at the Venice Biennal in 1958.

8 *Les Amants de Vérone (The Lovers of Verona)*   1949 B&W   *Director* André Cayatte; *Producer* CICC, Borderie; *Screenplay* André Cayatte; *Adaptation and Dialogue* Jacques Prévert; *Photography* Henri Alekan; *Music* Joseph Kosma; *Set* René Moulaert; *Sound* Antoine Petitjean; *Costumes* Rosine Delamare; *Editing* Christian Gaudin. Running time: 105 minutes.

Cast: Serge Reggiani, Anouk Aimée, Pierre Brasseur, Louis Salou, Marcel Dalio, Martine Carol, Marianne Oswald, Roland Armontel, René Génin, Philippe Lemaire, Claudie Carter, Solange Sicard, Yves Deniaud, Charles Deschamps, Max Dalban, Fréderic O'Brady, Palmyre Levasseur, Charles Blavette, Guy Favières, Claude Nicot, Marcel Pérès, Robert Rollis, Frank Maurice.

An adaptation of *Romeo and Juliet* set just after World War II. Angelo (Reggiani) is a glassblower from Murano and Georgia (Aimée) is the daughter of a Fascist magistrate. It is a passionate love story, but we all know how it ends.

A wonderful adaptation of Shakespeare's tragedy and a fine example of why literary filmmaking enjoyed the following that it did in France just after World War II. *The Lovers of Verona* was Cayatte's tenth movie and his first real success. It has a fabulous screenplay by the writer Jacques Prévert. It has wonderful photography, with the lovely light and water images adding to the beauty of the tragedy.

Critics applauded Cayatte's beautiful film. When it came out in the States in 1951, *Variety* called it "one of the better postwar French imports. It's an ingeniously contrived and beautifully told story ... technically excellent in all departments."

9 *Les Amants du Pont Neuf* 1991 Color *Director* Leos Carax; *Producer* Films Christian Fechner, Films A2; *Screenplay* Leos Carax; *Photography* Jean-Yves Escoffier; *Sound* Henri Morelle; *Set* Michel Vandestien; *Costumes* Robert Nardone; *Editing* Nelly Quettier. Running time: 125 minutes.

Cast: Denis Lavant, Juliette Binoche, Klaus-Michel Gruber.

A love story about Alex (Lavant), a poor acrobat/fire breather who makes his home on Paris' most famous bridge, the Pont-Neuf. One day on the bridge, he meets a beautiful young painter Michèle (Binoche), who lives in the streets with her cat and wears a patch over one eye because she is losing her vision. It turns out her eyesight began failing just when she lost her love Julien. Alex falls madly in love with Michèle and a passionate pursuit follows.

One of the most exciting films of the 1990s, by one of its most exciting young directors, *Les Amants du Pont Neuf* takes on one of France's newest social problems: homelessness and one of French cinema's greatest subjects *l'amour fou*, or crazy love. Until the romance takes off, Carax treats homelessness in modern Paris in a documentary fashion. Carax began the filming of this film, his third, in 1988, but went way over budget after completing only 40 minutes. A legal and financial battle halted production for two years. Another producer finally stepped in and saved the film in 1990. Binoche and Lavant form an unforgettable pair of lovers set against urban anguish and beauty. Lavant, who has been in all three of Carax's films, promises to be a major French actor.

Some critics had gripes with Carax's plot twists, but most hailed his rough, poetic filming as a major event, even calling him the most promising young talent at work in French film. *Cahiers du Cinéma* declared: "*Les Amants du Pont Neuf* is a great drunken film ... lyric, desperate, splendid and candid."

America Seen by a Frenchman *see* **L'Amérique insolite**

10 *L'Amérique insolite (America Seen by a Frenchman* or *L'Amérique vue par un français)* 1960 Color *Director* François Reichenbach; *Producer* Pierre Braunberger, Films de la Pléiade; *Screenplay* François Reichenbach; *Dialogue* François Reichenbach and Chris Marker; *Photography* Marcel Grignon; *Music* Michel Legrand; *Sound* Jean Neny, Pierre Fatosme; *Editing* Albert Jurgenson. Running time: 88 minutes.

A film about America as seen through the camera lens of French director François Reichenbach. He travelled from coast to coast, filming anything and everything that he felt was particularly American, including rodeos, ghost towns, Disneyland, New York's skyscrapers and religious communes.

This is a wonderful documentary of American culture. "I wanted to take the American citizen from his birth up to his death and follow him in all the odd and unusual circumstances of his life. I wanted to show his extraordinary youthfulness, his passions, his taste for violence, his kindnesses and eccentricities. To be a witness, a curious, unflagging witness, and yet remain unobtrusive; that was my aim. But I never let myself judge." Reichenbach's editing is superb; it keeps the film lively.

Some critics found the literary commentary a little at odds with the images. *Variety* said: "It does give an unusual closeup of the many sides of sprawling America that may have been seen before but not quite in this light of sympathetic curiosity."

L'Amérique vue par un français *see* **L'Amérique insolite**

11 *L'Ami de mon amie (Boyfriends and Girlfriends)* 1987 Color *Director* Eric Rohmer; *Producer* Les Films du Losange; *Screenplay* Eric Rohmer; *Photography* Bernard Lutic; *Music* Jean-Louis Valero; *Sound* Georges Prat; *Editing* Maria-Luisa Garcia. Running time: 102 minutes.

Cast: Emmanuelle Chaulet, Sophie Renoir, Anne-Laure Meury, Eric Viellard, François-Eric Gendron.

A romantic comedy about two young working women, Blanche (Chaulet) and Léa (Renoir), who become involved with the same two young men. When Blanche moves into a suburban apartment complex and befriends Léa, Léa is living with Fabien (Viellard). The two giggle over Blanche's crush on Alexandre (Gendron), but it is Léa who makes a move on him while Blanche is away. Betrayal among friends' does not end badly in this tale, though, because Blanche and Fabien fall as much in love as Alexandre and Léa.

This is the last of Eric Rohmer's six "Comedies and Proverbs," and sweet proof that games of love can be played out with freshness and wit in even the most sterile of modern backgrounds. *Boyfriends and Girlfriends* does not have the moral or philosophical weight of Rohmer's earlier films, but it is a fine vehicle for Rohmer's optimistic modern vision.

Gerald Nachman of *The San Francisco Chronicle* summed this film up as "Four French Yuppies Sort Out Love Lives." He found "Rohmer wraps it all up a little too snugly and cutely (especially for a director so good at ambivalence), something you might almost expect from Blake Edwards." Terrence Rafferty, however, called the film "an intellectual's dream of simplicity and unselfconsciousness."

12 *L'Amour en fuite (Love on the Run)* 1978 Color   *Director* François Truffaut; *Producer* Films du Carrosse, AMLF; *Screenplay* François Truffaut, Marie-France Pisier, Jean Aurel and Suzanne Schiffman; *Photography* Nestor Almendros; *Music* Georges Delerue; *Set* Jean-Pierre Kohut Svelko and Pierre Gompertz; *Sound* Michel Laurent; *Costumes* Monique Dury; *Editing* Martine Barraqué. Running time: 94 minutes.

Cast: Jean-Pierre Léaud, Marie-France Pisier, Claude Jade, Dani, Dorothée, Rosy Varte, Marie Henriau, Daniel Mesguich, Julien Bertheau, Jean-Pierre Ducos, Pierre Dios, Alain Ollivier, Monique Dury, Emmanuel Clot, Christian Lentretien, Roland Thenot, Julien Dubois, Alexandre Janssen, Chantal Zaugg, Patrick Auffey, Claire Maurier, Albert Rémy, Jean Douchet, Guy Decomble, François Darbon.

This is the last film in Truffaut's autobiographical Antoine Doinel series, which began with *The 400 Blows*. Antoine (Léaud), who has just divorced his wife, reflects on the important turning points in his life and reminisces about all the

L'Amour l'après-midi (Chloe in the Afternoon), 1972; directed by Eric Rohmer.

women whom he has loved. The solution to his melancholy he discovers, though, is to fall in love once again, this time when he sees a photograph of a young woman, Sabine (Dorothée). He pursues her with eternal boyish romanticism.

Truffaut uses footage from his earlier films for flashbacks, which is possible because Pisier, Léaud and Jade were in those films ten and fifteen years earlier; the "reality" this lends to the film's autobiography of the actor and the director is fascinating. It is a real trip down memory lane for Truffaut and Dionel fans.

Some critics complained of Antoine's eternal adolescence. Won't he ever grow up? They cried. No. This was the last of Truffaut's Antoine series.

13 *L'Amour l'après-midi (Chloe in the Afternoon)* 1972 Color *Director* Eric Rohmer; *Producer* Les Films du Losange; *Screenplay* Eric Rohmer; *Photography* Nestor Almendros; *Music* Arié Dzierlatka; *Set* Nicole Rachline; *Sound* Jean-Pierre Ruh; *Editing* Martine Kalfon. Running time: 97 minutes.

Cast: Bernard Verley, Zouzou, Françoise Verley, Daniel Ceccaldi, Malvina Penne, Babette Ferrier, Tina Michelino, Irène Skobline, Frédérique Hender, Claude Jean-Philippe, Jean-Louis Livi, Pierre Nuni, Sylvie Badesco, Claude Bertrnind, Sylvaine Charlet, Danièle Malat, Suzy Randall, Françoise Fabian, Aurora Cornu, Laurence de Monagham, Béatrice Romand.

Frédéric (Verley) is happy with his wife, until an old friend with freer morals and sexual ideas than Frédéric tempts him to contemplate some fantasies. He almost succumbs to acting on his newfound desires, but he does not. He makes love to his wife Chloe (Zouzou) in the afternoon, instead.

This is the sixth and last movie in Rohmer's series "Six Moral Tales," and like all of them, at the heart of the movie is a moral struggle. Rohmer is a master of sensitivity and restraint. His characters grow and change on screen, bringing real human lives into the movies in a way that rarely has been achieved before or since. Verbal acrobatics replace physical acrobats; if you like good talk, Rohmer delivers it.

Many critics find that he has a better understanding of the issues confronting men in modern society than most. Vincent Canby wrote of the film: "Rohmer's method is one of contradiction, between word and deed, sound and image, even between performer and performance . . . . The marvel of Rohmer's method is that Chloë, sometime model, bar girl, waitress, and salesgirl, grows into a woman of immense physical appeal, wit and courage, for us as well as for Frédéric, in the course of the film." In *The New Yorker* Pauline Kael predicted that *Chloë in the Afternoon* "will probably be called a perfect film."

The Anatomy of a Political Assassination *see* **Z**

And God Created Woman *see* **Et dieu créa la femme**

14 *L'Année dernière à Marienbad (Last Year at Marienbad)* 1960 B&W *Director* Alain Resnais; *Producer* Terra Films, Société Nouvelle des Films Cormoran, Précitel, Como Films, Argos Films, Les Films Tamara, Cinétel, Silver Films, Cineriz; *Screenplay* Alain Robbe-Grillet; *Photography* Sacha Vierny; *Music* Francis Seyrig; *Set* Jacques Saulnier; *Sound* Guy Villette, Jean-Claude Marchetti; *Costumes* Bernard Evein; *Editing* Henri Colpi, Jasmine Chasney. Running time: 93 minutes.

Cast: Delphine Seyrig, Giorgio Albertazzi, Sacha Pitoeff, Françoise Bertin, Luce Garcia-Ville, Helena Kornel, François Spira, Karin Toeche-Mittler, Pierre Barbaud, Wilhelm von Deek, Jean Lanier, Gérard Lorin, David Montemuri, Gilles Queant, Gabriel Werner.

The plot of the film involves a man, "X" (Albertazzi), and a woman, "A" (Seyrig), who are both vacationing at a baroque chateau hotel somewhere in Europe. The man attempts to convince the woman that they had an affair the year before at the German spa Marienbad and that this present meeting had been arranged at that time. She claims never to have seen him before. While he pursues her, she wonders if he is telling the truth or merely trying to seduce her.

This is a landmark film that proved the interior psychological life could be material for the big screen. Resnais worked closely with author Alain Robbe-Grillet to create a film that challenges traditional ideas of structure and storytelling, travelling into the past, the future, and the thoughts of X and A, where visuals are more important than narrative. It has been compared to Cubist painting for the cinema. People either love this puzzling movie or hate it.

Before the movie's premiere at the Venice Film Festival, producers and distributors feared the movie would alienate moviegoers. "We hope that the lyrical dream world that is to be found in the picture will appeal to the collective unconscious of people in all countries," said Resnais on opening night. Not only did it win the Festival's Lion d'Or, but for a complex film, it did quite well commercially. Almost every critic had his own interpretation of the film, from mythical and allegorical to Freudian and existential interpretations. It was nominated for an Oscar for Best Original Screenplay in 1962, and won the French Critics' Prix Méliès in 1961.

Antoine and Antoinette *see* **Antoine et Antoinette**

15 *Antoine et Antoinette (Antoine and Antoinette)* 1947 B&W *Director* Jacques Becker; *Producer* SNEG; *Screenplay and Dialogue* Jacques Becker, Maurice Griffe, and Françoise Giroud; *Photography* Pierre Montazel; *Music* Jean-Jacques Grünenwald; *Set* Robert-Jules Garnier; *Sound* Jacques Lebreton; *Editing* Marguerite Renoir. Running time: 78 minutes.

Cast: Roger Pigaut, Claire Mafféi, Noël Roquevert, Annette Poivre, Jacques Mayran, Paulette Jan, Emile Drain, Gérard Oury, Huguette Faget, Pierre Trabaud, Yvette Lucas, Gaston Modot, Maurice Marceau, Pierre Leproux, Paul Barge, Charles Camusic, René Stern, Made Siamé, Marthe Mellot, Odette Barancey, François Joux, Charles Vissières, Léon Bary, Nicolas Amato, Marcelle Hainia, Renée Thorel, Bob Ingarzo, Jean-Marc Thibault, Nicole Courcel, Jacqueline Carlier, Louis de Funès, Jean-Marc Tennberg, Maurice Régamey, Pierre Leproux, René Berthier, Henri Piestat, René Sauvaire.

The story of a working-class Parisian couple (Mafféi and Roquevert). He works in a printing shop; she at a Prisunic. Their simple life of petty quarrels and tender moments of forgiveness is turned upside when they first find, and then lose, and then re-find a winning lottery ticket.

In his first film made after World War II, Becker presented a fascinating look at the life of Paris' working class after the war. Through the myriad details of one married couple's life, he builds a complex portrait of his subjects. While it may not have been the social realism some hoped French cinema would produce, as the Italians had, Becker was more concerned with presenting a convincing slice-of-life than a stereotypical scenario.

While Becker presents a vivid and sympathetic portrait of working-class life in recently liberated France, some critics accused him of ignoring the pressing social problems that existed. Admirers of the film, many of whom consider it one of Becker's greatest works, rejoice in its poetic quality and its portrayal of Parisian domesticity at its truthful best. It won the prize for Best Psychological and Dramatic Film at Cannes in 1946.

16 *L'Argent* 1983 Color *Director* Robert Bresson; *Producer* Marions Films; FR3, EOS Films, Cinecom International; *Screenplay* Robert Bresson, based on Leo Tolstoy's story "The False Note"; *Photography* Emmanuel Machuel, Pasqualino De Santis; *Music* Johann Sebastian Bach; *Set* Pierre Lefait; *Costumes* Monique Dury; *Editing* Jean-François Naudon. Running time: 90 minutes.

Cast: Christian Patey, Sylvie van den Elsen, Michel Briguet, Caroline Lang, Vincent Risterucci, Beatrice Tabourin, Didier Baussy, Marc Ernest Fourneau, Brune Lapeyre, André Cler, Claude Cler, Jeanne Aptekman, François Barrier, Alain Aptekman, Dominique Mullier, Jacques Behr, Gilles Durieux, Alain Bourguignon, Anne de Kervazdoue, Bernard Lamarche Vadel, Pierre Tessier, Eric Franklin, Jean-Louis Berdot, Yves Martin, Luc Solente, Valerie Mercier, Alexandre Pasche, Jean-Michel Coletti, Stéphane Villette.

This is the story of a deliveryman, Yvon Targe (Patey), who enters a tragic chain of events when he is given counterfeit money and is arrested when he uses the bills to pay for a drink in a café. Though he is eventually acquitted, as the real criminals cover their tracks, this run-in has ruinous consequences as Targe loses his job, goes to jail, and suffers the death of his child and the abandonment of his wife. He is an innocent man whom the system turns into a brutal killer.

A Kafkaesque drama from the great director Bresson, this bleak tragedy is brilliantly rendered. Bresson made it at age 84, after a six-year absence from cinema, and it is marked by his trademark austerity. By paring everything down and focusing on the actions and objects that propel the personal tragedy, Bresson emphasized how money can elevate the rich and sink the poor. Despite its apparent focus on materialism, Bresson believed he had created a very spiritual work.

In France some conservative critics were very unhappy that Bresson chose Caroline Lang, who is Minister of Culture Jacques Lang's daughter, for the movie; they believed the choice stank of liberal political ties. Others called it his greatest work since *Pickpocket*. *The Christian Science Monitor* said the film had "both a dramatic and an intellectual depth." The film won Bresson the award for Best Director at Cannes in 1983.

17 *L'Argent des autres (Other People's Money)*   1978 Color   *Director* Christian de Chalonge; *Producer* Fildebroc, FR3, SFP, Films de la Tour; *Screenplay* Pierre Dumayet and Christian de Chalonge, based on the novel by Nancy Markam; *Photography* Jean-Claude Picavet; *Music* Patrice Mestral; *Set* Eric Simon; *Sound* Jacques Merrien, Pierre Parigi; *Editing* Jean Ravel. Running time: 105 minutes.

Cast: Jean-Louis Trintignant, Claude Brasseur, Michel Serrault, Catherine Deneuve, François Perrot, Gérard Sety, Jean Leuvrais, Michel Berto, Juliette Berto, Umberto Orsini, Francis Lemaire, Liza Braconnier, Raymond Bussières, Françoise Giret, Michel Delahaye, Pierre Sentier, Gérard Caillaud, Maurice Vallier, René Bouloc, Marc Chapill, Van Doude, Laura Kornbluth, Michèle Kornbluth.

This is an exciting thriller about one man taking on the bureaucracy of the banking system. Rainer (Trintignant) works as a managing director for a large bank. He unwittingly becomes tangled up in a financial scam. After an investigation, he discovers that he is being used to cover up shady dealings. He has to figure out whether his bosses, friends or clients are behind it — or are also victims. Two women help him sort through the mess and take on the powers that be.

This Kafkaesque film is mixed with a love story involving the lovely Catherine Deneuve. De Chalonge said of the film: *"Other People's Money* is the money of the millions of people who put their fortunes in banks, savings banks or less conspicuous private organizations . . . . Our purpose was to imagine the underhanded dealings of a financial scandal as seen through the life of a man caught in its meshes." The film is frightening because of the possibilities of such financial webs actually being woven.

Other People's Money was the biggest movie in France the year it was released. Critics and audiences loved the use of a bank as the bad guy and the duo of Trintignant and Deneuve. It won the César for Best Film and Best Director and the Prix Louis Delluc in 1978.

18 *L'Argent du Poche (Small Change)*   1976 Color   *Director* François Truffaut; *Producer* Films du Carrosse, Artistes Associés; *Screenplay* François Truffaut and Suzanne Schiffmann; *Photography* Pierre William Glenn; *Music* Maurice Jaubert and Charles Trenet; *Set* Jean-Pierre Kohut Svelko; *Sound* Michel Laurent; *Costumes* Monique Dury; *Editing* Yann Dedet. Running time: 105 minutes.

Cast: Jean-François Stévenin, Virginie Thévenet, Chantal Mercier, Nico Félix, Tania Torrens, Francis Devlaeminck, Marcel Berbert, Jean-Marie Carayon, Christian Lentretien, Roland Thénot, Thi Loan N'Guyen, Christine Pellé, Jane Lobre, Monique Dury, François Truffaut, Laura Truffaut, Paul Heyraud, Michèle Heyraud, Geory Desmouceaux, Bruno Staab, Philippe Goldmann, Corinne Boucart, Claudio and Franck Deluca, Eva Truffaut, Sylvie Grézel, Sébastien Marc, Laurent Devlaeminck, Pascale Bruchon, Little Gregory, Bruno Staab Jr., Richard Golfier, Katy Carayon, Annie Chavaldonne, Michel Dissart, Vincent Touly.

This is the story of the adventures of a class of schoolchildren in Thiers. Patrick (Desmouceaux) is an introverted boy, who cares for his crippled father and fantasizes about the mother of one of his classmates. Julien (Goldmann) is an unkempt "wild child" who is separated from his mother and grandmother after burns are discovered on him during a school check-up. The teacher, Monsieur Richet (Stévenin), tenderly tries to effect a positive influence on his charges. These are some of the cutest child moments ever caught on film — for example, the scene when two boys try to be barbers for their friend, with disastrous results.

This is without doubt one of the best movies ever made on childhood. The secret to this film's genius is how natural the scenes are, a trick that Truffaut mastered by using real children instead of child actors. He had the children read for the film, but then he worked around them. The director makes all of this look easy, but very few could effect such a brilliantly light touch.

Critics and audiences were united in their love for this film when it came out. *Film News* called it "a sunny kaleidoscope of childhood which shows its buoyant little miracles, its slapstick, its innocence, and in one battered child, its poignancy."

19 *L'Armée des ombres (The Army of Shadows)* 1969 Color *Director* Jean-Pierre Melville; *Producer* Corona, Fono Roma Productions, Dorfmann; *Screenplay* Jean-Pierre Melville, based on the novel by Joseph Kessel; *Photography* Pierre Lhomme; *Music* Eric Demarsan; *Set* Théo Meurisse; *Sound* Jacques Carrère; *Editing* Françoise Bonnot. Running time: 150 minutes.

Cast: Lino Ventura, Paul Meurisse, Simone Signoret, Jean-Pierre Cassel, Claude Mann, Christian Barbier, Serge Reggiani, Alain Libolt, Paul Crauchet, Albert Michel, Hubert de Lapparent, Colin Mann, Jean-Marie Robain, Georges Huart, Marco Perrin, Denis Sadier, Henri Daquin, Michel Fréttault, Alain Mottet, Anthony Stuart, Decock, André de Wawrin, Georges Sellier, Jacques Marbeuf, Michel Daquin, Percival Russel, Gaston Meunier, Marcel Bernier, Adrien Cayla-Legrand, Pierre Vaudier, Franz Sauer, Nathalie Delon.

This is a dark look at the lives of Resistance fighters, both male and female, during World War II. Denounced to the Gestapo, the characters are questioned and released. They exact revenge on their informers, arrange escapes for their captive members, and try to protect their loved ones while performing dangerous patriotic acts.

The film was based on the accounts of the Resistance fighter Lucie Aubrac. It was one of the films at the end of the 1960s that the critics claimed was mythologizing the era of DeGaulle and the war. Melville believed that his characters were far from romantic conceptions, because their human failings were revealed along with their moments of heroic courage. The film was on Melville's mind for years before he made it and is a very personal vision because he was in the Resistance himself.

Critics applauded Melville's ability to navigate a course between objective

L'Argent du Poche (Small Change), 1976; directed by François Truffaut.

realism and heroic melodrama. When it was released in the United States, *Variety* wrote: "Jean-Pierre Melville gives a painstaking reconstruction of the period and brings off a sober, well-observed tale of the early workings of the French Resistance."

The Army of Shadows *see* **L'Armée des ombres**

20 *L'As des as (The Ace of Aces)* 1982 Color *Director* Gérard Oury; *Producer* Gaumont, Cerito, Rialto; *Screenplay* Gérard Oury and Danièle Thompson; *Photography* Xavier Schwarzeneger; *Music* Vladimir Cosma; *Set* Marc Frédérix, Herbert Strabel; *Sound* Alain Sempé; *Editing* Albert Jurgenson. Running time: 100 minutes.

Cast: Jean-Paul Belmondo, Marie-France Pisier, Rachid Ferrache, Frank Hoffman, Benno Sterznbach, Gunter Meisner, Jean-Roger Milo.

This is the story of a former World War I ace flyer turned French boxer (Belmondo) at the Olympic Games in Berlin. When a sexy reporter (Pisier) introduces him to an orphaned young Jewish boy, the boxer undertakes to protect him and tries to help sneak the boy and his grandparents out of Hitler's Germany. Of course, the boxer's sympathies lead him right to Hitler.

One of Jean-Paul Belmondo's best movies, this film was one of the biggest box-office hits of the year in France with almost half a million tickets sold the first week it opened. Belmondo is everything he has ever been touted to be: sexy, sincere, tough and charming. The film was shot in Germany and, as usual, Belmondo performed all of his own stunts. The comedy-suspense plot is somewhat predictable, but consistently entertaining.

Some critics complained this was merely a vehicle built around Belmondo, even including the obligatory Belmondo in his undershorts scene. Others took offense at some of the Jewish and Hitler jokes. But for Belmondo fanatics, the movie proved a great showcase for his talents.

21 *L'Ascenseur pour l'échafaud (Elevator to the Gallows* or *Frantic)*
1957 B&W　*Director* Louis Malle; *Producer* Nouvelles Editions de Films; *Screenplay* Louis Malle and Roger Minier, based on the novel by Noël Calef; *Photography* Henri Decaë; *Music* Miles Davis; *Set* Rino Mondellini and Jean Mandaroux; *Sound* Raymond Gauguier; *Editing* Jean-Louis Misar. Running time: 87 minutes.

Cast: Jeanne Moreau, Maurice Ronet, Georges Poujouly, Elga Anderson, Yori Bertin, Ivan Petrovitch, Félix Marten, Jean Wall, Jean-Claude Brialy, Lino Ventura, Hubert Deschamps, Jacqueline Staup, Sylviane Aisenstein, François Joux, Charles Denner, Jacques Hilling, Marcel Cuvelier, Marcel Jounet, Gérard Darrieu, Lucien Desagneaux, Guy Henry, Micheline Sarfati, Gisèle Grandpré, Michèle Bona.

This is a story of the perfect crime. A wealthy wife (Moreau) persuades her lover Bernard Tavernier (Ronet), to kill her husband, who is also his boss (Wall). The murder goes smoothly until a series of misfortunes, including a stuck elevator and a stolen car, make the crime not so perfect after all.

This was Louis Malle's first feature film, which he made at the tender age of 25. It was an astounding directorial debut from a cinema student who had worked with Jacques Cousteau and Robert Bresson. The way in which Malle filmed Paris at night and the use of Miles Davis' music raised this movie way above the curse of being just another thriller. Malle captured Paris in the late 1950s with freshness and an exciting personal vision. His direction of Ronet and Moreau was credited with eliciting their best performances ever.

Georges Sadoul acknowledged some amateur awkwardness in the film, but that did not stop him from championing it in the French press and as a judge of the young director's Prix Louis Delluc, which Malle won. In fact, he called it "excellent" and "extraordinary."

Assassins and Thieves *see* **Assassins et voleurs**

22 *Assassins et voleurs (Assassins and Thieves* or *Lovers and Thieves)*
1956 B&W　*Director* Sacha Guitry; *Producer* CLM, Gaumont; *Screenplay* Sacha Guitry; *Photography* Paul Cotteret; *Music* Jean Françaix; *Set* Jean Douarinou; *Sound* Jean Bertrand; *Editing* Paulette Robert. Running time: 85 minutes.

Cast: Jean Poiret, Michel Serrault, Magali Noël, Darry Cowl, Clément Duhour, Lucien Baroux, Zita Perzel, Pierre Larquey, Pauline Carton, Marcel Vallée, Jacques Varennes, Pierre-Jean Vaillard, Fernand Raynaud, Marguerite Pierry.

Philippe d'Artois (Poiret), a wealthy dilettante, catches a burglar (Serrault) in his house. He pours his guilty heart out to the thief, telling him how he killed his mistress' husband years ago after the husband had strangled his wife in a jealous rage, but that coincidentally a thief had entered the house and the police arrested him and charged him with the murder. After a bout of insanity and a thieving life of his own, Philippe has become bored. That very morning, though, he learned that the thief who had gone to jail in his place had been freed, and Philippe fears he will come after him for revenge. Albert, it turns out, is that thief, but after their heart-to-heart, he tries to persuade Philippe not to worry; he promises he will not kill him, unless Philippe really is bored with life and wants to die, in which case he can leave everything to Albert to ease his guilt. While they stage the suicide, there is a so-called accident.

Guitry's last film, which he finished just before he died, is a wonderful satire on the film noir and one of his best postwar films. Poiret and Serrault dance around and manipulate each other and the audience superbly. It is a fascinating suspense tale with great crime and courtroom scenes.

Many critics found the film wonderfully amusing with a picaresque quality of finding hilarity in the grotesque that resembled the great authors Defoe and Diderot. Others complained that it was jumbled and had too many unlikely coincidences.

At the Meeting with Joyous Death *see* **Au rendez-vous de la mort joyeuse**

23 *L'Attentat (The French Conspiracy* or *The French Plot)*   1971 Color *Director* Yves Boisset; *Producer* Transinter, Terza, Corona; *Screenplay* Jorge Semprun, based on a story by Ben Barzman and Basilio Franchina; *Photography* Ricardo Aronovitch; *Music* Ennio Morricone; *Set* Marc Desages and Théo Meurisse; *Editing* Albert Jurgenson. Running time: 113 minutes.

Cast: Jean-Louis Trintignant, Jean Seberg, Michel Piccoli, Gian Maria Volonte, Michel Bouquet, Philippe Noiret, François Périer, Bruno Cremer, Daniel Ivernel, Karine Schubert, Roy Schneider, Jean Bouise, Georges Staquet, Pierre Santini, Denis Manuel.

This is a political thriller based on the French scandal that occurred in 1965 when the exiled leader of the Left Wing Moroccan opposition, Ben Barka, was kidnapped with the help of French and Moroccan officials and the French mafia. Darien (Trintignant) is a journalist whose involvement in the plot evolves from initial complicity to last-minute heroism.

This is one of the best of France's political genre films, so popular in the 1970s. Boisset assembled an amazing cast, and they prove to be one of the main strengths of the film. The twists and turns of the plot with characters suddenly shifting from guilty to innocent and back again provides great suspense.

The French Conspiracy opened to great fanfare in Paris with the leftist *Le Nouvel Observateur* running a six-page article on the real incident the film was based on. Though some complained that Boisset exploited the real story with a flashy cast and plot, many argued it was one of the better political pictures made. Some critics compared Boisset's ability to create suspense to Hitchcock's. When it came out in the United States, *Variety* called it: "A sharply made and potent political thriller on the line of *Z*."

24 *Au-delà des grilles (The Walls of Malapaga)*   1949 B&W   *Director* René Clément; *Producer* Francoriz Production, Alfredo Guarini Produzione; *Screenplay* Cesare Zavattini, Suso Cecchi d'Amico and Alfredo Guarini; *Adaptation and Dialogue* Jean Aurenche and Pierre Bost; *Photographer* Louis Page; *Music* Roman Vlad; *Set* Filippone; *Editing* Mario Serandrei. Running time: 95 minutes.

L'Ascenseur pour l'échafaud (*Elevator to the Gallows*), 1957; directed by Louis Malle.

Cast: Jean Gabin, Isa Miranda, Vera Talchi, Andréa Cecchi, Robert Dalban, Ave Ninchi, Carlo Tamberlani, Dina Romano, Checco Risoni, Vittorio Duse, Renato Mavasi, Fulvia Fulvi, Claudio Ermelli, Agnese Dublini, Giulio Tommassini, Giuseppe Garello.

To evade the police who are after him for the murder of his mistress, Pierre (Gabin) hides on a ship bound for Italy. He leaves the safety of the ship in Genoa because a toothache bothers him. When he falls in love with an Italian, Marta (Miranda), he thinks he has found happiness, but his past troubles catch up with him.

This was the last film of the great Jean Gabin, the tough-guy hero, so treasured by postwar France, and it did him justice. Love in the ruins rarely has been made so beautiful or poignant. The script is spare and yet the characters speak in their silences. The sad atmosphere of the port destroyed by war adds a haunting honesty to the desperate situation. All of the characters have depth and dimension. Gabin is truly at his best.

The New York Herald Tribune called it "a bitter account of a romance that blossomed too late, but it is tinged with beauty from beginning to end." The film won the awards for Best Director and Best Actress at Cannes in 1949. It won an honorary Oscar for Best Foreign Film in 1950.

25 *Au hasard, Balthazar* 1966 B&W *Director* Robert Bresson; *Producer* Argos Film, Parc Films, Athos Films, Svensk-Filmindustri, Svensk Filminstitutet; *Screenplay* Robert Bresson; *Photography* Ghislain Cloquet; *Music* Franz Schubert and Jean Wiener; *Set* Pierre Charbonnier; *Sound* Antoine Petitjean; *Editing* Raymond Lamy. Running time: 95 minutes.

Cast: Anna Wiazemsky, François Lafarge, Philippe Asselin, Nathalie Joyaut, Walter Green, Jean-Claude Guilbert, Pierre Klossowski, François Sullerot, Marie-Claude Frémont, Jean Remignard, Jacques Sorbets, Mylène Weyergans, Tord Paag, Sven Frostenson, Dominique Moune, Roger Fjellstrom, Jean-Joël Batbier, Rémy Brozek, Guy Bréjac, Gilles Sandier, Isabelle de Winter, Henri Fraisse.

This is a film that looks at the brutality of life through the eyes and fortunes of a donkey. He begins life as the pet of children in rural France, then is put to work. The donkey's misfortunes parallel those of his various owners. For a brief period his life improves when he joins a circus, but he is then sent back to work in the fields, before he winds up appearing in a processional as a saint.

Jean-Luc Godard said this movie "is really the world in an hour and a half." One of Bresson's masterpieces, *Au hasard, Balthazar* does seem to encompass all of the beauty and brutality of the world. With a mix of Christian overtones, eroticism, jazz and motorcyclists, this is Bresson at his most innovative. As usual, the photography is exquisite with a donkey's life set against the world beautifully.

French critic Georges Sadoul exclaimed: "This handsome film is truly one of the most complete and most perfect films produced in the world during the first six years of the '60s." He believed that *Balthazar* "is as rich and enriching as the best novel."

26 *Au rendez-vous de la mort joyeuse (At the Meeting with Joyous Death)* 1973 Color *Director* Juan Buñuel; *Producer* Serge Friedman; *Screenplay* Pierre-Jean Montigneux and Juan Buñuel; *Photography* Ghislain Cloquet; *Music* Vieutemps, Beethoven; *Set* Robert Clavel; *Editing* Geneviève Vaury. Running time: 90 minutes.

Cast: Yasmine Dahm, Françoise Fabian, Jean-Marie Bory, Jean-Pierre Darras, Michel Creton, Claude Dauphin, Gérard Depardieu, André Weber, Renato Salvatoir.

This is a fantastical story about the strange relationship between an old house and a young girl, Sophie (Dahm). Sophie's parents buy a lovely old house near the woods, but as soon as they move in strange things begin to happen. Frightened by the inexplicable occurrences, they decide to move out. A television crew comes to film the hauntings, but they too are chased away. The house wants only Sophie.

Surrealist Luis Buñuel's son takes on the old haunted house story, sets it in modern times and works magic in his first movie. Like his father, he was interested in taking the everyday to its wildest extreme. The film was made at a time when filmmakers around the world were playing with occult subjects in films such as *Rosemary's Baby* which came out a few years before. The plays on the girl's sexual awareness and her possible supernatural powers are interesting.

French critics hailed the film as a work of great promise. *Variety* called it a "sprightly occult romp." It was never distributed in the United States. The film won the Prix Georges Sadoul in 1972.

27 *Au revoir les enfants (Goodbye, Children)* 1987 Color *Director* Louis Malle; *Producer* Nouvelles Editions de Films S.A., MK2 Productions, Stella Film, NEF; *Screenplay* Louis Malle; *Photography* Renato Berta; *Music* Schubert and Saint-Säens; *Set* Willy Holt; *Sound* Jean-Claude Laureux; *Costumes* Corinne Jorry; *Editing* Emmanuelle Castro. Running time: 103 minutes.

Cast: Gaspard Manesse, Raphaël Fejto, Francine Racette, Philippe Morier-Genoud, Stanislas Carré de Malberg, François Berléand, François Négret, Peter Fitz, Pascal Rivet, Benoît Henriet, Richard Leboeuf, Xavier Legrand, Arnaud Henriet, Jean-Sébastien Chauvin, Luc Etienne, Daniel Edinger, Marcel Bellot, René Bouloc, Ami Flammer, Irène Jacob, Jacqueline Staup.

Three new students arrive at a boys' Catholic boarding school during World War II. One of the new students, Jean Bonnot (Fejto), slowly befriends another student, Julien (Manesse), who eventually figures out that Jean is Jewish, but he keeps quiet. Tipped off by an employee fired by the school, the Gestapo search the school and arrest the Jews and members of the Resistance, including the Catholic Father who heads the school.

Louis Malle's autobiographical film examining the costs of World War II in a school's daily life may be his best. He begins with the childhood vision of the world, where lights out, classes, and petty rivalries dominate the days, but a growing awareness of the dangers and ominous cruelty of the adult world outside slowly invades his consciousness until Nazis literally command the schoolyard, and he watches them take boys and priests away to die. Malle made *Au revoir les enfants* after ten years of not making a film in French. It is a moving portrait of how the war touched Malle's life in particular and the life of France in general.

"Rarely have audiences' tears been more honestly wrung," wrote Peter Rainer in the *Los Angeles Herald Examiner*. It won the Golden Lion at the Venice Biennal and the Prix Louis Delluc in 1987.

28 *L'Auberge rouge (The Red Inn)* 1951 B&W *Director* Claude Autant-Lara; *Producer* Memnon Films; *Screenplay* Jean Aurenche; *Adaptation and Dialogue* Jean Aurenche, Pierre Bost and Claude Autant-Lara; *Photography* André

Bac; *Music* René Cloërec; *Set* Max Douy; *Sound* Le Breton; *Costumes* Jacques Cottin; *Editing* Madeleine Gug. Running time: 95 minutes.

Cast Fernandel, Françoise Rosay, Julien Carette, Marie-Claire Olivia, Jean-Roger Caussimon, Nane Germon, Jacques Charron, Didier d'Yd, Lud Germain, Grégoire Aslan, Andrée Viala, Robert Berri, Jacques Charon, André Dalibert, Manuel Gary, André Cheff, René Lefèvre-Bel.

This is a dark farce about a group of travelers huddled together in an inn during a winter storm. Their refuge, though, is the hotel of a husband (Carette) and wife (Rosay) who rob and murder their guests. The monk (Fernandel) knows about the hoteliers' hobby but cannot warn the guests because of his vow of silence, so instead he tries to save them with a series of religious antics.

This is one of the great comic Fernandel's best movies. It is high-drama, farce, tragedy, social commentary and thriller all rolled into one. One French critic described the film as a Pagnol character in a Hitchcock film. It was banned in England, and Fernandel supposedly felt he had to redeem himself with Catholics by doing *Don Camillo* shortly after *The Red Inn*. The title came from the Balzac novel, which Autant-Lara wanted to adapt. He did not have a big enough budget to reenact the Rhine Army, so he and Jean Aurenche adapted a true story about a crime at an inn in the Ardeches and kept Balzac's title.

When the film was released, the critics could not fit it neatly into a genre, so they dismissed it altogether. Good Catholics, of course, took great offense at the jokes poking fun at religious rites and sacraments. The public, however, is always the final judge, and they found it hilarious.

29 *Une Aussi Longue Absence (The Long Absence)* 1960 B&W *Director* Henri Colpi; *Producer* Procinex, Lyre, Galatea; *Screenplay* Marguerite Duras and Gérard Jariot, based on a novel by Marguerite Duras; *Photography* Marcel Weiss; *Music* Georges Delerue, Rossini, Donizetti; *Set* Maurice Colasson; *Sound* René Breteau, Séverin Frankiel, Jean-Claude Marchetti; *Editing* Jasmine Chasney. Running time: 105 minutes.

Cast: Alida Valli, Georges Wilson, Jacques Harden, Charles Blavette, Diana Lepvrier, Amédée, Catherine Fontenay, Nane Germon, Paul Faivre, Pierre Parel, Georges Bielec, Charles Bouillaud, Corrado Guarducci, Clément Harari, Jean Luisi, Pierre Mirat.

Thérèse Langlois (Valli), whose husband was deported during World War II, runs a small café by herself. When a bum (Wilson), suffering from amnesia, begins spending his time in front of her café, she tries to help him recover his memory, and, in doing so, she recovers her lost feelings of love.

The combination of Marguerite Duras' reflections on love, loss, grief and memory with the subtle camera artistry of Henri Colpi and George Delerue's exquisite score make this an extraordinarily moving and beautiful film. It was Colpi's first feature, and he elicited superb performances from both Valli and Wilson.

French critics hailed it as a profoundly moving and beautiful film. Though the film never attracted much attention in the United States, it did manage to get international distribution. It won the Prix Louis Delluc in 1960 and the Palme d'Or at Cannes in 1961.

30 *Aux yeux du monde* 1991 Color *Director* Eric Rochant; *Producer* Productions Lazennec, FR3 Films, Société Générale de Gestion Cinématographique, Générale d'Images, Canal Plus; *Screenplay* Eric Rochant; *Photography* Pierre Novion; *Music* Gérard Torikian; *Set* Pascale Fenouillet; *Editing* Catherine Quesemand. Running time: 95 minutes.

Cast: Yvan Attal, Marc Berman, Kristin Scott-Thomas, Charlotte Gains-bourg, Francine Olivier, Michèle Foucher.

Bruno (Attal) is unhappy with his place in the world. He falls madly in love with a young hairdresser, Juliette (Gainsbourg). To get her attention, he hijacks a schoolbus. But when the police pursue him with a vengeance, and he has to deal with getting rid of the children and adults whom he has taken hostage, he is caught in something bigger than he expected.

Eric Rochant's second feature is a portrait of teenage turmoil and another example of French filmmakers of the late 1980s, early 1990s pitting passionate characters against a hostile world. Rochant succeeds in creating a *No Exit* sort of atmosphere by keeping almost all of the film's action inside the schoolbus.

Some critics found the film to be a poor man's version of *Betty Blue* or *Love Without Pity*. Others applauded Rochant's sincerity and his success in establishing a modern road movie with deep meditations on society's extreme reactions to youthful confusion.

Les Aventures de Holly and Wood *see* **Le Rose et le blanc**

31 *L'Aveu de Casta (The Confession)* 1970 Color   *Director* Constan-tin Costa-Gavras; *Producer* Corona, Pomereu, Fono Roma Productions, Sélénia; *Screenplay* Jorge Semprun, based on a story by Lise and Arthur London; *Photography* Raoul Coutard; *Music* Mikis Théodorakis; *Set* Bernard Evein; *Sound* William-Robert Sivel; *Editing* Françoise Bonnot. Running time: 160 minutes.

Cast: Yves Montand, Simone Signoret, Gabrielle Ferzetti, Michel Vitold, Jean Bouise, Laszlo Szabo, Antoine Vitez, Monique Chaumette, Guy Mairesse, Marc Eyraud, Gérard Darrieu, Charles Moulin, Antoine Vitez, Georges Aubert, Marcel Cuvelier, Michel Robin, Pierre-Jacques Moncrobier, Michel Beaune, Jacques Rispal, Jean Lescot, François Marthouret, Partick Lancelot, Umberto Raho, Claude Vernier, Jacques Marbeuf, Marc Arian, Jacques Chevaler, Gilles Segal, Maurice Jacquemont, André Cellier, Jean-Paul Cisife, Jean-François Gobbi, Pierre Vielescazes, Marc Bonseignour, Thierry Bosc, Pierre Decazes, Pierre Delaval, Basile Diamantopoulos, Jacques Emin, William Jacques, Jean-Pierre Janic, Henri Marteau, André Falcon, Paul Savatier, Nicole Vervil.

This is the story of an important communist politician, Gérard (Montand), in Eastern Europe during the Cold War, who is accused of a crime, arrested and sent to prison. As he suffers hunger, cold and all other discomforts of prison life, he is sustained through his torture by his communist fervor and forgives his captors because he believes they believe they are fighting for the communist cause. His wife Lise (Signoret) denounces him for the sake of the party. He is never cleared of his charges, but is not condemned to death. When he finally gets out of prison, the Soviet tanks enter Prague, and he and his wife leave for Paris.

With *Z* and *The Confession*, Costa-Gavras was credited with saving the political thriller genre in France. This was certainly one of the best political films of the decade. It was complete condemnation of totalitarianism. Yves Montand's performance is staggering. During the filming he lost over 25 pounds and wore his wrists raw with handcuffs to deliver one of his best performances ever.

The Confession was hailed as a masterpiece by critics on both sides of the Atlantic when it came out. Vincent Canby in *The New York Times* called Costa-Gavras "a movie master." He declared "*The Confession* is vastly more interesting than *Z*! Much more complex, much more human! . . . A harrowing film of intellectual and emotional anguish."

Bad Blood *see* **Mauvais Sang**

Bad Girls *see* **Les Biches**

The Bad Liaisons *see* **Les Mauvaises Rencontres**

32 *Les Baisers de secours (Emergency Kisses)* 1989 B&W   *Director* Philippe Garrel; *Producer* Les Films de l'Atlante, La Sept, Planète de compagnie; *Screenplay* Philippe Garrel; *Photography* Jacques Loiseleux; *Music* Barney Wilson; *Sound* Claudine Nougaret; *Editing* Sophie Coussein. Running time: 83 minutes.
   Cast: Brigitte Sy, Philippe Garrel, Anémone, Maurice Garrel, Yvette Etiévant, Louis Garrel, Jacques Kébadian, Valérie Dréville.
   A filmmaker (Philippe Garrel) decides to make a movie about his marriage, but when he casts himself as himself but doesn't cast his wife (Sy) as herself the problems begin. She is angry that he has chosen another actress (Anémone) to play her, and in the course of the filming, their real-life marriage falls apart. They finally mend things between them and the film project is shelved.
   This movie marked a new level of personal auteur filmmaking, with Garrel casting all the important people of his life in a movie about his life. His live-in lover and mother of his child plays his wife; he plays himself; his child plays his child; and his father plays his father. This is a family affair on film, the likes of which had never been tried before. The lessons on life, love and living together can be a bit over done, but Garrel's attempt at stretching the concept of personal filmmaking are very interesting.
   Some critics found the movie had taken introspection way too far. They accused Garrel of airing his dirty laundry for therapeutic purposes not artistic ones. *La Revue du Cinéma* applauded Garrel for "always putting himself on the frontier of the experimental."

33 *Baisers volés (Stolen Kisses)* 1968 Color   *Director* François Truffaut; *Producer* Films du Carrosse, Artistes Associés; *Screenplay* François Truffaut, Claude de Givray and Bernard Revon; *Photography* Denys Clerval; *Music* Antoine Duhamel; *Set* Claude Pignot; *Sound* René Levert; *Editing* Agnès Guillemot. Running time: 90 minutes.
   Cast: Jean-Pierre Léaud, Claude Jade, Daniel Ceccaldi, Claire Duhamel, Michel Lonsdale, Delphine Seyrig, André Falcon, Harry Max, Catherine Lutz, Marie-France Pisier, Jean-François Adam, Paul Pavel, Christine Pelée, Léon Ekelbaum, Jacques Rispal, Martine Brochard, Serge Rousseau, Noël Simon, Pascale Dauman, Carine Jeantet, Jacques Robiolles, François Darbon, Albert Simono, Jacques Delord, Carole Noe, Robert Cambourakis, Christine Pellé, Chantal Banlier, Marcel Mercier, Joseph Mériau, Léon Elckenbaum, Roger Trapp, Marcel Berbert, Madeleine Parard, France Monthell, Elisabeth Braconnier, Martine Ferrière.

Baisers volés (Stolen Kisses), 1968; directed by François Truffaut.

On returning from his military service, which he joined after a fight with his girlfriend, Antoine Doinel (Léaud) has difficulty finding and keeping a job. He works for a while in a seedy hotel, then becomes a private detective hired to find out why a shoe salesman is disliked by everyone. After he has a fling with the shoe salesman's wife (Seyrig), he turns to television repair and reunites with his girlfriend (Jade).

This is the third of the five-part Antoine Dionel series that began with *The 400 Blows*, and is one of Truffaut's best movies. It is funny, moving and charming. Antoine was Truffaut's screen alter-ego and, probably because he felt so close to the material, he was beautifully able to capture a youthful anguish and aimlessness. Truffaut dedicated the film to Henri Langlois and the Cinémathèque Française, during a bureaucratic struggle in which André Malraux ordered Langlois removed.

Some critics claimed that the film was too simplistic and pat. Bruce Bahrenburg said, "*Stolen Kisses* is a marvelous film, and shows that with the right themes Truffaut is one of the best directors in any country." The film was nominated for the Oscar for Best Foreign Film in 1968. It won the Grand Prix du Cinéma Français, the Prix Louis Delluc and the French Critics' Prix Méliès in 1968.

34 *Bako, l'autre rive* 1979 Color *Director* Jacques Champreux; *Producer* Orpham Productions; *Screenplay* Jacques Champreux and Cheikh Doukouré; *Photography* Jacques Ledoux; *Music* Lamine Konté; *Set* Charles Finelli; *Editing* Andrée Davanture, Marie-Christine Rougerie and Diap Alassane. Running time: 110 minutes.

Cast: Sikidi Bakaba, Doura Mané, Cheik Doukouré, Guillaume Corréa,

Amadou Camara, Konate Kassim, N'Demba Sidibe, Jean-Claude Yebga, Elias Cherif, Konate Lassana, Vince, Sylla, Florencio, Harouna N'Diaye, Awa N'Diaye, Abdoulaye Seck, Pathe Diop, Amidou Sow, Taierno Sow, Pierre Biet, Liliane Bertrand, Martin Trévières, Gérard Pichon, Arlette Tephany, Souleymane Koulibali.

This is the journey of a man hoping to escape from the poverty of his African village to Paris where he can earn money to send back to his loved ones. The hardships of the trip take so much out of him that the day he arrives in Paris, he dies.

This film, which incorporates three languages (Bambara, Ouoloff and French) sheds light on the immigrant situation in France in a way infrequently explored. It examined where France's African immigrants have come from, why and at what personal cost.

French critics rejoiced in *Bako*'s originality and its honesty. Perhaps because it focuses on the French immigrant experience, it has never been distributed in the United States. Claire Clouzot wrote in *Le Matin de Paris*: "*Bako* is the most clear, authentic and moving film one can see on the issue of immigration." It won the Prix Jean Vigo in 1978.

35 *Le Bal (The Ball)* 1983 Color   *Director* Ettore Scola; *Producer and Screenplay* Ruggero Maccari, Jean-Claude Pettchenat, Furio Scarpelli, Ettore Scola, based on the Théâtre du Campagnol; *Photography* Ricardo Aronovitch; *Music* Vladimir Cosma; *Set* Luciano Ricceri; *Sound* Bruno Le Jean, Corrado Volpicelli; *Costumes* Ezio Altieri, Françoise Tournafond; *Editing* Raimondo Crociani. Running time: 112 minutes.

Cast: Etienne Guichard, Francesco de Rosa, Regis Bouquet, Martine Chauvin, Lilian Delval, Rossana di Lorenzo, Raymonde Heudeline, Arnault Lecarpentier, Olivier Loiseau, Nani Noel, Jean-Claude Penchenat, Christophe Allwright, Aziz Arbia, Jean-François Perrier, Geneviève Rey-Penchenat, Marc Berman, Chantal Capron, Anita Picchiarini, François Pick, Danielle Rochard, Monica Scattini, Michel Toty, Michel Van Speybroeck.

Fifty years of life in a French ballroom with only the music and dance telling the story. From the popular favorites before, during and after World War II, up to the Beatles and through the early 1980s. The dancers are characters as colorful as the steps they perform, from Gallic lounge lizards to nerdy two-steppers.

This is a great visual comedy from the director of *La Cage aux folles* which proved that musicals and nostalgia can still find critical and commercial success. It was adapted from the play, which was a huge French hit. The music is great, with tunes from Piaf to Chevalier classics. Scola said of the film: "All my characters avoid words .... They try to communicate differently; by looks, gestures, physical contact and brief meetings which replace these words .... *The Ball* is the solitude of people who do not need words."

When it came out in the United States, *The Aquarian* called it "a chance to immerse oneself in all the deepest mortal grace notes, the richest popular icons, the most mellifluous sounds of several different eras." *The Ball* won three Césars, for best film, direction and music, and the Silver Bear for Best Film at the Berlin Film Festival. It was nominated for an Oscar for Best Foreign Language Film, which raised some eyebrows because it has no dialogue and the songs are in many languages.

36 *La Balance (The Nark)* 1982 Color   *Director* Bob Swain; *Producer* Films Ariane; *Screenplay* Bob Swain; *Photography* Bernard Zitzermann; *Music*

Roland Bouquet; *Set* Eric Moulard; *Sound* Jean-Charles Ruault; *Editing* Françoise Javet. Running time: 102 minutes.

Cast: Nathalie Baye, Philippe Léotard, Richard Berry, Maurice Ronet,
Christophe Malavoy, Florent Pagny, Tcheky Karyo, Jean-Paul Connart, Bernard
Freyd, Albert Dray, Jean-Daniel Laval, Luc-Antoine Diquero, Anne-Claude
Salimo, Michel Anphoux, Raouf Ben Yaghlane, Robert Atlan, Guy Dhers, Fran-
çois Berleand, Sam Karmann, Audrey Lazinni, Fiorella De Gennaro, Claude
Villers, Mostefa Zerguine, Marc Ballis, Patrick Guillaume, Christian Gaubert,
David Overbey, Catherine Le Dall, Geoffrey Carey.

Investigating a murder, Inspector Paluzzi (Berry) sets out to get the truth from
one of two sources. He tries alternately to crack the petty criminal Dédé (Léotard)
and the prostitute Nicole (Baye), with whom Dédé is in love. Nicole finally panics
and tells on Dédé, whom the police trap and kill.

Made by American director, Bob Swaim, who spent six months with neighborhood gangsters to ensure the authenticity of the film, this epitomizes the
modern thriller genre à la Française. It owes more to B-movies and television
shoot-'em-up series than it does to Sam Spade or *Pickpocket*, as cops and crooks
alike favor jeans over trenches. Though it breaks no new cinematic ground, it is
probably the best and most successful of the many French police thrillers that tried
to give Hollywood a run for the action market in the 1980s before just about aban-
doning the genre altogether. Nathalie Baye is wonderful as a tacky Paris prostitute
set against the elegant façade of La Madeleine.

While some critics wrote it off as just another cops-and-robbers, the French
audiences loved this Gallic gangster film. When the film was released in the United
States, Jay Carr of *The Boston Globe* wrote: "Aside from demolishing forever the
idea that police work is based on flashes of Sherlockian deduction, *La Balance* is
tough, tangy, stylish and immediate." It was one of the biggest box-office successes
of the decade. It won a number of 1983 Césars, including Best Film and one for
Baye for Best Actress.

The Ball *see* **Le Bal**

37 *Le Ballon rouge (The Red Balloon)*   1957 Color   *Director* Albert
Lamorisse; *Producer* Films Montsouris; *Screenplay* Albert Lamorisse; *Photography* Edmond Séchan; *Music* Maurice le Roux; *Editing* Pierre Gillette. Running
time: 35 minutes.

Cast Pascal Lamorisse.

The story of a boy and his red ballon. One day on the way to school, six-year-
old Pascal (Lamorisse) frees a red balloon from a streetlamp, where its string is
caught. The balloon follows Pascal to school, where it waits for him outside the
window, and then goes with him to mass, then to a pastry shop. But a gang of boys
pop the balloon. All the balloons in Paris come to comfort Pascal, and lift him
up in the air.

A classic film that many will remember from their grade school or high-school
French class. The red balloon against the background of the old gray buildings of
Montmartre is visually astounding. In fact, the photography throughout is
remarkable. This is a fairy tale of France in the 1950s, but also a work that preaches
the philosophy that one should look at the world anew to see its myriad possibilities.

This film was an instant crowd pleaser. All of France adored *The Red Balloon* when it came out, except, of course, for some critics. François Truffaut, for instance, said despite admirable photography, he found "no poetry, fantasy, sensibility nor truth" in the film. It won the Palme d'Or at Cannes in 1956.

Band of Outsiders *see* **Bande à part**

38 *Bande à part (Band of Outsiders* or *The Outsiders)* 1964 B&W *Director* Jean-Luc Godard; *Producer* Anouchka, Orsay Films; *Screenplay* Jean-Luc Godard, based on Dolorès and Bernard Hitchens' novel *Fool's Guide*; *Photography* Raoul Coutard; *Music* Michel Legrand; *Set* Outdoors; *Sound* René Levert; *Editing* Agnès Guillemot. Running time: 95 minutes.

Cast: Anna Karina, Sami Frey, Claude Brasseur, Luisa Colpeyn, Ernest Menzer, Chantal Darget, Danièle Girard, Michèle Seghers, Georges Staquet, Claude Makovski, Jean-Luc Godard, Jean-Claude Remoleux, M. Jojot, Michel Delahaye.

A parody of a drama about two friends, Frantz (Frey) and Arthur (Brasseur), who meet a schoolgirl-cum-maid, Odile (Karina), who tells them about a stash of money. The trio have been weaned on dime novels and gangster movies and decide to make a pulp fiction plot into their reality. When the three go to hold up the woman who is in possession of the bundle, they find no treasure and the old woman and Arthur are shot.

One of Godard's most interesting and respected films, which mixes Shakespeare with B-movies, this is a parody of a *serie noires*. The tone goes beyond satire to become cynical and makes for quite a depressing film. Against a montage of wonderful Paris street scenes, including a car race and café dancing, Godard explores everything from lovers' betrayal to literary jokes. Ultimately, the characters, who are very well played, are of less interest than Godard's unique vision.

Some critics found the movie to be a Godard "miss" rather than one of his usual hits. They complained that his parody of everything became irritating. When it came out in the United States, *Newsweek* declared: "Godard is the cinematic Fitzgerald of the pop generation. His band of outsiders are the beautiful and damned, whose grace and flair can dance into folly and explode into fatality."

39 *La Bande des quatres (The Gang of Four)* 1989 Color *Director* Jacques Rivette; *Producer* Pierre Grise Productions, Limbo Film, La Sept, Canal Plus, Le CNC; *Screenplay* Jacques Rivette, Pascal Bonitzer, and Christine Laurent; *Photography* Caroline Champetier; *Music* Monteverdi; *Set* Emmanuel de Chauvigny; *Sound* Florian Eidenbenz; *Editing* Catherine Quesemand. Running time: 160 minutes.

Cast: Bulle Ogier, Benoît Régent, Laurence Côte, Fejria Deliba, Bernadette Giraud, Inès de Medeiros-d'Almeida, Nathalie Richard, Karine Bayard, Dominique Rousseau, Caroline Gasser, Irène Jacob, Françoise Muxel, Pascale Salkin, Agnès Sourdillon, Irinia Dalle.

A story about four women in an acting class: Anna (Deliba), Claude (Côte), Joyce (Giraud) and Lucia (de Medeiros-d'Almeida). When a man appears and tells them their friend and fellow acting student, Cécile (Richard), is in trouble because of an illegal plot involving her boyfriend, they all try to help her. But the man who has informed them of Cécile's troubles is not what he seems.

Rivette is known as the least commercial of the New Wave directors, and this is easily one of his most accessible and entertaining films. With rehearsals of Racine, Corneille and Molière plays alternating with "girl talk" about Cécile and her problems, Rivette focuses on that age-old favorite theme of French film theater and life. The film's strength is Rivette's meditations, not the suspense line of the plot. Ogier, who plays the acting teacher, is wonderful.

Some critics were bothered by Rivette's balance between art house intellect and suspense thriller. Others loved it. *The Village Voice*'s critic, Elliott Stein, found the film to be Rivette's most "engaging" film in over a decade. "This is a gracefully fluent and deceptively simple work, nearly three hours long but consistently engrossing," he wrote.

40 *La Bataille de l'eau lourde (The Heavy Water Battle)* 1948 B&W   *Director* Titus Vibe Muller and Jean Dréville; *Producer* Hero Films and Le Trident; *Screenplay* Jean Marin; *Adaptation* Jean Marin, Jean Dréville, Titus Vibe Muller, Knut Haukelid, A. Feldborg, Yves Ciampi, Jens Poulsor Roberson and C. Helberg; *Photography* Hilding Bladle and Marcel Weiss; *Music* Gunnar Stenvstovald; *Editing* Jean Feyte. Running time: 95 minutes.

Cast: Frédéric Jolio-Curie, Alban Kowarski, Raoul Dautry and the French-Norwegian parachutists corps.

The story of a sabotage mission undertaken by a group of Norwegians, who travel from England, where they are refugees during World War II, to parachute back into Norway to destroy a distillation factory that supplies the Germans with deuterium oxide, commonly called "heavy water," which is integral to the Germans' atomic energy and destruction research.

A wonderful war drama–cum-documentary that captures with hard facts the spirit of war-time efforts. Some of the men who actually participated in the real mission appeared in the reenactment scenes, and real scientists explain how and why "heavy water" was important to the Germans' atomic bomb and energy efforts.

The film received a lot of publicity when it was released in Europe, because it was backed by a number of Resistance groups. American critics found the mixture between fact and drama did not succeed as well.

41 *Bataille du rail (Battle of the Rails)* 1945 B&W   *Director* René Clément; *Producer* CGCF; *Screenplay* René Clément and Colette Audry; *Dialogue* Colette Audry; *Photography* Henri Alekan; *Music* Yves Baudrier; *Sound* Constantin Evangelou; *Editing* Lucien Desagneaux. Running time: 85 minutes.

Cast: Jean Clarieux, Jean Daurand, Tony Laurent, Robery Leray, Lucien Desagneaux, Léon Pauléon, Jean Rauzéna, Redon, Max Well, Pierre Mindaist, Michel Salina, François Joux, Pierre Latour, Jean Lozach, Barreault.

A docu-drama about French railway workers who worked for the Resistance during World War II. Among the real war events reenacted were spy runs and the workers' sabotage of the train the Nazis were using to take reinforcements to Normandy as the liberating troops were landing.

This powerful movie crossed the formerly unbridgeable gap between great documentaries and great dramas. René Clément's first feature, it was inspired by the railway workers' own experiences. The movie is dedicated to the 4,000 French railway men who died during the war and was financed with donations from the workers who wanted to preserve and share their story. Clément travelled through

La Bataille de l'eau lourde (*The Heavy Water Battle*), 1948; directed by Titus Vibe Muller and Jean Dréville.

railyards and stations for months researching the details. It was the first film in which an entire train was destroyed; as it was sent off of a ravine. It inspired John Frankenheimer's *The Train*.

This brilliant evocation of the Occupation and the heroic human war efforts and sacrifices was an immediate and enormous success with critics and the public. Some critics found Clément's merging of fictional plot and documentary less successful than others, but all recognized it as one of the most important films about the war. This was one of the four films chosen to represent France in the first Cannes Film Festival in 1946. It won the Jury Prize and Best Director at Cannes, the Grand Prix du Cinéma Français and the French Critics' Prix Méliès in 1946.

Battle of the Rails *see* **Bataille du rail**

The Bear *see* **L'Ours**

A Beating Heart *see* **Un Cœur qui bat**

Betty Blue *see* **37.2 degrés le matin**

42 *Le Beau Mariage (The Well Made Marriage)*   1982 Color   *Director* Eric Rohmer; *Producer* Films du Losange, Films du Carrosse, Menegoz Productions; *Screenplay* Eric Rohmer; *Photography* Bernard Lutic, Romain Winding and Nicolas Brunet; *Music* Roman Girre and Simon Des Innocents; *Sound* Georges Prat, Gérard Lecas, Dominique Hennequin; *Editing* Cécile Decugis. Running time: 97 minutes.

Cast: Béatrice Romand, André Dussolier, Feodor Atkine, Huguette Faget, Arielle Dombasle, Thamila Mezbah, Sophie Renoir, Hervé Duhamel, Pascal Greggory, Virginie Thévenet, Denise Bailly, Vincent Gauthier, Anne Mercier, Catherine Réthi, Patrick Lambert.

A charming film about a young girl, Sabine (Romand), who lives in Le Mans and studies art history in Paris. One day, not long after breaking up with her boyfriend, she decides that she is dying to get married. She sets her sights on a "good marriage" — a lawyer named Edmond (Dussolier), who will be her husband. She puts up a good chase, but he prefers his independence, and she soon spots another victim.

Rohmer, who has been called "the satirical poet of the French bourgeoisie," parodies love and marriage in the second film in his series, *Comedies and Proverbs*. With exquisite photography and acting, Rohmer explores the sexual traditions and freedoms of men and women in the late twentieth century.

Critics on both sides of the Atlantic found this charming and funny. "Nothing happens," wrote the critic in *Screen International*, "yet not a move or a mood or a revealing comment is without relevance to how we try to fit awkwardly shaped truths into pretty patterns." It won the Grand Prix du Cinéma Français in 1982.

43 *Beau Père*   1981 Color   *Director* Bertrand Blier; *Producer* Sara Films, Antenne 2; *Screenplay* Bertrand Blier, based on his novel; *Photography* Sacha Vierny; *Music* Philippe Sarde and Johann Sebastian Bach; *Set* Théobald Meurisse; *Sound* Jean-Pierre Ruh; *Editing* Claudine Merlin. Running time: 122 minutes.

Cast: Patrick Dewaere, Ariel Besse, Nicole Garcia, Nathalie Baye, Maurice

Ronet, Macha Méril, Maurice Rich, Michel Berto, Geneviève Mnich, Pierre Leru-meur, Yves Gasc, Rose Thierry, Henri-Jacques Huet, Guy Teisseire, Catherine Alcover, Maurice Biraud, Jacques Rispal.

A musician, Rémi (Dewaere), finds himself responsible for a 14-year-old girl, when his live-in girlfriend is killed in a car accident and her daughter (Besse) would rather stay with him than move in with her real father. The girl's designs on her "stepfather" are not entirely innocent though, and, after much moral anguish, he gives in to her seduction, but all does not end happily.

What may seem to begin as one more Lolita film becomes an exploration of the moral responsibilities and depravities of a grown man. Blier handles the complexities of male–female and father–daughter relationships in both innovative and timeless ways. The lessons he shares are sad, but sweet in the fashion of real evolving relation-ships. Few will think of parenting in quite the same way after seeing this gem.

Kathy Schulz Huffhines called *Beau père* "Blier's tenderest movie." She hailed it as "a story about the hazards girls will face as daughters, wives, and mother." Others found it long and bogged down by a bad script and poor photography, and Blier found himself defending his Catholicism daily in the press.

44 *Le Beau Serge (Handsome Serge)* 1958 B&W *Director* Claude Chabrol; *Producer* Ajym Films, Marceau; *Screenplay* Claude Chabrol; *Photog-raphy* Henri Decaë and Jean Rabier; *Music* Emile Delpierre and Géo Legros; *Set* Outdoors in Sardent; *Sound* Jean-Claude Marchetti; *Editing* Jean Cotet. Running time: 97 minutes.

Cast: Gérard Blain, Jean-Claude Brialy, Bernadette Lafont, Michèle Méritz, Edmond Beauchamp, Claude Cerval, Jeanne Perez, André Dino, Claude Chabrol, Philippe de Broca, Jacques Rivette.

François (Brialy) goes home to the village of his childhood in Sardent, where he finds his best friend, Serge (Blain), has become an alcoholic after the birth of his mongoloid child. Despite François' valiant efforts to save his friend's marriage, he discovers that some lives are not easily redeemed. François eventually realizes his motives may be wrapped up in his own lack of purpose and, although very ill with tuberculosis, he goes out into a snowy night to drag a drunken Serge home, where they witness the birth of Serge's new son.

Hailed by many as the official start of the New Wave, *Handsome Serge* was Claude Chabrol's first feature. Chabrol financed the film with money his wife in-herited. Somewhat autobiographical, the film proved Chabrol was a master direc-tor from the first. Henri Decaë's photography of the wintertime village is lovely. Both Blain and Brialy prove themselves to be fine actors.

An immediate success with critics and the public. Some critics objected to the dissonance between the violent drama and the picturesque pastoral backdrop and the heavy Christian overtones, which is ironic because Chabrol considered this film to be his adieu to Catholicism. Others applauded as surprisingly fresh Chabrol's daring, rough filming and use of non-professional actors. It won the Prix Jean Vigo in 1959.

Beauties of the Night *see* **Les Belles de nuit**

The Beautiful Nut *see* **La Belle Noiseuse**

Beauty and the Beast *see* **La Belle et la bête**

45 *Le Bel Âge (The Wonderful Age)* 1959 B&W *Director* Pierre Kast; *Producer* Films d'Aujourd'hui, Centaure; *Screenplay* Pierre Kast and Jacques Doniol Valcroze, based on Alberto Moravio's novel *Un Vieil Imbécile*; *Photography* Gishlain Cloquet and Sacha Vierny; *Music* Georges Delerue and Alain Coragher; *Set* Jacques Saulnier; *Sound* Michel Fano; *Editing* Yannick Bellon. Running time: 100 minutes.

Cast: Françoise Prévost, Loleh Bellon, Gianni Esposito, Alexandra Stewart, Jean-Claude Brialy, Françoise Brion, Ursula Kubler-Vian, Marcel Pagliero, Virginie Vitry, Edith Scob, Barbara Aptekman, Anne Colette, Roland Tisseire, Marcello Pagliereo, Jacques Doniol-Valcroze, Boris Vian, Hubert Nöel.

Three men who manage a bookstore and a poet/patron swap their romantic war stories. Jacques (Doniol-Valcroze) pursues the lovely young woman Alexandra (Stewart), who is hired as a bookkeeper. He fails because of his worries about being too old. Claude (Esposito) tries to seduce Anne (Bellon), but his smooth moves give him away as an incorrigible ladies' man. Finally, four women on a ski vacation decide to play the pursuers rather than the pursued.

In this New Wave look at men and women in love, Kast wanted to explore the nature of love from scientific, philosophical and abstract angles. Without being a militant feminist or a male chauvinist, he manages to illuminate both feminine and masculine reactions to the rituals, traditions and constraints of love, because the men and women involved in each episode give their side of the story. Kast was more interested in psychology and morals than feelings, particularly how women struggle with achieving an equal role in courtship. The photography and narrative are wonderful.

Some critics found the film too intellectual, too didactic. One French critic wondered whether it should be termed "sentimental science-fiction." Others found Kast's meditation on love to be a fresh, original way to present a love story and credited him with achieving a large degree of depth.

46 *Bel Ami* 1954 Color *Director* Louis Daquin; *Producer* Les Films Malesherbes, Projecktograph Film; *Screenplay* Roger Vaillan, Vladimir Pozner and Louis Daquin, based on the novel by Guy de Maupassant; *Photography* Nicolas Hayer; *Music* Hans Eisler; *Set* Léon Barsacq; *Costumes* André Bakst. Running time: 85 minutes.

Cast: Jean Danet, Anne Vernon, Renée Faure, Christel Mardayn, Jean-Roger Caussimon, René Lefèvre, Egon Jordan, Jacqueline Duc, Mario Emo.

Set in Paris at the end of the nineteenth century, this film shows the rise of the ambitious Georges Duroy (Danet), a journalist who arrives from the colonies in Paris and manages to take the city by storm as he marries and seduces his way through a series of powerful and wealthy women.

The chronicle of an arriviste who is viewed as both a cold manipulator and a victim of society's ills. The film was censored because of references to North Africa which at the time, were viewed as inflammatory. Despite the wonderful photography and performances, the film was relegated to the art house scene in the United States, because an American adaptation had been made a decade earlier by Albert Lewin. Americans felt familiar with the story, even though, in this one the "bel ami" does not get the punishment for his sins that he did in the American version.

Variety called it "a faithful transcription of the book ... backed up by good atmosphere .... This is more of a social study than a real drama, which makes the characters somewhat sketchy rather than full-blooded."

47 *Belle de jour* 1967 Color   *Director* Luis Buñuel; *Producer* Robert and Raymond Hakim, Paris Film Productions, Five Films; *Screenplay* Luis Buñuel and Jean-Claude Carrière, based on the novel by Joseph Kessel; *Photography* Sacha Vierny; *Set* Robert Clavel; *Sound* René Longuet; *Costumes* Hélène Nourry; *Editing* Louisette Hautecoeur. Running time: 105 minutes.

Cast: Catherine Deneuve, Jean Sorel, Michel Piccoli, Pierre Clémenti, Geneviève Page, Françoise Fabian, Francisco Rabal, Maria Latour, Francis Blanche, Georges Marchl, François Maistre, Macha Méril, Muni, Dominique Dandrieux, Bernard Musicson, Brigitte Parmentier, Claude Cerval, Iska Khan, Marcel Charvey, Marc Eyraud, Pierre Marcay, Michel Charrel, D. De Roseville, Adélaïde Blasquez.

The story of a young married woman (Deneuve), who is bored in her marriage to a handsome young doctor (Sorel). Though she loves her husband, she finds her sadomasochistic fantasies consuming her, and even driving her to spend her afternoons as a prostitute. When one of her regular customers (Clémenti), a petty criminal, becomes obsessed with "Belle de Jour," as she calls herself, her two separate lives collide in a tragic fashion.

A masterpiece by cinema's greatest surrealist director. The combination of Buñuel's play with fantasy and reality verging on the pornographic and the beautiful, innocent Deneuve as a sadomasochist struck a chord in audiences. Buñuel, who was used to critical, but not commercial success, was astounded when the film became a huge hit. Deneuve is wonderful.

Some critics found the film stilted and accused Buñuel of making an arty pornographic film to attract the crowds. Others loved the surreal fairy tale–like farce with its open-ended relationship to reality and compared it to a Freudian fairy tale. Godard said of *Belle de Jour* that Buñuel seemed to be playing the cinema in the way that Bach played the organ. It won the Lion d'Or at the Venice Biennal and was co-winner of the French Critics' Prix Méliès in 1967.

48 *La Belle et la bête (Beauty and the Beast)* 1945 B&W   *Director* Jean Cocteau; *Producer* René Clément; *Screenplay* Jean Cocteau, based on the story by Madame Leprince de Beaumont; *Dialogue* Jean Cocteau; *Photography* Henri Alekan; *Music* Georges Auric; *Art Director* Christian Bérard; *Set* Christian Bérard, René Moulaert and Lucien Carré; *Costumes* Marcel Escoffier and Castillo; *Sound* Jacques Lebreton and Jacques Carrère; *Editing* Claude Héria. Running time: 100 minutes.

Cast: Josette Day, Jean Marais, Marcel André, Mila Parély, Nane Germon, Michel Auclair, Raoul Marco, Gilles Watteaux, Noël Blin, Christian Marquand.

Cocteau brings new magic to an old fairy tale. A spell has been cast on Prince Charming. He is trapped in the body of a beast and destined to die unless Beauty (Day) falls in love with him. Of course, she sees beyond his hideous appearance and recognizes a beautiful soul. So the two manage to foil the evil plans of their enemies and love conquers all. As in the fairy tale, a beautiful girl gets her Prince Charming from a beast.

This is Cocteau's glorious poetic adaptation of a fairy tale. The poet, playwright,

La Belle et la bête (Beauty and the Beast), 1945; directed by Jean Cocteau.

artist, director wished to make a truly fantastical fairy tale of a film, but also to treat love and death seriously. With enchanting costumes, masks and sets, the film accomplishes the first goal, and with the performances of Day and Marais, the second aim is approached. In making this visual masterpiece, Cocteau faced numerous difficulties, such as five-hour daily make-up sessions for Marais and finding supplies in war-torn France. The magical realm he created with his castle that has human hands coming out of the wall to act as candlebras, set the standard for all *Beauty and the Beast*s to follow. The beast/prince is Jean Marais' greatest role, though some loved his beast so much they were disappointed by his prince — apparently when Greta Garbo saw the film and the prince appeared, she screamed: "Give me back my beast!"

When it was released in the United States, *The New York Times* hailed it as "a sensuously fascinating film .... Priceless, gorgeous, exquisite." *Newsweek* declared it: "A brilliant example of what cameras can do with a poet in charge." When Disney's animated version came out in 1992, Jerry Tallmer of *The New York Post* maintained Cocteau's "stunning, seminal" *Beauty* was still the best. It won the Prix Louis Delluc in 1946.

49 *La Belle Meunière (The Pretty Miller Girl)* 1947 Color *Director* Marcel Pagnol; *Producer* Société du Film La Belle Meunière; *Screenplay* Marcel Pagnol; *Découpage* Max de Rieux; *Photography* Willy; *Music* Franz Schubert; *Arrangement* Tony Aubin; *Set* Robert Giordani; *Costumes* Azaïs, Boyer and Nina Ricci from models by Robert Giordani; *Editing* Jeannette Rongier. Running time: 120 minutes.

Cast: Tino Rossi, Jacqueline Pagnol, Lilia Vetti, Raphaël Patorni, Pierrette

Rossi, Raoul Marco, Suzanne Després, Alexandre Fabry, Emma Lyonel, Pierre Labry, Edouard Hemme, Nicolas Amato, Louis Lions, Jean Deschamps, Gustave Hamilton, Jules Dorpe, René Maupré.

An episode from the dream life of Franz Schubert. As he searches the countryside for inspiration, Schubert (Rossi) follows a stream that leads to a windmill. He agrees to work for the miller after having seen his beautiful daughter (Pagnol) bathing in the stream. More touched by money than music, she prefers to become the mistress of a wealthy count and Schubert is left alone with his music.

A lovely Pagnol film, not up to his prewar films, but still his best picture after 1945. He had almost finished the movie in black and white, when he learned about the Roux-color process. He was so intrigued by it that he reshot the entire movie. It was the second French film shot in color after the war, and though some scenes are beautiful there were still some problems with the process, which resulted in blurred close-ups and strange effects on the inside shots.

The French critics loved the novelty of the color and how masterfully Pagnol managed it in some scenes. American critics accused Pagnol of having "sacrificed everything else" for the color.

50 *La Belle Noiseuse (The Beautiful Nut)*   1990 Color   *Director* Jacques Rivette; *Producer* FR3 Films, Centre National de la Cinématographie, Canal Plus, La Sofica Investimage 2 and 3; *Screenplay* Pascal Bonitzer, Christine Laurent, and Jacques Rivette, based on Balzac's novella *The Unknown Masterpiece*; *Photography* William Lubtchansky; *Set* Emmanuel de Chauvigny; *Sound* Florion Eidenbenz; *Costumes* Laurence Struz; *Editing* Nicole Lubtchansky. Running time: 240 minutes.

Cast: Michel Piccoli, Emmanuele Béart, Jane Birkin, Marianne Denicourt, David Bursztein, Gilles Arbona, Bernard Dufour.

A famous painter (Piccoli), who has lost his creative urge, lives in fame and comfort in the south of France. He stumbles around his chateau, pondering the reasons he has never finished his masterpiece. Then a young collector and a beautiful young woman (Béart) visit him and inspire him to paint again.

This is an examination of the creative process by one of the great New Wave directors, Jacques Rivette, and will probably be remembered as his masterpiece. Despite, its four-hour length it remains his most accessible film, and thanks to the beautiful cinematography of Lubtchansky, is his most beautiful as well. Rivette based the screenplay on Balzac's novella, *The Unknown Masterpiece*. He explores the relationship between life and art and demystifies the process by showing how painstaking and painful it is to create a masterpiece. He also focuses on the role of the muse as adored and abused subject. Emmanuelle Béart is exquisite and utterly convincing as the human object of beauty inspiring enough to end a decade-long artistic block.

The film was a unanimous hit with critics at Cannes when it opened. Vincent Canby called it in *The New York Times*, "an incredibly beautiful, roomy sort of film whose views of art reflect the tradition of what might be called academic romanticism." *New York* magazine raved: "Filmmaking doesn't come purer than *La Belle Noiseuse*." It won the Grand Prix du Cinéma at Cannes in 1991.

51 *La Belle Vie (The Good Life)*   1963 B&W   *Director* Robert Enrico; *Producer* Films du Centaure; *Screenplay* Robert Enrico and Maurice Pons;

Photography Jean Boffety; *Music* Henri Lanoé; *Set* François de Lamothe; *Sound* Pierre Vuillemin; *Editing* Denise de Casabianca and Jacqueline Meppiel. Running time: 110 minutes.

Cast: Frédéric de Pasquale, Josée Steiner, Lucienne Hamon, Françoise Giret, Odile Geoffroy, Gregory Chmara, Nane Germon, Aline Bertrand, Nicole Desailly, Alice Reichen, Edwine Moatti, Roger Jacquet, Jean-Pierre Lituac, André Zibral, Pierre Frag, Stéphane Fey, Jacques Ramade, Philippe Moreau.

Frédéric (de Pasquale) is released from his military service after 27 months in Algeria. When he returns to Paris, he marries his childhood sweetheart, Sylvie (Steiner), but the "good life" is not long lived. With employment and lodging troubles and an unwanted baby on the way, the couple is desperate. Then, just when things seem to turn around, Frédéric is called back into the army.

A simple, but realistic story that highlighted the human costs of the Algerian War, which were rarely taken into consideration. In his first feature, Enrico explored many troubling issues during a time when the Algerian War was consuming more and more of the French population's concern. Enrico used news footage for the background. It was released in 1964 after cuts were made by the censorship board.

American critics were less taken by the historical issues. *Variety* complained that "it lacks an insight into the characters to make their plight engrossing, real, or interesting." French critics, however, found it to be a deeply sincere human drama that captured the period and the anguish it evoked very well. It won the Prix Jean Vigo in 1964.

52 *Les Belles de nuit (Beauties of the Night)* 1952 B&W   *Director* René Clair; *Producer* Franco London Films, Rizzoli; *Screenplay* René Clair in collaboration with Jean-Pierre Grédy, and Pierre Barillet; *Photography* Armand Thirard, Robert Juillard and Louis Née; *Music* Georges Van Parys; *Set* Léon Barsacq; *Sound* Antoine Petitjean; *Costumes* Rosine Delamare; *Editing* Louisette Hautecoeur. Running time: 85 minutes.

Cast: Gérard Philipe, Martine Carol, Gina Lollobrigida, Magali Vendeuil, Marilyn Buffert, Raymond Bussières, Jean Parédès, Bernard Lajarrige, Raymond Cordy, Albert Michel, Pierre Palau, Paolo Stoppa, René-Jean Chauffard, Paul Demange, Bernard Dhéran, Christian Chantal, Monique Darval, Marcelle Legendre, Chantal Tirède, Pierre Fléta, Bernard Musson, Jane Pierson, Madeleine Barbulée, Mathilde Casadesus, Monique Aïssasta, Dominique Marcas, Jean Daurand, Albert Michel, René Fluet, Henri Marchand, Léon Larive, Georges Bever, Paul Faivre, Henri Niel, Bernard Farell, Julien Maffre, Jean Ozenne, Balpo, Marcel Charvey, André Dalibert, Eugène Stuber, Roger Vincent, Jackie Blanchot, Piot, Joe Davray, Gil Delamare, Beauvais, Jean Morel, François Nadal, François Richard, Frank Maurice.

A handsome music teacher (Philipe) frustrated by his life in the provinces travels through time in his dreams. In his fantasies he becomes a hero in different historical periods: in turn-of-the-century Paris he dazzles ladies at a salon; under Louis-Philippe's reign he takes part in the conquest of Algeria; during the French Revolution he plays warrior and poet musician; in the time of Louis XII he seduces the lover of France's greatest musketeer, d'Artagnan. Of course, in each era he also has a beautiful and adoring woman at his side. In reality, he winds up marrying the daughter of the village mechanic.

Les Belles de nuit (*Beauties of the Night*), **1952; directed by René Clair.**

The best of René Clair's postwar films and a wonderful romantic farce. At the time of the movie's release, René Clair said his purpose was pure amusement, because "of all the periods which [the film] evokes, we feel that it is ours which has the greatest need for distraction. And so we willingly admit that we have only tried to amuse you in relating this fictitious adventure which does not try to prove anything whatsoever, which champions no cause, and which, in one word, is as perfectly useless as the nightingale and the flower which bear the same name."

"René Clair has made a perfectly delightful satirical comedy for anyone who is willing to engage in a little suspension of disbelief," wrote the critic in *1,000 Eyes*. It won the French Critics' Prix Méliès in 1952, and the following year it won the Grand Prix du Cinéma Français.

Benjamin *see* **Benjamin ou les mémoires d'un puceau**

53 *Benjamin ou les mémoires d'un puceau (Benjamin)* 1967 Color
Director Michel Deville; *Producer* Parc Films, Mag Bodard, Marianne Productions; *Screenplay* Lille and Nina Companeez; *Photography* Ghislain Cloquet; *Music* Mozart, Haydn, Bocchernini; *Set* Claude Pignot; *Sound* André Hervée; *Costumes* Rita Bayance; *Editing* Nina Companeez. Running time: 105 minutes.

Cast: Michèle Morgan, Michel Piccoli, Pierre Clémenti, Catherine Deneuve, François Bergé, Catherine Rouvel, Anna Gaël, Odile Versois, Jacques Dufilho, Simone Bach, Madeleine Damien, Jean Lefvre, Tania Torrens, Angelo Bardi, Brigitte Defrance, Sacha Briquet, Jacques Filh, Danièle Gérard, René Bazart, Cécile Vassort, Eve Cloquot, Lyne Chardonnet.

Set in the eighteenth century, this is the story of the very unsentimental education of Benjamin (Clémenti) at the hands of his worldly aunt, the Countess of Valandry (Morgan). While he is initiated into the ways of love, Benjamin is being used by his aunt to exact revenge on the Count (Piccoli) who abandoned her years before. She has Benjamin seduce the Count's young fiancée (Deneuve).

This is a deliciously cruel tale of love and vengence in the tradition of Laeclos' famous *Les Liaisons Dangereuses* and Renoir's *Rules of the Game*. With the music of Mozart and Haydn, the eighteenth century is beautifully evoked and is an exquisite backdrop for such a sordid tale. Deneuve is lovely, and Deville inspires great feeling.

The New Wave critics faulted Deville for setting his twisted love story in an early era, complete with classical furniture and classical camera moves. Old guard critics applauded his return to established ways. It won the Prix Louis Delluc in 1968.

The Best Way to Get Along *see* **La Meilleur Façon de marcher**

Between Us *see* **Coup de foudre**

54 *Les Biches* (*Bad Girls* or *The Does* or *The Heterosexuals*) 1968 Color   *Director* Claude Chabrol; *Producer* Films la Boétie, Alexandra; *Screenplay* Claude Chabrol and Paul Gégauff; *Photography* Jean Rabier; *Music* Pierre Jansen; *Set* Marc Berthier; *Costumes* Maurice Albray; *Sound* Guy Chichignoud; *Editing* Jacques Gaillard. Running time: 88 minutes.

Cast: Jean-Louis Trintignant, Stéphane Audran, Jacqueline Sassard, Dominique Zardi, Henri Attal, Nane Germon, Serge Bento, Henri Francis, Claude Chabrol, Laure Valmée.

What begins as a lesbian love affair between a wealthy older woman, Frédérique (Audran), and a penniless young girl named Why (Sassard) becomes a very volatile love triangle when an architect becomes involved first with Why and then with Frédérique. The jealousy inspired is perhaps deeper than the love, but the young girl's confusion and hurt lead her to murder and madness.

This film is credited with spawning a slew of films that explored society's ills. It focuses on the mechanics of love, homosexual and heterosexual relations, and money. Hitchcock's influence on Chabrol is quite evident in the detached tone. Chabrol beautifully weaves a social critique with a suspenseful plot. All of the actors, but particularly the two leading ladies, deliver fantastic performances.

When it came out, French critics called *Bad Girls* Chabrol's best work, ranking him with his New Wave brethren Godard and Truffaut, and it is still

Le Blé en herbe (*The Game of Love*), 1953; directed by Claude Autaut-Lara.

considered among his finest films. One American critic, however, dismissed it as a "futile and empty exercise" with two very pretty faces. *The Sunday Observer*'s critic obviously disagreed, because he declared it "one of the most beautifully composed films I have ever seen: nothing is superfluous, nothing mis-paced, no detail extraneous."

The Big Blue *see* **Le Grand Bleu**

The Big Feast *see* **La Grande Bouffe**

The Big Wash! *see* **La Grande Lessive!**

Birds of a Feather *see* **La Cage aux folles**

Bitter Fruit *see* **Les Fruits amers**

Black and White in Color *see* **La Victoire en chantant**

Black Orpheus *see* **Orfeu Negro**

Black Victory *see* **La Victoire en chantant**

55 *Le Blé en herbe (The Game of Love)* 1953 B&W *Director* Claude Autant-Lara; *Producer* Franco-London Films; *Screenplay* Jean Aurenche, Pierre Bost and Claude Autant-Lara, based on Colette's novel; *Photography* Robert Lefebvre; *Music* René Cloërec; *Set* Max Douy; *Sound* Antoine Petitjean; *Costumes* Léon Zay; *Editing* Madeleine Gug. Running time: 106 minutes.

Cast: Edwige Feuillère, Nicole Berger, Pierre-Michel Beck, Renée Devillers, Charles Deschamps, Louis de Funès, Hélène Tossy, Josiane Lecomte, Julienne Paroli, Madeleine Suffel, Janette Lucas, Simone Duhart, Yannick Malloire, Pierre-Michel Beck, Charles Camusic, Robert Berri, Claude Berri, Louis Saintève, Philippe Chauveau.

Set on the coast of Brittany in the 1920s. Two teenage sweethearts (Berger and Beck) struggle with desire and innocence, until the boy meets "the lady in white" (Feuillère). A woman who feels her beauty waning, she seduces the boy. After his young girlfriend grows jealous, he in turn introduces her to sex.

The sexual subject matter of this film caused scandals on both sides of the Atlantic. Religious organizations objected to the film's "immoral" subject matter. It was banned in Chicago and Nice and boycotted in Caen, Le Havre and Lyon. In the United States, it was used in a case to argue against the unconstitutionality of censoring film releases. Today, it stands as a delicate, sincere treatment of physical love. The original screenplay adapted by Aurenche and Bost, the same team who adapted the *Diary of a Country Priest* for Autant-Lara, added a lesbian twist to Colette's novel, which was cut just before shooting on the film began.

Some critics found little more than titillating entertainment guaranteed to generate scandal and ticket sales. Others believed that Autant-Lara captured youthful infatuation remarkably well. The film won the Grand Prix du Cinéma Français 1954. Shown the movie on her deathbed, Colette said: "The magic of the cinema has brought my characters before me."

Blonde in a White Car *see* **Toi, le venin**

Blood of the Beasts *see* **Le Sang des bêtes**

Blow Out *see* **La Grande Bouffe**

Bluebeard *see* **Landru**

56 *Bob le flambeur (Bob the Gambler)* 1955 B&W   *Director* Jean-Pierre Melville; *Producer* OGC, Jenner, Play Art, La Cyme; *Screenplay* Auguste Lebreton and Jean-Pierre Melville; *Photography* Henri Decaë; *Music* Eric Barclay; *Set* Claude Bouxin; *Sound* Jean Carrère and Pierre Philippenko; *Editing* Monique Bonnot. Running time: 100 minutes.

Cast: Isabelle Corey, Roger Duchesne, Daniel Cauchy, André Garret, Claude Cerval, Colette Fleury, Simone Paris, Howard Vernon, Gérard Buhr, Guy Decomble, Germaine Licht, Jean-Marie Rivière, François Gir, Jean-Marie Robain, André Tételman, Durieux, Chris Kersan, Jean-François Drach, Annick Bertrand, Emile Cuvelier, Yannick Arvel, André Salgues, Couty, Cichi, Alleaume, Roland Charbeaux, René Havard, Yvette Amirante.

A great film noir set in the Montmartre quarter of Paris. Robert Montagné (Duchesne) is a former bank robber who has been gambling for 20 years. When he gets lured back into crime with the set-up of a lifetime—a chance to rob the casino at the beach resort of Deauville—things do not go smoothly. The night of the crime he gets carried away at the gaming tables and forgets the time. He wins the

800 million francs he was supposed to steal, but the police have been tipped off, and his partner is killed and he arrested.

A Hollywood-style film noir with a fantastic French flair that allows a hard-boiled crime tale to be funny, sweet and full of romance. From the streets of Pigalle to the perfectly Parisian jazz, this is a Melville masterpiece. The black and white photography is probably some of the best work of one of France's finest twentieth century cinematographers, Henri Decaë. The music mixes jazz with rhumba, piano and accordion to set a perfect sound stage for gangsters' gestures.

Made in 1955, not released in the United States until 1982. Stephen Schiff wrote: "*Bob le flambeur* makes you feel the way the New Wave directors must have felt watching it — as though anybody who loved movies with all his heart could take a camera out into the streets and capture the mysterious beauty waiting there."

Bob the Gambler *see* **Bob le flambeur**

The Body of My Enemy *see* **Le Corps de mon ennemi**

57 *Le Bon Dieu sans confession (Good Lord without Confession)*
1953 B&W   *Director* Claude Autant-Lara; *Producer* Les Films Gibé; *Screenplay* by Claude Autant-Lara, Ghislaine Auboin and Roland Laudenbach, based on the novel by Paul Vialar; *Photography* André Bac; *Music* René Cloërec; *Set* Max Douy; *Sound* Robert Biard; *Costumes* Monique Plotin; *Editing* Madeleine Gug. Running time: 112 minutes.

Cast: Henri Vilbert, Danielle Darrieux, Myno Burney, Claude Laydu, Isabelle Pia, Grégoire Aslan, Ivan Desny, Julien Carette, Jean Dunot, Madeleine Suffel, Claude Berri, Marcelle Ferry, Georges Bever, René Lacourt, Jo Dest, Michel Dumur, Marie-Chantal Fefert, Pierre Duncan.

At the burial of François Dupont (Vilbert), his wife, daughter, son, mistress (Darrieux) and business associate all pay their respects, revealing their different relations with the deceased. Through their eyes, Dupont is shown to be a many faceted man.

A wonderful literary film with an interesting and unusual narrative structure. It is part bourgeois morality tale, part human drama. Autant-Lara elicits superb performances from his actors. Darrieux comes across as being as evil as she is pretty.

The film was poorly received in the United States. *Variety* called it "an uneven film which splits emphasis between two protagonists, and remains a series of literary sketches rather than a cohesive film." French critics were kinder, delighting in Darrieux and the film's literary quality. Henri Vilbert won the Best Actor at the Venice Biennal in 1953.

58 *Le Bonheur (Happiness)*   1965 Color   *Director* Agnès Varda; *Producer* Parc Films; *Screenplay* Agnès Varda; *Photography* Jean Rabier and Claude Beausoleil; *Music* Mozart; *Set* Hubert Monloup; *Sound* Michel Choquet; *Editing* Janine Verneau. Running time: 80 minutes.

Cast: Jean-Claude Drouot, Claire Drouot, Paul Vecchiali, Marie-France Boyer, Marc Eyraud, Sandrine Drouot, Olivier Drouot.

A happily married man, François (Drouot), falls madly in love with a young woman (Boyer), and for a short while he finds his affair only increases the happiness of his marital life. Though he believes he can love both his wife and his mistress, the day that he reveals his affair to his wife, she kills herself. Grief does not overwhelm François, rather he moves in with his mistress.

Varda's most beautiful and lyrical film. The husband, wife and children in the film are a family in real life. Varda found inspiration for the film in Jean Renoir's *Picnic on the Grass*, a clip of which is included in the film. What interested Varda was not the psychology that motivated the husband and the wife's actions, but the tradition of blame and how people buy into it.

Happiness inspired intense reactions from viewers, with some women infuriated by the ending. Some critics found the lyrical, flowery music and scenery at odds with the strangely unemotional film. Others who expected a political slant from Varda were disappointed that she focused only on a domestic situation. All agreed, however, that Varda's artistic sense was at its height. It won the Prix Louis Delluc.

59 *Les Bonnes Femmes (The Good Girls)* 1960 B&W *Director* Claude Chabrol; *Producer* Paris Films, Panitalia; *Screenplay* Paul Gégauff and Claude Chabrol; *Photography* Henri Decaë and Jean Rabier; *Music* Paul Misraki and Pierre Jansen; *Set* Jacques Mély; *Sound* Jean-Paul Marchetti; *Editing* Jacques Gaillard. Running time: 104 minutes.

Cast: Bernadette Lafont, Stéphane Audran, Clotilde Joano, Lucile Saint-Simon, Ave Ninchi, Sacha Briquet, Mario David, Claude Berri, Albert Dinan, Jean-Louis Maury, Pierre Bertin, Serge Bento, Dominique Zardi, Karen Blanguernon, Jean Barclay, Gabriel Gobin, Liliane David, France Asselin, Dolly Bell, Simone Landry, Louise Roblin, Jenny Doria, Charles Bayard, Charles Belmont, Henri Attal, Philippe Castelli, Claude Chabrol, Laszlo Szabo.

Two days in the lives of four salesgirls in a hardware store. All of them dream of lives very different from their present tedious existences. One dreams of being a bourgeois housewife. Another is revealed to work part-time in a cheap music-hall. The third thinks she will find happiness when she goes off with two men. The sweet, shy one thinks she has found her knight in shining armor in a motorcyclist, who takes her into the woods and strangles her.

A wonderful film, in which Chabrol tried to draw attention to the inferior position of women in society. He said of the movie: "It is the story of the good woman .... My good women, all during work, they can't wait to stop working. And finally, when they don't have to work anymore, all four focus on their parallel obsessions: to break out, to make money, to be famous, to get out of their daily routine."

Instead of being hailed as an early feminist filmmaker, Chabrol was accused of making a nasty, cold movie, because people missed his irony. For example, the many references to animal cages in the film provoked cries of treating the women like animals, whereas Chabrol meant to show how sorrowful was their condition. Upon its release, *Variety* wrote: "Chabrol is a clever craftsman but he shows no definite attitude towards his poor puppet girl victims." Chabrol pities the sad, escapist dreams the women choose to hold on to, he's not critical of them.

60 *Borsalino* 1970 Color *Director* Jacques Deray; *Producer* Adel Films, Marianne Productions, Mars Film Produzione; *Screenplay* Jean-Claude Carrière, Claude Sautet and Jacques Deray, based on Eugène Saccomano's novel *Bandits à Marseilles*; *Photography* Jean-Jacques Tarbès; *Music* Claude Bolling; *Set* François de Lamothe; *Sound* Jacques Maumont; *Costumes* Jacques Fonterey; *Editing* Paul Cayatte. Running time: 120 minutes.

Borsalino, 1970; directed by Jacques Deray.

Cast: Jean-Paul Belmondo, Alain Delon, Catherine Rouvel, Michel Bouquet, Corinne Marchand, Françoise Christophe, Julien Guimoar, Arnoldo Foa, Nicole Calfan, Laura Adani, Christian de Tilière, Mario David, Daniel Ivernel, Dennis Berry, André Bollet, Hélène Rémy, Odette Piquet, Lionel Vitrant, Jean Aron, Pierre Koulak.

Set in Marseille during the 1930s, the story of two low-level gangsters, Capella (Belmondo) and Siffredi (Delon), who manage to murder their way to the top of the heap by assassinating the two reigning bosses. Tired of the dangerous lifestyle, Capella decides to run off with his girl, but the same night that he tells Siffredi of his plan, he is killed. Siffredi is the one who disappears.

A light nostalgic Gallic look at America's old gangster movies, this film is fun and has Belmondo at his best. All the leads in this are marvelous, with Delon in one of his finest roles. The authentic evocation of Marseille's underworld before World War II is very well done, but it does not trap the film's mafia ruminations in the past, because what it explores about gang rites remains relevant.

This film was touted in one of France's biggest publicity pushes ever mounted for a film. The reactions of American critics covered both extreme ends of the spectrum. *The New York Times* called it "a failure of stupendous proportions," because of the wasted talent and elaborate set work that failed to carry the plot. While *The New Republic*'s Stanley Kauffmann declared it "an attempt to recreate a Cagney-Bogart crime epic, and with a nice double view: the past 30 years never happened; on the other hand, the past 30 years give the film an ambience of affection." *Films in Review* simply hailed it as "a top gangster film."

61 *Le Boucher (The Butcher)* 1969 Color *Director* Claude Chabrol; *Producer* Films La Boëtie; *Screenplay* Claude Chabrol; *Photography* Jean Rabier; *Music* Pierre Jansen; *Set* Guy Littaye; *Sound* Guy Chichignoud; *Costumes* Joseph Poulard; *Editing* Jacques Gaillard. Running time: 95 minutes.

Cast: Stéphane Audran, Jean Yanne, Antonio Passalia, Pasquale Ferone, Mario Beccaria, Roger Rudel, William Guerault, André Genovès.

A thriller about a very cultured and repressed school teacher (Audran) who becomes romantically involved with the local butcher (Yanne). While their intimacy intensifies, a serial killer is terrorizing the area. As the school teacher finds herself more and more involved with the butcher, the bodies of young girls are found near the schoolyard and where she picnics with her schoolchildren. She grows suspicious about coincidences linking the butcher to one of the bodies. Of course, love and intrigue can lead to all sorts of tragedy.

Chabrol explores guilt again, but also the relationships between civilization and brutality, decorum and passion. The killer is complicated, portrayed somewhat sympathetically along the he-can't-help-himself lines. The fact that Chabrol chose to set the film in the Dordogne region of Cro-Magnon caves effectively emphasizes the bestial nature of man. Audran was married to Chabrol in real life.

Critics called this one of Chabrol's best and most intriguing films. Some found his portrait of village life absolutely on target, except of course for the violence, which is not lurking beneath the surface of every provincial town. The deceptively simple tale is full of complex meaning and human struggles.

62 *La Bourse et la vie* 1966 B&W *Director* Jean-Pierre Mocky; *Producer* Orsay Films, Balzac Films, Société d'Expansion du Spectacle; *Screenplay* Fernand

À bout de souffle (*Breathless*), 1959; directed by Jean-Luc Godard.

Marzelle, Jean-Pierre Mocky, Alain Moury; *Dialogue* Marcel Aymé, Jean Tournier; *Music* André Domage; *Set* Rino Mondellini; *Sound* Antoine Petitjean;
Editing Gabriel Rongier. Running time: 88 minutes.

    Cast: Fernandel, Jean Poiret, Heinze Ruhmann, Michel Galabru, Jean
Carmet, Darry Cowl, Jean-Claude Remouleux, André Gabriello, Marilu Tolo,
Jacques Legras, Marcel Pérès, Roger Legris, Christa Nelli, Michel Lonsdale,
Colette Teissèdre, Rudy Lenoir, Claude Piéplu, Edmond Ardisson, Simone
Duhart, Andrex, Dominique Zardi, Gisèle Grimm, Léonce Corne, Claude Man-
sard, Anne Marescot, Pierre Durou, Henri Arius, Maryse Martin, Philippe Cas-
telli, Françoise Arnaud, Raymond Jourdan, Henri Poirier, Pierre Gualdi, Albert
Dagnan, Michel Dupleix, Yves Elliot, Albert Daumergue, Serge Bento, Max
Amyl, Joachim Westhof, Gilbert Robin, Max Montavon, Henri Attal.

    A man from Toulouse, Pélepan (Poiret), promises 10 million francs to the
Robinhoudes who need to get it to a lawyer in Paris the next day. A cashier
(Fernandel) and an accountant (Ruhmann) are given the job of delivering it, but
of course, they run into all sorts of obstacles.

    Mocky believed this to be one of his most personal works, though he later
decided it was poorly done and dismissed it as of no interest to anyone. Fernandel
is hilarious, though, and Mocky's humor is in evidence.

    Some critics called Mocky's thriller a poor imitation of the great *Pig Across
Paris*. *The London Observer* said that it "indicates that Jean-Pierre Mocky's unerr-
ing bad taste is still way ahead of his ability as a director." But among die-hard
Mocky fans, of which there are many, Mocky can do no wrong and his humor is
side-splitting.

63 *À bout de souffle (Breathless)* 1959 B&W   *Director* Jean-Luc Godard; *Producer* D. de Beauregard, SNC; *Screenplay* François Truffaut and Jean-Luc Godard; *Photography* Raoul Coutard; *Music* Martial Solal; *Set* Claude Chabrol; *Sound* Jacques Maumont; *Editing* Cécile Decugis. Running time: 89 minutes.

Cast: Jean-Paul Belmondo, Jean Seberg, Henri-Jacques Huet, Van Doude, Jean-Pierre Melville, Daniel Boulanger, Roger Hanin, Claude Mansard, Liliane David, Michel Favre, Jean Domarchi, Jean-Luc Godard, André S. Labarthe, Jean Herman, Jean Douchet, Richard Balducci, François Moreuil.

A handsome young criminal (Belmondo), who fancies himself to be a hip Bogartesque gangster, is on the run from the police because he stole a car and killed a motorcycle cop who was chasing him for speeding. He finds refuge in the arms of a beautiful young American newspaper salesgirl (Seberg), who steals his heart and eventually turns him into the police.

Called the beacon of the New Wave, it is certainly the most famous film of the movement. The idea came from a newspaper story Truffaut read about a man who killed a policeman and hid out at his girlfriend's until she turned him in. Truffaut gave the idea to Godard when he was unable to use it in a film he was working on. Shooting the film in one month with a budget of $90,000, Godard used jump cuts, innovative camera angles and a hand-held camera to create what has been described as a "sense of living in the moment." Shot on city streets and in friends' bedrooms, this low-budget film revolutionized French filmmaking. Riding around Paris in one stolen car after another, Seberg is lovely. The film's freshness has not aged. Belmondo was a former boxer and his rough face is amazingly tender and beautiful.

When *Breathless* came out in Paris, some found it scandalous, others dismissed it as sloppy, but the great critic Georges Sadoul recognized Godard for who he would become. "*Breathless* reveals an undeniable, a very great talent. Jean-Luc Godard, who is not yet thirty, is "an animal of the movies .... He has film in his bones." It won the Prix Vigo and was the co-winner of the French Critics' Prix Méliès in 1960.

64 *Boy Meets Girl* 1984 B&W   *Director* Leos Carax; *Producer* Agilène; *Screenplay* Leos Carax; *Photography* Jean-Yves Escoffier; *Music* Jacques Pinault; *Set* Serge Marsolff, Jean Bauer; *Sound* Jean Umanski; *Editing* Nelly Meunier, Francine Sandberg. Running time: 100 minutes.

Cast: Denis Lavant, Mireille Perrier, Carroll Brooks, Elie Poicard, Maïté Nahyr, Christian Cloarec, Hans Meyer, Anna Baldaccini, Jean Duflot, Frédérique Charbonneau, Jacques Pinault, Anne Dieumegard, Ardag Basmadjian, Evelyne Schmitt, Robert Benavente, Georges Castorp, Dominique Reymond, Marc Desclozeaux, Albert Braun, Lolo Pigalle.

Heartbroken, Alex (Lavant) wanders the nocturnal streets of modern Paris. His girlfriend has left him for his best friend. Assaulted by the sounds of lovers' quarrels and the sight of lovers' embraces, he wanders from the Métro, to a bar, to a stranger's party, where he finally makes a connection with the beautiful and suicidal Mireille (Perrier).

This was Carax's first feature film. He made it when he was only 23 years old, and it became the talk of the 1984 Cannes Film Festival. Carax's combination of an odd intimacy and a chilling detachment recalls early New Wave films and yet the film has a very 1980s atmosphere. Apparently, quite autobiographical, the film may be the first elegy to France's "Generation X," teenagers and twentysomethings who search for meaning in a postwar world.

Though the film caused a huge sensation when it was released at the Cannes Film Festival, it received both raves and pans from critics. *Variety* called it "an offbeat tale ... his actors register effectively and the eerie combination of images, music and location provides an indelible quality." *Film Comment* represented the less flattering position: "*Boy Meets Girl* is emblamed in a sludge of paralyzing self-consciousness."

Boyfriends and Girlfriends *see* **L'Ami de mon amie**

The Brain *see* **Le Cerveau**

Breathless *see* **À bout de souffle**

65 *Buffet froid (Cold Cuts)* 1979 Color   *Director* Bertrand Blier; *Producer* Alain Sarde, Sara Films, Antenne 2, Gaumont; *Screenplay* Bertrand Blier; *Photography* Jean Penzer; *Music* Johannes Brahms; *Set* Théo Meurisse; *Sound* Jean-Pierre Ruh; *Editing* Claudine Merlin. Running time: 95 minutes.

Cast: Gérard Depardieu, Bertrand Blier, Jean Carmet, Geneviève Page, Jean Rougerie, Bernard Crommbey, Denise Gence, Carole Bouquet, Michel Serrault, Liliane Rovere, Michel Fortin, Nicole Desailly, Maurice Travail, Jean Benguigui, Marco Perrin, Pierre Frag, Eric Wasberg, Roger Riffard.

A satiric comedy verging on the surreal, about Alphonse Tram (Depardieu), who the same night that he discovers his knife lodged in the stomach of an unknown man in the subway, also finds that his wife has disappeared. He teams up with a police inspector who believes in keeping criminals out of jail and a paranoid killer who is afraid of the dark. They form a hysterical trio. When the three take off for the country for a little rest and recreation after various murders, the daughter of the unknown man in the subway tracks them down, seeking revenge.

A surreal comedy/farce that is as dark as it is absurd. Blier's great talent and uniquely twisted humor as both writer and director are at their strongest here. He has created a sick nightmare that grows ever darker with tight control. The photography is wonderful, with Paris slick and empty in a completely new way. Depardieu, once again playing a bumbler, delivers a fantastic performance. Blier's father, the actor Bernard, is also great. It has some of the funniest scenes in French film.

Alan Brien of the London *Sunday Times* described the film as "more of a curiosity than a pleasure." *Variety* called this "a marvelous new impertinence .... The weaving of a texture of deepening nightmare, undergirded by a grimly funny sense of disconnected logic, is masterfully done and sustained." It won the César for Best Screenplay in 1980.

The Burglars *see* **Le Casse**

The Butcher *see* **Le Boucher**

A Butterfly on the Shoulder *see* **Un Papillon sur l'épaule**

66 *La Cage aux folles (Birds of a Feather* or *The Mad Cage)* 1978
Color   *Director* Edouard Molinaro; *Producer* Les Productions Artistes Associés,
Da Ma Produzione Spa; *Screenplay* Mercello Danon, Edouard Molinaro, Francis
Veber and Jean Poiret, based on Jean Poiret's play; *Photography* Armando Man-
nuzzi; *Music* Ennio Morricone; *Set* Mario Garbuglia; *Sound* Mario Dallimonti,
Danilo Moroni; *Costumes* Piero Tosi and Ambra Danon; *Editing* Robert Isnar-
don. Running time: 103 minutes.

Cast: Ugo Tognazzi, Michel Serrault, Michel Galabru, Claire Maurier, Rémy
Laurent, Benny Luke, Carmen Scarpitta, Luisa Maneri, Venantion Venantini,
Peter Boom, Carlo Reali.

A family farce about two male lovers, one is a drag queen star (Serrault), the
other (Tognazzi) runs the Saint-Tropez nightclub, La Cage Aux Folles, where his
lover performs. The couple has to pretend to be man and wife when they meet the
very morally upright family of their son's fiancée. Despite their humorous efforts to
hide their gay lifestyle, much goes awry and in the end, the fiancée's father, who is
the secretary of the Union of Moral Order, has to dress up in drag to avoid reporters.

This screen adaptation of the very successful play is every bit as funny as the
stage version. Though homosexual stereotypes abound, Molinaro's touch is light
and loving, so nothing offends. Michel Serrault as the drag queen, Zaza, is absolutely delightful. This is easily one of the best postwar French comedies.

La Cage aux folles was the biggest-grossing foreign language film ever released
in the United States, earning more than $40 million. It was nominated by the
Academy of Motion Picture Arts and Sciences for Direction, Screenplay and
Costume Design. Serrault won the César for Best Actor.

67 *Camille Claudel* 1988 Color   *Director* Bruno Nuytten; *Producer*
Lilith Films, Gaumont, Antenne 2, Films A2, DD Productions, CNC, Sofica Créa-
tions, Sofimage, Sofica Investimage, Images Investissements, Soffia; *Screenplay*
Bruno Nuytten, Marilyn Goldin, based on the book by de Reine-Marie Paris;
Photography Pierre Lhomme; *Music* Gabriel Yared; *Set* Bernard Vezat; *Sound*
Guillaume Sciama; *Costumes* Dominique Borg; *Editing* Joëlle Hache, Jeanne Kef.
Running time: 149 minutes.

Cast: Isabel Adjani, Gérard Depardieu, Laurent Grevill, Alain Cuny,
Madeleine Robinson, Philippe Clévenot, Katrine Boorman, Jean-Pierre Sentier,
Danièle Lebrun, Maxime Leroux, Aurelle Doazan, Philippe Painblanc, Roger
Planchon, Denise Chalem, Madeleine Marie, Gérard Darier, François Berleand.

Based on the tumultuous love affair of the sculptor Auguste Rodin (Depardieu) and his pupil, the sculptress Camille Claudel (Adjani), this is a tragic love
story that merges art and love. While the artists' passion for one another inspired
some of their finest work, one artist's temperament was better able to handle the
heart ache.

This beautiful film is a portrait of an artist so obsessed with love that she loses
all hold on reality and on her art. In his directorial debut, Nuytten breathes great
life into his meditations on artists' passion for their art and their loves. He uses
Rodin's and Claudel's works to deepen their portraits. The photography plays
beautifully with darkness and light to emphasize Camille's state of mind. Adjani
reportedly came up with the idea for the movie, and it is without doubt her greatest
role, as she plays a famous woman insane with passion, not unlike her role in *The
Story of Adèle H.*

A great commercial success, *Camille Claudel* disappointed some critics who found it too written and elaborately photographed at the expense of the character development. For the most part, though American critics loved it. *Film Journal* wrote: "This is bold, sweeping moviemaking which totally suits the dizzying fin de siècle world that Camille inhabited and the one which eventually swept her away. *Camille Claudel* takes you into the heart of creative darkness and spins its appalling tale with an unblinking eye for the truth seldom found in movies." It received a record number (12) of César nominations and won Best Film, Best Actress, Best Costumes, Best Art Direction and Best Photography.

68 *Le Camion (The Truck)* 1977 Color   *Director* Marguerite Duras; *Producer* Cinéma 9, Auditel; *Screenplay* Marguerite Duras; *Photography* Bruno Nuytten; *Music* Beethoven's *Variations on the Theme of Diabelli*; *Sound* Michel Vionnet; *Editing* Dominque Auvray and Caroline Camus. Running time: 80 minutes.
Cast: Marguerite Duras, Gérard Depardieu.
A cinematic essay by Marguerite Duras in which Depardieu and Duras discuss the essence and the limits of film. The camera is focused on Duras as she writes a script for Depardieu, who listens and interrupts her. The script is about a female hitchhiker and the truck driver who picks her up, but, of course, we never see them.

This is a political film that showcases Duras' greatest talents as experimental writer, actress, director and political thinker. She described her intent by saying: "Cinema on the road to ruin is the only real cinema. The world on the road to ruin is the only real political issue." By constructing a film within a film, where images challenge traditional film narrative and having her characters debate social ills in a communist/anti-communist struggle, she achieved her aims. She filmed the entire film in one week, with no rehearsal, which brought an element of freedom and chance to her work.

Some critics disliked Duras' disjointed pessimism. Others loved her radical politicking with art. *Variety* summed up most critics' feelings by calling the film "a bit of a downer" that like her other work, "should be applauded as attempts to find a literary form of filmmaking."

69 *Le Caporal épinglé (The Elusive Corporal* or *The Vanishing Corporal)* 1962 Color   *Director* Jean Renoir; *Producer* Films du Cyclope; *Screenplay* Jean Renoir and Guy Lefranc, based on the novel by Jacques Perret; *Photography* Georges Leclerc and Jean-Louis Picavet; *Music* Joseph Kosma; *Sound* Antoine Petitjean; *Editing* Renée Lichtig. Running time: 108 minutes.
Cast: Jean-Pierre Cassel, Claude Brasseur, Claude Rich, Cornelia Froebes, Jean Carmet, Mario David, Raymond Jourdan, Guy Bedos, Jacques Jouanneau, Philippe Castelli, Gérard Darnieu, Sacha Briquet, François Darbon, Lucien Rainbourg, Elisabeth Marcus, Helmut Janatsch, Elisabeth Stiepel, Bill Kearns.
Just as the armistice is being signed at the end of World War II, a French corporal (Cassel) and two of his soldiers still captive in a German Army camp decide to escape. The corporal's first attempt is a failure and he is returned to a new camp, but he refuses to give up and with the help of a young German girl, he and his comrades eventually reach Paris.

In many ways, this film is Renoir's reprise of his masterpiece *The Grand Illusion*. Both are escape movies, the first set in World War I; the second set in World

War II. Renoir's beautiful way with a camera still manages to bring warmth to even prison landscapes. The morality and integrity of the filmmaker imbues the character's struggle and the film's success. The focus is on human weakness and the intoxication of freedom. Unfortunately, Renoir's style was out of fashion in the New Wave climate of the 1960s. The film did not do well, and producers were reluctant to work with him after its lackluster reception.

Critics could not help comparing this to *The Grande Illusion*, and while it does come up short against Renoir's greatest work, there is much in the film to be lauded. Andrew Sarris of the *Village Voice* was one of the few American critics to recognize Renoir as the old master he was. He called it "the apparently effortless achievement not of an old man, but of an old master."

70 *Les Carabiniers (The Soldiers or The Riflemen)* 1963 B&W *Director* Jean-Luc Godard; *Producer* Rome Paris Films, Marceau, Cocinor; *Screenplay* Jean Guault, Roberto Rossellini and Jean-Luc Godard; *Adaptation* Benjamino Joppolo; *Photography* Raoul Coutard; *Music* Philippe Arthuys; *Set* Jean-Jacques Fabre; *Editing* Agnès Guillemot. Running time: 75 minutes.

Cast: Marino Mase, Albert Juross, Geneviève Galéa, Catherine Ribeiro, Gérard Poirot, Jean Brassat, Jean-Louis Comolli, Odile Geoffroy, Vladimir Faters, Jean Gruault, Catherine Durante, Jean Monsigny, Gilbert Servien, Barbet Schroeder, Roger Coggio, Pascale Audret, Alvaro Gheri.

Godard's parody of a war film follows two illiterate peasants, Ulysses (Mase) and Michelangelo (Juross), who are drafted into the cavalry. They go to war, where they kill, rape and pillage like good soldiers, all the while sending home postcards of their exploits. When they return home, the king has made peace, and they are killed for their overzealousness.

This is one of Godard's most experimental films. He said of his intention: "The action and the events described in the film could happen anywhere, on the left or on the right, at anytime and any place." He meant to provoke the audience to respond to the horrors of war, instead they responded to the horrors of his film, but it is nonetheless quite a troubling and important work. Godard's style paid tribute to early filmmakers such as Lumière, with silent film conventions and newsreel footage of war, which added confusion to the film, not clarification. Still there are wonderful Godardian moments.

This film received very bad reviews when it first came out. Many critics deemed it stupid and vulgar. *Variety* called it "a way out anti-war fable" and said that it "has the brash inventiveness, progression and continuity of the growing changes in film narrative methods." Kenneth Tynan of London's *Observer* ended his review with the high praise: "It eats into the mind like acid. If this is not a masterpiece, it will do until one comes along."

71 *La Carrosse d'or (The Golden Coach)* 1953 Color *Director* Jean Renoir; *Producer* Panaria Films, Hoche Production, Corona; *Photography* Claude Renoir, Ronald Hill and Rodolpho Lombardi; *Music* Vivaldi, Corelli, Olivier Metra with arrangements by Gino Marinuzzi; *Set* Mario Chiari and Gianni Polidori; *Sound* Joseph de Bretagne and Ovidio Del Grande; *Costumes* Mario de Matteis; *Editing* David Hawkins. Running time: 100 minutes.

Cast: Anna Magnani, Odoardo Spadaro, Duncan Lamon, Paul Campbell, Riccardo Rioli, Nada Fiorelli, Georges Higgins, Gisela Mathews, Ralph Truman,

La Carrosse d'or (The Golden Coach), 1953; directed by Jean Renoir.

Elena Altieri, Renato Chiantoni, Alfredo Kolner, Alfredo Medini, Giulio Tedeschi, Dante, Cecil Mathews, Rino, John Pasetti, Jean Debucourt, Fredo Keeling, William Tubbs, Raf della Torre, Jean Perez, Augusto, Alfredo, Franco, and Giulio Medini.

Set in the eighteenth century, a troupe of Italian actors travel to South America to make their fortune. When they reach the court, the star of the troupe, the beautiful Camilla (Magnani), catches the fancy of a celebrated toreador Ramon (Rioli), a dashing Italian (Spadaro), and the Viceroy Ferdinand (Lamon). The court is scandalized when Ferdinand offers Camilla, as a token of his affection, the glorious golden carriage that he had had sent over from Europe. To avoid bloodshed, Camilla gives the carriage to the church and departs with her one love: the theater.

This is Renoir's last masterpiece. An ode to the aesthetic and spiritual splendors of the world of theater, the film is visually breathtaking. Renoir focuses on the themes of true love and creative passion. He would return to the idea of a woman choosing her art over a man in *French Cancan*, but not quite so elegantly. Like a play, the film can be divided into three scenes: the farmhouse, the palace and Camilla's apartments.

When it was released, *The Golden Coach* was not received very well by the critics nor by the general public. Some found that the Commedia dell'Arte scenes interrupted the narrative, but Truffaut said it was probably Renoir's greatest work. "The most noble and refined film ever made," he said. "*The Golden Coach* is of an absolute, profound beauty."

72 *Casque d'or (Golden Marie)* 1952 B&W   *Director* Jacques Becker; *Producer* Sepva Films, Discina; *Screenplay* Jacques Becker and Jacques Companeez; *Photography* Robert Lefebvre; *Music* Georges Van Parys; *Set* Jean d'Eaubonne; *Sound* Antoine Petitjean; *Costumes* Georgette Fillion, M. Mayo; *Editing* Marguerite Renoir. Running time: 96 minutes.

Cast: Simone Signoret, Serge Reggiani, Claude Dauphin, Raymond Bussières, Gaston Modot, Daniel Mendaille, Loleh Bellon, William Sabatier, Claude Castaing, Roland Lesaffre, Paul Azaïs, Dominique Davray, Odette Barencey, Paul Barge, Emile Genevois, Fernand Trignol, Yvonne Yma, Pierre Goutas, Yvette Lucas, Jean Clarieux, Pauléon, Corteggiani, Roger Vincent, Léon Bary, Raphael Patorni, André Méliès, Marcel Rougé, Marcel Metrac, Jean Degrave, Suzanne Grey, Paquerette, Odette Talazac, Joëlle Bernard, Jacqueline Marbaux, Christiane Minazzoli, Simone Jarnac, Pomme, Henri Coutet, Jean Berton, René Pascal, Roger Dalphin, Pierre Leproux, Solange Cortain, Julien Maffre, Abel Coulon, Marianne Borgue, Gisèle Delzen, Anna Béressi, Jacqueline Cantrelle, Martine Arden.

The tragic love story of a beautiful blond prostitute, Marie (Signoret), nicknamed "Casque d'or," which translates to "Golden helmet," and a gang of young hoodlums. When Marie is out with the gang one afternoon, she and one of the boys, Manda (Reggiani), fall in love at first sight. In a jealous rage, the gang's leader, Felix (Dauphin), incites a fight in which Manda kills another member of the gang. Felix's betrayal does not go unpunished, but it is Manda who eventually goes to the guillotine before Marie's eyes.

Hailed as one of the most beautiful films of the postwar era, this cinematic masterpiece reveals Becker's genius. It is "an ode to loyalty" that succeeds in making believable the idea of a lasting love that was conceived at first sight. Signoret considered it to be her greatest role, and she really is magical as Marie. Becker brings an old era to new life with wonderful scenes, a great cast and a story of violence and passion.

Golden Marie opened in Belgium and was not well received by the critics. It didn't fare much better when it moved to Paris, except in the eyes of Georges Sadoul, who believed it ranked with the great works of Renoir and Clair. After the British Film Academy awarded Simone Signoret recognition as Best Foreign Actress in 1952, it was reconsidered.

73 *Le Casse (The Burglars)* 1971 Color   *Director* Henri Verneuil; *Producer* Henri Verneuil; *Screenplay* Henri Verneuil and Vahé Katcha, based on David Goodis' novel *The Burglar*; *Photography* Claude Renoir; *Music* Ennio Morricone; *Set* Jacques Saulnier; *Sound* Jean Rieul; *Editing* Pierre Gillette. Running time: 100 minutes.

Cast: Jean-Paul Belmondo, Omar Sharif, Robert Hossein, Renato Salvatori, Dyan Cannon, Nicole Calfan, José Luis de Villalonga, Robert Duranton, Myriam Colombi, Raoul Delfosse, Steve Eckardt, Daniel Verite, Marc Arian.

A remake of the 1950s film noir *The Burglar*, in which Azad (Belmondo) and his crew break into a wealthy Greek man's suburban home with the help of a high-tech computer and steal his million dollar emerald collection. They are hunted by a corrupt Greek cop (Sharif), who wants to keep the jewels for himself. The cop's nasty methods do not help him in the end, and Azad manages to trap him in a grain elevator and smother him.

A great action film for Belmondo to strut and stunt his stuff with Omar Sharif and Dyan Cannon providing extra star power. There is a wonderful car chase with Belmondo performing his trademark daring stunts on his own. Verneuil is a master of cops and robbers movies and handles the twists and turns of suspense very well. This is not groundbreaking, but it is good entertainment.

Some critics called it just another Belmondo vehicle and complained that it was a bit long even for his fanatical fans. *Variety* praised it as "a canny, well-concocted caper pic."

74 *Les Casse-pieds (The Spice of Life)* 1948 B&W   *Director* Jean Dréville; *Producer* Cinéphonic; *Screenplay* Noël-Noël; *Photography* Léonce-Henry Burel and André Thomas; *Music* René Cloérec; *Set* Lucien Carré; *Sound* René C. Forget; *Editing* Jean Feyte. Running time: 90 minutes.

Cast: Noël-Noël, Marguerite Deval, Bernard Blier, Jean Tissier, Henri Crémieux, Pierre Destailles, René Blancard, Paul Frankeur, Georges Questiau, Jean-Pierre Mocky, Claire Olivier, Elisa Lamothe, Marion Tourès, Gaby Bruyère, Jacques Mattler, Charles Vissières, Guy Saint Clair, Titys, Lucien Frégis, Jean Varennes, Emile Rémongin, Aline Andrée, La Houppa, Madeleine Barbulée, Christine Arden, Micheline Rolla, Cécile Eddy, Paul Clergue, Georges Rollin, Charles Bayard, Lucien Guervil, Maryse Martin, Maguy Horiot.

A singer's lively discussion of all the bores whom he has known. He recounts his run-ins with bores in the theater; the bad female driver bore; the short-winded bore; the constant kidder, and many others. In short, he pokes fun at the stereotypical pains in the neck that populate everyday existence.

This is the great comedian Noël-Noël's greatest film. It is full of good humored fun as every banal dullard gets his due. Released just after World War II, its childlike humor that laughed at people's quirky characteristics hit France's funny bone in just the right spot. This hilarious movie is carried by Noël-Noël's great comedic talent.

The Times of London raved: "It is a tour-de-force carried out with immense verve and ingenuity." It won the Prix Louis Delluc and the Grand Prix du Cinéma Français in 1948.

Cat and Mouse *see* **Le Chat et la souris**

The Cat and the Mouse *see* **Le Chat et la souris**

75 *Le Cavaleur (Practice Makes Perfect)* 1978 Color   *Director* Philippe de Broca; *Producer* Alexandre Mnouchkine; *Screenplay* Michel Audiard, Philippe de Broca; *Photography* Jean-Paul Schwartz; *Music* Ludwig van Beethoven; *Set* Eric Moulard; *Sound* Jean Labussière; *Editing* Henri Lanoë. Running time: 104 minutes.

Cast: Jean Rochefort, Nicole Garcia, Danielle Darrieux, Annie Giradot, Catherine Alric, Jean Desailly, Jacques Jouanneau, Lila Kedrova, Catherine LePrince, Carole Lixon, Peggy Besson, Julie Besson, Sophie Holtham, Serge Coursan, José Noguero, Yvon de Broca, Jacques Jouhanneau, Xavier Saint Macary, Florent Boffard, Jean-Marie Bon, Raoul Guy, Thomas Hnevsa, Oleg Gboldouieff, Gaëtan Noël, Michel Degand, Bernard Musson, Michel Oudart, Catherine Floch, Lucienne Legrand, Madeleine Colin, Frédérique Lafond, Georges Anderson, Eurydice, Alain Gomis, Mame Awa Indoye, Anna Gaylor, Gilbert Prenneron, Dominique Probst, Philippe Castelli, Arnaud Bompis, Philippe Cachet.

Casque d'or (Golden Marie), 1952; directed by Jacques Becker.

A comedy about a famous pianist, Edouard Chosieul (Rochefort), who has too many romantic attachments. His wife, Marie-France (Garcia), threatens to leave him, so he takes the family to the seashore, only to run off with his mistress, whom he soon dumps for the granddaughter of an old lover. He winds up living in the country with a friend who runs a hardware store, but then his daughter shows up pregnant. Her wedding turns into a happy reunion.

This light-hearted romantic comedy is one of Philippe de Broca's best films. Yves Montand was originally slated to play the role of Edouard, but Jean Rochefort took his place and delivered a sweet and subtle performance of a man in mid-life crisis. De Broca keeps a fast, fun pace throughout the film, which keeps amusement high at all times. It is a beautifully photographed film with gorgeous shots of Brittany. Nicole Garcia is wonderfully elegant and intelligent as the neglected wife.

When the film came out in the United States, *The Hollywood Reporter* said: "*Practice Makes Perfect* is a pleasant diversion which should give pleasure to fans of French film. De Broca has captured France beautifully in the film, moving his scenario from Paris to the seashore to the chateaus in the country, all of which are appealingly lensed." Nicole Garcia won the César for Best Actress in 1980.

Celine and Julie Go Boating *see* **Céline et Julie vont en bateau**

76 *Céline et Julie vont en bateau (Celine and Julie Go Boating)*   1975
Color   *Director* Jacques Rivette; *Producer* Films du Losange, Action Fechner,

Renn Productions, Saga Simar, Films 7, VM Productions; *Screenplay* Eduardo de Gregorio, Juliet Berto, Bulle Ogier, Marie-France Pisier, Jacques Rivette and Dominique Labourier; *Photography* Jacques Renard; *Music* Jean-Marie Sénia; *Set* Eric Simon; *Sound* Paul Lainé; *Editing* Nicole Lubtchansky. Running time: 190 minutes.

Cast: Juliet Berto, Dominique Labourier, Bulle Ogier, Marie-France Pisier, Barbet Schroeder, Nathalie Asnar, Jean-Claude Romer, Jean Douchet, Philippe Clevenot, Adèle Taffetas, Anne Zamire, Monique Clément, Jérôme Richard, Michael Graham, Jean-Marie Sénia, Jean-Claude Biette.

A fantastical story about two young women. Julie (Labourier) is a sensible librarian, and Céline (Berto) is a magical girl who lives in her fantasies and calls herself a magician. Céline transports Julie to a fantasy world with her stories, and Julie introduces Céline to her childhood, which is not without its dangerous implications. Fantasy becomes reality and vice versa.

One of Rivette's best and most entertaining films, *Celine and Julie Go Boating* was hailed by *Film Comment* as the most important film to come out of France since 1968. Rivette plays with magic and myth, time and place, literature and fantasy, and the idea of the little girl going through the looking glass. His allusions to *Alice in Wonderland* are obvious, with mirrors and double images playing a major role. He also alludes to Cocteau, Borges and Proust.

Some critics found it a very beautiful film, while others complained that they never figured out what happened. It was the hit of the 1974 New York Film Festival. London's *Observer* called it an "extraordinary, enchanting, maddeningly elusive kaleidoscope."

77 *Le Cercle rouge (The Red Circle)*   1970 Color   *Director* Jean-Pierre Melville; *Producer* Corona, Selenia Films; *Screenplay* Jean-Pierre Melville; *Photography* Henri Decaë; *Music* Eric de Marsan; *Set* Théobald Meurisse; *Sound* Jacques Carrère; *Editing* Jean-Pierre Melville. Running time: 150 minutes.

Cast: Alain Delon, Bourvil, Yves Montand, François Périer, Gian Maria Volonte, André Eycan, Paul Crauchet, Anna Douking, Paul Amiot, Stéphanie Fugain, René Berthier, Robert Favart, Jean Franval, Jean Champion, Yves Arcanel, Robert Rondo, Pierre Collet, André Ekyan, Jean-Pierre Posier, Guy Henry, Yvan Chiffre, Roger Fradet, Pierre Lecomte, Edouard Francomme, Jean Pignol, Jacques Galland, Jacques Leroy, Jean-Marc Bory, Jean-Pierre Janic.

A thriller about a gangster, Corey (Delon), who is released from prison and teams up with two other men to pull off a major jewelry heist on the Place Vendôme. Along with an escaped prisoner (Volonte) and an alcoholic ex-policeman (Montand), Corey succeeds in lifting the jewels, but then is pursued by a sharp inspector (Bourvil).

From the master of French thrillers, this film benefits from Melville's mastery and great performances by some of France's best actors. Melville plays on the idea of a special loyalty and comradeship among thieves and Montand and Delon deliver fine performances that uphold this theory. Melville builds suspense beautifully, even after the jewelry heist. Henri Decaë's camerawork is superb as always.

The Red Circle did very well in France when it came out in 1970, but it was not released commercially in the United States, until 1993. *The London Times* called it: "Ingenious, it is exciting, it is never dull." *The New York Times'* review said: "Understatement is the method of the film, from Melville's pared-down screenplay to the performances by the three trenchcoated principals, even to the muted photography by Henri Decaë, which is in color but has the chilly effect of black and white."

78 *Le Cerf-volant du bout du monde (The Kite from Across the World)* 1958 Color *Director* Roger Pigaut; *Producer* Garance Films, J. Tourane, Cocinor, Studios de Pékin; *Screenplay* Roger Pigaut and Antoine Tudal; *Photography* Henri Alekan; *Music* Louis Bessières and Tuan Se Tchung; *Set* Claude Moesching; *Sound* Jean-Claude Marchetti, William Sivel, and Tchen Yen Hsi; *Editing* Marinette Cadix. Running time: 82 minutes.

Cast: Patrick de Bardine, Gérard Szymanski, Sylvaine Rozenberg, Jacques Faburel, Alain Astié, Henri Blanchard, Georges Desplaces, Raphaël Hassan, Claude Bougis, Annie Noël, Gabrielle Fontan, Guy Delorme, Claire Gérard, Charles Vissières, Tchen Ming Tchen, Lou P'Ung, Ying-Ghi-Yun, Yuang Di Wang, Thcan Tchum Wha, Sie T'Ien, Jacques Kubista.

A sort of fairy tale in which Pierrot (de Bardine) and a band of street kids from the Montmartre quarter of Paris discover an amazing Chinese kite caught on a tree branch. Two kids' gangs fight over the kite, with one gang tearing off the tail. There is a note hidden in the kite from a Chinese boy who wants a Western friend. The leader of the gang has the note translated and enters into a series of imaginary adventures with a band of Chinese children.

One of France's best children films blends fantasy with beautiful shots of Paris and Peking. The flights of fantasy contain important life morals about enemies and friends, rivalries and peacemaking. The vivid colors, kites and the magic Chinese Monkey King add a deep visual beauty to the film. It is a sweet, sincere work that dazzles children and amuses adults.

When the film debuted at Cannes in 1958, *Variety* said: "Director Roger Pigaut shows sensitivity and the ability to translate warmth and sentiment short of getting maudlin or precious."

79 *Le Cerveau (The Brain)* 1969 Color *Director* Gérard Oury; *Producer* Gaumont International, Dino de Laurentiis; *Screenplay* Gérard Oury; *Adaptation* Gérard Oury, Marcel Jullian, Danièle Thompson; *Photography* Armand Thirard, Vladimir Ivanov; *Music* Georges Delerue; *Set* Jean André; *Sound* Jean Rieul; *Editing* Albert Jurgenson. Running time: 115 minutes.

Cast: Bourvil, Jean-Paul Belmondo, David Niven, Eli Wallach, Silvia Monti, Frank Valois, Henri Genès, Sophie Grimaldi, Dominique Zardi, Frank Valois, Tommy Dugan, Yves Barsacq, Micha Bayard, Guy Delorme, Robert Dalban, Raymond Gérôme, Jacques Balutin, Fernand Guiot, Marcel Charvey, Patrick Préjean, Henri Attal, Jacques Ciron, Paul Mercey, John Rico, Max Montavon, Roger Lumont, Raoul Delfosse, Mario David, Arch Taylor, Roland Monk, Pierre Tornade, Gérard Hernandez, Georges Steinbach, Charles Dallin, Pipo Merisi, Luigi Cortese, Jean-Paul Gouaze, Bob Ingarao, Bob Lerick, Jean Minisini, Roger Pappini, César Torrès, Christina Walls, Kim Camba, Daniel Crohem, Mick Besson, Yvon Dihé, Jean Borodine, Jerry Brouer, Jean-François Barre, Gordon Lacy, Michel Garland, Jean-Pierre Posier, Douglas Read, Jean Gabert, Gérard Streiff, Jacques Van Dooren, Pierre Roussel, Raymond Pierson, Guy Bonnafous.

A comedy about three sets of crooks, all planning the same train robbery. The Brain (Niven) is a famous British train robber, who plans to pull off a job in France.

Two petty French thiefs (Belmondo and Bourvil) have the same idea, as does an Italian mobster. The three contending teams continuously manage to frustrate each other's efforts, until all the money is lost; but then they plan to join forces.

A great, accessible comedy with a star-studded cast from the master of postwar French comedies, Gérard Oury. This big-budget film cost over $4 million to make. Belmondo, Bourvil and Niven are wonderful as the quintessential bumblers and the sophisticated swindler. Oury uses elaborate and innovative gags to great effect, as well as tributes to Buster Keaton and Charlie Chaplin.

Some French critics dismissed it as a great expense for mediocre results. When it came out in France, *Variety* called it: "An elaborate comedy-actioner takeoff on the British *Great Train Robbery*."

Cesar and Rosalie *see* **César et Rosalie**

80 *César et Rosalie (Cesar and Rosalie)* 1973 Color   *Director* Claude Sautet; *Producer* Fil Lebroc, UPF, Méga Films, Paramount, Orion Films; *Screenplay* Jean-Loup Dabadie, Claude Sautet and Claude Néron; *Photography* Jean Boffety; *Music* Philippe Sarde; *Set* Pierre Guffroy; *Sound* William Sivel; *Editing* Jacqueline Thiédot. Running time: 110 minutes.

Cast: Yves Montand, Romy Schneider, Samy Frey, Umberto Orsini, Bernard Lecoq, Isabelle Huppert, Eva Maria Meineke, Jacques Dhéry, Pipo Merisi, Henri Jacques Huet, Carlo Nell, Gisela Hahn, Dimitri Petricenko, Carol Lixson, Céline Galland, Hervé Sand, Martin Lartigue, Muriel Deloumeaux, Betty Beckers, Marcel Gassouk, Henri Coutet, Robert Le Beal, Jerry Brouer, Nicolas Vogel, Arcady, Brigitte Defrance, Jean-Claude Susfeld, Lucienne Legrand, Colin Drake and the voice of Michel Piccoli.

The tale of a woman, Rosalie (Schneider), and the two men whom she loves. Rosalie first moved in with César (Montand), a rich and dependable man, after her divorce from a painter. When she bumps into a sweetheart from her youth, David (Frey), she realizes she is still in love with him and goes to live with him. When César and David become friends, she leaves them both, but returns a year later.

A wonderful tender and realistic portrayal of quotidian love by one of France's great chroniclers of the 1970s. This is a quintessential French love story in the tradition of *A Man and a Woman* and *Jules and Jim*, but much modernized. Montand and Schneider are both wonderful, vulnerable and utterly charming. Sautet called the film "a tonic fantasy ... [in] a sophisticated manner of reality." He explained the film's dilemma by saying: "It's very difficult to balance freedom and love. Rosalie believes there's freedom in love, and she can't get it. Cesar believes in possession of her and that's his freedom. Neither one of them is satisfied. It's a draw."

Critics in France and abroad almost universally raved over this film. In fact, the harshest criticism it received was being brushed off as "a pleasant piece of romantic fluff" by *The New Republic*'s critic. Judith Christ in *New York* magazine called it "An enchanting story of what love is all about with Yves Montand never better and Romy Schneider never lovelier." Norma Stoop in *After Dark* said: "Claude Sautet's direction is keen, and his eye for detail is evident in all of the small touches which combine so beautifully to construct a tender, imagist sort of love story—nothing cosmic, nothing universal, just an admirable direct look into the hearts of three very appealing people." It won the Grand Prix du Cinéma Français in 1972.

81 *Cet Obscur Objet du désir (That Obscure Object of Desire)* 1977
Color   *Director* Luis Buñuel; *Producer* Greenwich-Les Films Galaxie-In Cine
Productions; *Screenplay* based on Pierre Louys' novel *La Femme et le pantin*;
Photography Edmond Richard; *Music* Flamenco and Richard Wagner; *Set* Pierre
Guffroy; *Sound* Guy and Olivier Villette; *Costumes* Sylvie de Ségouzac; *Editing*
Hélène Plémiannikov. Running time: 100 minutes.

Cast: Fernando Rey, Carole Bouquet, Angela Molina, André Weber, Julien
Bertheau, Piéral, Bernard Musicson, Milena Vukotic, Maria Asquerino, Muni,
Ellen Bahl, Valérie Bianco, Jacques Rebray, Augusta Carrière, Antonio Duque,
André Lacombe, Rita Luluch-Piero, Isabelle Rattier, Jean Santamaria, Mario
David, David Rocha, Isabelle Sadoyan, Jean-Claude Montalban, Dick Winslow,
Mélody Thomas.

Mathieu (Rey), an upper-class Parisian, falls for a beautiful, young and im-
poverished Spanish woman named Conchita (played alternately by Bouquet and
Molina), who teases him along. She even goes so far as to move in with him, sharing his bed, but never quite being ready to make love. Set in Paris and Seville, the
object of desire and her pursuer make for great Buñuel wit.

Buñuel's last film is one of his best. He made it when he was 77 years old, and
took cinematic deconstruction so far as to have the leading lady played by two
different actresses. The film deals with all of Buñuel's obsessions — destructive love,
random violence, social codes, liberation, sex and more — as he deconstructs the
femme fatale once and for all with his characteristic wit.

Critics hailed this film as the last word on Buñuel's wild and wonderful world,
and unfortunately it was. Even those who did not believe it stood up to his masterpieces, credited Buñuel with bringing one more breath of fresh air to film. It was
nominated for the Oscar for Best Foreign Film and Best Screenplay Adaptation
in 1977.

82 *Le Chagrin et la pitié (The Sorrow and the Pity)* 1971 *Director*
Marcel Ophuls; *Producer* SSR, TV Rencontre, NDR; *Screenplay* Marcel Ophüls,
André Harris; *Photography* André Gazut, Jürgen Thieme; *Music* songs sung by
Maurice Chevalier; *Sound* Bernard Migy; *Editing* Claude Wazda. Running time:
250 minutes.

Interviews with: Emmanuel d'Astier de la Vigerie, René de Chambrun,
Georges Bidault, Emile Coulaudon, Marcel Fouché-Deglieme, Jacques Duclos,
Christian de la Mazière, Georges Lamirand, Claude Lévy, Pierre Mendès-France,
Anthony Eden, Maurice Buckmaster, General Spears, Denis Rake, Helmut Tau-
send, Dr. Elmer Michel, General Walter Warlimont, Dr. Paul Schmidt, Corporal
Bleibinger.

A documentary about Clermont-Ferrand and the Auvergne from 1940 to 1945,
this film covers the beginning of World War II, France's defeat, the Occupation,
the Resistance, the Liberation, and the departure of the Nazis, using photographs
and films from British, French and German archives, mixed in with interviews with
people who played very different roles in the war.

One of the most important films, if not the most important film, made on
World War II. Marcel Ophüls, the son of Max Ophüls, was a young Israeli filmmaker when he spent nine months making this movie for television. When it opened
April 5, 1971, in Paris, it was so shocking that it continued to play for 12 years in
the theater, before it ever went to television. The film demystified Europe in this

period by showing it as it really was — full of contradictions and ambiguities — for the first time since the war. The film absolutely destroyed previous conceptions that people had had about the Vichy government. It began a movement in literature and film called "la mode rétro," which questioned established historical ideas.

The Sorrow and the Pity was a success in both France and the United States It ran for over 39 weeks in New York. *The Nation* said, "*The Sorrow and the Pity* offers insight not only into the specific character of one moment in French and European history but into history in general. This film persuades one — as do few books, novels, plays or eyewitness reportage — of the truth of Karl Marx's aphorism: 'History walks on two feet,' in other words, that it is enacted by ordinary as well as extraordinary men and women." The film won the Prix Georges Sadoul in 1970.

83 *Une Chambre en ville (A Room in Town)* 1983 Color *Director* Jacques Demy; *Producer* Technisonor, Progefi, TF1; *Screenplay* Jacques Demy; *Photography* Jean Penzer; *Music* Michel Colombier; *Set* Bernard Evein; *Sound* André Hervée; *Costumes* Rosalie Varda; *Editing* Sabine Mamou. Running time: 92 minutes.

Cast: Dominique Sanda, Richard Berry, Danielle Darrieux, Michel Piccoli, Fabienne Guyon, Jean-François Stevenin, Anna Gaylor, Jean-Louis Rolland, Marie-France Roussel, Georges Blanes, Marie-Pierre Feuillard, Monique Créteur, Gil Warga, Nicolas Hossein, Yann Dedet, Patrik Joly, Antoine Nikola, Denis Epstein, Jean Porcher.

Set in Nantes, 1955, this is the tragic story of two strangers who share an ill-fated passion. After renting a room from a widow, François (Berry), a blue-collar worker is visited one night by a woman who is naked except for her fur coat. They spend a passionate night together. The woman, who is the widow's daughter, is married to a man who is impotent. Soon after François and Edith's night together, all three meet tragic ends.

Another musical love story from the French master Jacques Demy, *A Room in Town* may not be *The Umbrellas of Cherbourg*, but it is a lovely work. It was the first film Demy made after an eight-year hiatus, and though the music is not as great as in *Umbrellas*, few could pull off such drama and singing as well as Demy. It was a project that he had started in film school and nurtured for years before he could make it. His choreography is spectacular. Darrieux is lovely, and the melodramatic plot proves to be moving.

When *A Room in Town* did badly at the French box-office, 76 French critics paid $4,100 to run an ad in *Le Monde* encouraging people to go see the film. A reporter explained the critics' unusual support of the film as a political act. "For some of its most engaged supporters in Socialist France [the film] has the kind of Frenchness, intellectual ambition and leftist point of view that they would hope marks culture here in the 1980s." Another band of French critics claimed that if the movie was a failure it "would be that of all of French cinema — nothing more, nothing less." It won the French Critics' Prix Méliès in 1982.

84 *La Chambre verte (The Green Room)* 1978 Color *Director* François Truffaut; *Producer* Films du Carrosse, Artistes Associés; *Screenplay* François Truffaut and Jean Gruault, based on the stories "L'Autel des morts," "Les Ami des amis," and "La Bête de la jungle" by Henry James; *Photography* Nestor Almen

Cet Obscur Objet du désir (*That Obscure Object of Desire*), 1977; directed by Luis Buñuel.

dros; *Music* Maurice Jaubert; *Set* Jean-Pierre Kohut Svelko; *Sound* Michel Laurent; *Editing* Martine Barraqué. Running time: 94 minutes.

Cast: François Truffaut, Nathalie Baye, Jean Dasté, Jean-Pierre Moulin, Antoine Vitez, Jean Lobre, Patrick Maléon, Jean-Pierre Ducos, Annie Miller, Marie Jaoul, Monique Dury, Laurence Ragon, Marcel Berbert, Thi Loan N'Guyen, Guy d'Ablon, Christian Lentretien, Henri Bienvenu, Alphonse Simon, Anna Paniez, Carmen Sarda Canovas, Jean-Claude Gasche, Serge Rousseau, Jean-Pierre Kohut Svelko, Roland Thénot, Martine Barraque Curie.

A few years after World War I, Julien Davenne (Truffaut) devotes first a room of his house, then his life to the memories of his dead wife and friends. He writes obituaries for the local newspaper. When he bumps into an old acquaintance Cécilia (Baye), who understands his feelings for the dead, he is on the verge of returning to the world of the living. But once he learns that she has been involved with the childhood friend who introduced Julien to adult cynicism, he shuts himself off from the world permanently. Cécilia loves him, but it is too late.

Truffaut's most somber film, although not marked by the humor for which he is known, is still remarkably beautiful and possibly one of his best and most sophisticated works. Starring in his last acting role, as Davenne, Truffaut presents an interesting meditation on human obsession from his character's struggle to remain optimistic to his ultimate defeat. The germ for the movie, he said, was the fact that at some point in your life you know more people who are dead than living.

The Green Room was a commercial failure, maybe because it was not what people expected from him. Some critics hailed it as Truffaut's most original film ever, but they acknowledged that death and morbidity were the kiss of death as film subject matter, especially in France.

La Chambre verte (*The Green Room*), 1978; directed by François Truffaut.

Charlotte and Lulu *see* **L'Effrontée**

85 *Le Charme discret de la bourgeoisie (The Discreet Charm of the Bourgeoisie)* 1972 Color *Director* Luis Buñuel; *Producer* Greenwich Film Production, Jet Film, Dean Film; *Screenplay* Luis Buñuel and Jean-Claude Carrière; *Photography* Edmond Richard; *Set* Pierre Guffroy; *Sound* Guy Villette; *Costumes* Jacqueline Guyot; *Editing* Hélène Plemiannikov. Running time: 105 minutes.

Cast: Fernando Rey, Delphine Seyrig, Jean-Pierre Cassel, Stéphane Audran, Bulle Ogier, Paul Frankeur, Claude Piéplu, Julien Bertheau, François Maistre, Maria Gabriella Maione, Michel Piccoli, Muni, Georges Douking, Pierre Maguelon.

A black comedy about three bourgeois drug-traffickers—one of whom is a South American ambassador (Rey)—their amorous adventures, their nightmares, their martini cocktail hours and their inability to sit down to a civilized meal together.

A masterpiece of surrealistic comedy, in which the same premise—how this group of people are interrupted as they have a meal together (by funerals, by armies, by the police)—is taken up again and again in a spiraling form of nightmare. "I now say with humor what I used to say with violence," said Buñuel of this film, which he made at age seventy-two and in which he once again tackles his favorite topics: sex, religion and the middle-class.

Jonathan Rosenbaum believed *The Discreet Charm of the Bourgeoisie* was "arguably the first contemporary, global masterpiece to have come from France in the seventies." It won the Oscar for Best Foreign Film and the French Critics' Prix Méliès in 1972.

Le Charme discret de la bourgeoisie (*The Discreet Charm of the Bourgeoisie*), **1972; directed by Luis Buñel.**

86 *Le Chat et la souris (Cat and Mouse* **or** *The Cat and the Mouse)*
1976 Color   *Director* Claude Lelouch; *Producer* Les Films 13; *Screenplay* Claude Lelouch; *Photography* Jean Collomb; *Music* Francis Laï; *Set* Eric Moulard; *Sound* Jean-Louis Ducarne; *Editing* Georges Klotz. Running time: 107 minutes.

Cast: Serge Reggiani, Michèle Morgan, Jean-Pierre Aumont, Philippe Aumont, Valerie LaGrange, Judith Magre, Philippe Labro, Anne Libert, Michel Peyrelon, Christine Laurent, Jacques François, Arlette Emery, Jean Mermet, Yves Alfonso.

A mystery that begins with the death of a Parisian millionaire, Monsieur Richard (Aumont). Despite a good alibi, all evidence points to his lovely wife, Madame Richard (Morgan), as the killer. The police inspector (Reggiani) in charge of the investigation goes from being convinced of her guilt to finding her more and more charming and innocent. Lovers, clues and missing art works complicate the situation.

A very enjoyable who-dunit and one of Lelouch's best, in which the audience is just as much a part of the cat-and-mouse game as the actors. Lelouch said of his intent: "In this film the main idea is that criminals are a product of circumstances, not of evil. There are no real rats in my film, simply people who make the most of circumstances when they come up." This was the first film Michèle Morgan did in eight years, and it was a great come back for her talents. Lelouch successfully uses flashbacks to build romantic and plot suspense.

This was a great commercial success in France and a critical triumph abroad. Rex Reed praised it in *Vogue* as "Superior to anything Hitchcock has come up with in the past decade! Totally unique. A star-spangled canvas — clever, amusing and devilishly labyrinthian."

87 *Le Château de ma mère (My Mother's Castle)* 1990 Color *Director* Yves Robert; *Producer* Gaumont, Productions de la Guéville, TF1 Films; *Screenplay* Yves Robert, based on Marcel Pagnol's novel *Souvenirs d'enfance*; *Photography* Robert Alazraki; *Music* Vladimir Cosma; *Set* Jacques Dugied; *Sound* Alain Sempé; *Costumes* Agnès Nègre; *Editing* Pierre Gillette. Running time: 100 minutes.

Cast: Philippe Caubère, Nathalie Roussel, Didier Pain, Thérèse Liotard, Julien Ciamaca, Jean Carmet, Jean Rochefort, Georges Wilson, Philippe Uchan, Julie Timmerman, Victorien Delamare, Paul Crauchet, Patrick Préjean, Joris Molinas, Ticky Holgado, Pierre Maguelon, Michel Modo, Jean-Marie Juan, René Loyon, Maxine Lombard, André Chameau, Alain Ganas, Ivan Romeuf, Jean Maurel, Elizabeth Macocco, Michel Combale, Philippe Car, Raoul Curet, Paul Vilalte, Christina Karian, Josy Andreiu, and the voice of Jean-Pierre Darras.

A family drama about Augustine (Roussel), the mother of Marcel, who desperately wants to return to her family's country house as soon as possible. The family starts taking a shortcut on the weekends. The shortcut requires trespassing on someone's property and using a key illegally, which could make the father, who is a civil servant, lose his job.

One of the three Pagnol films by director Yves Robert that evoke bucolic France in a more tender era, *My Mother's Castle* is a beautiful film. Pagnol described the novel the film was based on as "a testimony of a bygone age and a little song of filial piety which in our day, perhaps, may pass for a great novelty." The plot is not what is important, it is the photography and the slowly building sentiment that matter.

Serge Toubiana, the editor of *Cahiers du Cinéma*, summed up the movie's appeal when he wrote: "Pagnol describes a France in all its simplicity — before mass media, before modern times. There is no menace. It's the opposite of what people see today in their lives: drugs, AIDS, violence. It's the inviolable myth of France, the family, the children; Pagnol is harmony and unity."

The Cheat *see* **Manèges**

The Cheaters *see* **Les Tricheurs**

88 *La Chèvre (The Goat)* 1981 Color *Director* Francis Veber; *Producer* Alain Poiré; *Screenplay* Francis Veber; *Photography* Alex Philips; *Music* Vladimir Cosma; *Set* Jacques Bufnoir; *Sound* Bernard Rochut; *Editing* Albert Jurgenson. Running time: 91 minutes.

Cast: Gérard Depardieu, Pierre Richard, Michel Robin, Corynne Charbit, André Valardy, Michel Forin, Robert Dalban, Jean-Louis Fortuit, Pedro Armenderiz, Jr.

Marie Bens (Charbit), the daughter of an industrialist, has always had horrible luck. When she disappears on a trip to Mexico, her father hires a private detective named Campana (Depardieu) to find her. He has no luck, until someone suggests Mr. Bens find someone as accident-prone as Marie to go looking for her; surely this person will fall into the same traps and misfortunes. Campana gets saddled with an unlucky accountant, François Perrin (Richard), from Mr. Bens' company, and the two run into mishaps that yield clues. Of course, they find Marie, and she and François fall in love.

A wonderful comedy by Veber, one of France's master's of the light, romantic touch. Depardieu and Richard are a hilarious odd couple. Veber creates gags around Depardieu's organized detective methods and Richard's bumbling ways. This was Veber's second comedy as director.

The Goat was a huge success in France and was quite successful abroad. Upon its release, *Variety*'s critic wrote: "*La Chèvre* is an amiable little comedy .... It's modest and relaxed, a neatly assembled series of calamities in which Richard, unusually low-keyed and all the more amusing for it, and Depardieu, appealing in an essentially foil role, generate a breezy charm."

Children of Paradise *see* **Les Enfants du paradis**

Chloe in the Afternoon *see* **L'Amour l'après-midi**

89 *Chocolat* 1988 Color *Director* Claire Denis; *Producer* MK2, Cerito Films, La Sept, TF1 Films, CNC, La Sofica Sofima, WDR; *Screenplay* Claire Denis and Jean-Paul Fargeau; *Photography* Robert Alazraki; *Music* Abdullah Ibrahim; *Set* Thierry Flamand; *Sound* Jean-Louis Ughetto, Dominique Hennequin; *Editing* Claudine Merlin. Running time: 105 minutes.

Cast: Guilia Boschi, Isaach de Bankolé, François Cluzet, Cécile Ducasse, Mireille Perrier, Jean-Claude Adelin, Laurent Arnal, Jacques Denis, Didier Flamand, Jean Bediebe, Emet Judson Williamson, Jean-Quentin Chatelain, Emmanuelle Chaulet, Clémentine Essono, Kenneth Cranham, Essindi Mindja.

A memoir of life and friendship in colonial Africa in the 1950s. France (Perrier), who grew up in Cameroon when it was still a French colony, returns to find that very little remains of the place that she remembers. Memories of her close childhood friendship with Protée (de Bankolé) reveal the tensions and tenderness that underlay black–white racial relations at the time.

Claire Denis' first film marked an exciting directorial debut as well as the advent of a new approach to colonial history. With a personal approach (Denis drew on her own African childhood), she explores the complexities of race relations. She manages to avoid political preachiness while clearly revealing the costs of colonialism to both oppressed and oppressor.

Applauded for the objective tone that revealed the attitudes and sentiments of both the French colonists and the native Cameroons, *Chocolat* was well-received in the United States and France. "[Denis] expresses the subject of racial difference photographically if not dramatically, sensually if not politically," wrote Armond White.

90 *Les Choses de la vie (The Things of Life)* 1969 Color *Director* Claude Sautet; *Producer* Lira Films, Sonocam; *Screenplay* Claude Sautet, Paul Guimard and Jean-Loup Dabadie, based on the novel by Paul Guimard; *Photography* Jean Boffety; *Music* Philippe Sarde; *Set* André Piltant; *Sound* René Longuet; *Editing* Jacqueline Thiédot. Running time: 90 minutes.

Cast: Michel Piccoli, Romy Schneider, Léa Massari, Gérard Lartigau, Jean Bouise, Bobby Lapointe, Dominique Zardi, Hervé Sand, Henri Nassiet, Marcelle

Arnold, Jean-Pierre Zola, Roger Crouzet, Gabrielle Doulcet, Jacques Richard, Claude Confortès, Jerry Brouer, Jean Gras, Gérard Streiff, Betty Beckers, Dominique Zardi, Marie-Pierre Casey, Béatrice Buffety, Max Amyl, Isabelle Sadoyan, Maurice Carmet, Henri Coutet, Raoul Delpard, Pierre Londiche, Christian Bertola, Clément Bairam, Lucien Frégis, Luigi, Karine Jeantet, Mme. Blome, Mme. Duval.

A romantic comedy, in which a near-fatal automobile accident causes an architect (Piccoli) to reflect on the two things he cares most about in life: his wife (Schneider) and his mistress (Massari). A chronically indecisive man, who has left his wife, but thinks of returning to her, Pierre realizes he has lost his son's respect. But before he can act to set things right, he learns that decisions are not the only means through which one's life can change.

This is the film that marked Claude Sautet as a great French film "auteur." It established his psychological realist style and the themes and characters that would resurface in many of his later films. His look at bourgeois dilemmas is compassionate, not critical. Though his style is musical, with a memorable slow-motion car crash, his ending is brutal. The film was a huge hit in Paris and did quite well abroad. Piccoli and Schneider are both very good.

French critics raved over the film's sophistication and subtlety. Many American critics found it laborious. Robert Hatch in *The Nation* brushed it off as proof that "The French, for reasons obvious to anyone who has driven their national highways, are obsessed by motor fatalities." In 1994 it was made into a slick adaptation in the United States as *Intersection,* starring Richard Gere and Sharon Stone. It won the Prix Louis Delluc in 1969.

Clair's Knee *see* **Le Genou de Claire**

Clean Slate *see* **Coup de torchon**

91 *Cleo de cinq à sept (Cleo from 5 to 7)* 1962 B&W   *Director* Agnès Varda; *Producer* Rome Paris Films; *Screenplay* Agnès Varda; *Photography* Jean Rabier; *Music* Michel Legrand; *Set* Bernard Evein; *Sound* Julien Coutellier, Jean Bavussière and Jacques Maumont; *Editing* Janine Verneau. Running time: 90 minutes.

Cast: Corinne Marchand, Dominique Davray, Loyse Payen, José Luis de Villalonga, Michel Legrand, Serge Korber, Dorothée Blanck, Antoine Bourseiller, Robert Porte, Jean Champion, Lucienne Marchand, Jean-Pierre Taste, Jean-Luc Godard, Anna Karina, Danièle Delorme, Renée Duchateau, Sami Frey, Eddie Constantine, Arthur Brunet, Jean-Claude Brialy, Yves Robert.

A tarot card reader sees death in the future of a beautiful singer, Cléo (Marchand), a prediction that coincides with a troubling doctor's visit. Cléo convinces herself that the test results she awaits will reveal that she has cancer. She spends two hours wandering the streets of Paris, seeing both the people with whom she is most intimate and complete strangers in a new way as she comes to grips with her sudden mortality.

A lyrical voyage through Paris' Left Bank, home of the New Wave and the leftist intellectuals, some of whom make cameo appearances in the film. The impending doom, the absolute solitude with which Cleo must face death is palpable, especially as the film presents the wait in real time. The photography in

Varda's second film is wonderful. One great scene sums up the gist of the movie as Jean-Luc Godard, Anna Karina, Sami Frey and other New Wave greats lift up their dark glasses to see things as they really are.

When *Cléo from 5 to 7* came out in 1962, critic Marcel Lobet called it "a subtle dose of intelligence and sensibility." Georges Sadoul applauded Varda's ability to make "Ninety minutes in the life of a Parisian contain the anguish and preoccupations of an entire nation, France." When it opened in the United States, Pauline Kael declared that in *Cleo from 5 to 7* "Agnes Varda sustains an unsentimental yet subjective tone that is almost unique in the history of movies."

Cleo from 5 to 7 *see* **Cleo de cinq à sept**

The Clockmaker *see* **L'Horloger de Saint-Paul**

92 *Un Cœur en hiver (A Heart in Winter* or *A Heart of Stone)* 1991 Color *Director* Claude Sautet; *Producer* Film par Film, Cinéa, Orly Films, Sédif, Paravision, D.A. Films, FR3 Films; *Screenplay* Claude Sautet, Jacques Fieschi, and Jérôme Tonnerre; *Photography* Yves Angelo; *Music* Maurice Ravel; *Set* Christian Marti; *Sound* Pierre Lenoir; *Costumes* Corinne Jorry; *Editing* Jacqueline Thiedot. Running time: 105 minutes.

Cast: Emmanuelle Béart, Daniel Auteuil, André Dussollier, Elizabeth Bourgine, Myriam Boyer, Brigitte Catillon, Maurice Garrel, Jean-Luc Bideau.

A sweet, sad love story set in the classical music world of modern-day Paris. Shy and reserved Stéphane (Auteuil) and the extroverted Maxime (Dussollier) are best friends and partners in a violin repair shop. But when Maxime leaves his wife for a beautiful young violinist, Camille (Béart), who develops a crush on Stéphane, the friendship is jeopardized and passions erupt.

A restrained and beautiful thinking–person's love story that brings a new twist to the tired idea of a love triangle. Claude Sautet's direction is subtle and brilliant. All of the performances are extraordinary, especially those of Béart and Auteuil, who live together in real life and appeared together as star-crossed lovers of a different sort in *Manon of the Spring*. Ambiguity and misinterpretation run rampant for the characters and viewers, but this adds great depth and is surprisingly refreshing in an era when love stories tend to be so neatly tied up.

Upon its release *Variety* called *A Heart in Winter*: "extremely subtle and intensely enjoyable." *Newsday*'s critic John Anderson wrote: "Thoughtful and well-acted, *A Heart in Winter* also is highly ambitious, and by giving us a three-character study devoid of the usual cookie-cutter personalities, executes a rather delicate balancing act of its own." It won Césars for Best Director, Best Supporting Actor, André Dussollier, and the Grand Prix de l'Académie Nationale du Cinéma, the Prix de la Critique and the Prix Méliès in 1993.

93 *Un Cœur gros comme ça! (A Heart as Big as That!)* 1962 B&W *Director* François Reichenbach; *Producer* Films de la Pléiade; *Screenplay* François Reichenbach; *Photography* François Reichenbach and Jean-Marc Ripert; *Music* Michel Legrand, Georges Delerue with songs by Edith Piaf and Léo Ferré; *Sound* Bernard Meusnier, J.J. Campignon and René Renault; *Editing* Kenout Peltier. Running time: 80 minutes.

Cast: Michèle Morgan, Jean-Paul Belmondo, Luce Vidi, Abdou Faye, Bruchard, Milou Pladner.

The few moments of glory in the life of a Senegalese boxer Abdou Faye. Before a championship match, he dreams of famous women such as Michèle Morgan, he wanders the not-so-welcoming streets of Paris, visits a clairvoyant, and eventually loses the match and goes back to work in a factory.

Part fiction and part documentary, this unique film takes a look at a lifestyle and a segment of the population rarely brought to the screen. By mixing scenes from the boxer's life with his thoughts, Reichenbach gives a deep meditative quality to this film. As the boxer wanders the streets of Paris as an urban initiate, the city takes on a new feel. Photography is superb, and the acting quite good.

"This gives insight into a negro boxer's needs and attitudes," wrote *Variety*'s critic upon its release, "and the fact that this vocation gives him a standing in a white world. The final fight is well done. In short, another of the French essay-like films that use film to capture truth." It won the Prix Louis Delluc and the Grand Prize at the Festival of Locarno in 1961.

94 *Un Cœur qui bat (A Beating Heart)* 1991 Color   *Director* François Dupeyron; *Producer* Hachette Première, UGC, Avril Sa-FR3 Films Production; *Screenplay* François Dupeyron; *Photography* Yves Angelo; *Music* Jean-Pierre Drouet; *Set* Carlos Conti; *Sound* Pierre Gamet; *Editing* Françoise Collin. Running time: 100 minutes.

Cast: Dominique Faysee, Thierry Fortineau, Jean-Marie Winling, Roland Amstutz, Christophe Pichon, Steve Kalfa, Coralie Seyrig, Daniel Laloux.

The story of a married Parisian woman, Mado (Faysee), who enters into an intense, adulterous affair with a stranger (Forbineau) on a Montmartre-bound subway train. She is happily married to an antique dealer (Winling) and they have a child. But what began with eye contact on the Métro is followed by an immediate interlude in a hotel. More hotel rendezvous follow and her affair soon takes over her life, because she cannot choose between her passions nor reconcile both.

What could have been just another love triangle movie is much more profound in the hands of Dupeyron. In small everyday details, he cultivates the most important moments and passionate emotions of a lifetime and paints deep psychological portraits. He explores how a soul can feel divided between a physical and a spiritual passion. Set in the eighteenth Arrondissement of Pigalle and Montmartre, the film explores a neighborhood that often was used in films noirs, but is not so familiar in its modern manifestation. The shots of Paris are extraordinary, with the city almost becoming a full-fledged character on its own. Faysee, who is married to the director in real life, is wonderful.

The French critics applauded this film as a confirmation of the talent that Dupeyron revealed in his first film. *Cinéma* declared, "We are in the presence of an authentic major filmmaker." *La Revue du Cinéma* concurred: "*A Beating Heart* is a film that vibrates, that beats wildly, that has the fever."

The Co-Fathers *see* **Les Compères**

Cold Cuts *see* **Buffet froid**

95 *Les Compères (The Co-Fathers)* 1983 Color   *Director* Francis Veber; *Producer* Fideline Films; *Screenplay* Francis Veber; *Photography* Claude Agostini; *Music* Vladimir Cosma; *Set* Gérard Daoudal; *Sound* Bernard Aubouy; *Costumes* Corinne Jorry; *Editing* Marie-Sophie Dubus. Running time: 92 minutes.

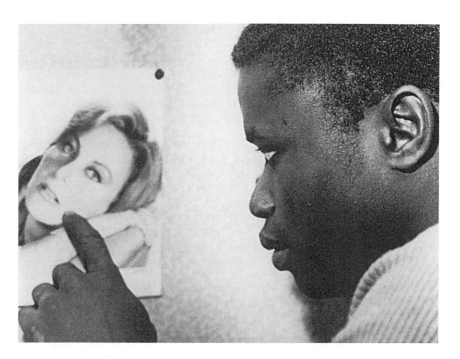

Un Cœur gros comme ça! (*A Heart as Big as That!*), 1962; directed by François Reichenbach.

Cast: Pierre Richard, Gérard Depardieu, Anny Duperey, Michel Aumont, Stéphane Bierry, Giselle Pascal, Roland Blanche, Jean-Jacques Scheffer, Philippe Khorsand, Maurice Barrier, Charlotte Maury, Jacques Frantz, Jacques Maury, Robert Dalban, Patrick Blondel, Florence Moreau, Bruno Allain, François Bernheim, Philippe Brigaud, Pulchier Castan, Robert Dalban, Luc-Antoine Duquiero, Natacha Guinaudeau, Sonia Laroze, Patrick Laurent, Jean-Claude Martin, Guy Matchoro, Patrick Melennec, Jacqueline Noëlle, Christian Bianchi, Gérard Camp, Patrick Le Barz, Philippe Ribes, Claude Rossignol.

A comedy about a woman (Duperey) who is desperate to find her runaway son (Bierry). While her husband searches for the child, she calls two of her old lovers, a journalist (Depardieu) and a teacher (Richard) and tells each of them that they are the father of her son, so they set out in search of him as well. The two meet and discover the mother's ruse, but even when they realize that neither is the real father, they help to reunite the boy with his parents.

One of the greatest modern French comedies by the great comedy director of the 1980s, Francis Veber. Depardieu and Richard recreate the hilarious odd couple they first teamed up to form in Veber's *The Goat*. This was the third biggest boxoffice seller of the decade after *Three Men and a Cradle* and *My New Partner*.

This film was generally well liked by French and American critics. Upon its release, *Variety*'s critic declared: "*The Co-Fathers* is brisk, amusing and warm hearted, and far and away the best of Francis Veber's male-bonding farces...."

96 *Un Condamné à mort s'est échappé* **or** *Le Vent souffle où il veut* *(A Man Escaped)* 1957 B&W *Director* Robert Bresson; *Producer* SNEG; *Screenplay* Robert Bresson, based on André Devigny's memoir *Le Vent souffle où il veut*; *Photography* Léonce Henri Burel; *Music* Mozart; *Set* Pierre Charbonnier; *Sound* P.A. Bertrand; *Editing* Raymond Lamy. Running time: 95 minutes.

Cast: François Leterrier, Charles Le Clainche, Roland Monod, Jack Ertaud, Maurice Beerblock, Roger Tréherne, Jean-Paul Delhumeau, Roger Planchon, César Gattegno, Max Schoendorff, André Collombet, Jean-Philippe Delamare, Jacques Oerlemans, Klaus Detlef Grevenhorst.

A French lieutenant (Leterrier) captured by the Germans during the Occupation and condemned to death has planned a way to escape from the Nazi prison. His only tools for escape are his spirit and a wooden spoon. When another prisoner (La Clainche) is put in his cell, his freedom is jeopardized. He decides to include the young boy in his plans, and the two manage to escape together.

One of the most brilliant French films ever made. By basing the film on the true story of the Resistance fighter André Devigny, who narrowly escaped execution by the Nazis by breaking out of a high-security prison in 1943, Bresson created an amazingly faithful and suspenseful tale of escape, as well as a fascinating forum in which to explore the spiritual/existential issue of how connected are God's will and man's will. Are they at odds? Or always the same? Bresson often said of his vocation: "Film is to have a dialogue with oneself." He wanted the lieutenant's imprisonment to be felt by the audience. Made five years after the great success of *Diary of a Country Priest*, he used only non-professional actors. The film was shot in the same prison that Devigny was kept in, even using his cell.

François Truffaut called it "not only the most beautiful of Bresson's films, but also the most decisive French film of the past ten years." It won the Best Director at Cannes and was co-winner of the French Critics' Prix Méliès in 1957.

The Confession *see* **L'Aveu de Casta**

Confidentially Yours *see* **Vivement dimanche**

Contempt *see* **Le Mépris**

97 *Le Corniaud (The Sucker* or *The Jerk)* 1965 Color *Director* Gérard Oury; *Producer* Robert Dorfmann, Films Corona, Explorer Films; *Screenplay* Gérard Oury, based on the story by Oury; *Adaptation* Gérard Oury and Marcel Jullian; *Photography* Henri Decaë; *Music* Georges Delerue; *Set* Robert Giordani and Francesco Carletta; *Sound* Antoine Bonfanti; *Editing* Albert Jurgenson. Running time: 111 minutes.

Cast: Bourvil, Louis de Funès, Venantino Venantini, Beba Loncar, Alida Ghelli, Henri Virlojeux, Guy Delorme, Saro Urzi, Pierre Roussel, Germaine de France, Nando Buzzanca, Henri Genès, Guy Grosso, Michel Modo, Jack Ary, Jean Droze, Jacques Ferrière, Jean Meyer, Jacques Eyser, Jean-Marie Bon, Yvon Jeanclaude, Robert Duranton, Jean Minisini, Marius Gaidon, Louis Viret, Bernard Meunier, Bob Lerick, Nino Vingelli.

Hired to drive a Cadillac to Italy, Antoine Maréchal (Bourvil) is seen by the gangster paying him as the perfect "sucker." The car is filled with diamonds, gold and drugs. Of course, Antoine becomes the prey of another greedy gang who are after the goods. In the end, the sucker dupes them all.

One of the great French comedies of the postwar period, *The Sucker* is highly entertaining, though not groundbreaking, filmmaking. Bourvil and de Funès make a great duo. Using the old chase plot, this film's humor and jokes are fresh, funny and French in an accessible way. Oury, who was an actor before he started directing, used a light touch that worked beautifully.

This film was a huge success in France. Upon its release, *Variety*'s critic proclaimed: "Flippant title hides a breezy comedy that has some first-rate comics and enough inventiveness and perky progression to have this slanted for solid returns...."

98 *Le Corps de mon ennemi (The Body of My Enemy)* 1976 Color *Director* Henri Verneuil; *Producer* Cerito Films; *Screenplay* Henri Verneuil, Michel Audiard and Félicien Marceau, based on the novel by Félicien Marceau; *Photography* Jean Penzer; *Music* Francis Lai; *Set* François de Lamothe; *Sound* Jacques Maumont; *Editing* Pierre Gillette. Running time: 120 minutes.

Cast: Jean-Paul Belmondo, Marie-France Pisier, René Lefèvre, Bernard Blier, Daniel Ivernel, Suzy Prim, Nicole Garcia, Yvonne Gaudeau, François Perrot, Charles Gérard, Claude Brosset.

A film noir about an ambitious nightclub owner, François Leclerc (Belmondo), who was wrongly accused of murder. He knows he has been set up by the drug traffickers who he was planning to blow the whistle on, so when he finally clears his name after spending seven hard years in prison, he sets out to seek revenge.

This is an engrossing thriller and another fabulous Belmondo vehicle. It was the seventh film Belmondo and Verneuil made together. The title comes from a William Blake poem that included the lines: "In the morning I saw much to my joy/ My enemy lying under the tree." François' story is told in flashbacks that slowly build the portrait of a man and the history of the social ascent and fall that make him so hungry for revenge. Verneuil hoped to make a larger social comment on corruption in the upper classes by adapting a gripping story that was set in the midst of this world.

When it came out in France, *Variety*'s critic hailed Belmondo's new serious role. "Technically assured, elegantly dressed up, with gadgets and luxurious living quarters and pliable women and hoods, Belmondo does not do his usual sloppy but workable acrobatics in this."

99 *Coup de foudre (Entre Nous* **or** *Between Us)* 1983 Color   *Director* Diane Kurys; *Producer* Alexandre, Hachette, Films A2, SFPC, Partners; *Screenplay* Diane Kurys and Alain Le Henry; *Photography* Bernard Lutic; *Music* Luis Bacalov; *Set* Jacques Bufnoir; *Sound* Harald Maury, Alix Comte; *Costumes* Michel Cheminal; *Editing* Joëlle van Effenterre. Running time 110 minutes.

Cast: Miou-Miou, Isabelle Huppert, Guy Marchand, Jean-Pierre Bacri, Robin Renucci, Patrick Buchau, Jacques Alric, Jacqueline Doyen, Patricia Champagne, Saga Blanchard, Guillaume Le Guellec, Dominique Lavanant, Christine Pascal, Jacques Blal, Sonia Pfirmann, Bernard Cazassus, Anne Fabien, Jean-Claude de Goros, Anne Lévy, Serge Ruben, Catherine Margaillan, Corinne Anzionnaz, François Cluzet, Niels Tavernier, Denis Lavant, Pascal Pistacio.

Two women, Léna (Huppert) and Madeleine (Miou-Miou), who are both unhappily married, meet and forge a friendship that changes their lives. Set in Lyon in the 1950s, the film explores the love between two female friends, which not only transports them out of the boredom of their daily lives but transforms them completely.

A fascinating and innovative love story with an unusual twist to the stock adultery movies of the late 1970s, early 1980s. In her third feature, Diane Kurys explores a loving, but not quite lesbian, relationship between women. Their feminine rapport is at once liberating and sad. The material was taken from Kurys' life. One gathers she was the child of one of these women, and therefore also the child of one of the deceived and deserted husbands.

Some French critics said Kurys' films had the artistic style of television melodramas, others commended her realistic approach to social issues. When the film was released in the United States, one American critic wrote: "*Entre Nous* explores previously unexplored terrain in the no man's land that often separates male and female notions of love, honor, and duty."

100 *Le Coup de grâce* 1966 Color   *Director* Jean Cayrol; *Producer* Sofracina, Soquema; *Screenplay* Jean Cayrol and Claude Durand; *Photography* J.M. Bousaguet; *Music* Jean Ferrat; *Sound* André Louis; *Editing* Odile Terzieff. Running time: 90 minutes.

Cast: Michel Piccoli, Danielle Darrieux, Emmanuelle Riva, Jean-Pierre Bouyxou, Janine Delannoy, Florence Guerfy, Jean-Jacques Lagarde, Bernard Tiphaine, Jacqueline Laurent, Jacques Letourneau, Olivier Hussenot, Alain Saury, Marcel Roche.

Twenty years after the end of World War II, Bruno Capri (Piccoli) returns to Bordeaux, where as a student during the war he denounced many members of the Resistance to the Germans. He has had plastic surgery and tries to start a new life in Bordeaux, but a woman in his building recognizes him and a manhunt ensues.

Jean Cayrol's masterpiece is a great meditation on the war and the role guilt

Coup de foudre (*Entre Nous* or *Between Us*), 1983; directed by Diane Kurys.

and blame play in the postwar world. He based the film on his own experiences during the war; he worked for the Resistance and someone informed on him to the Nazis. Cayrol had previously worked with Resnais, and his mentor's obsession with time and memory is apparent in this work.

Some critics hailed this as a beautiful realization of an abstract idea. American critics were less enamored of the film than the French. *Variety*'s critic complained that the "valid subject" was "handled in a too talky, static manner to make this anything but arty house fodder abroad and limited at this."

101 *Coup de torchon (Clean Slate)* 1981 Color *Director* Bertrand Tavernier; *Producer* La Tour, Little Bear, A2 (Adolphe Viezzi, Henri Lassa); *Screenplay* Bertrand Tavernier and Jean Aurenche, based on Jim Thompson's novel *Pop. 1280*; *Photography* Pierre William Glenn; *Music* Philippe Sarde; *Set* Alexandre Trauner; *Sound* Michel Desrois, Dominique Levert; *Costumes* Jacqueline Laurent; *Editing* Armand Psenny. Running Time: 128 minutes.

Cast: Philippe Noiret, Isabelle Huppert, Jean-Pierre Marielle, Stéphane Audran, Eddy Mitchell, Guy Marchand, Irene Skobline, Michel Beaune, Jean Champion, Victor Garrivier, Gérard Hernandez, Abdoulaye Dico, Daniel Langlet, François Perrot, Raymond Hermantier, Mamadou Dioum, Samba Mané, Irene Martin.

A black comedy set in 1938, in a colonial outpost in West Africa. Police Chief Lucien Codier (Noiret), who has long been kicked around by the townspeople whom he is meant to protect and whose laws he is meant to enforce, turns from a meek man into a tyrant. He decides to clean up corruption by murdering anyone whom he finds to be immoral, including his wife (Audran), her lover (Mitchell), and his mistress's husband.

A cinematic satire of the highest order. Tavernier looks and laughs at racism and fascism and how they occur. Noiret does a magnificent job of playing someone who can be at once horrifying and sympathetic. Though his character begins by seeing himself on a moral mission, he so quickly commits his own slew of misdeeds that Tavernier subverts morality completely and the audience is left in an ethical limbo. As with so many surreal works, the many levels of meaning can be frustrating or entertaining. Huppert and Audran prove themselves to be wonderful comedic actresses.

Clean Slate was one of the biggest box-office successes in France the year it came out. "It's a black comedy of the richest kind: a film that teeters on the edge," wrote David Kerr. Judy Stone of *The San Francisco Chronicle* agreed: "Never has stupidity or mock-stupidity been so acutely and hilariously portrayed as by this superb cast." It was nominated for 12 Césars and was the co-winner of French Critics' Prix Méliès in 1981.

102 *Cousin, Cousine* 1975 Color *Director* Jean-Charles Tacchella; *Producer* Films Pomereu, Gaumont; *Screenplay* Jean-Charles Tacchella and Danièle Thompson; *Photography* Georges Lendi; *Music* Gérard Anfosso; *Sound* Pierre Lenoir; *Editing* Agnès Gullemot. Running time: 95 minutes.

Cast: Marie-Christine Barrault, Victor Lanoux, Marie-France Pisier, Guy Marchand, Ginette Garcin, Sybil Maas, Catherine Verlor, Jean Herbert, Pierre Plessis, Hubert Gignoux.

Two cousins by marriage, Marthe (Barrault) and Ludovic (Lanoux), who are

Cousin, Cousine, **1975; directed by Jean-Charles Tacchella.**

both unhappily married, find themselves terribly attracted to each other. Causing a family crisis, which is just what their spouses want to avoid at any cost, they announce at Christmas dinner that they are leaving their spouses and moving in together.

A joyous romance that celebrates the grandeur of love set against the petty pretensions of bourgeois niceties. The beautiful and talented Marie-Christine Barrault is the niece of the great Jean-Louis Barrault, whose most famous role was Baptiste in the *Children of Paradise*. She and Lanoux create lovers for whom it is impossible not to cheer. Ironically, this film was more successful in the United States than in France, where it was expected to be particularly familiar and troubling because family and marriage are still held sacred to a greater degree than they are here. In the United States, it was seen as the quintessential French film, full of charm and romance.

A few French critics were offended by the unadulterated celebration of adultery in the film, but most admired it. One American critic raved: "It is literate, expert, witty, and handsome, and it touches again the romantic strand without which the movies do not long endure." The critic for *Grand Illusions* wrote: "The sparkle and defiance of *Cousin, Cousine* leaves a sense of glowing victory. It does not probe inner conflicts, but, instead, maintains the lightness of a new love." It was nominated for four Césars and won the Prix Louis Delluc in 1975. In 1976, it was nominated for an Oscar for Best Foreign Film, and it inspired a poor American remake called *Cousins.*

103 *Les Cousines (The Cousins)* 1959 B&W   *Director* Claude Chabrol; *Producer* Ajym Films, SFC; *Screenplay* Claude Chabrol and Paul Gégauff;

Les Cousines (The Cousins), 1959; directed by Claude Chabrol.

Photography Henri Decaë and Jean Rabier; *Music* Paul Misraki; *Set* Jacques Saulnier and Bernard Evein; *Sound* Jean-Claude Marchetti; *Editing* Jacques Gaillard. Running time: 110 minutes.

Cast: Gérard Blain, Jean-Claude Brialy, Juliette Mayniel, Claude Cerval, Guy Decomble, Stéphane Audran, Corrado Guarducci, Geneviève Cluny, Jeanne Pérez, Jean-Pierre Moulin, Michèle Merritz, Françoise Vatel, Paul Bisciglia, André Jocelyn, Sophie Grimaldi, Jean-Louis Maury, Laszlo Szabo, Virginie Vitry, Chantal Bouchon, Gaby Blandé, Clara Gansard, Simone Vannier, Catherine Candida, Sabine Moussali, Taty Rocca, Colette Teissèdre, Anne Zamire, Gilbert Edard, Jacques Kemp, André Zamire, André Chanal, Christian Pezey, Emmanuel Pierson, Jean-Marie Arnoux, Robert Barre, Michel Benoist, Jacques Deschamps, Abdou Filali, Yann Groël, Jacques Ralf, Jean-Paul Thomas.

A shy country cousin, Charles (Blain), comes to Paris to study for the French equivalent of the bar exam and to live with his sophisticated and dilettantish cousin Paul (Brialy). The cousins prove to be unevenly matched in everything — love, luck and ultimately in longevity — as Paul kills Charles by accident with the gun Charles had dreamed of using on Paul.

Chabrol manages to turn what could have been seen as simply two characters representing good and evil into a pair of complicated individuals, each of whom inspires sympathy and blame for their own tragedy. Chabrol made *The Cousins* at age 27 with a budget of only $160,000, but the final product is beautifully shot and polished, which may be the characteristic that later earned him the sobriquet of "showman of the New Wave."

When it came out in the United States, *The Cousins* was dismissed by just about every critic as depressing. *The New York Times* critic Bosley Crowther wrote that "M. Chabrol is the gloomiest and most despairing of the new creative French directors. His attitude is ridden with a sense of defeat and ruin." It won the Golden Bear at the Berlin Film Festival in 1959.

The Cousins *see* **Les Cousines**

104 *Le Crabe-tambour (The Drummer Crab)* 1977 Color *Director* Pierre Schoendoerfer; *Producer* Bela, AMLF, Lira Films; *Screenplay* Pierre Schoendoerfer and Jean-François Chauvel, based on the novel by Schoendoerfer; *Photography* Raoul Coutard; *Music* Philippe Sarde; *Set* Outdoors; *Sound* Raymond Adam; *Editing* Nguyen Long. Running time: 119 minutes.

Cast: Jean Rochefort, Claude Rich, Jacques Perrin, Jacques Dufilho, Odile Versois, Aurore Clément, Morgan Jones, Hubert Laurent, Joseph Momo, Pierre Rousseau, François Dyrek, Bernard Lajarrige, François Landolt, Jean Champion.

A ship's captain (Rochefort) and ship's doctor (Rich) travel to Newfoundland years after they served together with the Drummer Crab Willsdorff (Perrin). They reminisce about Willsdorff, who was nicknamed "The Drummer Crab," because he pounded his belly like a drum after eating crabs. He fought in Vietnam, was captured by the Vietcong, and then took his dead brother's place fighting in Algeria. The ship's doctor regrets not having stayed with him in Vietnam but, instead, having returned to France to marry. The captain agonizes over his failure to help the "Crab" lead a successful coup in Algeria, for which attempt he was eventually sent to jail, partly because of the captain's testimony. Before he dies of lung cancer, the captain is determined to find the Crab, who runs a fishing boat off Newfoundland.

A mythic rendering of military heros whose time has past. Those who fought for an ideal find themselves at sea, literally and metaphorically, in a modern world of moral complexities and contradictions. The photography is beautiful, as is the acting. The film evokes a real feeling for the bonds men form in wartime. Schoendoerfer uses every shot, every sound of waves and wind, to emphasize the inevitable loneliness and loss of his subjects.

The film inspired comparisons from French and American critics to Conrad's *Heart of Darkness*. *The Drummer Crab* was not released in the United States until 1984. When it came out in the United States, Vincent Canby of *The New York Times* declared it: "a hugely romantic film about war and honor and empire .... From the opening shots to the last, *Le Crabe Tambour* is spellbinding." It won the Grand Prix du Cinéma Français in 1977. Dufilho won the César for Best Actor, and Raoul Coutard won a César for Best Photography.

The Crimson Curtain *see* **Le Rideau cramoisi**

The Crying Woman *see* **La Femme qui pleure**

Cybele *see* **Les Dimanches de ville d'Avray**

105 *Cyrano de Bergerac* 1990 Color *Director* Jean-Paul Rappeneau; *Producer* Hachette, Antenne 2, Groupe Europe 1; *Screenplay* Jean-Paul Rappeneau and Jean-Claude Carrière, based on the novel by Edmond Rostand; *Photography* Pierre Lhomme; *Music* Jean-Claude Petit; *Set* Ezio Frigerio; *Sound* Pierre Gamet;

Cyrano de Bergerac, 1990; directed by Jean-Paul Rappeneau.

Costumes Franca Squarciapino; *Editing* Noëlle Boisson. Running time: 138 minutes.

Cast: Gérard Depardieu, Anne Brochet, Vincent Perez, Jacques Weber, Roland Bertin, Philippe Morier-Genoud, Pierre Maguelon, Josiane Stoléru, Anatole Delalande, Ludivine Sagnier, Alain Rimoux, Philippe Volter, Jean-Marie Winling, Louis Navarre, Gabriel Monnet, François Marie, Catherine Ferran, Amélie Gonin, Madeleine Marion.

Set in the eighteenth century, this is the story of the very large-nosed soldier and poet, Cyrano de Bergerac (Depardieu), and his love for Roxanne (Brochet). When he must go off to war, Roxanne makes him vow to protect the handsome Christian she has fallen in love with. Christian is lovely to look at, but it is Cyrano who provides him with the words to woo the intelligent Roxanne. Cyrano writes the love letters that inspire Roxanne to come to the battle front. When Christian is killed, Roxanne enters a nunnery. Cyrano visits her faithfully. One afternoon, when they are old, Cyrano is hit on the head with a rock and in his daze he lets slip some of the lines from one of the love letters he wrote her. As he lies dying in her arms, she realizes the man she has loved — for she loved the man behind the words, not the pretty face — has been with her, without her knowing, for years.

This is an extravagant revival of one of the world's saddest love stories, and offers the great Depardieu in one of his best performances ever. Anthony Burgess translated the dialogue for the English subtitles and did quite an impressive job putting them into rhyme.

Some dismissed Rostand's classic as melodramatic drivel, but such cynicism is their loss. One American critic said: "Depardieu is the definitive romantic Cyrano . . . . It's a towering performance, magnificent and moving, that does just what any honest telling of the Cyrano legend should do: set us all dreaming." It was nominated for an Oscar for Best Foreign Film, and Depardieu won Best Actor at Cannes in 1990.

106 *Les Dames du Bois de Boulogne (Ladies of the Park)* 1945 B&W *Director* Robert Bresson; *Producer* Films Raoul Ploquin; *Screenplay* based on a story in *Jacques le fataliste et son maître* by Denis Diderot; *Adaptation* by Robert Bresson; *Dialogue* Jean Cocteau; *Photography* Philippe Agostini; *Music* Jean-Jacques Grünenwald; *Set* Max Douy; *Costumes* Madame Grès and Elsa Schiaparelli; *Sound* René Louge, Lucien Legrand and Robert Ivonnet; *Editing* Jean Feyte. Running time 90 minutes.

Cast: Maria Casarès, Elina Labourdette, Lucienne Bogaert, Paul Bernard, Jean Marchat, Bernard La Jarrige, Yvette Etiévant, Lucy Lancy, Nicole Regnault, Emma Lyonel, Marcel Rouzé, Marguerite de Morlaye, Kastou the dog.

A tale of a mistress's revenge, in which Hélène (Casarès) devises a plan to get back at Jean (Bernard), the lover who has stopped caring for her. She sets up a cabaret dancer, Agnès (Labourdette), in an apartment with her mother and masterminds the marriage of Agnès and Jean. The day of the wedding, Hélène reveals to Jean that his wife is no more than a prostitute.

Taken from a story in Diderot's *Jacques le fataliste et son maître*, Bresson's second film has many of the great characteristics of his later works. As in his other films, Bresson here very faithfully adapts literature for the screen. Cocteau wrote the dialogue, updating Diderot with great wit. The leading ladies, Casarès and Labourdette, are both fantastic. Despite all this, Bresson repudiated the film after it proved to be a critical and commercial failure.

The film was received very poorly when it came out soon after the end of World War II. Critics and the public found a bourgeois revenge story to be out of touch with the pressing social issues of the day. *Ladies of the Park* did not come to the United States until almost twenty years after it was made, by which time its director had an international reputation. When the film became popular with critics and ciné-clubs in France years later, Truffaut cited Cocteau's expression: "It won its trial on appeal."

The Damned *see* **Les Maudits**

Dangerous Moves *see* **La Diagonale du fou**

107 *Danton* 1983 Color *Director* Andrézej Wajda; *Producer* Gaumont, Les Films du Losange; *Screenplay* Andrezej Wajda, Jean-Claude Carrière, based on Stanislawa Przybyszewska's play *The Danton Affair*; *Photography* Igor Luthor; *Music* Jean Prodromidès; *Set* Allan Starski, Gilles Vaster; *Sound* Jean-Pierre Ruh, Dominique Hennequin, Piotr Zawadzki; *Costumes* Yvonne Sassinot de Nesle; *Editing* Halina Prugar-Ketling. Running time: 136 minutes.

Cast: Gérard Depardieu, Wojciech Pszoniak, Patrice Chéreau, Roger Planchon, Boguslaw Linda, Jacques Villeret, Angela Winkler, Andrezej Seweryn, Roland Blance, Emmanuelle Debever, Serge Merlin, Lucien Melki, Bernard Maître, Erwin Nowiaszack, Marian Kociniak, Gérard Hardy, Anna Albaro, Stéphane Jobert, Marek Kondrat, Alain Mace, Jean-Loup Wolff, Krzysztof Globisz.

The story of the French Revolutionary figure Danton (Depardieu), who along with his friend Camille Desmoulins (Chéreau) tried to encourage Robespierre (Pszoniak) to use less violent methods than those employed during the Reign of Terror. Robespierre resists them and ultimately orders their arrest, and despite Robespierre's efforts to save them from death, they are guillotined.

A fabulous historical film, in which the director Wajda found parallels between the Reign of Terror in France and the situation in his native Poland when Poland was under martial law. He originally planned to produce the film in Poland, but because of the political turmoil there, he ended up shooting it in France. The cruelty of a political process is well demonstrated and the historical figures come to life in a way that is very realistic. Though both the French and Polish governments contributed funds to the making of *Danton*, neither was thrilled with the film's political implications. Poland, in fact, delayed the film's release and Mitterrand's socialist government admitted to being "disconcerted" by the film, which Wadja said showed Danton as the West and Robespierre as the East.

In France, the film incited arguments, not only over present political parties, but also over its interpretation of the Revolution. When it was released in the United States, the *Columbia Film Review* declared: "*Danton* is the kind of film that cannot be easily forgotten, for all its imperfections .... *Danton* is as garish, bloody and unsubtle as its subject matter; it is a glorious mess." It won the Prix Louis Delluc and the César for Best Director in 1982.

Day for Night *see* **La Nuit américaine**

A Day in the Country *see* **Une Partie de campagne**

Deadly Circuit *see* **Mortelle randonnée**

Death in Full View *see* **La Morte en direct**

Death in the Garden *see* **La Mort en ce jardin, cela s'appelle l'Aurora**

Death Watch *see* **La Morte en direct**

108 *De bruit et de fureur (The Sound and the Fury)* 1988 Color *Director* Jean-Claude Brisseau; *Producer* Les Films du Losange, Sofica Investimage; *Screenplay* Jean-Claude Brisseau; *Photography* Romain Winding; *Sound* Louis Gimel; *Editing* Maria-Luisa Garcia, Jean-Claude Brisseau, Annick Hurst. Running time: 95 minutes.

Cast: Vincent Gasperitsch, François Négret, Bruno Cremer, Fabienne Babe, Lise Hérédia, Antoine Fontaine, Luc Ponette, Isabelle Hurtin, Thierry Helaine, Sandrine Arnault, Victoire Buff, Françoise Vatel.

A story about lost youth in today's urban landscape. Teenage Bruno (Gasperitsch) moves in with his working mother, who lives in a high-rise where crime and violence are common. He becomes friends with Jean-Roger (Négret) who teaches him how to have fun by stealing, vandalizing and assaulting people. Though both boys have their tender sides, their lives lead toward a violent, ill-fated end.

A sad and realistic look at children's lives in the midst of urban violence, this is one of the films that marked the new naturalism in French filmmaking and announced the emergence of one of the decade's most important new filmmakers. To achieve the film's authenticity, Brisseau drew on his own childhood spent in the eighteenth Arrondissement of Paris and his work as a high school teacher. He believed the film, like life, is marked with "violence, but also with poetry, tenderness, humor, even grotesqueness and buffoonery."

The Sound and the Fury caused a critical sensation at the Cannes Film Festival where it premiered. Its hard look at a nasty childhood world inspired great acclaim. No one under the age of 18 was allowed to see it, even though it won the Special Youth Prize. It also won the Prix Perspectives du Cinéma Français and Best Screenplay at Cannes in 1988.

109 *Dédée d'Anvers (Woman of Antwerp)*　1948 B&W　*Director* Yves Allégret; *Producer* Sacha Gordine; *Screenplay* based on a novel by Ashelbé; *Adaptation* Jacques Sigurd and Yves Allégret; *Dialogue* Jacques Sigurd; *Photography* Jean-Serge Bourgoin; *Music* Jacques Besse; *Set* Georges Wakhévitch based on designs by Maurice Colasson; *Sound* Pierre Calvet; *Editing* Léonide Azar. Running time: 100 minutes.

Cast: Simone Signoret, Bernard Blier, Marcelo Pagliero, Marcel Dalio, Jane Marken, Marcel Dieudonné, Michel Jourdan, Marcelle Arnold, Claude Farrell, Mia Mendelssohn, Denise Clair, Frédéric Fisher, Arsenio Freygnac, Maurice Petitpas.

Set in the port town of Anvers, this is the story of Dédée (Signoret), a showgirl/streetwalker in a bar/dance hall, who catches the eye of an Italian ship captain, Francesco (Pagliero). He promises to take her away from her seedy life. The man who Dédée lives with — the bar's bouncer, Marco (Dalio) — kills Francesco out of jealousy and fear of losing his prize performer. Dédée and the bar owner, René (Blier), get revenge on Marco, and life at the bar goes on.

One of the most famous French film noirs of the late 1940s, this is a very depressing but beautiful film, which represented the popular poetic, but hopeless frame of mind of French filmmakers just after the war. Their films reflected the sad despair of their countrymen. The sensitive screenplay was written by Ashelbé, who wrote the prewar masterpiece *Pépé le Moko*. The photography, pacing and acting are superb. Dédée is one of Simone Signoret's finest performances.

The film was very popular when it came out in France. Critics were divided along extreme lines, with some finding it irritatingly youthful and others recognizing Allégret and Signoret as the very promising talents that they proved to be.

110 *Delicatessen*　1990 Color　*Director* Marc Carot and Jean-Pierre Jeunet; *Producer* UGC, Hachette Première; *Screenplay* Jean-Pierre Jeunet, Marc Carot and Gilles Adrien; *Photography* Darius Khondji; *Music* Carlos d'Alessio; *Set* Jean-Philippe Carp; *Sound* Jérôme Thiault, Vincent Arnardi; *Costumes* Valerie Pozzo Di Borgo; *Editing* Hervé Schneid. Running time: 95 minutes.

Cast: Dominique Pinon, Marie-Laure Dougnac, Jean-Claude Dreyfus, Karin Viard, Rufus, Ticky Holgado, Anne-Marie Pisani, Edith Ker, Mickael Todde, Boban Janevski, Jacques Mathou, Chick Ortega, Howard Vernon, Jean-François Perrier, Sylvie Laguna, Maurice Lamy, Marc Carot, Dominique Zardi, Pascal Benezech.

A comedy set in a post-apocalyptic suburban apartment building inhabited by a band of absolute odd balls who battle the people living in the sewer. When a clown, Loison (Pinon), moves in and catches the fancy of the butcher/landlord's

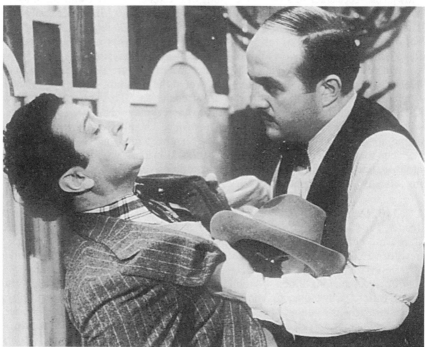

Dédée d'Anvers (*Woman of Antwerp*), 1948; directed by Yves Allégret.

near-blind daughter, Julie (Dougnac), the two discover how her father continues to provide meat when no livestock exists, which also solves the mystery of what is happening to the neighbors who mysteriously disappear at night.

A mad and modern comedy of the highest order, with references as diverse as Carné and cartoons. One of the film's directors explained their intent: "Be it the humorous scenes, the action scenes or the love scenes, we tried to bring out the tenderness within the madness." Not only did the low-budget film mark the auspicious debut of two talented young directors, who previously worked in animation, but it also introduced some great new acting talent, such as Marie-Laure Dougnac. The sets are wild and wonderful, as are the outrageous characters, who include a suicide fanatic and an escargot lover whose apartment teems with snails. The animation background from which the creators spring is clearly evident.

Delicatessen became an instant cult favorite when it came out in France and still runs once a week at an art house in Paris. Some French and American critics complained that the directors had bitten off more than they could chew. Others loved its wild daring. *Downtown* declared it "the best example on film in a good while of what a well-developed idea and a rip-roaring cast working together can accomplish if given the chance." It won the Golden Hugo for Best Film at the Chicago Film Festival and a Felix at the annual European Film Awards.

111 *Les Demoiselles de Rochefort (The Young Girls of Rochefort)*
1967 Color *Director* Jacques Demy; *Producer* Parc Films, Madeleine Films; *Screenplay* Jacques Demy; *Photography* Ghislain Cloquet; *Music* Michel Legrand; *Set* Bernard Evein; *Sound* Jacques Maumont; *Choreography* Norman Maen; *Costumes* Jacqueline Moreau, Marie-Claude Fouquet, Jean-Marie Armand, Jean Barthet; *Editing* Jean Hamon. Running time: 120 minutes.

Cast: Catherine Deneuve, Françoise Dorléac, Danielle Darrieux, Georges Chakiris, Gene Kelly, Michel Piccoli, Jacques Perrin, Henri Crémieux, Geneviève Thénier, Jacques Ribérolles, Grover Dale, Patrick Jeantet, Pamela Hart, René Bazart, Leslie North, Daniel Maquay, Daniel Gall, Pierre Caden, Jacques Baratier, Dorothy Blank, Alain Franchet, Bernard Fradet, Véronique Duval, Rémy Brozek, Agnès Varda, Pierre Durussy, Maureen Evans, Peter Ardan, Taiza Fernando, Lindsay Dolan, Sarah Elmington, John McDonald, Alix Krista, Keith Drummond, Nicky Temperton, Johnny Greenland, Barrie Wilkinson, Léo Guérard, Maureen Willsher, David Hepburn, Sarah Butler, Bob Howe, Ann Chapman, Jerry Manley, Jane Darling, Tony Manning, Tom Merrifield, Connel Miles, Albin Pahernik, Wendy Barry, Tudor Davies, Sue Allen, George Becker, W. Earl Brown, Ronald Hicklin, Frank Allen Howren, Thomas Kenny, Judith Lawler, Bill Lee, Diana Lee, Gilda Maiken, Gene Merlino, Joseph Pryor, Ronald Reeve, Sally Stevens, Sara Jane Tallman, Robert Tebow, Jackie Ward, Bernard Fradet, Rémy Brozek, Daniel Gall, Véronique Duval, Pierre Caden.

A musical about two sisters who run a ballet school and music shop in Rochefort. The twins dream of love, and for Solange (Dorléac) it appears as a sailor (Perrin), who painted a picture of his ideal woman, only to find her residing in Rochefort as Solange. When a piece of music Delphine (Deneuve) has written gets into the hands of a handsome American concert pianist (Kelly), love soon follows. Even their mother (Darrieux) finally realizes her dream, when she wins the man she has long been pining for (Piccoli).

This is the charming sequel to *The Umbrellas of Cherbourg*. Demy's trademark sets and music are wonderful. For this tribute to American musicals, the town of Rochefort was delightfully painted to be the set, as Demy did with Cherbourg, and the town got a major tourism boost from the film. Deneuve and Dorléac, who play the lovely sisters were sisters in real life, and Dorléac died in an automobile accident not long after the film was released.

While most critics did not find this film as musically or dramatically appealing as *The Umbrellas of Cherbourg*, many conceded that it had plenty of charm. *The Saturday Review* critic wrote: "*Rochefort* is no more substantial than a soufflé, but master chef that Demy is, he sees to it that it doesn't fall for a moment."

112 *La Dentellière (The Lacemaker)* 1976 Color   *Director* Claude Goretta; *Producer* Citel Films, Actions Films, FR3, Filmproduktion Janus; *Screenplay* Claude Goretta and Pascal Lainé, based on the novel by Lainé; *Photography* Jean Boffety; *Music* Pierre Jansen; *Set* Serge Etter; *Sound* Pierre Gamet; *Editing* Joëlle Van Effenterre. Running time: 108 minutes.

Cast: Isabelle Huppert, Yves Beneyton, Florence Giorgetti, Christian Baltauss, Renata Schroeter, Anne-Marie Düringer, Michel de Ré, Monique Chaumette, Jean Obé, Odile Poisson.

A shy, sweet girl (Huppert) named "Pomme" (translated, Apple) meets and falls in love with a literature student, François (Beneyton), while vacationing by the sea. They get an apartment together in Paris, but their social and educational differences become a problem. Pomme is not ambitious, and François breaks up with her when he decides that he needs a woman who shares his interests. Pomme ends up in a mental home; François ends up alone.

A quiet and devastating film that explored the subtleties of social barriers and made Isabelle Huppert a star. At age 22, it was her first major role, and her performance is extraordinary. A feminist reading of the film could view the cost of Pomme's inability to express herself as a metaphor for how women have been kept powerless in society. Goretta said of the film: "Pomme and François are fragile characters, lonely and ordinary, but who find self expression hard and can't integrate into society and therefore don't understand one another."

Most critics loved *The Lace Maker's* delicate sensibility, though Vincent Canby of *The New York Times* called it "only interesting and moving in a theoretical way." Leo Lerman in *Vogue* hailed it as "a pure perfect movie experience." The British Film Academy awarded Huppert the award for Most Promising Newcomer. The film won the special prize at Cannes.

113 *Le Dernier Combat (The Last Battle)* 1983 B&W   *Director* Luc Besson; *Producer* Films du Loup; *Screenplay* Luc Besson, Pierre Jolivet; *Photography* Carlo Varini; *Music* Eric Serra; *Set* Christian Grosrichard, Thierry Flamand, Patrick Lebere; *Sound* Jean-Paul Loublier; *Costumes* Martine Rapin, Marie Beau; *Editing* Sophie Schmit. Running time: 90 minutes

Cast: Pierre Jolivet, Fritz Wepper, Jean Bouise, Jean Reno, Christiane Kruger, Maurice Lemy, Pierre Carrive, Michel Doset, Bernard Havé, Petra Muller, Jean-Michel Castanié, Marcel Berhomier, Garry Jode.

One man's (Jolivet) adventures in post-apocalyptic France. After living alone in the ruins of a skyscraper, he makes a one-man attack on the dictator (Wepper) of a neighboring compound. He flees in an airplane he has fixed up, bearing one of the dictator's fingers as his trophy. When the plane crashes in burnt-out Paris, he gets involved with a doctor (Bouise), a thug (Reno), and an imprisoned woman (Muller) before he returns to take the dictator's place as ruler of the last community on earth.

This science-fiction cult favorite was Luc Besson's first movie. He made it at age 23, and it announced his original vision as a filmmaker. Its star is also the film's screenwriter, who chose not to give himself any lines. In fact, there is no dialogue in the film at all. But what it lacks in speech it more than makes up for in effects. Besson's idea was to take a "stroll through the imagination," which yields, among other things, downpours of fish and a nuked landscape of sand.

French critics loved the film when it came out. Americans critics were less captivated. Judy Stone of *The San Francisco Chronicle* said in her review: "This is a movie that has nothing to say so it's just as well they skipped the dialogue." James Verniere of *The Aquarian* saw the beauty of Besson's vision: "*Le Dernier Combat* is a lyrical contemplation of ordinariness and its virtues." It was nominated for a César for Best First Feature in 1983 and won many prizes at small European film festivals.

114 *Le Dernier Métro (The Last Métro)* 1980 Color   *Director* François Truffaut; *Producer* Films du Carrosse, Sédif, TF1, SFP; *Screenplay* François Truffaut, Suzanne Schiffman; *Photography* Nestor Almendros; *Music* Georges Delerue; *Set* Jean-Pierre Kohut Svelko; *Sound* Michel Laurent; *Costumes* Lisele Roos; *Editing* Martine Barraqué. Running time: 133 minutes.

Cast: Catherine Deneuve, Gérard Depardieu, Heinz Bennent, Jean Poiret, Andrea Ferreol, Sabine Haudepin, Maurice Rich, Paulette Dubost, Jean-Pierre Klein, Richard Bohringer, Jean-Louis Richard, Alain Tasmat, Jean-José Richer, Martine Simonet, Hénia Ziv, René Dupré, Laszlo Szabo, Renata, Marcel Berbert, Franck Pasquier, Rose Thierry, Pierre Belot, Jessica Zucman, Catherine Frot, Jacob Weisbluth, Christian Baltauss, Alexandra Aumond, Marie-Dominique Henry.

Marion Steiner (Deneuve), the wife of a German Jew, has taken over running the Théâtre Montmartre during the German Occupation of Paris. The Germans are looking for her husband, Lucas Steiner (Bennent), a famous director who has been unable to flee Paris and is hiding out in the bowels of the theater. He even eavesdrops on the rehearsals of the new play, which stars Marion and Bernard Granger (Depardieu), so he can continue to direct. When things heat up between Marion and Bernard, loyalty and betrayal are explored on political and romantic fronts.

This was Truffaut's twentieth picture and his greatest commercial success, as well as the most successful picture ever by a New Wave director. It is also one of the best films on France during the Occupation. He explores some of the same themes that occupied him in his earlier films—a woman loved by two good men (*Jules and Jim*); the theater as a refuge (*Shoot the Piano Player*); and the relationship between acting and reality (*Day for Night*). The film could be viewed as a parable on the role of art in war, as both men are creative types engaged in politics through art. Truffaut managed to depict the Occupation in personal and political terms in a meaningful way. He wrote the role of Marion for Deneuve, and it is one of her finest performances.

When *The Last Metro* and Godard's *Every Man for Himself* were shown together at the New York Film Festival, Godard categorically dismissed Truffaut and his work. The critics, however, loved the film. Janet Maslin of *The New York Times* believed Truffaut "is at his very best with *The Last Metro.*" Even Andrew Sarris, who had many problems with the film, declared that "*The Last Metro* must be seen by anyone seriously interested in the cinema." It won the Best Picture at Cannes, ten Césars, including Best Film, Best Director, Best Actor and Best Actress, and was nominated for an Oscar for Best Foreign Film.

115 *Les Dernières Vacances (The Last Holiday)* 1947 B&W *Director* Roger Leenhardt; *Producer* LPC–Pierre Gérin; *Screenplay and Adaptation* Roger Leenhardt; *Dialogue* Roger Leenhardt and Roger Breuil; *Photography* Philippe Agostini; *Music* Guy Bernard; *Set* Léon Barsacq; *Sound* René Forget; *Editing* Myriam Borsoutzky. Running time: 95 minutes.

Cast: Odile Versois, Michel François, Renée Devillers, Pierre Dux, Jean d'Yd, Berthe Bovy, Christiane Barry, Raymond Farge, Frédéric Murié, Marcelle Monthil, Suzanne Demars, Jean Varas, Lucie Valnor, Arlette Wherly, Gérard Gervais, Liliane Maguy, Didier d'Yd, Jacques Sergy, Paul Faivre, Roger Leenhardt, Henri Bossuet.

Set in the 1920s at a country house in the Languedoc region, the film is about childhood friends passing their last hours of innocent pleasure together, as their parents discuss the need to sell their family estate. They must leave the place that has been their childhood idyll, just as they make the transition from childood to adulthood. They must adjust to their first painful feelings of love, as their parents adjust to reduced social status.

Leenhardt worked as a film critic and documentary maker before he made this film, which proved to be a cult classic, and the last feature he made for another 15 years. The plot's jumping off point — the selling off a family property — was a common occurrence in France during the depressed years between the wars. "I really made *Les Dernières Vacances* like one writing a novel without thinking of the editor," Leenhardt said.

Some criticized Leenhardt for focusing too much on the romantic problems of the parents and for spreading his talents too thin by adapting, directing and even acting in the film. But most adored his handling of the melancholy atmosphere and the children — the primary elements of the film. Critic Georges Sadoul wrote that *Les Dernières Vacances*' excesses should be excused "by two qualities too rare in cinema: sincerity and freshness of feeling."

116 *La Désenchantée (The Disenchanted)* 1990 Color *Director* Benoit Jacquot; *Producer* Cinéa, La Sept, CNC, Sofica Sofinergie 2; *Screenplay* Benoit Jacquot; *Photography* Caroline Champetier; *Music* Jorge Arriagada; *Set* Sylvie Barthet; *Sound* Michel Vionnet; *Editing* Dominique Auvray. Running time: 79 minutes.

Cast: Judith Godrèche, Marcel Bozonnet, Ivan Desny, Thérèse Liotard, Malcolm Conrath, Thomas Salsman, Hai Tuhong-tu, Francis Magé, Marion Perry, Stéphane Auberghen, Caroline Bonmarchand.

Three days in the life of a brilliant 17-year-old lycée student, Beth (Godrèche), who wants to escape her miserable home life. She passionately studies Rimbaud, who used his poetry to escape his own life. She lives with an invalid mother and brother. All of them survive on handouts from the mother's lover, who has his eyes on the budding young Beth. The other men in her life include a man whom she meets in a disco, a boyfriend she breaks up with, and a man who collects knives.

This film offers much more than just a pretty face, though a pretty face it does have in Godrèche, who is the perfect modern girl on the verge of ripe womanhood. Jacquot wanted to make a film about the ecstasy and anguish of being a woman at this particular age and from the beginning of planning the film he had Godrèche in mind. She is impulsive, torn between her desires and her defiance toward the adult world.

Critics loved this study of a girl/woman on the verge of life. Some even compared Jacquot to Truffaut and Bresson. *Cahiers du Cinéma* raved, "Speed, conciseness, a sense of the ellipse, these are the qualities that make *The Disenchanted* the best French film in a long time."

117 *Le Désert des Tartares (The Desert of the Tartars)* 1977 Color *Director* Valerio Zurlini; *Producer* Jacques Perrin, Michelle de Broca, G. Silvagni, Cinema Due, FR3, l'Apostrophe, Janus; *Screenplay* André Brunelin and Jean-Louis Bertucelli, based on the novel by Dino Buzzati; *Photography* Luciano Tovoli; *Music* Ennio Morricone; *Set* Giancarlo Bartolini-Salimberi; *Sound* Bernard Bats; *Costumes* Giancarlo Barolini-Salimberi; *Editing* Raimondo Crociani. Running time: 140 minutes.

Cast: Vittorio Gassman, Jacques Perrin, Giuliano Gemma, Philippe Noiret, Francisco Rabal, Jean-Louis Trintignant, Max von Sydow, Fernando Rey, Helmut Griem, Laurent Terzieff.

Lieutenant Drogo (Perrin) is posted to a frontier camp on the edges of the Tartar desert. Despite his desire to build a strong defense against the Tartars, whose threatening presence is never firmly established, he is slowly destroyed by sickness and must abandon his responsibility on the day the Tartars attack.

This beautiful adaptation of Dino Buzzati's classic novel captures the waiting for war and the toll it takes on soldiers. It was filmed mainly in Iran, and the scenery and vistas are extraordinary. It explores the soldier's sick quest for war, as pent-up soldiers existing on hierarchical military rituals anxiously await the arrival of their enemies. The film was years in the making, with the project first conceived in 1940. Creative and financial troubles delayed its production for over thirty years.

The Desert of the Tartars received heaps of praise from critics in France and abroad who celebrated its deep meditations on human nature and its Kafkaesque atmosphere set against the glorious desert. Some American critics found it was too literary and plodding. *Variety*'s critic called it "Technically fine, with the fort and locations in Iran emerging the most effective aspects of this ambitious attempt to put a labyrinthine novel on film." It won the Grand Prix du Cinéma Français in 1976.

The Desert of the Tartars *see* **Le Désert des Tartares**

118 *Deux Heures moins le quart avant Jésus Christ (A Quarter to Two Before Jesus Christ)* 1982 Color   *Director* Jean Yanne; *Producer* Claude Berri, Tarak Ben Amar; *Screenplay* Jean Yanne; *Photography* Marco Vulpiani; *Music* Jean Yanne; *Set* Théobald Meurisse and Enrico Fiorentini; *Sound* Georges Prat; *Editing* Hervé de Luze. Running time: 97 minutes.

Cast: Coluche, Michel Serrault, Jean Yanne, Françoise Faban, Michel Auclair, Mimi Coutelier, Darry Cowl, Paul Préboist, Daniel Emilfork, André Pousse, Michel Constantin, Philippe Clay, Valérie Mairesse, Yves Mourousi, Léon Zitrone, José Arthur, Moustache, Laurence Riesner, Paul Mercey, Ibrahim Seck,

Lionel Rocheman, Maurice Vamby, Jean-Pierre Dravel, Michel Tugot-Doris, Daniel Laloux.

A comedy set in the Roman colony of Rahatlcoum in North Africa. Jules César's (Serrault) expensive vacation incites grumbling amongst the populace, who want mechanic Ben Hur Marcel (Coluche) to become their new leader. After a short stint in jail, Cleopatra (Coutelier) proclaims him to be her long-lost half-brother, and he is named pharaoh Aminemphet. When he represents his country in the televised circus games, he is the underdog winner.

This star-studded comedy was one of the biggest movies of the early 1980s. It cost over 40 million francs ($5 million) to make, and when it came out, it broke all box-office records with over a million spectators. It may be one of the most perfect examples of cultural and national differences in humor because as good an example as this film is of Gallic gags and jokes, many non–French found little reason to laugh. Its plot is in the tradition of Monty Python's *The Life of Brian* and Hanna-Barbera's *Flintstones,* with stone-age men and women equipped with modern conveniences and problems.

It remains a favorite with many French critics, but *Variety*'s reviewer represented the views of many American critics by dismissing it as "a witless and leaden historical spoof" with "a script that is sub-sub Mel Brooks at best."

Devil in the Flesh *see* **Le Diable au corps**

The Devil, Probably *see* **Le Diable probablement**

119 *Le Diable au corps (Devil in the Flesh)* 1947 B&W *Director* Claude Autant-Lara; *Producer* Transcontinental; *Screenplay* Jean Aurenche and Pierre Bost, based on the novel by Raymond Radiguet; *Photography* Michel Kelber; *Music* René Cloérec; *Set* Max Douy; *Costumes* Monique Dunan and Claude Autant-Lara; *Sound* William Sivel; *Editing* Madeleine Gug. Running time: 110

Cast: Gérard Philipe, Micheline Presle, Jean Debucourt, Germaine Ledoyen, Denise Grey, Pierre Palau, Jeanne Pérez, Jean Varas, Michel François, Marthe Mellot, Maurice Lagrenée, Albert Michel, Richard Francoeur, Edmond Beauchamp, Charles Vissières, Albert Rémy, Jacques Tati, André Bervil, Henri Gaultier, Jean Berton, Tristan Sévère, Léon Larive, Jean Relet, Roger Vieulille, Jean Fleury.

In the middle of World War I, a 17-year-old schoolboy, François (Philipe), and a married woman, Marthe (Presle), who had fallen in love before her marriage, meet again and realize they still love one another. Marthe's husband is away at the front, and the two lovers find perfect happiness together until the armistice, when Marthe, pregnant with François' child, flees to Brittany to have the baby and dies in childbirth. Her husband raises the child despite the fact that it is not his.

This is Autant-Lara's great masterpiece. When the book was published in 1923, five years after World War I, people were horrified by the immorality of encouraging sympathy for people who indulged in adulterous love affairs while their spouses were risking their lives on the front. Autant-Lara faced some of the same criticism when he made this film at the end of World War II. That young people could be portrayed sympathetically at such a time of national crisis, when good sons were dying in battle, was unthinkable. Autant-Lara's later films would come back to the themes in *Devil in the Flesh*, and the crew he amassed for this film worked with him for years. Micheline Presle's performance was the best of her career, and the role of François made Philipe a great leading man in France.

The film was a great success. New York State censors banned the film, and it was not shown there until an edited version came out in 1949. The Roman Catholic reviewing group complained that it "presents immorally and indecently a sympathetic portrayal of illicit actions." When it was released in the United States, *The Christian Science Monitor*'s reviewer called it "another example of the French film makers' boldly creative, searchingly perceptive gift for using the film to study character." It won the International Critics' Prize at the First World Film Festival in 1947.

120 *Le Diable boiteux (The Lame Devil* **or** *The Limping Devil)* 1948 B&W *Director* Sacha Guitry; *Producer* Union Cinématographique Lyonnaise; *Screenplay* Sacha Guitry; *Photography* Nicolas Toporkoff; *Music* Louis Beydits; *Set* René Renoux; *Sound* Jean Rieul; *Editing* Jeannette Berton. Running time: 138 minutes.

Cast: Sacha Guitry, Lana Marconi, Emile Drain, Maurice Teynac, Henry Laverne, Jeanne Fusier-Gir, Philippe Richard, José Noguéro, Jacques Varennes, Catherine Fonteney, Renée Devillers, Robert Seller, Georges Grey, José Torrès, Maurice Escande, Jean Debucourt, Pierre Bertin, André Randall, Robert Favart, Michel Lemoine, Georges Spanelly, Maurice Schutz, André Brunot, Denis d'Inès, Jean Piat, Howard Vernon, Roger Gaillard, Georges Bréhat, Pierre Lecoq, Michel Nastorg, Georges Rivière, Jean-Claude Briet, Léon Walther, Robert Hossein, Robert Dartois, Daniel Ceccaldi, Jane Daury, Pauline Carton, Yvonne Hébert, Anne Campion, Philippe Derevel, Sophie Mallet, Dominique Davray, Simone Logeart, Renée Bouzy.

The life of Charles-Maurice de Talleyrand-Périgord (Guitry), who is better known simply as Talleyrand. One of the great architects of the French Revolution, Talleyrand was born with a clubfoot and was ordained as a priest before he became Napoleon's most important minister and was finally called a betrayer of France. The movie explores the public, private and political life of this complicated historical legend.

Guitry's wives often played the leading female roles in his film, as was the case in *The Lame Devil*. His wife at the time, Lana Marconi, played his wife in the movie. Guitry made the movie as an homage to the man he considered to be "one of the most intelligent men who ever lived." His chameleon-like ability to use whatever talents he had to best please whomever was in power at the time, in Guitry's view, made him the consummate skilled survivor. Guitry said that he loved playing the sophisticated, wily Talleyrand. He completed the film in only 16 days.

The Lame Devil was accorded neither the acclaim nor the success of Guitry's prewar films, which really were his greatest. It was his first film since the war and many considered it to be a poor justification for his own cooperation with the collaborationist Pétain government. He was lambasted for sacrificing historical accuracy for dramatic effect. What infuriated people the most, though, was Guitry's apparent comparison of Hitler to Napoleon. Whatever his personal reasons were for making the film, Guitry does give his all, as both actor and director in paying tribute to his hero.

121 *Le Diable probablement (The Devil, Probably)* 1977 Color *Director* Robert Bresson; *Producer* Sunchild, GMF; *Screenplay* Robert Bresson; *Photography* Pasqualino de Santis; *Music* Philippe Sarde; *Set* Eric Simon; *Sound* Georges Prat; *Editing* Germaine Lamy. Running time: 100 minutes.

Cast: Antoine Monnier, Tina Irissari, Henri de Maublanc, Laetitia Carcano, Régis Hanrion, Nicols Deguy, Geoffroy Gaussen, Roger Honorat, Vincent Cottrell, Laurence Delannoy, Leatitia Martinetti, Miquel Irissari, Nadine Boyer Vidal, Dominique Lyon, Roland de Corbiac, Thadé Klossowsky, Martine Schlumberger.

A group of young people, Charles (Monnier), Michel (de Maublanc) and Alberte (Irissari), struggle with finding answers to world problems. They worry about the world's unsolvable disasters, famine, pollution, nuclear destruction and spiritual corruption. The church, the state, and psychoanalysis offer little aid. Michel finds his hope in militant ecology, but 20-year-old Charles (Monnier) opts for suicide.

This beautiful film is probably Bresson's most depressing, which says a lot when applied to one of the century's most somber and serious filmmakers. Bresson said of his intention in making his twelfth film: "What pushed me to make this film, is the mess we've made of everything. It's this mass civilization where soon the individual will not exist any more. This crazy agitation. This immense industry of destruction where which we die by or believe we've lived by. It is also the stupefying indifference of people, except for a few lucid young people." As usual, Bresson's luminous photography imbues the film with great spirituality despite the main character's despair.

The film was well received by most critics, but did not do well at the box-office. Truffaut called it "voluptuous." When it was shown at the New York Film Festival in 1977, the festival program text captured its essence: "Even though Bresson has painted a picture of wasted youth and beauty, one comes out of the film with a sense of exaltation: when a civilization can produce a work of art as perfectly achieved as this, it is hard to believe there is no hope for it."

The Diabolical Ones *see* **Les Diaboliques**

Diabolique *see* **Les Diaboliques**

122 *Les Diaboliques (Diabolique* or *The Fiends* or *The Diabolical Ones)* 1954 B&W *Director* Henri-Georges Clouzot; *Producer* Filmsonor; *Screenplay* Henri-Georges Clouzot, Jérôme Géronimi, Frédéric Grendel, and René Masson, based on Boileau-Narcejac's novel *Celle qui n'était plus*; *Photography* Armand Thirard; *Music* Georges Van Parys; *Set* Léon Barsacq; *Editing* Madeleine Gug. Running time: 90 minutes.

Cast: Simone Signoret, Vera Clouzot, Paul Meurisse, Charles Vanel, Jean Brochard, Noël Roquevert, Pierre Larquey, Thérèse Dorny, Michel Serrault, Jacques Varennes, Georges Chamarat, Robert Dalban, Jean Temerson, Georges Poujouly, Yves Marc Maurin, Madeleine Suffel, Jean-Pierre Bonnefous, Michel Dumur, Roberto Acon Rodgrigo, Henri Humbert, Jean Lefebvre, Jacques Hilling, Camille Guérini, Aminda Monserrat, Henri Coutet, Jean Clarieux, Jimmy Urbain, Dominique Brun.

A chilling suspense classic, in which Michel Delasalle (Meurisse), who operates a very run-down boarding school for boys, makes life miserable for everyone around

Les Diaboliques (*Diabolique*), 1954; directed by Henri-Georges Clouzot.

him, including his wife Christina (Clouzot) and his mistress Nicole (Signoret). The two women conspire to murder Michel. The plan succeeds until the body disappears, and, after seeing Michel's ghost, Christina has a heart attack. Inspector Fichet (Vanel) puts the pieces together and uncovers the real murderers.

Diaboliques is one of Clouzot's greatest film noir masterpieces. It is a classic of 1950s French cinema. Clouzot is a master of suspense, and the plot is full of twists that keep one guessing. The dark, shabby setting of the school creates a perfectly sinister atmosphere. The performances are all wonderful, especially from the wily detective played by Charles Vanel, French femme fatale Simone Signoret, and Vera Clouzot, the director's real-life wife.

French critics raved over this film when it came out. They praised its originality, suspense and horror. American critics were less impressed. Some, like *Variety*, dismissed it as "a creaky-door type melodrama." In time, though, most have come to agree that it is a film noir masterpiece of the highest order. It won the Prix Louis Delluc in 1954.

123 *La Diagonale du fou (Dangerous Moves)* 1983 Color *Director* Richard Dembo; *Producer* La Cecilia, Gaumont; *Screenplay* Richard Dembo; *Photography* Raoul Coutard; *Music* Gabriel Yared; *Set* Ivan Mussion; *Sound* Alix Comte. Running time: 110 minutes.

Cast: Michel Piccoli, Alexandre Arbatt, Liv Ullmann, Leslie Caron, Jean-Hughes Anglade, Hubert Saint Macary, Michel Aumont, Pierre Vial, Serge Avedikian, Wojciech Pszoniak, Daniel Olbrychski, Pierre Michael, Bernhard Wicki, Jacques Boudet, Jean-Paul Eydoux, Albert Simono, Benoît Régent, Sylvie Granotier, Willy Nicoidski, Marcel Tassinot.

Set in Geneva in 1983, the world championship chess match sets a Soviet, Liebskind (Piccoli), against a defector to the West, Fromm (Arbatt). Aside from the chess battle, there is the struggle of master against prodigy, East against West, Communism against Capitalism, but in the end the two are men who become friends despite their innumerable differences.

This wonderful suspense film was Richard Dembo's first feature and was inspired by the Karpov versus Korchnoi match in 1978. Piccoli and Arbatt do superb jobs of portraying chess fanatics who play the game to the exclusion of all else and who end up being used as pawns by their governments. The film's producer, Arthur Cohn, the only producer to win four Oscars, said of his intent: "What attracted me to the story was the originality of the main characters. Both are determined to use every trick to undermine the confidence of their opponents. What bothered me was that most people do not play chess, so the game had to remain in the background." To achieve this, Dembo manages to turn the chess matches into heroic battles between individuals. The photography by Coutard is, of course, exquisite.

When it came out in the United States, *Time* magazine said: "*Dangerous Moves* offers chic, vigorous entertainment." *The Aquarian Weekly* raved: "This is the kind of film that renews one's faith in filmmaking, and it is also the kind of film that seems only to come from outside the borders of the U.S." It won the Oscar for Best Foreign Film and the César for Best First Film in 1984.

Diary of a Chambermaid *see* **Le Journal d'une femme de chambre**

Diary of a Country Priest *see* **Journal d'un curé de campagne**

To Die of Love *see* **Mourir d'aimer**

124 *Dieu a besoin des hommes (God Has Need of Men)*   1950 B&W
Director Jean Delannoy; *Producer* Fox-Trans Continental; *Screenplay* Jean
Aurenche and Pierre Bost, based on Henri Queffelec's novel *Un Recteur de l'île de
Seine*; *Photography* Robert Lefebvre; *Music* René Cloéric; *Set* René Renoux;
Sound Jacques Carrère; *Costumes* Marcel Escoffier; *Editing* James Cuenet. Run-
ning time: 100 minutes.
    Cast: Pierre Fresnay, Madeleine Robinson, Andrée Clément, Daniel Gélin,
Daniel Ivernel, Jean Brochard, Jean d'Yd, Antoine Balpêtré, Louise Sylvie, Ger-
maine Kerjean, Lucienne Bogaert, Marcele Géniat, Marcel Delaître, Jean-Pierre
Mocky, Jean Carmet, Rapheal Patorni, René Génin, Fernand René, Jérôme
Goulven, Cécile Marcyl, Charles Bouillaud, Pierre-Jacques Moncorbie, Louise
Andrès, Jeanne Herviale, Albert-Michel, Jean Favre-Bertin, Pierre Latour, Serge
Lecointe, Christian Martaguet, Georges Cerf, Pierre Salas, Henri Maïk.
    A religious drama set in the nineteenth century on a poor, desolate Breton
island. When a new sexton, Thomas Gourvennec (Fresnay), arrives at this remote
wilderness where the inhabitants' irreligious ways have scared away one priest, he
faces initial difficulties with the islanders, but a tragedy unites them and brings
faith back to the people.
    One of the most representative films of French filmmaking in the 1950s, this
religious film is part of the literary tradition, with a screenplay faithfully adapted
by the great literary team of Aurenche and Bost and direction by one of the most
ambitious directors of the period, Delannoy. It is imbued with lyricism, humanity
and artistic sensibility. It is one of Delannoy's greatest works, with its themes and
spiritual meditations more important than its characters. The ever-so precise direction so perfected in this work and in other films of the era are just what New Wave
filmmakers were breaking away from a decade later.
    When it debuted at the Venice Biennal, *Variety* called it "an interesting study
of faith and religion" with " a sincere and important air." Despite some religious
rumblings about Delannoy's interpretation of the scriptures, it won the International Grand Prize at the Venice Biennal in 1950.

125 *Un Dimanche à la campagne (A Sunday in the Country)*   1984
Color   *Director* Bertrand Tavernier; *Producer* Sara Films, Antenne 2; *Screenplay*
Bertrand and Colo Tavernier, based on Pierre Bost's novella *Monsieur l'admiral
va bientôt mourir*; *Photography* Bruno de Keyser; *Music* Gabriel Fauré, Louis
Decreux, Marc Perrone; *Set* Patrice Mercier; *Sound* Guillaume Sciama; *Costumes*
Yvonne Sassinot de Nesles; *Editing* Armand Psenny. Running time: 94 minutes.
    Cast: Louis Ducreux, Sabine Azéma, Michel Aumont, Geneviève Mnich,
Monique Chaumette, Claude Winter, Thomas Duval, Quentin Ogier, Katia
Wostrikoff, Valentine Suard, Erika Faivre, Marc Perrone, Jean-Roger Milo,
Pascale Vignal, Jacques Poitrenaud.
    A beautiful movie about a day in the life of an Impressionist painter named
Monsieur Ladmiral (Ducreux). His children visit, they dine, discuss life and art,
enjoy the spectacular countryside, go for a drive, dance, drink and the day ends.
    One of Tavernier's best films, *A Sunday in the Country* is in many ways a

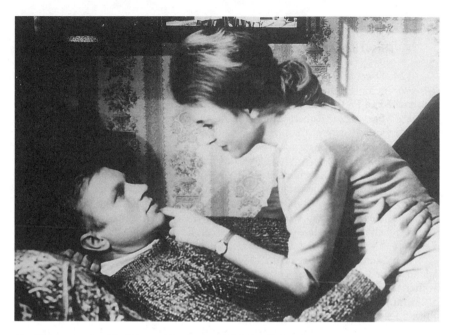

Les Dimanches de ville d'Avray (Sundays and Cybele), 1962; directed by Serge Bourguignon.

tribute to Impressionist painters as well as to filmmakers who have worked with them in mind, such as Renoir and Bergman. It also marked the conscious return to the tradition of fine French filmmaking, which cared less for innovation than for masterful craftsmanship. Tavernier and his wife adapted the script from a 1945 novel, though Tavernier also drew heavily on his relationship with his father. He explained the film by saying: "I wanted to make a film that would be based entirely on feelings. A film where emotions could reach a peak simply because a young woman leaves her father a bit early on a Sunday afternoon—that's the only dramatic moment in the film. I found it irresistible." And so did many others.

The very simple plot serves as a perfect vehicle for a gorgeous film that was a great hit internationally with both critics and the public. Jay Carr of *The Boston Globe* raved: "It's been a long time since any film gave as much to the eye and the heart as Bertrand Tavernier's *A Sunday in the Country*." Tavernier won Best Director at Cannes in 1984, and the film won Best Foreign Film of 1984 by the New York Film Critics and the National Board of Review and the Grand Prix du Cinéma Français.

126 *Les Dimanches de ville d'Avray (Sundays and Cybele* or *Cybele)*
1962 B&W   *Director* Serge Bourguignon; *Producer* Trocadéro, Fidès, Orsay, Terra Films, Romain, Pinès; *Screenplay* Serge Bourguignon, Antoine Tudal and Bernard Eschassériaux, based on the novel by Bernard Eschassériaux; *Photography* Henri Decaë; *Music* Maurice Jarre, Albinoni, Respighi, Handel and Marc-Antoine Charpentier; *Set* Bernard Evein; *Sound* Robert Teisseire and Jean Neny; *Editing* Léonide Azar. Running time: 110 minutes.

Cast: Hardy Krüger, Nicole Courcel, Daniel Ivernel, André Oumansky,

Patricia Gozzi, Anne-Marie Coffinet, Michel de Ré, Jocelyne Loiseau, Lisette Lebon, Denise Péron, Alain Bouvette, Gilbert Edard, Bibiane Stern, Malka Ribowska, Martine Ferrière, René Clermont, Renée Duchateau, France Anglade, Antoine Tudal, Albert Hughes, Raymond Pélissier, Paul Bonifas, Serge Bourguignon, Florence Blot, Dominique Maurin, Jacques Prévot, Jacques Robiolles, Jacques Tessier, Maurice Garrel, Roger Trapp, Pierre Mirat.

Pierre (Krüger), who has lost his memory after a plane crash in which he killed a child, believes that he once had a child. When he meets a little orphan girl, Françoise (Gozzi), he pretends to be her father and visits her every Sunday. Though the two become a sort of family, eventually the nuns at the orphanage become concerned about the man and his attachment. When the two go off to celebrate Christmas together in the woods, the police fear Pierre plans to hurt the girl. They ambush them and kill Pierre.

This sad, sensitive picture about two lost souls searching for identity and connection was Bourguignon's first feature. He said of the film: "I was fascinated by the contrast between a man who is very much a child and the child who is very much an adult." The photography and performances are hauntingly beautiful.

Some French critics complained about an "arty" self-conscious quality. Others felt the film marked an important debut. *Cue* said, "Serge Bourguignon directed his own screenplay with great delicacy and poetic sensitivity, making of it a most exquisite, and memorable film." *Sundays and Cybeles* was received more warmly in the United States. The film won the Oscar for Best Foreign Film in 1962.

Dirty Like an Angel *see* **Sale comme un ange**

Dirty Mary *see* **La Fiancée du pirate**

The Discreet *see* **La Discrète**

The Discreet Charm of the Bourgeoisie *see* **Le Charme discret de la bourgeoisie**

127 *La Discrète (The Discreet)* 1990 Color *Director* Christian Vincent; *Producer* Alain Rocca; *Screenplay* Christian Vincent and Jean-Pierre Ronssin; *Photography* Romain Winding; *Music* Jay Gottlieb with themes from Schubert and Scarlatti; *Set* Sylvie Olivé; *Sound* Jean-Jacques Ferran; *Costumes* Marie Malterre; *Editing* François Ceppi. Running time: 95 minutes.

Cast: Fabrice Luchini, Judith Henry, Maurice Garrel, Marie Bunel, François Toumarkine, Brice Beaugier, Yvette Petit, Nicole Félix, Olivier Achard, Serge Riaboukine, Katia Popova, Amy Laviètes, Hélène Ardouin, Maria Verdi, Pierre Gérald, Sophie Broustal.

Antoine (Luchini), a young writer, is dumped by his girlfriend before he can break up with her. To help Antoine get over his humiliation, his friend Jean (Garrel) devises a game for Antoine. Why not choose a woman by chance, make her fall in love with him, break it off, and chronicle the adventure in a book? Antoine finds his victim, Catherine (Henry), by running an ad for a typist. Despite her plain looks and an unsightly mole (discrète in French) on her face, Antoine goes through with the plan, with Jean playing the strategist. But when Antoine wants to stop the game because of his real feelings for Catherine, Jean decides to seek his own revenge.

Diva, 1981; directed by Jean-Jacques Beineix.

This fascinating film could be called a deconstructionist love story or the quintessential psychological French drama. One critic compared Vincent's gaze to both "a scienticist's curiosity and a jeweler's eye." This was Vincent's first feature film and his elaborate meditation on love and attraction make for a fabulous and frustrating game of seduction. A great depth of intelligence and emotion is built in the simply photographed and well scripted scenes. The influences of Pagnol and Guitry are strong. The role of Catherine catapulted Judith Henry to the inner circle of great young French actresses.

Critics loved *La Discrète*. Molly Haskell in *Film Comment* called the film: "Wonderful! Exuberant! ... a blend of Renoir and Rohmer." Andrew Sarris in *The New York Observer* exclaimed: "Judith Henry's incarnation of the perverse ingenue who erupts deliciously and unexpectedly in spasms of sensuality is hard to beat for top honors."

The Disenchanted *see* La Désenchantée

128 *Diva* 1981 Color   *Director* Jean-Jacques Beineix; *Producer* Galaxie-Greenwich-Silberman; *Screenplay* Jean-Jacques Beineix and Jean Van Hamme, based on the novel by E. Delacorta; *Photography* Philippe Rousselot; *Music* Vladimir Cosma, Charles Gounod, Catalini; *Set* Hilton McConnico; *Sound* Jean-Pierre Ruh; *Editing* Marie-Joseph Yoyotte. Running time: 115 minutes.

Cast: Wilhelmenia Wiggins Fernandez, Frédéric Andréï, Richard Bohringer,

Thuy An Luu, Jacques Fabbri, Chantal Dermaz, Anny Romand, Roland Bertin, Dominique Piron, Gérard Darmon, Jean-Jacques Moreau, Patrice Floersheim.

A suspenseful thriller about the adventures of a young post-office employee, Jules (Andréï), who is obsessed with a famous opera diva. She (Fernandez) has never allowed her voice to be recorded, but Jules secretly tapes one of her concerts. A prostitute who is about to be murdered stashes a tape with incriminating evidence against her killers into his bootleg tape bag. All sorts of intrigue follows, with pimps and Taiwense record pirates after Jules and his moped. A sexy young Vietnamese girl on roller skates named Alba (Luu) and her 40-some-year-old lover (Borhinger) help Jules get rid of the hoodlums and gain the diva's friendship.

This is one of the most stylish movies of the early MTV era and Beineix's first feature. *Diva* became a cult film of the 1980s, and its aesthetic established a whole modern "cool" cinematic vocabulary. Thirty-five-year-old Beineix, who once worked for Jerry Lewis, made wonderful use of Puccini and Verdi set against the slick urban nightlife of Paris. *Diva* was the first of a slew of French films, such as those of Luc Besson and Leos Carax, that were called by their detractor Serge Toubiana of *Cahiers du Cinéma* "all for image" and by a defender Raphaël Bassan, who applauded their rejection of naturalism and successful melange of high art, postmodernism, and pop culture as "neo-baroque."

Some French critics complained that *Diva*'s "chic, trendy" style brought Beineix an enormous amount of undeserved success and acclaim. They cried slick style, zero substance. But they mistook a sweet easiness for lack of meaning. Many American critics loved it. "Nimble and pretty and lighter than air," wrote Stephen Schiff. "*Diva* is a delicious little movie, and part of what one loves about it is its Frenchness."

The Does *see* **Les Biches**

129 *Le Dossier 51* 1978 Color *Director* Michel Deville; *Producer* Eléfilm -SFP, Maran Film; *Screenplay* Michel Deville and Gilles Perrault, based on a novel by Gilles Perrault; *Photography* Claude Lecomte; *Music* Franz Schubert and Jean Schwarz; *Set* Noëlle Galland; *Sound* Jean Pantaloni; *Editing* Raymonde Guyot. Running time: 108 minutes.

Cast: François Marthouret, Anna Prucnal, Françoise Lugagne, Roger Planchon, Laszlo Szabo, Didier Sauvergrain, Jean Martin, Jean-Pierre Barlier, Sabin Glaser, Hubert Bouthion, Claude Marcault, Uta Taeger, Philippe Roulleau, Jean Dautremay, Daniel Mesguich, Patrick Chesnay, René Bouloc, Gérard Dessalles, Nathalie Juvet, Jenny Clève, Isabelle Ganz, Corinne Clève, Liliane Gaudet, Jacques Zabor, Stephan Meldegg, Pierre Mailland, Julie Rossini, Françoise Béliard, Olivier Nolin, Jean-Luc Terrade, and the voices of Sacha Pitoeff, Liliane Coutanceau, Hélène Arié, Michel Aumont, Jean Mermet, Rosanna Sacco, Yan Brian, Michel Fortin, Daniel Mesguich, Jean-Marc Dupuis.

"Dossier 51" is the file that refers to Dominique Auphal (Marthouret), a young diplomat who is put under surveillance when he is assigned to work on a currency committee with the Third World. He learns that, despite his solid career and family life, nothing can be hidden from the methods of modern espionage, and when his homosexuality is revealed, he kills himself.

A truly horrifying exploration of how modern intelligence gathering methods, which involve agents and bugs, can so easily destroy a person's life. Filmed in a very objective, documentary style, the cold, distance of the director makes the film that much more chilling.

Some critics complained that Deville focused more on the high-tech gadgetry than on the human drama. Others, like the critic in *After Dark*, called the film "a brilliant, riveting work." It won the French Critics' Prix Méliès in 1978.

130 *Le Doulos (The Fingerman* or *The Stoolie)* 1963 B&W *Director* Jean-Pierre Melville; *Producer* Rome Paris Films, C.C. Champion Rome; *Screenplay* Jean-Pierre Melville, based on the novel by Pierre Lesou; *Photography* Nicolas Hayer; *Music* Paul Misraki; *Set* Daniel Guéret; *Sound* Julien Coutellier; *Editing* Monique Bonnot. Running time: 108 minutes.

Cast: Jean-Paul Belmondo, Serge Reggiani, Fabienne Dali, Jean Desailly, Michel Piccoli, René Lefèvre, Aimé de March, Marcel Cuvelier, Jack Léonard, Monique Hennessy, Christian Lude, Charles Bayard, Georges Sellier, Charles Bouillaud, Carl Studer, Paulette Briel, Jacques de Léon, Daniel Crohem, Philippe Nahon, Andrès, Robert Blome, Dominique Zardi.

A film noir about Silien (Belmondo), an incorrigible squealer, who agrees to help Maurice (Reggiani) with a robbery and then tells the police of the plan. Maurice is wounded getting away and hires a man to kill Silien, but in the end both have orchestrated their own deaths.

Melville's third film noir after *Bob the Gambler* and *Deux Hommes Dans Manhattan* is more of an homage to film noirs, particularly *The Asphalt Jungle*, which was Melville's favorite American film, than a simple cops-and-robber film. He has once again created a fabulous black-and-white world, where gangsters never remove their hats and Belmondo's beat-up beauty is classical. Sad strains of jazz cinch the haunting moments.

"*The Fingerman* is a bittersweet examination of deceit," wrote the French critic Claude Beylie. It is also what Melville believed it to be: "the story of a friendship and the end of a friendship."

The Drummer Crab *see* **Le Crabe-tambour**

130a *Du Rififi chez les hommes (Rififi)* 1955 B&W *Director* Jules Dassin; *Producer* Indus Films, Société Nouvelle Pathé Cinéma, Prima Film; *Screenplay* Jules Dassin, René Wheeler, Auguste Le Breton, based on the novel by Auguste Le Breton; *Photography* Philippe Agostini; *Music* Georges Auric; *Set* Auguste Capelier; *Sound* Jacques Lebreton; *Editing* Roger Dwyre. Running time: 116 minutes.

Cast: Jean Servais, Carl Mohner, Robert Manuel, Perlo Vita, Marie Sabouret, Janine Darcey, Claude Sylvain, Marcel Lupovici, Pierre Grasset, Robert Hussein, Magali Noël, Dominique Maurin, Marcelle Hainia, Jules Dassin, Daniel Mendaille, Maryse Paillet, Marcel Lesieur, Armandel, Alain Bouvette, Marcel Rouzé, René Hell, Fernand Sardou, Emile Genevois, Teddy Billis, André Dalibert, Jacques David, Jenny Doria, Gilbert Moreau.

A wonderful suspense story about a gang of robbers who plan and execute a masterful jewelry heist from a Paris jewelry store. But when one of the gang members lets slip news of the job to a rival gang, a gruesome chain of events, including kidnapping and murder, follows.

The first great French robbery film; it set off a wave of neo-realist thrillers.

Rififi's famous breaking-and-entering scene is 28 minutes long with no dialogue or music. The audience cannot help but feel a part of the job, as the camera shows the gang entering through the roof of the store, turning off the alarm and cracking the safe. The tension created is unbelievable. The director himself appears in the picture as the safecracker. Crime as a subject of high art works, and its success spawned many other such films. The film was made after Dassin was chased out of Hollywood by McCarthyism. He had made dark thrillers in the United States, but this was his first such effort in France, and it was widely copied by his countrymen.

Rififi was an enormous success with critics on both sides of the Atlantic. William Zinsser of *The New York Herald Tribune* said, "it has no pity on sentimentality, but it is strong, manly and strangely hypnotic." Bosley Crowther of *The New York Times* exclaimed, "This is perhaps the keenest crime film that ever came from France, including *Pépé le Moko*." Dassin was awarded Best Director at Cannes.

Dying of Love *see* **Mourir d'aimer**

The Earrings of Madame de ... *see* **Madame de ...**

131 *L'Eau vive (The Girl and the River* or *The Live Water)* 1956 Color *Director* François Villiers; *Producer* Films Caravelle; *Screenplay* Jean Giono and Alain Allioux; *Photography* Paul Soulignac; *Music* Guy Béart; *Set* Pierre Thévenet; *Editing* Edouard Berne. Running time: 96 minutes.

Cast: Pascale Audret, Charles Blavette, Andrée Debar, Henri Arius, Milly Mathis, Maurice Sarfati, Germaine Kerjean, Odette Barencey, Arlette Thomas, Jacques Moncorbier, Hélène Gerber, Hubert de Lapparent, Madeleine Silvain, Robert Lombard, Jean Panisse, Harry Max, Jean Clarens, Jean-Marie Serreau, Jean Toscane.

A drama about the end of farming life, in which a young girl's loss of innocence is paralleled with industrial technology arriving in the countryside where she lives. Hortense's family tries to get control of the wealth her father left her that he received when he sold his land to an electric company for a dam site. But just as the mighty river will not be stopped by a dam, neither will Hortense be defeated by her family. The pros and cons of agricultural life versus technological progress are played out in the struggle.

A great example of cinéma vérité, *The Girl and the River* is a mix of documentary and fiction that uses the best of both to create a powerful story. This was the one film adaptation of his work that pleased the author, Jean Giono. He and Villiers began the project with the support of the French electric company, which was building a controversial dam on the Durance River. Villiers said of their intention in a *Cahiers du Cinéma* interview: "*L'Eau vive* is a synthesis of human problems presented in a dramatized form, a synthesis which takes into consideration two principal characters whose destinies are always parallel and occasionally intertwined—a river (La Durance) and a young girl (Hortense)."

The Girl and the River received very positive reviews at home and abroad. *The Daily Telegraph* compared it to an unimpressive American film about the Tennessee River and praised *The Girl and the River* for handling a similar situation "with the lightest, most original touch."

Edouard and Caroline *see* **Édouard et Caroline**

132 *Édouard et Caroline (Edouard and Caroline)* 1951 B&W *Director* Jacques Becker; *Producer* UGC; *Screenplay* Annette Wademant and Jacques Becker; *Photography* Robert Lefebvre; *Music* Jean-Jacques Grunenwald; *Set* Annette Wademant; *Sound* William Sivel; *Editing* Marguerite Renoir. Running time: 100 minutes.

Cast: Daniel Gélin, Anne Vernon, Elina Labourdette, Jacques François, Betty Stockfeld, William Tubbs, Jean Galland, Jean Toulout, Jean Marsac, Yvette Lucas, Jean Riveyre, Jean-Pierre Vaguer, Grégoire Gromoff, Edmond Ardisson, Louis Vonelly, Hélène Duc, Charles Bayard, Micheline Rolla, Pierre Marnat.

A romantic comedy about a young married couple, Edouard (Gélin) and Caroline (Vernon). He is a pianist who dreams of great success. When the two go to a party at Caroline's uncle's house, the success of their social outing causes the two to fight. Caroline decides to leave him. Ultimately, with the help of a little music, of course, the two are reunited.

One of Becker's social comedies, this film may just be one of the best cinematic looks at marriage ever made. It is also credited with setting the stage for the New Wave. The glance that Becker casts upon society is searching, amused, but never condescending. Beneath the traditions, expectations and bickering, Becker's couple seek love everlasting. Gélin and Vernon are wonderful young lovers.

François Truffaut, who found Becker could make a wonderful film out of almost anything said: *"Edouard and Caroline* is just a story of one evening in the world with a telephone and a tuxedo jacket as props."

133 *L'Effrontée (Charlotte and Lulu* or *The Impudent Girl)* 1985 Color *Director* Claude Miller; *Producer* Oliane Productions, Films A2, Téléma, Monthyon Films; *Screenplay* Claude Miller, Luc Béraud, Bernard Stora, Anne Miller; *Photography* Dominique Chapuis; *Music* Alain Jony, Beethoven, Mendelssohn, Mozart; *Set* Jean-Pierre Kohut Svelko; *Sound* Paul Lainé, Gérard Lamps; *Editing* Albert Jurgenson. Running time: 96 minutes.

Cast: Charlotte Gainsbourg, Bernadette Lafont, Jean-Claude Brialy, Clothilde Baudon, Jean-Philippe Escoffey, Julien Glenn, Raoul Billerey, Simon de la Brosse, Richard Guerry, Cedric Liddell, Luisa Chafa, Daniel Chevalier, Philippe Baronnet, Chantal Banlier, Armand Barbault.

Thirteen-year-old Charlotte (Gainsbourg), who lives with her widowed father, is fed up with her life and her long-time friend Lulu (Glenn). When she befriends a brilliant young pianist, Clara (Baudon), she thinks she has found a means of escape. Clara forgets Charlotte soon enough though, and when Lulu falls ill, Charlotte is reminded of her right place in the world.

Claude Miller has been called "a leader of the return to craft and tradition in the French cinema" and in this battle, *Charlotte and Lulu* was one of his greatest weapons. It is a masterpiece of quiet, beautiful, unsentimental, yet poignant filmmaking. Miller's poetic direction lends a childish dreaminess to the film, which was based loosely on Carson McCuller's novel *The Member of the Wedding*. Gainsbourg gives just the right mix of innocence and sexuality to create one of cinema's most memorable gamines.

Elliott Stein of *Film Comment* gave it three stars and called it "the best coming-of-age film in years." In 1985, the film won the Prix Louis Delluc and a César for Gainsbourg.

Elena and Her Men *see* **Eléna et les hommes**

134 *Eléna et les hommes (Elena and Her Men* or *Paris Does Strange Things)* 1956 Color *Director* Jean Renoir; *Producer* Franco London Film, Gibé, Electra Cinématografica; *Screenplay* Jean Renoir and Jean Serge; *Photography* Claude Renoir and Henri Tiquet; *Music* Joseph Kosma; *Set* Jean André and Jacques Saulnier; *Sound* William Sivel; *Costumes* Rosine Delamare and Monique Plotin; *Editing* Boris Lewin. Running time: 96 minutes.

Cast: Ingrid Bergman, Jean Marais, Mel Ferrer, Pierre Bertin, Jean Claudio, Dora Doll, Frédéric Duvallès, Magali Noel, Elina Labourdette, Juliette Gréco, Jean Richard, Jean Castanier, Jacques Jouanneau, Mirko Ellis, Jacques Hilling, Renaud Mary, Gaston Modot, Jacques Morel, Michèle Nadal, Albert Rémy, Olga Valéry, Léo Marjane, Léon Larive, Grégori Chmara, Paul Demange, Jim Gérald, Claire Gérard, Robert Le Béal, Hubert de Lapparent, Jaques Catelain, Jean Ozenne, Simone Sylvestre, Palmyre Levasseur, Robert Mercier, René Berthier, Gérard Buhr, Lyne Carrel, Pierre Duverger, Corine Jansen, Liliane Ernoult, Louisette Rousseau, Jean-Claude Brialy, François Valorbe.

At the turn of the century in Paris, Elena Sokorowska (Bergman) is a widowed Polish princess who has run out of jewelry to sell. She decides to marry a wealthy industrialist for money, not love. But after her engagement, both the charming Count Henri (Ferrer) and the heroic General Rollan (Marais) fall in love with her. Persuaded that only she can convince General Rollan to seize power and save France, Princess Elena enters into a political drama. Her amorous games finally come to an end when she realizes that she has fallen for Count Henri.

In what he termed a musical fantasy, Renoir once again creates a dazzlingly beautiful saga. He was inspired by the true story of General Boulanger, who attempted to become dictator of Paris in the 1880s. From a boisterous Bastille Day celebration to the costumes in the caravan of gypsies, there is plenty of opportunity for Renoir to exercise his colorful mastery of spectacular costumes and scenes and to turn a critical eye on the unduly wealthy and ambitious.

Some critics found the plot did not stay as interesting as the scenery and the costumes. Truffaut, however, believed it was Renoir's ideal world come to life on screen.

Elevator to the Gallows *see* **L'Ascenseur pour l'échafaud**

The Elusive Corporal *see* **Le Caporal épinglé**

Emergency Kisses *see* **Les Baisers de secours**

135 *Emmanuelle* 1974 Color *Director* Just Jaeckin; *Producer* Trincara Films, Orphée Productions; *Screenplay* Jean-Louis Richard, based on Emmanuelle Arsan's novel *Laure*; *Photography* Robert Fraisse; *Music* Pierre Bachelet; *Editing* Claudine Bouche. Running time: 90 minutes.

Cast: Sylvia Kristel, Alain Cuny, Marika Green, Daniel Sarky, Jeanne Colletin, Christine Boisson, Samantha.

An erotic film about a young woman, Emmanuelle (Kristel), who goes to meet her husband, who has been posted in Bangkok. When she arrives she is introduced to an older man who initiates her in all ways of sadistic pleasure. Against the lush, exotic landscapes of the Far East, he reveals the deeper meaning of sex to Emmanuelle.

Probably the most famous soft-porn, erotic movie ever released, *Emmanuelle* was a huge box-office success, as it earned the dubious distinction of being the respectable sex movie everyone could see. It ran for 529 weeks straight in Paris with a record number of eight million spectators. The theater showing the English-language version became a regular tourist attraction. Giscard d'Estaing abolished censorship in film when he became president, and *Emmanuelle* was merely the most popular and successful of a slew of pornographic films that hit the big screen in France in the early 1970s. The close attention to clothing and sets and the soft photography comes from director Jaeckin's first career as a fashion photographer and took the hard-core edge out of the porn and made it more palatable for mass audiences. The film spawned six sequels.

Critics complained that Jaeckin had merely filmed fashion models in humiliating sex scenes. One distributor called the film's discreet sexual content "coffee table sex." But despite critics' objections to its glossy, glamorous superficiality, *Emmanuelle* proved to be the one X-rated movie housewives queued up for in broad daylight.

The End of Desire *see* **Une Vie**

136 *L'Enfance nue (Me* **or** *Naked Childhood* **or** *Nude Childhood)*
1969 Color   *Director* Maurice Pialat; *Producer* Parc Films, Renn Productions, Carosse; *Screenplay* Maurice Pialat and Arlette Langmann; *Photography* Claude Beausoleil; *Set* Outdoors; *Sound* Henri Moline. Running time: 77 minutes.

Cast: Henri Puff, Michel Terrazon, Pierrette Deplanque, Raoul Billery, René Thierry, Marie Louise Thierry, Linda Gutenberg, Marie Marc, Maurice Coussoneau, Claire Thierry.

The story of young boy, François (Terrazon), in foster care. He is moved from one miserable family situation to another. He finally finds compassion and understanding when he moves in with an elderly couple. But his happiness does not last long. He ends up in a sort of reform school with only the hope of returning to the last family that sustained him.

This is the first film by one of France's most socially sensitive modern filmmakers. The austere, intelligent look at complicated social issues introduced in this film would become a hallmark of Pialat's work and inspire a movement of socially conscious young French filmmakers such as Jean Eustache. The film treats the child as a complicated human being, not just a difficult, unstable social problem. This is a powerful condemnation of how social institutions and their necessary bureaucracy are inherently maladept at dealing with the children in their charge. Pialat used the secret of his cinematic forefathers, Truffaut and Bresson, to achieve real humanity—he used mainly non-professionals as actors.

Many critics compared the film with Truffaut's *The 400 Blows* when it came out. *Variety*'s critic admired the film's perception and sincerity. "Rarely has a young rebel been defined with such insight on film," he wrote. It won the Prix Jean Vigo in 1969.

137 *L'Enfant sauvage (The Wild Child)*   1970 Color   *Director* François Truffaut; *Producer* Films du Carrosse, Artistes Associés; *Screenplay* François

Les Enfants du paradis (*Children of Paradise*), 1945; directed by Marcel Carné.

Truffaut and Jean Gruault, based on the reports of Jean Itard on Victor de l'Aveyron; *Photography* Nestor Almendros; *Music* Antoine Duhamel; *Set* Jean Mandaroux; *Sound* René Levert; *Costumes* Gitt Magrini; *Editing* Agnès Guillemot. Running time: 90 minutes

   Cast: Jean-Pierre Cargol, François Truffaut, Françoise Seigner, Paul Ville, Jean Dasté, Pierre Fabre, Claude Miller, Annie Miller, René Levert, Jean Mandaroux, Jean Grualt, Mathieu Schiffman, Robert Cambourakis, Laura Truffaut, Gitt Magrini, Eva Truffaut, Jean-François Stévenin, Frédérique Dolbert, Nathan Miller, Dominique Levert, Guillaume Schiffman, Eric Dolbert, Tounet Cargol.

   The story of a savage child (Cargol), discovered in 1797 by peasants in Aveyron. He is sent to an asylum in Paris, where he is treated cruelly, until open-minded Dr. Itard (Truffaut) takes him into his own house and treats him kindly. Some of the lessons the boy must learn are painful, and after one particularly difficult incident he runs away. Eventually, though, he does return.

   Based on the diaries of the doctor who was involved in teaching and caring for the child, this film is one of Truffaut's real tributes to children and their special view on the world, and some believe it is his most beautiful film. Truffaut, who himself plays the doctor in the movie, grew up in an orphanage and found a similar kind of caregiver and mentor in André Bazin, the editor of *Cahiers du Cinéma*, who took him in off the streets. He was interested in what culture could make of something uncultured. This true story was perfect material for Truffaut, as some of his best movies, *The 400 Blows* and *Small Change*, focused on children and education. In fact, he used his own children in the film.

Some critics could not get over their disappointment after hoping for another *The 400 Blows* from Truffaut. Those who could forgive him for indulging in trying something new hailed this as a film of the greatest artistry. *The Evening News* raved, "*The Wild Child* is an almost flawless exercise in film making." *The Village* declared, "*The Wild Child* is such a moving, even inspiring, experience in what intelligence, love and patience can accomplish that it should hold strong appeal for any audience." The film won the French Critics' Prix Méliès in 1970.

138 *Les Enfants du paradis (Children of Paradise)*   1945 B&W   *Director* Marcel Carné; *Producer* Pathé-Cinéma; *Screenplay and Dialogue* Jacques Prévert; *Photography* Roger Hubert; *Music* Maurice Thiriet, Josephy Kosma and Georges Mouqué; *Set* André Baracq, Raymond Gabutti and Alexandre Trauner; *Sound* Robert Teisseire and Monchablon; *Costumes* Mayo; *Editing* Henri Rust and Madeleine Bonin. Running time: 385 minutes.

Cast: Arletty, Jean-Louis Barrault, Pierre Brasseur, Maria Casarès, Marcel Herrand, Louis Salou, Pierre Renoir, Gaston Modot, Etienne Decroux, Jane Marken, Fabien Loris, Marcel Pérès, Pierre Palau, Léon Larive, Raymond Rognoni, Albert Rémy, Maurice Schutz, Jean Dussol, Paul Frankeur, Auguste Boverio, Paul Demange, Jean Diener, Robert Dhéry, Marcelle Monthil, Jacques Castellot, Lucienne Vigier, Jean Gold, Ginette Quéro, Gustave Hamilton, Jean Lanier, Louis Florencie, Guy Favières, Raphaël Patorni, Jean-Pierre Delmon, Lucien Walter, Habib Bengalia.

An epic love story in two parts: "The Boulevard of Crime," and "The White Man." The film is set against Paris' colorful Boulevard of Crime in the 1820s and 1830s. The beautiful Garance (Arletty) is loved by four men, all of whom are based on historical characters from the nineteenth century: a mime, Baptiste Debureau (Barrault); an actor, Frédéric Lemaître (Brasseur); a writer/assassin, Lacenaire (Herrand); and the Count of Montray (Salou). Over a period of years, the fortunes of Garance and her suitors rise and fall. Saved from jail by the Count's influence, Garance becomes his mistress. When she disappears, Baptiste, who has always loved her, marries the devoted Nathalie (Casarès). Finally, Garance returns to Paris. She and Baptiste spend one night together confessing their love. The next day, Garance is swallowed up in the crowd on "The Boulevard of Crime," where the lovers had first laid eyes on each other.

The most famous and loved of all French movies. Carné began *The Children of Paradise* in 1943, but the war caused many disruptions. It was finally finished in secret, as many of its cast and crew were either Jewish, and therefore forbidden to work on films, or members of the French Resistance, who evaded the Gestapo by day and filmed or worked on sabotage by night. Considering the impossible circumstances under which this movie was made — with air raids, power outages and disappearing actors (one of the stars, Pierre Renoir, who played Jericho, was actually a replacement for Robert Le Vigan who was suspected of being a collaborator and disappeared partway through the making of the movie) — it is truly amazing that out of such production chaos, a classic was born. It is one of the greatest tales of impossible love ever imagined, full of meditations on morality, happiness and the theater.

As Carné had wished, the *Children of Paradise* was the first film to open after the Liberation. It was immediately hailed as the "monument of French cinema" and has since been called France's *Gone with the Wind*. Arletty was in her forties

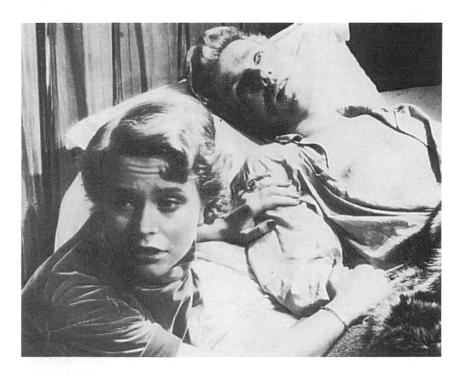

Les Enfants terribles (*The Strange Ones*), 1949; directed by Jean-Pierre Melville.

when the movie was made, but she is still very convincing as a beauty able to capture so many men's hearts. After the movie was released, she was sent to prison briefly because she had had an affair with a German officer. When it was released on video in the United States, Pauline Kael called it "a film poem on the nature and varieties of love—sacred and profane, selfless and possessive." Prévert was nominated for an Oscar for Best Original Screenplay in 1946.

139 *Les Enfants terribles (The Strange Ones)* 1949 B&W   *Director* Jean-Pierre Melville; *Producer* Melville Productions; *Screenplay* Jean-Pierre Melville and Jean Cocteau, based on the novel by Jean Cocteau; *Dialogue* Jean Cocteau; *Photography* Henri Decaë; *Music* Vivaldi; *Set* Jean-Pierre Melville constructed by Emile Mathys; *Sound* Jacques Gallois and Jacques Carrère; *Editing* Monique Bonnot. Running time: 107 minutes.

Cast: Edouard Dhermite, Nicole Stéphane, Renée Cosima, Jacques Bernard, Adeline Aucoc, Mel Martin, Maria Cyliakus, Maurice Revel, Annabel, Roger Gaillard, Jean-Marie Robain, Emile Mathys, Rachel Devirys, Hélène Rémy, Etienne Aubray.

A psychological drama about the relationship between a brother, Paul (Dhermite), and his sister, Elizabeth (Stéphane). When Paul falls in love with a beautiful model, Agathe (Cosima), Elizabeth intercepts a telegram from Paul declaring his love and encourages Agatha toward Paul's friend Gérard (Bernard). Paul poisons himself, but tells Agatha he loves her before he dies. Elizabeth shoots herself in despair.

This is "the Father of New Wave," Melville's best known film. It is a fascinating story that was one of Melville's favorite books when he was young, though it was Cocteau who approached Melville about making the movie. Cocteau wrote *Les Enfants terribles* while recuperating from an opium addiction, and it became a cult favorite in the 1930s. Cocteau had seen Melville's first feature, *Le Silence de la mer*, and was attracted to Melville's "free-lance air." The dialogue, music and photography are fantastic, and the commentary is narrated by Cocteau himself. Melville was born under the name Grumbach but changed his name out of adoration for Herman Melville— a fact that informs the great literary bent of his film career. The film was made on a low budget, with some scenes actually shot at the Théâtre Pigalle, and it launched the career of Edouard Dhermite, just as Cocteau hoped it would. Despite a difficult working relationship between Cocteau and Melville during the film, Cocteau believed it was the best film adaptation of any of his works.

When it first came out, many critics admired Melville's intelligence and the psychological subject, but most doubted it would become the great hit that it did. Truffaut claimed it was one of the few films in the history of cinema to evoke a sense of smell, in particular the smell of a child's sickroom. Of the film's lasting impact, he wrote: "This hospital-born poetry will never be outdated as long as we—the young and the old—will remain susceptible to the disease of love."

Entre Nous *see* **Coup de foudre**

140 *Escalier C (Stairway C)* 1985 Color   *Director* Jean-Charles Tacchella; *Producer* Films 7, FR3 Films; *Screenplay* Jean-Charles Tacchella, based on a novel by Elvire Murail; *Photography* Jacques Assuerus; *Music* Raymond

Alessandrini; *Set* Georges Lévy; *Sound* Pierre Lenoir; *Editing* Agnès Guillemot. Running time: 102 minutes.

Cast: Robin Renucci, Jean-Pierre Bacri, Catherine Leprince, Jacques Weber, Claude Rich, Jacques Bonnafé, Michel Aumont, Hugues Quester, Fiona Gelin, Florence Giorgetti, Catherine Frot, Gilles Gaston-Dreyfuse, Mony-Rey, Constance Schacher, Maite Maille, Peronille Moss, Oliver Lebeau.

The story of a cynical young man and his neighbors in a building in the 14th Arrondissement. Forster (Renucci) is an art critic, whose life is dramatically changed by his interactions with his neighbors. He befriends a gay neighbor; has a passionate affair with a young publicist, Florence (Leprince); finally discovers a painter (Weber) whose work he thinks is brilliant; and is profoundly affected by the suicide in the building of an old woman (Mony-Rey), to whom he had never spoken.

Another wonderfully perceptive comedy-cum-psychological study, this film cemented Tacchella's reputation as one of the important modern auteurs. Based on an award-winning novel that was originally set in Manhattan, the film revolves around the stairway C, which is used as the scene of the events that transform Forster from cynical egoist to a caring young man. Tacchella has once again captured a slice of the French lifestyles.

French critics generally received this complex film warmly. *La Revue du Cinéma* declared that with this film, Tacchella earned the title of heir apparent to Jacques Becker. It has never been distributed in the United States.

141 *L'Espoir (Sierra de Teruel* or *Man's Hope)* 1945 B&W *Director* André Malraux; *Producer* Corniglion, Molinier; *Screenplay* André Malraux, assisted by Denis Marion, based on Malraux's own novel *Espoir*; *Photography* Louis Page; *Music* Darius Milhaud; *Set* Vincent Petit; *Editing* André Malraux, Georges Grace. Running time: 78 minutes.

Cast: Andres Mejuto, Nicolas Rodrigues, José Lado, Julio Pena, Members of the International Brigade, Spanish peasants.

Set in 1937, the film is an historical drama about the Spanish Civil War, focusing on the battles of the Sierra de Teruel, in which a Loyalist battalion is on a mission to destroy a bridge. Republicans fight Francoists. Patriots defend democracy with the help of volunteers from other countries, and peasants pitch in. One airplane crashes into a mountain. As the dead and the wounded are carried from the summit, heroic resistance flares and the battle for freedom rages.

Though intensely patriotic, Malraux's only film goes beyond pure propaganda to represent one of France's first examples of cinéma vérité. Malraux used real footage from the war. He wrote, directed and edited the film. Like many artists of the 1930s, such as Hemingway and Orwell, Malraux was involved in the Spanish Civil War, as a concerned citizen of the world, not just as an artist. He joined the International Air Squadron, and when a mission he was involved in ran into trouble, he organized search parties. This incident formed the basis of his novel and then of this film. Social and political contexts were very important to him. The film was shot in Spain in 1937, and smuggled into Occupied France. Because the Nazis planned to destory it as anti–Fascist propaganda, it was hidden and not released until 1945, when the war was over. The film was strongly influenced by Russian cinema, in particular Malraux's idol Eisenstein.

Man's Hope has been called the masterpiece of an engaged artist. Malraux beautifully married his political sentiments with a story to create a thrilling commentary. The film was awarded the Prix Louis Delluc in 1945.

142 *Et Dieu créa la femme* (*And God Created Woman*) 1956 Color *Director* Roger Vadim; *Producer* Iéna, UCIL, Cocinor; *Screenplay* Roger Vadim and Raoul Lévy; *Photography* Armand Thirard; *Music* Paul Misraki; *Set* Jean André; *Sound* Pierre Calvet; *Editing* Victoria Mercanton. Running time: 92 minutes.

Cast: Brigitte Bardot, Mary Glory, Jane Marken, Isabelle Corey, Jany Mourey, Jacqueline Ventura, Curd Jürgens, Jean-Louis Trintignant, Christian Marquand, Georges Poujouly, Jean Tissier, Paul Faivre, Claude Véga, Jean Lefèbvre, André Toscano, Philippe Grenier, Jacques Ciron, Léopoldo Frances, Raoul Lévy, Guy Henry, Roger Vadim.

Juliette Hardy (Bardot) is an 18-year-old beauty who drives the men of Saint-Tropez crazy. A wealthy older bar owner (Jürgens) and the two Tardieu brothers (Trintignant and Marquand) desperately try to win her love. All three fight over the lovely young Juliette, with the sweet, shy brother finally asserting himself and overcoming the other two's advances to succeed in winning her love and admiration.

The sociological importance of this film outweighs its artistic significance. The film's liberal sexual attitude, which presented Bardot's sexual appetites as healthy, not immoral, marked an important step in the liberation of woman's sexuality on screen and, possibly, off screen as well. Bardot's sensual power is revealed to the fullest, as she renders mad, not only the men in the film, but also the men in the audience. She was married to Vadim when the movie was made; it was his first feature. This was the film that made Bardot a sex symbol and a mythic character of the Riviera.

The film was an enormous success, albeit a scandalous one, grossing over $25 million. Many claimed that it had a youthful and lively quality that long had been missing in French cinema, and called it the first film of the New Wave. In *Cahiers du Cinéma*, Jacques Rivette declared that it was the only "alive" French movie that he saw all year. The American ad exclaimed: "*And God Created Woman*, but the devil invented Brigitte Bardot."

143 *État de siège* (*State of Siege*) 1972 Color *Director* Constantine Costa-Gavras; *Producer* Reggane-Unidis-Geissler Film; *Screenplay* Franco Solinas and Constantine Costa Gavras; *Photography* Pierre William Glenn; *Music* Mikis Théodorakis; *Editing* Françoise Bonnot. Running time: 120 minutes.

Cast: Yves Montand, Renato Salvatori, Otto E. Hasse, Jacques Weber, Jean-Luc Bideau, Maurice Teynac, Evangéline Peterson, Yvette Etiévant, Harold Wolff, Nemesio Antunes, André Falcon, Mario Montilles, Jerry Brouer, Jean-François Boggi, Eugenio Guzman, Maurice Jacquemont, Roberto Navarette, Gloria Lass, Alejandro Cohen, Martha Contreras, Jacques Perrin, Gérard Manneveau, Aldo Francia, Gilbert Brandini, Douglas Harris, Robert Holmes, Alegandro Sieverina, Alejandro Misle, Julio Zarata.

A political drama about a government agent, Philip Michael Santore (Montand), who is kidnapped and killed by South American rebels. In flashback, Santore's story is revealed. Although he claimed he was in Uruguay to teach traffic control, the rebels did not buy it. After tense negotiations and many mind games, the rebels decide to kill him.

Et Dieu créa la femme (And God Created Woman), 1956; directed by Roger Vadim.

This is one of the best political films ever made, and it, along with Costa-Gavras' earlier works, *Z* and *The Confession*, sparked a whole slew of political thrillers, which marked a new era in the idea of the "engaged" filmmaker. *State of Siege* was so controversial that it was not allowed to be shown at the American Film Institute in Washington because the film was seen as anti–American and pro-assassination. The film was based on the life of Daniel Mitrione, an agent who worked for the U.S. Agency for International Development, who also was killed amidst murmurings that his job was not really traffic control but anti-rebel activities.

A political firestorm raged about the just or unjust censorship of the film and its perceived "anti–American" bias. This occupied critics and the public more than the film's artistic merits. Critics opined about communism and dictatorships and shelved their artistic opinions; responses were passionately for or against the film. It won the Prix Louis Delluc in 1972.

144 *L'Été meurtrier (One Deadly Summer)* 1983 Color *Director* Jean Becker; *Producer* SNC TF1 Films Productions; *Screenplay* Sébastien Japriso, based

L'Été meurtrier (*One Deadly Summer*), 1983; directed by Jean Becker.

on his novel; *Photography* Etienne Becker; *Music* Georges Delerue; *Set* Jean-Claude Gallouin; *Sound* Guillaume Sciama; *Editing* Jacques Witta. Running time: 134 minutes.

Cast: Isabelle Adjani, Alain Souchon, Suzanne Flon, Maria Machado, Jenny Clève, Evelyne Didi, Jenny Gaven, François Cluzet, Manuel Gélin, Roger Carel, Michel Galabru, Cécile Vassort, Martin Lamotte, Edith Scob, Jacques Dynam,

Yves Alfonso, Max Morel, Raymond Meunier, Daniel Langlet, Evelyne Didi, Jacques Nolot, Marie-Pierre Casey, Catherine Le Gouey, Maiwen Lebesco, Virginie Vignon, Patrice Melennec, Pierre Gallon, Renaud Bossert.

A beautiful young woman (Adjani) returns to her native village to seek revenge on the three men who raped and beat her mother years before. She marries Pin-Pon (Souchon), because she believes he will be of help in finding the men. She mistakenly believes she has found them, learning that one man has already died and finding the other two. She makes the mistake because her step-father has already killed the three responsible for the rape. A vicious cycle of violence has been set in motion.

This beautiful suspense thriller announced the ascent of one of France's most talented modern actresses. Isabelle Adjani is in one of her finest roles in this film, which was directed by Jean Becker, the son of the great filmmaker Jacques Becker. The screenplay was adapted from a best-selling novel by Sebastien Japrisot, which delved even more deeply into the psychology of shame that motivates the woman's obsessive behavior.

"Adjani's performance of a disturbed young woman moving implacably towards madness is so electrifying it manages to forestall any questions one might have about the unlikely plot turns," wrote *Variety*'s reviewer. The film won a number of Césars, including Best Actress for Adjani's performance.

145 *Les Étoiles de midi (Stars at Noon)* 1959 Color *Director* Marcel Ichac; *Producer* Filmartic, Films du Centaure, Les Requins Associés; *Screenplay* Gérard Herzog and Marcel Ichac; *Photography* Georges Strouve and René Vernadet; *Music* Maurice Jarre; *Editing* Pierre Gillette. Running time: 78 minutes.

Cast: Lionel Terray, Pierre Rousseau, Roger Blin, Pierre Dany, Michel Vaucher, René Desmaison, René Collet, Pierre Paret, Jean Favre, Maurice Claret.

A documentary about various mountain climbers who have scaled the Alps, including a fabulous rescue sequence and the story of how a German prisoner escaped over the Alps during the World War II.

This is one of the finest documentaries of the postwar period. Its breathtaking views and photography of the Alps bring nature and the great outdoors to the big screen in a splendor rarely captured on film. Some of the world's greatest climbers can be seen scaling the peaks in reenactments of the climbers' true accounts.

Critics admired the film's photography and stunt daring. It won the Grand Prix du Cinéma Français in 1959.

146 *Une Étrange Affaire (A Strange Affair)* 1981 Color *Director* Pierre Granier-Deferre; *Producer* Sara Films, Antenne 2; *Screenplay* Pierre Granier-Deferre, Christopher Frank and Jean-Marc Roberts, based on Jean-Marc Robert's novel *Affaires étrangères*; *Photography* Etienne Becker; *Music* Philippe Sarde; *Set* Dominique André; *Sound* Guillaume Sciama; *Editing* Isabelle Garcia de Herreros. Running time: 105 minutes.

Cast: Michel Piccoli, Nathalie Baye, Gérard Lanvin, Jean-Pierre Kalfon, Jean-François Balmer, Madeleine Cheminat, Victor Garrivier, Dominique Blanchar, Pierre Michael, Ariane Lartéguy, Suzy Rambaud, Christian Peireira, Sophie Deschamps, Nicole Vogel, Humbert Balsan, Jacques Boudet, Dominique Zardi, Katie Kriegel, Christophe Odent, Jean-Paul Solal, Philippe Roussel, André Chaumeau, Jean Trégomain, Niombi, Dominique Lablanche, Elisabeth Catroux.

A young advertising executive, Louis Coline (Lanvin), throws himself completely into his job at a department store. To serve a demanding new boss, Bertrand Malair (Piccoli), he sacrifices his marriage, family and friends. Although his wife (Baye) warns Coline of his boss's true nature, he refuses to heed her warning, and she leaves him before disaster hits.

A fascinating drama with one of Michel Piccoli's greatest performances, this is also one of Granier-Deferre's best pictures. His touch is light, with nothing spelled out, but a lot suggested. The dangerous seduction of the workplace and employer could not have been more aptly timed than the early 1980s when yuppies threw themselves into advancement with abandon.

Critics hailed Piccoli's performance and Granier-Deferre's masterful direction. Gilles Colpart in *La Revue du Cinéma* admired how *A Strange Affair* explored servitude with psychoanalysis and revealed how "the traps of ambition ensnare their victims with illusions of power." It won the Prix Louis Delluc in 1981.

147 *Un Étrange Voyage (On the Track)* 1981 Color   *Director* Alain Cavalier; *Producer* La Guéville, Antenne 2; *Screenplay* Alain Cavalier and Camille de Casabianca; *Photography* Jean-François Robin; *Music* Maurice Leroux; *Set* Bernard Evein; *Sound* Alain Lachassagne; *Editing* Joëlle Hache. Running time: 100 minutes.

Cast: Jean Rochefort, Camille de Casabianca, Arlette Bonnard, Dominique Besnehard, Patrick Depeyrrat, Gérard Challion, Patrick Bonnel, Alain Lachassagne, Hubert Saint Macary, Gérard Darrier, Jean-François Robin, Jean-Pierre Bagot, Roland Amstutz, François Berleand, Laurent Guérin.

When Pierre's mother is not on the train from Troyes to Paris and the police and the train company offer no explanation for her disappearance, the middle-aged picture restorer (Rochefort) sets out in search of her on foot with his college-student daughter, Amélie (de Casabianca). After walking for days, they find her body in a bush on the side of the railroad tracks.

On the Track is a moving journey picture by one of France's greatest and least prolific modern moviemakers. Cavalier wrote the screenplay with his 24-year-old daughter, who also made her screen debut in the film. The voyage referred to in the French-language title is as much an emotional voyage as a geographical one. The trek beside the railroad tracks parallels a quest for a father and daughter connection.

Some critics applauded the film's quiet emotional drama. Others felt it was too heavy and slow. *La Revue du Cinéma*'s critic summed up the opinion of many when she wrote that *On the Track* could have been a strong and original film. "The originality is there," she wrote, "as is the actors' talent, but the work itself leaves a feeling of dissatisfaction." It won the Prix Louis Delluc in 1980.

Every Man for Himself *see* **Sauve qui peut, la vie**

Everybody He Is Nice, Everybody He Is Beautiful *see* **Tout le monde il est beau, tout le monde il est gentil**

Evil Eden *see* **La Mort en ce jardin, cela s'appelle l'Aurora**

148 *Falbalas (Paris Frills)* 1945 B&W   *Director* Jacques Becker; *Producer* Essor Cinématographique; *Screenplay* Maurice Aubergé, Maurice Griffe, and Jacques Becker; *Photography* Nicolas Hayer; *Music* Jean-Jacques Grunenwald; *Set* Max Douy; *Costumes* Marcel Rochas; *Editing* Marguerite Houllé. Running time: 95 minutes.

Cast: Raymond Rouleau, Micheline Presle, Jean Chevalier, Jeanne Fusier Gir, Gabrielle Dorziat, Christiane Barry, Françoise Lugagne, Jean Marken, Rosine Luguet, Marcelle Hainia, Roger Vincent, Marc Doelnitz, Nicolas Amato, François Joux, Paul Barge, Paul Lluis, Rolande Forest, Evelyne Volney, Paulette Langlais, Renée Thorel, Marguerite de la Morlaye, Gaston Roullet, Georges Bréhat, Paul Delauzac, Catherine Romane, Lucy Lancy, Yolande Bloin, Maric Carld, Simone Gerbier, Celia Cortez.

A famous Parisian couturier, Philippe Clarence (Rouleau), falls in love with a young girl, Micheline (Presle), who is engaged to his friend Daniel. Inspired by his fatal muse, Philippe insists on making her wedding gown. The two become lovers and although she calls off her marriage, Philippe refuses to marry her. When she returns to her family, he is so devastated by his loss that he jumps out the window.

This is a postwar masterpiece. It is amazing how sumptuous the film is, considering that it was made during the war. Becker filmed it during the Occupation. He knew the intricacies of his subject, because his mother worked in a couture house. When it was released right after the Liberation, the film really transported people to an unknown world — after years of food rationing, they found themselves in the thick of haute couture Paris.

Hailed as a romance that was such an in-depth portrait of the fashion world as to be almost a documentary, the film did only so-so at the box office. Some critics complained that Becker lost his magic when the plot turned tragic.

The Fall of Lola Montes *see* **Lola Montès**

149 *Fanfan la tulipe (Fanfan the Tulip)*   1952 B&W   *Director* Christian-Jaque; *Producer* Ariane, Filmsonor-Amato; *Screenplay* René Wheeler, René Fallet, Christian-Jaque and Henri Jeanson; *Photography* Christian Matras; *Music* Maurice Thiriet and Georges Van Parys; *Set* Robert Gys; *Sound* Lucien Lacharmoise; *Costumes* Jean Zay; *Editing* Jacques Desagneaux. Running time: 102 minutes.

Cast: Gérard Philipe, Marcel Herrand, Gina Lollobrigida, Geneviève Page, Noël Roquevert, Sylvie Pelayo, Olivier Hussenot, Jean-Marc Tennberg, Jean Parédès, Henri Rollan, Lolita de Sylva, Georgette Anys, Gil Delamare, Irène Young, Joe Davray, Jacky Blanchot, Nerio Bernardi, Hennery, Lucien Callamand, Gérard Buhr, Georges Demas, Max Harry, Paul Violette, Françoise Spira, Guy Henry.

Set during the reign of Louis XV, the film recounts the adventures of Fanfan (Philipe), a soldier in the Aquitaine regiment. He falls in love with the lovely Adeline (Lollobrigida). After various military and court intrigues that threaten to forever separate the two lovers, Fanfan's bravery is brought to the attention of the king and the two are allowed to marry.

In this epic comedy, Gérard Philipe proves himself to be all that a leading man should be. He is charming, sincere, funny, great to look at, and adept at all manner of stunts. Poking fun at war, this film became a huge success after World War II. It somehow managed to balance glorifying the hero of war and satirizing the endeavor itself. The idea for the film came from a nineteenth century song about a young soldier who loves women, wine and war.

Fanfan the Tulip was the biggest hit of the year in France. Director Claude Autant-Lara called the film "ravishing." *The Herald Tribune* hailed it as a "rollicking, fantastic comedy of soldier life during the reign of Louis XIV — a sort of *Gil Blas* of the screen." Christian-Jaque won Best Director at Cannes 1952.

Fanfan the Tulip *see* **Fanfan la tulipe**

150 *Le Fantôme de la liberté (The Phantom of Liberty* or *The Specter of Freedom)* 1974 Color   *Director* Luis Buñuel; *Producer* Serge Silberman; *Screenplay* Luis Buñuel and Jean-Claude Carrière; *Photography* Edmond Richard; *Set* Pierre Guffroy; *Sound* Guy Villette; *Editing* Hélène Plemiannikov. Running time: 103 minutes.

Cast: Adrianna Asti, Julien Bertheau, Jean-Claude Brialy, Adolfo Celi, Paul Frankeur, Michel Lonsdale, Claude Piéplu, Monica Vitti, François Maistre, Hélène Perdrière, Jean Rochefort, Michel Piccoli, Milena Vukotic, Muni, Pierre Maguelon, Pascale Audret, Marie-France Pisier, Bernard Verley, Marcel Perez, Paul Le Person, Hélène Perdière, Pierre-François Pistorio.

A series of surrealistic episodes that are not narratively connected. In one, two young girls sitting in a garden are approached by a satyr bearing obscene postcards of monuments in Paris. In another, a man is condemned to death and then liberated. In another, a nurse spends the night in a very strange guesthouse, where she meets a masochist and a professor. There is also a great dinner party scene with guests on toilet seats.

Buñuel, the Salvador Dalí of films, made this uproarious comedy at age 75 and although he had long been admired by critics and film buffs, the commercial success of this disjointed film established him as a recognized auteur and internationally beloved filmmaker. Wielding his surreal style, Buñuel begins and ends scenes abruptly, to fly in the face of narrative expectations, which complements, rather than disrupts, the chaotic world he depicts. He satirizes the bourgeois with liberty and imagination as his major weapons to create a highly amusing film.

Critics called this Buñuel's return to his prewar *Un Chien Andalou*, and surprisingly this surrealist gem was very popular.

151 *Le Farceur (The Joker)* 1961 B&W   *Director* Philippe de Broca; *Producer* Lopert; *Screenplay* Philippe de Broca; *Photography* Jean Penzer; *Music* Georges Delerue; *Set* Jacques Saulnier; *Editing* Laurence Mery. Running time: 86 minutes.

Cast: Anouk Aimée, Jean-Pierre Cassel, Geneviève Cluny, Anne Tonietti, Pierre Palau, Georges Wilson, François Maistre, Jean-Pierre Rambal, Liliane Patrick, Iréne Chabrier.

A romantic comedy about Edouard Berlon (Cassel), an incorrigible philanderer. One day, while leaving one woman's bedroom by the skylight, he falls into the garden of another woman, Hélène (Aimée). He decides to give up his errant ways and to marry the implacable woman. He bends over backwards wooing her. When she finally consents to go off with him to a country inn, she turns out not to hold his interest.

Another wonderful light comedy by sentimentalist de Broca, *The Joker* is one more successful attempt by the director to lighten up the filmmaking of his day. De Broca made this film on the heels of the great success of his first movie, *The Love Game*. He used the same crew and leading man. The film's emphasis on antiques and old ways and traditions was a harkening back to the comfortable, simple life of days gone by, in a time when France found the march of modernity unwelcome. Cassel was once again delightful and was even compared to Tati's wonderful Monsieur Hulot.

Some ardent fans of de Broca's *The Love Game* were disappointed with *The Joker*, but most critics loved it. *The New York Herald Tribune* called it "inspired lunacy" and "an endearing plea for a life that never was and, alas, probably never will be." And *The New Yorker*'s reviewer confessed to wanting to applaud the screen.

152 *Farrebique* 1946 B&W   *Director* Georges Rouquier; *Producer* Ecran Français and Films Lallier; *Screenplay* Georges Rouquier; *Photography* André Dantan; *Music* Henri Sauguet; *Sound* René Lécuyer; *Editing* Madeleine Gug. Running time: 100 minutes.

A documentary about one Aveyronnaise family and their farm life, followed through a year's four seasons. In between the daily and seasonal rituals of bread-making, praying, plowing and harvesting, a child is born, and the patriarch of the family dies. More modern methods of farming are resisted, and the installation of electricity is debated. It is a record of farm life on the verge of modernization.

This magnificent film remains one of the benchmarks by which all French documentaries are judged. It was filmed in the Massif Central just after the war, a region that truly had yet to enter the twentieth century as we know it. The film is a wonderful record of the traditional farming life that once dominated the world. Rouquier spent a year with this family and rather than creating a straight documentary, he fashioned a lyrical, poetic film about this way of life. Rouquier returned to the same village almost forty years later to make *Biquefarre*, which starred his own family, but once again used the seasons to relay a way of life, now dominated by machines, but still full of poetry.

Hailing it as a glorious homage to farming life, critics were right in declaring *Farrebique* to be Rouquier's masterpiece. It was one of the great hits of the year. Critic Georges Sadoul believed the film was realism in its highest form and that the grandfather's burial scene was one of cinema's best moments. *Farrebique* was chosen as the official selection at Cannes in 1946, where it won the Critics' International Grand Prize. It went on to win the Grand Prix du Cinéma Français.

153 *La Femme d'à côté (The Woman Next Door)* 1981 Color   *Director* François Truffaut; *Producer* Les Films du Carrosse, TF1 Films Productions; *Screenplay* François Truffaut, Suzanne Schiffman and Jean Aurel; *Photography* William Lubtchansky; *Music* Georges Delerue; *Set* Jean Pierre Kohut-Svelko; *Sound* Michel Laurent; *Editing* Martine Barraqué. Running time: 106 minutes.

Cast: Gérard Depardieu, Fanny Ardant, Henri Garcin, Michèle Baumgartner, Véronique Silver, Roger Van Hool, Philippe Morier-Genoud.

A passionate, modern love story about two former lovers who married other people, but when they end up living next door to each other, cannot keep from getting involved again. Mathilde (Ardant) and Bernard (Depardieu) are in a vicious cycle of love, with one growing cool, just as the other gets hot.

This is one of Truffaut's last and most passionate films. Playing the bucolic, almost suburban setting off the violent emotional states of the two lovers, Truffaut beautifully underscored interior and exterior lives. In discussing the film, Truffaut touched on many enigmatic heroines of twentieth century French film, including Catherine in his own classic *Jules and Jim*. "Our femmes fatales are different," he said, "vulnerable, in danger, and this provides the pull. With Mathilde, even if she was the pursuer, each of her glances was a call for help."

When the film opened at the New York Film Festival, Truffaut was beseiged with criticisms couched as questions about the film's relevance and its depressing nature. Fanny Ardant responded to Americans' apparent confusion about the picture by saying, "Love is the *only* thing that is universal." Richard Eder of *The New York Times* called this a "tale of two monstrous innocents who almost literally devour each other."

154 *Une Femme douce (A Gentle Creature)* 1969 Color *Director* Robert Bresson; *Producer* Parc Films, Marianne Productions; *Screenplay* Robert Bresson, based on Dostoevsky's novella *A Gentle Spirit*; *Photography* Ghislain Cloquet; *Music* Jean Wienier, with selections from Purcell and Mozart; *Set* Pierre Charbonnier; *Sound* Urbain Loiseau; *Editor* Raymond Lamy. Running time: 88 minutes.

Cast: Dominique Sanda, Guy Frangin, Jane Lobre, Claude Ollier, Dorothy Blank, Gilles Sandier, Jacques Kébadian.

A man (Frangin) sits over the body of his wife (Sanda), who has committed suicide, and he goes over their past in an effort to understand her despair. From their wedding to the day she threw herself out of a window, this sweet young woman's marriage was a growing nightmare, as her husband bullied and neglected her, and her small acts of rebellion brought her no freedom or hope. Unfortunately, his realization of her emotional situation comes too late to save her.

A Bressonian masterpiece, this heavy-duty Dostoevsky adaptation is as fascinating as it is dark. Bresson discovered Sanda modeling in a fashion magazine. She was only 16 when she made *A Gentle Creature*, and it launched her movie career. Bresson used all of his directorial skills to reinforce the somber, claustrophobic feelings of the wife trapped by her petty, greedy pawnbroker of a husband. The work is both erotic and profoundly psychological in its disjointed narrative that builds a portrait of this ill-fated relationship.

Bresson's somber, serious, ascetic films were slow to garner acclaim. In France, he never received the cult fanfare awarded his contemporary New Wave filmmakers. Although most of his films were not distributed in the United States, *A Gentle Creature* was. *The Hollywood Reporter* declared it: "a careful, serious, and perfectly crafted film."

155 *La Femme infidèle (The Unfaithful Wife)* 1969 Color *Director* Claude Chabrol; *Producer* Films la Boëtie, Cinegay; *Screenplay* Claude Chabrol; *Photography* Jean Rabier; *Music* Pierre Jansen; *Set* Guy Littaye; *Editing* Jacques Gaillard. Running time: 98 minutes.

Cast: Stéphane Audran, Michel Bouquet, Maurice Ronet, Stéphane de Napoli; Michael Duchaussoy, Guy Marly, Serge Bento, Louise Chevalier, Louise Rioton, Henri Marteau, François Moro-Giafferi, Dominique Zardi, Michel Charrel, Henri Attal, Jean-Marie Arnoux, Donatella Turri.

An insurance salesman, Charles (Bouquet), suspects that his beautiful wife, Hélène (Audran), is cheating on him. The private detective he hires discovers that she is having an affair with a Parisian writer, Pégala (Ronet). When Charles goes to his house to confront Pégala, he first chats with him about his wife and then when jealousy overtakes him, he kills Pégala. Before the police arrest Charles, he and Hélène rediscover their passion.

One of Chabrol's greatest films once again tackles the turbulence beneath the calm and proper surface of a bourgeois life. Deceit, deception, murder and mystery are handled with a fine intelligence and sophistication, which are qualities his characters possess as well. It also stars his wife Stéphane Audran, who starred in *The Butcher.*

The Unfaithful Wife is universally acknowledged as Chabrol's best bedroom film. One critic declared: "The suspense is there, in the pure Hitchcockian tradition." When it came out in the United States, Margot Kernan of *Film Quarterly* exclaimed: "Few directors are more skillful at using a sensuous cinematic style to suggest a world of minimal feelings and reified relationships."

156 *La Femme Nikita* 1990 Color   *Director* Luc Besson; *Producer* tk; *Screenplay* Luc Besson; *Photography* Thierry Arbogast; *Music* Eric Serra; *Set* Dan Weil; *Sound* Pierre Befve and Gérard Lamps; *Costumes* Anne Angelini; *Editing* Olivier Mauffroy. Running time: 115 minutes.

Cast: Annie Parillaud, Jean-Hughes Anglade, Tcheky Karyo, Jeanne Moreau, Jean Reno, Jean Bouise, Philippe du Anerand, Roland Blanche, Philippe Leroy-Beaulieu, Marc Duret, Jacques Boudet.

A thriller and a love story about a convicted murderess who is given the choice between being executed and becoming a highly trained government agent. She opts for life, is declared dead and then is confined to a high-tech training center. Despite Nikita's violent rebellions, one agent, Bob (Karyo), believes he can train her. After months of grueling classes and workouts and some brutal government assignments, Nikita (Parillaud) evolves from a heartless street punk into a sophisticated, sensitive agent. But her troubles do not end there.

One of the most stylish modern thrillers, *La Femme Nikita* proved that French films can combine sex and violence with unparalleled Gallic flair. The film was the biggest grossing film in France the year it came out and set the all-time single-week record for a French language film in England. Made when Besson was 31 years old, this is his fourth feature. It contains his trademark sleek, modern style. "What I had wanted to show is that we shouldn't be to quick to judge people who seem, on the face of things, unredeemable," said Besson of the film. "Society doesn't forgive. Realistically, everyone of us would judge Nikita and find her guilty, and yet in the film we surprise ourselves when we find her beautiful, and begin to love her and hope that she can make good." When he met Annie Parillaud he wanted to cast her in a movie, so he wrote *Nikita*. Not only did she prove to be perfect for the role, Besson married her.

Critics and audiences loved *La Femme Nikita*. It was nominated for nine Césars. Besson was asked to make an American adaptation, but backed out of the deal when he learned they wanted a shot-for-shot remake in English with American stars. A different director made *Point of No Return* with Bridget Fonda, and even though he did copy Besson's film virtually frame for frame, it does not hold a candle to the original. One American critic raved when *Nikita* was released: "Imagine

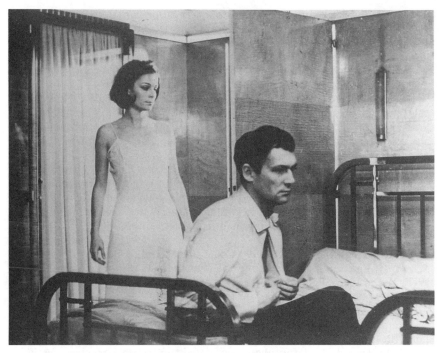

Le Feu follet (The Fire Within), 1963; directed by Louis Malle.

A Clockwork Orange transported from London to Paris in the post-feminist, post-punkish 1990s. That's only a hint of the perverse delights of *La Femme Nikita*, an exotic thriller and the hippest new movie of the year."

157 *La Femme qui pleure (The Crying Woman)*   1978 Color   *Director* Jacques Doillon; *Producer* La Guéville, Lola Films, Renn Productions; *Screenplay* Jacques Doillon; *Photography* Yves Lafaye; *Sound* Michel Kharat; *Editing* Isabelle Rathery. Running time: 90 minutes.

Cast: Dominique Laffin, Jacques Doillon, Haydée Politoff, Lola Doillon, J.D. Robert, Michel Vivian.

A woman, Dominique (Laffin), has been left by her husband (Doillon) for another woman (Politoff). She will do anything to get him back. One day, she calls both the husband and his lover and asks them to come over because their little girl has had an accident. First, she uses the opportunity to try to befriend the other woman, who leaves once she figures out what is going on. Then she tries to make up with her husband before finally leaving with the child.

This semi-autobiographical film, which Doillon wrote, directed and starred in, is an example of a new intimacy in French film, which characterized much of French filmmaking in the 1980s. Doillon wanted to present the interior lives of complicated liberated people, who were captive to feelings of jealousy and passion, despite their good, liberal intentions. It is a psychological portrait and a bittersweet story about a struggle to regain love lost. Unfortunately, as divorce is a growing phenomenon in France, its poignancy spoke to many. When Doillon could not get the actor he wanted to play the lead, he decided to play it himself. Much of the film was shot at his country house and his daughter plays his daughter.

French critics applauded Doillon's elegant, sophisticated tone. *Cahiers du Cinéma* declared that the film established Doillon among the most exciting filmmakers at work. The film has never been distributed in the United States.

158 *Le Feu follet (The Fire Within or A Time to Live and a Time to Die)* 1963 B&W *Director* Louis Malle; *Producer* Nouvelles Editions de Films; *Screenplay* Louis Malle, based on the novel by Pierre Drieu La Rochelle; *Photography* Ghislain Cloquet; *Music* Erik Satie; *Set* Bernard Evein; *Sound* Guy Villette; *Editing* Suzanne Baron. Running time: 104 minutes.

Cast: Maurice Ronet, Jeanne Moreau, Jean-Paul Moulinot, Mona Dol, Alexandra Stewart, Léna Skerla, Hubert Deschamps, Yvonne Clech, Pierre-Jacques Moncorbier, René Dupuy, Bernard Tiphaine, Bernard Noël, Ursula Kubler, Alain Mottet, François Gragnon, Romain Bouteille, Jacques Sereys, Tony Taffin, Henri Serre, Claude Deleusse, Madeleine Declercq, Véra Valdez, Michèle Mahaut, France Arnell.

After going through a detoxification program, alcoholic writer and playboy Alain Leroy (Ronet) decides he has no reason left to live. Once he picks the day for his death, he decides to spend his last 48 hours reviewing his life. But he finds no solace in the company of his friends. He gets completely drunk at a dinner party, and the following morning he shoots himself in the heart.

One of Malle's best pictures, if not his best, *The Fire Within* is a poignant exploration of human anguish. Adapted from the 1931 novel by Pierre Drieu La Rochelle, which was based on the surrealist writer Jacques Rigaut's suicide in 1929, the film is a shockingly realistic portrait of a man on the verge of suicide. After collaborating with the Nazis in World War II, La Rochelle himself committed suicide in 1945. The film was not a commercial success, despite its critical acclaim. "It is such a harsh subject and it's such a depressing movie," said Malle of why it failed to attract audiences. Maurice Ronet plays the desperate and doomed man beautifully; he believed it was the greatest role of his career.

When *The Fire Within* came out, many critics lauded the film as touching. One wrote, "a poignant film which touches us at the most profound level, even if the pitiable 'hero' is really nothing more than an old dandy." Others faulted Malle for not making Ronet more complicated. It won the Special Jury Prize at the Venice Biennal in 1963.

159 *La Fiancée du pirate (A Very Curious Girl or Dirty Mary or Pirate's Fiancée)* 1969 Color *Director* Nelly Kaplan; *Producer* Cythère Films; *Screenplay* Nelly Kaplan, Claude Makovski, Serguine and Michel Fabre; *Photography* Jean Badal; *Music* Georges Moustaki; *Set* Michel Landi, Jean-Claude Landi and P. Lafarge; *Sound* Claude Jauvert, P. Brisson and J. Lebreton; *Editing* Gérard Pollicand. Running time: 102 minutes.

Cast: Bernadette Lafont, Georges Géret, Michel Constantin, Claire Maurier, Gilberte Géniat, Renée Duncan, Julien Guiomar, Jean Parédès, Jacques Marin, Claire Olivier, Henri Czarniak, Mischa Bayard, Marcel Pérès, Pascal Mazzotti, Jacques Masson, Fernand Berset, Francis Lax, Louis Malle, Claude Makovski.

A pretty young peasant woman, Marie (Lafont), lives with her mother in horrible poverty in the country. Though all of the village men pursue her, she refuses their advances. When her mother dies in an accident, the people of the village refuse to help her pay for a proper burial. As revenge, Marie seduces the men of the town and records their most intimate secrets, which she then plays one morning over the town's loudspeaker.

This moral comedy shows social hypocrisy at its worst. When the film came out in 1969, the idea of a revolt against established society and bourgeoisie morality was in step with the mood in France. Kaplan saw her first feature as the tale of a "curious girl who teaches the leading citizens of a small French village a thing or two about life." Lafont, who was one of the preferred leading ladies of the New Wave directors, is wonderfully sensual as Marie. The film contains one of the first explicit lesbian love scenes in film and is often included in feminist and women's film festivals.

Marjorie Rosen of *Millimeter* described *A Very Curious Girl* as one of her favorite films because it is "a movie screaming with rage and indignation at woman's condition (indeed, it's the angriest movie by a woman I've ever seen) and also because the director rejects rhetoric, venting her outrage within the confines of a bizarre and witty black comedy." The film was the official French entry at the thirtieth International Film Art Festival in Venice in 1969.

The Fiends *see* **Les Diaboliques**

160 *Un Fils unique (An Only Son)* 1969 B&W   *Director* Michel Polac; *Producer* ORTF; *Screenplay* Michel Polac; *Photography* Eric Dalmat; *Music* Jean Drouet; *Sound* Mario Vinck; *Editing* Hervé Basle. Running time: 80 minutes.

Cast: Eric Ancian, Serge Hureau, Guy Schoeller, Eleanor Fronel, Francis Bouvet, Guy Schoeller, Paul Vanier-Baulier.

The story of a boy, Eric (Ancian), who is unhappy in his family life. When he finds a portrait of his mother, he becomes desperate to find the painter. He grows convinced that the painter is his real father and he dreams of escape.

A tender, perceptive movie about adolescent angst, which caught the mood of an entire country when it was made. Originally shot as a 16-millimeter film, this movie captured the prize for best first feature and was then blown up to 35 millimeter to be distributed to movie theaters. The director is a novelist, and his literary style comes through in this film. He used non-actors and created the wonderful adolescent world that Truffaut, Vigo, and Malle have also evoked.

Critics either loved its rough, literary intimacy or found it rambling and amateurish. It won the Prix Georges Sadoul in 1969.

Finally, Sunday *see* **Vivement dimanche**

The Fingerman *see* **Le Doulos**

The Fire Within *see* **Le Feu follet**

The Five-Legged Sheep *see* **Le Mouton à cinq pattes**

Forbidden Games *see* **Jeux interdits**

The 400 Blows *see* Les Quatre Cent Coups

Frantic *see* L'Ascenseur pour l'échafaud

Fraudulent Death *see* Mort en fraude

French Can Can *see* French Cancan

161 *French Cancan (French Can Can)* 1954 Color *Director* Jean Renoir; *Producer* Franco-London Films, Jolly Films; *Screenplay* Jean Renoir; *Photography* Michel Kléber; *Music* Georges Van Parys; *Set* Max Douy; *Sound* Antoine Petitjean; *Costumes* Rosine Delamare; *Editing* Boris Lewin. Running time: 104 minutes.

Cast: Françoise Arnoul, Jean Gabin, Maria Félix, Gianni Esposito, Edith Piaf, Valentine Tessier, Jean-Roger Caussimon, Philippe Clay, Max Dalban, Franco Pastorino, Dora Doll, Michel Piccoli, Jean Parédès, Michèle Philippe, Lydia Johnson, Annick Morice, Jacques Jouanneau, Jean-Marc Tennberg, Pierre Olaf, Gaston Gabaroche, Hubert Deschamps, Albert Rémy, Patachou, Anne-Marie Mersen, Philippe Clay, Gaston Modot, André Claveau, Albert Rémy, Jean Raymond, Jaque-Catelian, Jacques Marin, Léo Campion, René-Jean Chauffard, Lia Amendola, France Roche, Paquerette, François Jous, Palmyre Levasseur, André Numès, Sylviane Delannoy, Jean Sylvère, Michèle Nadal, Pierre-Jacques Moncorbier, Rosy Varte, Jean Mortier, Laurence Bataille, Jacques Hilling, Ursula Kubler, Jacques Ciron, Claude Arnay, Anna Amendola, Claude Berri, Paul Mercey, Martine Alexis, René Pascal, Carine Jansen, Henri-Roland Hercé, Maïa Jusanova, Dorothée Balnk, Bruno Balp.

The backdrop of this wonderful film is the backstage world of the music halls of Montmartre during the grand opening of the Moulin Rouge. Danglard (Gabin) is a master of metamorphosis, who turns French working girls into cabaret stars. But when he discovers a beautiful laundress, Nini (Arnoul), and decides to make her the queen of the Moulin Rouge, his jealous mistress (Félix) tries to keep the show from going on. Nini and the French cancan triumph.

A beautiful ode to the French music halls, which has inspired comparisons to the Impressionist paintings of Degas, Renoir and Toulouse-Lautrec. The talent of Renoir found a wonderful showplace in the music hall sequences with fabulous dancing and costumes. Gabin is wonderful. Arnoul gives the performance of her life.

While critics just about unanimously agree that *French Cancan* is not Renoir's best movie, they do admit it is a visual extravaganza.

The French Conspiracy *see* L'Attentat

The French Plot *see* L'Attentat

French Provincial *see* Souvenirs d'en France

162 *Les Fruits amers (Bitter Fruit)* 1966 Color *Director* Jacqueline Audry; *Producer* Terra Films, Avala Film, Bosna Film, Prodi Cinematografica, Le Terrier; *Screenplay* Colette and Jacques Audry, based on the play by Colette

Audry; *Photography* Maurice Fellous; *Music* Joseph Kosma; *Sound* Pierre Calvet; *Editing* Francine Gruber. Running time: 108 minutes.

Cast: Emmanuelle Riva, Laurent Terzieff, Beba Loncar, Roger Coggio, Rick Battaglia.

The story of a group of revolutionaries in South America and what happens when one of the members is arrested. Soledad (Riva) loves the leader of the band Sebastien (Battaglia). When she is arrested, her sister Tita (Loncar) offers herself to the chief of police to save Soledad's life. Soledad kills the chief of police to revenge her sister, but Tita had really loved him.

Based on a French play, this film explores a 1960s issue of how to reconcile revolutionary social aims with personal, emotional needs. Despite some far-fetched plot twists, the meditations on the costs of fighting for a cause are well drawn. Emmanuelle Riva, who rose to international prominence in *Hiroshima, mon amour*, does a very good job.

Some critics were not fans. *Variety*, for instance, called it "talky, lifeless." But many critics found the film to be intelligent and original. It won the Grand Prix du Cinéma Français in 1966.

163 *Les Fugitifs (The Fugitives or Three Fugitives)*   1986 Color   *Director* Francis Veber; *Producer* Fideline Films; *Screenplay* Francis Veber; *Photography* Luciano Tovoli; *Music* Vladimir Cosma; *Set* Gérard Daoudal; *Sound* Jean-Pierre Ruh; *Editing* Marie-Sophie Dubus. Running time: 89 minutes.

Cast: Gérard Depardieu, Pierre Richard, Anaïs Bret, Jean Carmet, Maurice Barrier, Jean Benguigui, Roland Blanche, Michel Blanc, Philippe Lelièvre, Yveline Ailhaud, Didier Pain, Michel Berto.

A comedy about a professional bank robber, Jean Lucas (Depardieu), who, when he is released from prison, decides to go straight. He is taken hostage by an amateur robber, François Pignon (Richard), and is forced to return to the life of crime. After a botched hold-up the two have to run from the police and when Lucas is charmed by Pignon's little girl, he decides not to abandon Pignon, but to help them reach the border safely.

This was Veber's third comedy with the hilarious odd couple of Depardieu and Richard, and it is as good as French comedy gets. The two Gallic goofballs, who appeared in Veber's *The Goat* and *The Co-Fathers*, complement each other wonderfully.

The film was a huge hit. *Présence du Cinéma Français* declared Veber had reached a new level for "alongside outright comedy, Francis Veber has created moments of optimism and tenderness." French critics declared *The Fugitives* "the height of film comedy." Hollywood gave it their highest form of praise by making a poor American version.

Fugitive in Saigon *see* **Mort en fraude**

The Fugitives *see* **Les Fugitifs**

Full Moon Over Paris *see* **Les Nuits de la pleine lune**

The Game of Love *see* **Le Blé en herbe**

The Gang of Four *see* **La Bande des quatres**

164 *Garde à vue (The Inquisitor)* 1981 Color   *Director* Claude Miller; *Producer* Ariane Films, TF1 Films Productions; *Screenplay* Claude Miller, Jean Herman and Michel Audiard, based on John Wainwright's novel *Brainwash*; *Photography* Bruno Nuytten; *Music* Georges Delerue; *Set* Eric Moulard and Lam-Lé; *Sound* Paul Laîné; *Editing* Albert Jurgenson. Running time: 90 minutes.

Cast: Lino Ventura, Michel Serrault, Romy Schneider, Guy Marchand, Elsa Lunghini, Jean-Claude Penchenat, Pierre Maguelon, Michel Such, Mathieu Schiffman, Patrick Depeyrrat, Yves Pignot, Didier Agostini, Serge Malik, Mohammed Bekireche.

A very respectable man, Jérome Martinaud (Serrault), is suspected of killing two young girls. He is held overnight, and the police questioning him are convinced of his guilt. After grueling hours of interrogation and because his own life is so unsatisfactory, Martinaud gives up arguing his innocence. Finally, he is released because a piece of evidence clears him, only to learn that his wife has killed herself.

This is one of France's best modern police thrillers, which plays cat and mouse with one character's image and reality. Miller's masterful direction allows the audience to see Martinaud in every possible light. It has been called a *No Exit* like film, because of the isolation of the police inspector who must rely on his hunches; of the accused who must try in vain to convince people of his innocence; and of the wife of the accused who is tormented by her doubts and her fears. Ventura and Serrault deliver some of the finest performances of their careers.

The critics were bowled over by the brilliance of Serrault's performance. The film won four Césars and the Grand Prix du Cinéma Français and was co-winner of the French Critics' Prix Méliès in 1981.

Gates of Lilacs *see* **Porte des Lilas**

Gates of Paris *see* **Porte des Lilas**

Gates of the Night *see* **Les Portes de la nuit**

165 *Le Genou de Claire (Claire's Knee)* 1970 Color   *Director* Eric Rohmer; *Producer* Films du Losange; *Screenplay* Eric Rohmer; *Photography* Nestor Almendros; *Sound* Jean-Pierre Ruh; *Editing* Cécile Decugis. Running time: 105 minutes.

Cast: Jean-Claude Brialy, Aurora Cornu, Beatrice Romand, Laurence de Monaghan, Michèle Montel, Gérard Falconetti, Fabrice Luchini, Sandro Franchina, Isabelle Pons.

A young diplomat and former lady's man (Brialy), staying in a resort town, where he waits for his fiancée to arrive from Stockholm, meets an old friend (Cornu). The friend introduces the diplomat to the family he is staying with and the young diplomat becomes obsessed with the daughter's knee. As he is committed to another woman, he can not bear to act upon his desire. His struggle is presented in the very comic, intelligent, sophisticated way of Rohmer.

This is the fifth of Rohmer's "Six Moral Tales." In his novelization, *Six Contes moraux*, Rohmer wrote: "One of the reasons that these Tales are called 'Moral' is that physical actions are almost completely absent: everything happens in the head of the narrator." The film is beautifully photographed, well acted, and deliciously visual and intellectual. Despite Rohmer's verbal acrobatics, he manages to evoke a great humanity. While the knee has a particular erotic fascination in France where poets have long written odes to the knee, the intense fetish quality of the taboo to a man about to be married is an idea that travels easily.

When the film came out in the United States, Vincent Canby of *The New York Times* wrote: "*Claire's Knee* has the qualities of pure crystal — it is original, complete, mysterious, clear...." It won the Prix Louis Delluc in 1970 and the French Critics' Prix Méliès and the National Society of Film Critics' Award as the Best Movie in 1971.

A Gentle Creature *see* **Une Femme douce**

166 *Gervaise*   1956 B&W   *Director* René Clément; *Producer* Silver Films, Agnès Delahaie, Cinematographiques; *Screenplay* Jean Aurenche, Pierre Bost, and René Clément, based on Emile Zola's novel *L'Assommier*; *Photography* Robert Juillard; *Music* Georges Auric; *Set* Paul Bertrand; *Sound* Antoine Archimbaud; *Costumes* Mayo; *Editing* Henri Rust. Running time: 111 minutes.

Cast: Maria Schell, François Périer, Suzy Delair, Armand Mestral, Jacques Harden, Jany Holt, Hubert de Lapparent, Mathilde Casadesus, Jacques Hilling, Ariane Lancel, Lucien Hubert, Amédée, Micheline Luccioni, Florelle, Yvonne Claudie, André Wasley, Chantal Gozzi, Christian Denhez, Christian Ferez, Patrice Catineaud, Yvette Cuvelier, Rachel Devirys, Pierre Duverger, Jacqueline Morane, Yvonne Dany, Palmyre Levasseur, Aram Stephan, Pierre Duverger, Jo Peignot, Max Elbèze, Jean Relet, Roger Dalphin, Armand Lurville, Jean Gautrat, Gilbert Sanjakian, Georges Paulais, Gérard Darrieu, Bernard Musson, Jean Daurand, Pascal Bessy.

Set in nineteenth century Montmartre, this is the story of Gervaise (Schell), a poor washerwoman abandoned by her lover. Left to cope with two children, she marries a sweet, dependable roofer named Coupeau (Périer). They find a brief happiness when they have a little girl, Nana (Gozzi), together. But when Coupeau is injured in an accident at work, he begins to drink. A series of additional misfortunes, both personal and financial, push Gervaise to drink as well. With both of her parents now alcoholics, Nana is left to fend for herself.

An example of cinematic realism in the literary tradition, this is the tragedy and misery of Zola beautifully, if somberly, rendered. Though Zola's novel focused more on alcoholism as a central subject, the movie presents Gervaise as the subject and alcoholism is just one of her many problems. Clément directs a beautiful movie with wonderful performances, but like so many Zola works this material is markedly depressing. It was quite a departure for Clément, as he primarily directed comedies not dramas, or in this case, tragedies. He was a stickler for historical accuracy, even installing an actual public wash house from the period on the set. In *Gervaise* Schell gives her greatest performance. Zola wanted to document working-class life in all its dirty detail, and Clément faithfully rendered his wish.

Some found it too perfectly "set" for the subject matter, others applauded the historical veracity. It won the Volpi Cup for Best Film at the Venice Biennal, was nominated for the Oscar for Best Foreign Film and won the New York Film Critics'

Award for Best Foreign Film in 1956. Maria Schell also won the prize for Best Actress at Venice.

Get Out Your Handkerchiefs *see* **Préparez vos mouchoirs**

The Ghost *see* **Un Revenant**

167 *La Gifle (The Slap)* 1974 Color *Director* Claude Pinoteau; *Producer* Gaumont; *Screenplay* Claude Pinoteau and Jean-Louis Dabadie; *Photography* Jean Collomb; *Music* Georges Delerue; *Editing* Marie-Josèphe Yoyotte. Running time: 100 minutes.

Cast: Lino Ventura, Annie Giradot, Isabelle Adjani, Jacques Spiesser, Francis Perrin, Nicole Courcel, Georges Wilson, Charles Gérard, Arlette Gordon.

A comedy about a geography professor (Ventura) who is raising his daughter (Adjani) alone. She is 18 and wants to get out from under his parental thumb, but when she fails an exam, the crisis comes to a head.

This wonderful domestic comedy was Pinoteau's first feature. He manages to mix comedy with tenderness and deliver a delicate treatment to weighty issues. It revealed Pinoteau to be an understudy to such great documenters of the French homelife scene as Chabrol. Generational conflicts were at the forefront of many people's minds in this era, and this film was unusual in its light handling of explosive material. Adjani, Ventura and Giradot, who plays the estranged mother, are all wonderful.

The film did well in France and only so-so in the United States. When it was released in the United States, *The New York Times*' Richard Eder saw "sparks of humor and style...." Andrew Sarris of *The Village Voice* wrote: "I did enjoy [it] even though it was something of a mess structurally and stylistically." The film won the Prix Louis Delluc in 1974, and Adjani won Best Actress of the Year from the National Society of Film Critics.

The Girl and the River *see* **L'Eau vive**

The Goat *see* **La Chèvre**

God Has Need of Men *see* **Dieu a besoin des hommes**

Going Places *see* **Les Valseuses**

The Golden Coach *see* **La Carrosse d'or**

Golden Marie *see* **Casque d'or**

The Good Girls *see* **Les Bonnes Femmes**

The Good Life *see* **La Belle Vie**

Good Lord Without Confession *see* **Le Bon Dieu sans confession**

Goodbye, Children *see* **Au revoir les enfants**

168 *Le Grand Amour (The Great Love)* 1969 Color   *Director* Pierre Etaix; *Producer* CAPAC, Madeleine Films, Productions de la Guéville; *Screenplay* Pierre Etaix and Jean-Claude Carrière; *Photography* Jean Boffety; *Music* Claude Stiermans; *Set* Daniel Louradour; *Sound* Jean Bertrand; *Editing* Henri Lanoë. Running time: 86 minutes.

Cast: Pierre Etaix, Annie Fratellini, Nicole Kalfan, Louis Maïss, Alain Janey, Ketty France, Jacqueline Rouillard, Claude Massot, Jean-Pierre Helga, Jean Beretta, Loriot, Renée Gardès, Odette Duc, Denise Péronne, Magali Clément, Josette Poirier, Paule Marin, Sandra Fratellini, Rolph Zavatta, Billy Bourbon, Luc Delhumeau, Georges Montax, Emile Coryn, Gino Fratellini, Tino Fratellini.

Pierre (Etaix) marries his wife, Florence (Fratellini), more from a sense of duty than from love. After 15 years of marriage, he is bored and spends much of his time daydreaming. When his sexy, new 19-year-old secretary, Agnès (Kalfan), walks into his ho-hum world, he thinks that he has found the key to changing his life, until he realizes how absurd the situation is and goes back to his wife.

This amusing film by one of France's most talented directors is more a collection of observations than a narrative. Pierre Etaix is a comic author, director and actor all rolled into one, and he showcases all of his talents in this zany film. The wedding scene, which plays with the various characters unspoken motives and musings, is memorable, and the movie's gags occasionally take off into the realm of the surreal.

Variety's reviewer lauded *The Great Love* as "a film of disarming charm." The film won the Grand Prix du Cinéma Français in 1969.

169 *Le Grand Bleu (The Big Blue)* 1988 Color   *Director* Luc Besson; *Producer* Gaumont; *Screenplay* Luc Besson, Robert Garland, based on a story by Luc Besson; *Photography* Carlo Varini; *Music* Eric Serra; *Set* Dan Weil; *Sound* Pierre Befve, Pierre Excoffier, Gérard Lamps, François Groult, Jacques-Thomas Gérard; *Editing* Olivier Mauffroy. Running time: 190 minutes.

Cast: Jean-Marc Barr, Jean Reno, Rosanna Arquette, Jean Bouise, Paul Shenar, Sergio Castellitto, Marc Duret, Griffin Dunne, Andreas Voutsinas, Valentine Vargas, Kimberly Beck, Patrick Fontana, Alessandra Vazzoler, Geoffrey Carey, Constantin Alexandrov, Claude Besson, Bruce Guerre-Berthelot, Gregory Forstner, Marika Gevaudan, Peter Semler.

As a child on a Mediterranean island, Jacques Mayol (Barr) watched his father, a diver, die before his eyes when his breathing tube blocked underwater. Thirty years later, an American girl (Arquette), who is working with a professor researching ice diving, meets Jacques and they fall in love. Jacques and his childhood friend and competitor, Enzo (Reno), compete for the free diving record, plunging to the greatest depth without breathing apparatus. But even when the competition is over, they continue trying to best each other, even after the professor has told them the depths they are attaining are dangerous. Enzo dies while diving off the island they grew up on. Though Johanna is pregnant, Jacques cannot stop diving.

This film is a wonderful mix of outdoor adventure and romance. Besson based the film on his own childhood memories of diving and the true experiences of the legendary free diver Jacques Mayol, who worked on the film as a technical director. It was Besson's first and only English-language film. The underwater shots and special effects are spectacular, as is the film's soundtrack, which went platinum in France.

The film was a huge hit when it debuted at the Cannes Film Festival. Word quickly spread to the United States, where a shorter version became a cult favorite. *Sight and Sound* called it an "infuriatingly erratic combination of the breathtaking and the banal." Lloyd Sachs of the *Chicago-Sun Times* said, "On the whole, it's a reasonably intelligent and frequently enchanting fantasy, populated by characters who are fun to spend time with."

170 *Le Grand Chemin (The Grand Highway* or *On Pain of Love)* 1987 Color   *Director* Jean-Loup Hubert; *Producer* Pascal Hommais, Jean-François Lepetit; *Screenplay* Jean-Loup Hubert; *Photography* Claude Lecomte; *Music* Georges Granier; *Set* Thierry Flamand; *Sound* Bernard Aubouy; *Costumes* Annick François; *Editing* Raymonde Guyot. Running time: 106 minutes.

Cast: Anémone, Richard Bohringer, Antoine Hubert, Vanessa Guej, Christine Pascal, Raoul Billerey, Pascale Roberts, Marie Matheron, Daniel Rialet, Jean-François Derec, André Lacombe, Denise Péron, Jean Cherlian, Eugénie Charpentier, Thierry Flammand, Marcelle Lucas, Jeanne Allaire, Christine Aubert, Robert Averty, Marie-Thérèse Allaire.

Set in the 1950s, a coming-of-age movie about nine-year-old Louis (Hubert), a boy from Paris who spends a summer in the Breton countryside with a childhood friend of his mother's, Marcelle (Anémone), and her husband, Pelo (Bohringer), the local carpenter. From a young country girl he learns about love, and from the couple, whom he grows to adore, he learns about loss. Through Louis, the couple rediscovers their love for each other, which had disappeared when their child died years before. When Louis returns to the city, it is with knowledge and regret.

In the great tradition of French coming-of-age films, this film was the surprise hit of 1987. It may follow a traditional narrative, but its surprising freshness and sincerity made it the second most popular film in France in 1987, after *The Name of the Rose*. Very autobiographical, the film is based on Hubert's memories of the village in which he grew up. He cast his own son, Antoine, who had no acting experience, to play the part that he most identified with, Louis. The film proved that even in modern times a movie without sex and violence could become a huge hit, renewing faith in the fundamentals of French filmmaking.

French critics lauded its originality, authenticity and depth of emotion. American critics such as Andrew Sarris compared it to the Swedish film *My Life as a Dog*. The film was nominated for five Césars. Both Anémone and Bohringer won Césars for Best Actress and Best Actor in 1987.

The Grand Highway *see* **Le Grand Chemin**

The Grand Maneuver *see* **Les Grandes Manoeuvres**

171 *La Grande Bouffe (The Grande Bouffe* or *The Big Feast* or *The Great Feed* or *Blow-Out)* 1973 Color   *Director* Marco Ferreri; *Producer* A. Salfa; *Screenplay* Marco Ferreri and Rafael Azcona; *Photography* Mario Vulpiani; *Music* Philippe Sarde; *Set* Michel de Brois; *Costumes* Gitt Magrini; *Editing* Claudine Merlin. Running time: 125 minutes.

Cast: Marcello Mastroianni Ugo Tognazzi, Michel Piccoli, Philippe Noiret, Andrea Ferreol, Monique Chaumette, Florence Giorgetti, Solange Blondeau, Michèle Alexandre, Rita Scherer, Eva Simonet, Henri Piccoli, Maurice Dorléac.

La Grande Bouffe (*The Grande Bouffe*), **1973; directed by Marco Ferreri.**

A comedy about four friends, a judge (Noiret), a restaurateur (Tognazzi), a pilot (Mastroianni) and a television director (Piccoli), who decide to give up humdrum daily life by gorging themselves to death. They hole up in a house in Paris, hire prostitutes and order supplies for an eternal banquet. A schoolteacher (Ferreol) joins them in their gourmet death quest and becomes their angel of death.

Director Marco Ferreri has been called the "master of bad taste," and this proves to be his ultimate testament to grand trash. It is a black comedy about overindulgence that verges on the repulsive and a satire on the consumer society and its quest for constant, immediate gratification. When the film was chosen to represent France at the Cannes Film Festival, its selection caused a huge scandal. Some even believe that it cost one of its backers his job as head of the governmental Centre du Cinéma. There was also a rumor that Catherine Deneuve blew up at her lover Mastroianni for appearing in such filth.

French critics hailed it as one of the great film comments of the 1970s, because it was a moral condemnation of wealthy countries and their excessive and selfish ways. Earl Wilson of *The New York Post*, however, called it "the most revolting, stomach-turning picture I've ever seen."

The Grande Bouffe *see* **La Grande Bouffe**

172 *La Grande Lessive! (The Big Wash!)* 1968 *Director* Jean-Pierre Mocky; *Producer* Méditerranée Cinéma Productions, Balzac Films, Firmament Films; *Screenplay* Jean-Pierre Mocky, Claude Pennec; *Adaptation* Alain Moury; *Photography* Marcel Weiss; *Music* François de Roubaix; *Set* Pierre Tyberghien; *Sound* René Sarrazin; *Editing* Marguerite Renoir. Running time: 95 minutes.

Cast: Bourvil, Jean Poiret, Francis Blanche, Michel Lonsdale, Karin Balm, Jean Tissier, Marcel Pérès, Roland Dubillard, Alix Mahieux, René-Jacques Chauffard, Roger Legris, Mischa Bayard, Jean-Claude Rémoleux, Numès Fils, Ruddy Lenoir, Philippe Brizard, René Gardès, René Fleur, Luc Delhumeau, Roger Lumont, Simone Duhart, Albert Pilette, Henri Poirier, Philippe Castelli, Daniel Crohem, Jean-Michel Molé, Pierre Durou, Jo Labarrère, Christian Chevreuse, Jean-Marie Richiez, Luc Andrieu, Claude Legros, Roland Malet, Marius Gaidon, Emile Riandreys, Agostino Castro, Jean-Marie Vayne, Maria Goud, Robert Andreozzi, Nicole Chaumeau, Georges Bruce, Françoise Arnaud, Frédéric Magne, Edith Ker, Raymond Tyczka.

A comedy about a literature teacher, Armand Saint-Just (Bourvil), who is so fed up with his students' lack of interest that he decides to sabotage their television antennas. He enlists the school's gym teacher and a young engineer, and the three cross the rooftops of Paris to accomplish their attack on the "boob tube." He is so thrilled when he gets away with his initial venture that he decides to rid the entire country of television. The police get involved and Saint-Just ends up taking refuge on the Eiffel Tower where he finally explains his purpose.

A riotous film that celebrates anarchy and individual obsession and, in Mocky's deft hands, makes for hilarious comedy. Bourvil's character was compared to a modern-day Don Quixote let loose across the rooftops of Paris. It requires a strong suspension of disbelief, but this comedy is sweet and funny. France's adoration for Mocky may not be easy to explain, but it is probably connected to their love for Jerry Lewis, and it is certainly part of their cinematic heritage.

This was Mocky's biggest commercial success. Critics, who were generally less kind to Mocky than his loyal fans, gave him some credit for his gentle humor, but complained that he took a simple idea too far.

173 *Les Grandes Manœuvres (The Grand Maneuver* or *Summer Manœuvres)* 1955 Color *Director* René Clair; *Producer* Filmsonor, Rizzoli;

Screenplay René Clair and Jérôme Géromini; *Photography* Robert Lefebvre and René Juillard; *Music* Georges Van Parys; *Set* Max Douy; *Sound* Antoine Petit-jean; *Costumes* Rosine Delamare; *Editing* Louisette Hautecoeur. Running time: 107 minutes.

Cast: Gérard Philipe, Michèle Morgan, Yves Robert, Jean Desailly, Brigitte Bardot, Lise Delamare, Simone Valère, Jacques François, Jacqueline Maillan, Magali Noël, Dany Carrel, Catherine Anouilh, Pierre Dux, Olivier Hussenot, Jacques Fabbri, Arlette Thomas, France Asselin, Gabrielle Fontan, Hélène Duc, Raymond Cordy, Madeleine Barbulée, Jacqueline Marbaux, Bruno Balp, Georges Bever, Colette Castel, Paul Faivre, Jacques Jouanneau, Judith Magre, Pierre Palau, Daniel Sorano, Claude Rich, Jacques Morel, Jean-Pierre Maurain, Clé-ment Thierry, Bernard Dhéran, Charles Debert, Jean Bayle, Guy Cosson, Pierre Maréchal, Daniel Ceccaldi, Georges Carrère, Pierre Langlet, Claude Magnier, Michel Piccoli, Pierre Roussel, Roger Vincent, Eugène Stuber, Robert Thomas, Madeleine Ganne, Anne-Marie Mersen.

Set in a small garrison town just before World War I, a brilliant lieutenant, Armand de la Verne (Philipe), makes a bet in an attempt to kill the boredom he suffers while waiting for the fighting to begin. He vows he can make the modest Marie-Louise Rivière (Morgan) his mistress. When he falls truly in love with her, she learns that she was merely the object of a bet and breaks off the relationship. Heartbroken, de la Varne heads to war.

A shining example of "poetic realism," this beautiful film was Clair's first color picture. It was the first time that he made a film that was not predominantly humorous, and it proved he could make a very moving film. He called it a love adventure, and considered ending it with a suicide scene, but decided against it in the editing room. Philipe and Morgan present one of the decade's most memorable pair of lovers. It is said that after a screening in Russia, a member of the audience said the film was "lacking in seriousness." "Lacking in seriousness?" Clair replied. "It deals only with love," the Russian said. To which Clair retorted, "For us, love is a very serious matter."

Some critics believed this was Clair's best and most heartfelt picture. It won the Prix Louis Delluc and was co-winner of the French Critics' Prix Méliès in 1955.

The Great Feed *see* **La Grande Bouffe**

The Great Love *see* **Le Grand Amour**

The Great Spy Chase *see* **Les Tontons flingueurs**

The Green Room *see* **La Chambre verte**

Grisbi *see* **Touchez pas au Grisbi**

174 *La Guerre des boutons (War of the Buttons)*   1962 B&W   *Direc-tor* Yves Robert; *Producer* La Guéville; *Screenplay* Yves Robert and François Boyer, based on the novel by Louis Pergaud; *Photography* André Bac; *Music* José Berghmans; *Set* Pierre-Yves Thévenet; *Sound* Pierre Calvet; *Editing* Marie-Josèphe Yoyotte. Running time: 90 minutes.

Cast: Jacques Dufilho, Jean Richard, André Treton, Michel Isella, Paul

Crauchet, Michel Galabru, Pierre Trabaud, Henri Labussière, Yvette Etiévant, Martin Lartigue, Claude Confortès, Michèle Meritz, Robert Rollis, Pierre Tchernia, Louisette Rousseau, Jean-Paul Quéret, Yves Peneau, François Boyer.

A comedy about a war between the children of two neighboring villages. The two sides take their captives' buttons as war spoils, knowing the missing buttons will bring punishment from their parents. To avoid this, one side decides to fight naked and soundly defeats their rival gang. When the fighting gets out of hand, the parents enter the fray. They send the leaders of both gangs off together to the same reform school.

This adolescent anti-war platform was a great commercial success and ranks up there with *Goodbye Children*, *Small Change* and *Zero for Conduct* as one of the greatest movies to capture children's sensibility. It was one of the first movies to benefit from a government effort to help filmmakers by giving producers an advance on sales. The screenplay was taken from a good novel and turned into a very fun movie.

One of the biggest box-office hits in French history, critics and audiences adored *War of the Buttons*. It was co-winner of the Prix Vigo in 1962.

175 ***La Guerre du feu (Quest for Fire)*** 1981 Color   *Director* Jean-Jacques Annaud; *Producer* John Kemeny, Denis Héroux, Jacques Dormann, Vera Belmont; *Screenplay* Gérard Brach and Jean-Jacques Annaud, based on the novel of the same name by Joseph-Hénri Rosny; *Photography* Claude Agostini; *Music* Philippe Sarde; *Set* Guy Comtois; *Sound* Claude Hazanavicious; *Costumes* John Hay and Penny Rose; *Special Effects* Martin Malivoire; *Editing* Yves Langlois. Running time: 98 minutes.

Cast: Everett McGill, Rae Dawn Chong, Ron Perlman, Nameer El Kadi, Gary Schwarz, Frank Olivier Bonnet, Jean-Michel Kindt, Kurt Schiegl, Terry Fitt, Naseer El Kadi, Brian Gill, Michel Francomer, Peter Eliott, Josuah Melnick, Benoit Levesque, Butch Lynch, Dann Lynch, Luke McMasters, Adrian Street, Walter Masaï, Mohamed Siad Coockney, Hassan Ali Damji, Tarlok Sing Sera, Michelle Leduc.

A film about a prehistoric people, the Ulams tribe, who when attacked by another tribe lose their fire, which is a necessary tool of survival in the Stone Age. Three of the strongest tribesmen, Noah (McGill), Amoukar (Perlman) and Gaw (El Kadi), are sent in search of another flame. On their journey, they meet other tribes, save a little girl from cannibals and learn how to light a fire.

This is not just another caveman movie. Using no dialogue, only gestures, Annaud worked with ethnologists and historians in an effort to create a scientifically, historically accurate portrait of Stone Age people. Desmond Morris, who wrote *The Naked Ape*, developed an entire body language vocabulary based on actual ape signals for the film. Annaud succeeded in making a fascinating and historically believable film.

A huge hit in France, *Quest for Fire* was hailed by Alain Garel in *La Revue du Cinéma* as "a collective adventure which traced the evolution ... of beast to man." It won Césars for Best Film and Best Director in 1981.

176 ***La Guerre est finie (The War Is Over)*** 1966 B&W   *Director* Alain Resnais; *Producer* Sofracima, Europa Films; *Screenplay* Jorge Semprun; *Photography* Sacha Vierny; *Music* Giovanni Fusco; *Set* Jacques Saulnier; *Sound*

Antoine Bonfani; *Costumes* Marie Martine; *Editing* Eric Pluet. Running time: 121 minutes.

Cast: Yves Montand, Ingrid Thulin, Geneviève Bujold, Dominique Rozan, Anouk Ferjac, Jean Bouise, Paul Crauchet, Michel Piccoli, Jean-François Rémi, Marie Mergey, Roland Monod, Bernard Fresson, Marcel Cuvelier, Laurence Badie, Pierre Decazes, Jacques Wallet, Françoise Bertin, Yvette Etiévant, Annie Fargue, Gérard Séty, Catherine de Seynes, Jean Dasté, Jean Bolo, Claire Duhamel, Antoine Bourseiller, Pierre Barbaud, René-Jean Chauffard, Gérard Lartigau, Jean Larroquette, Martin Vatel, Laure Paillette, M. Jacques Robnard, Antoine Vitez, José-Maria Flotats.

Set in 1965, Diego (Montand), a Spanish communist, crosses the border into France. He makes contact with communist activists in Paris, but he finds his views are very different from theirs. He decides to return to Spain, but the woman (Bujold) with whom he has been involved learns that the police have set a trap for him. She warns his wife (Thulin), who will try to get to him before the police.

This is one of the greatest political films ever. It is beautiful, complicated and thought-provoking. It helped to establish the struggle against Franco as a mythic fight for Leftists around the world. The crisis in the Communist Party between lifelong members who made careers and commitments to the cause versus feverish young converts would explode a few years later with the May 1968 riots. Resnais chose a more traditional use of the film medium than in his usual avant-garde films, such as *Last Year in Marienbad*, but by keeping the heart of the film — Spain — out of the film, he remained an avant-garde experimenter.

Cahiers du Cinéma's reviewer Michel Caen declared that the love scene between Bujold and Montand "makes us rediscover black and white cinema." It won the Prix Louis Delluc and was the co-winner of French Critics' Prix Méliès in 1966.

Hail Mary! *see* **Je vous salue, Marie**

The Hairdresser's Husband *see* **Le Mari de la coiffeuse**

Handsome Serge *see* **Le Beau Serge**

Happiness *see* **Le Bonheur**

A Heart as Big as That! *see* **Un Cœur gros comme ça!**

A Heart in Winter *see* **Un Cœur en hiver**

A Heart of Stone *see* **Un Cœur en hiver**

The Heavy Water Battle *see* **La Bataille de l'eau lourde**

The Heterosexuals *see* **Les Biches**

177 *Hiroshima, mon amour* 1958 B&W   *Director* Alain Resnais; *Producer* Argos Films, Como Films, Pathé Overseas Production, Daici Motion Picture Company; *Screenplay* Marguerite Duras; *Photography* Sacha Vierny, Michio

Hiroshima, mon amour, **1958; directed by Alain Resnais.**

Takahashi; *Music* Georges Delerue, Giovanni Fusco; *Set* Esaka, Mayo, Petri; *Sound* Pierre Calvet, Renault, Yamamoto, Khozubara; *Editing* Henri Colpi, Jasmine Chasney, Anne Sarraute. Running time: 88 minutes.

Cast: Emmanuelle Riva, Eiji Okada, Stella Dassas, Pierre Barbaud, Bernard Fresson.

A French actress (Riva) picks up a Japanese architect (Okada) while she is filming a movie in Hiroshima. They have an affair, during which they learn that each is happily married and each is a survivor of the ravages of war—she lost a German lover and suffered a nervous breakdown after being punished for fraternizing with the enemy; he survived the blast at Hiroshima. Like much of the movies that followed in the 1960s, the drama is more about visual experience than sequential narrative.

This is an avant-garde classic. The synopsis greatly simplifies this unconventional movie, which was hailed as a cinematic breakthrough by some and an utterly bewildering existential experience by others. As newsreel footage is intercut with sensual sex scenes, love and war, and memory and forgetting are what are supposed to come to mind. Resnais' first feature was begun as a documentary, but Hiroshima's horror seemed too mammoth, so Resnais asked Duras to write a love story in which the atomic bomb would be the background. "I intended to compose a sort of poem in which the images would act as counterpoint to the text," Resnais has said.

Some credit *Hiroshima, mon amour* with signalling an entirely new approach to narrative film. Andrew Sarris wrote upon its video release: "Anyone even remotely interested in the sheer art of cinema cannot afford to pass up this work

L'Histoire d'Adèle H. (*The Story of Adèle H.*), 1975; directed by François Truffaut.

of exquisite taste and craftsmanship." Others frustrated by the avant-garde were less impressed. The film was the co-winner of the French Critics' Prix Méliès in 1959. It won the International Critics Award at Cannes in 1958, the New York Film Critics' Award for Best Foreign Film in 1960 and was nominated for an Oscar for Best Original Screenplay in 1960.

178 *L'Histoire d'Adèle H. (The Story of Adèle H.)*   1975 Color *Director* François Truffaut; *Producer* Films du Carrosse, Artistes Associés; *Screenplay* François Truffaut, Jean Gruault, and Suzanne Schiffman, in collaboration with Frances Guille, the author of *The Journal of Adèle Hugo*; *Photography* Nestor Almendros; *Music* Maurice Jaubert; *Set* Jean-Pierre Kohut Svelko; *Sound* Jean-Pierre Ruh; *Costumes* Jacqueline Guyot; *Editing* Yann Dedet. Running time: 97 minutes

Cast: Isabelle Adjani, Bruce Robinson, Sylvia Marriott, Reubin Dorey, Joseph Blatchley, M. White, Sir Raymond Falla, Sir Cecil de Sausmarez, Care Hathwell, Ivry Gitlis, Roger Martin, Mme. Louise, Jean-Pierre Leursse, Louise Bourdet, Clive Gillingham, Ralph Williams, François Truffaut, Edward Jackson, Thi Loan N'Guyen, Aurélia Mansion, David Footé, Chantal Durpoix, Jacques Fréjabru, Geoffrey Crook.

Based on the diaries of Adèle Hugo, the youngest daughter of Victor Hugo, this is the story of Adèle's (Adjani) obsessive mission to force an English officer, Lieutenant Pinson (Robinson), into loving her. She follows him to Nova Scotia in the 1860s and does not waver from her mad obsession when he makes it clear that he has no intention of marrying her. She becomes a virtual vagrant before she is returned to her concerned father.

Considered to be one of France's finest psychological films, *The Story of Adèle H.* masterfully explores the line between one individual's perception or fantasy and the real world in which they live. It is also in the tradition of French films on *l'amour fou*, or crazy love. The role of Adèle was one of Adjani's best performances, as she portrays the passion, torment and insanity of this young woman.

Critics hailed this work as a great historical drama and a Truffaut achievement. It won the Grand Prix du Cinéma Français in 1975 and the French Critics' Prix Méliès in 1976. Adjani was nominated for an Oscar for Best Actress in 1975.

179 *Histoire de Paul* 1976 B&W   *Director* René Féret; *Producer* Les Films de l'Arquebuse; *Screenplay* René Féret; *Photography* Nurith Aviv; *Set* Jean Haas; *Sound* Francis Bonfanti; *Editing* Vincent Pinel. Running time: 80 minutes.

Cast: Paul Allio, Michel Amphoux, Roland Amstutz, Philippe Clévenot, Richard Elbaz, Yves Kerboul, Olivier Perrier, Pierre Ascaride, Jean Benguigui, Philippe Clévenot, Bernard Bloch, Claude Bouchery, Gildas Bourdet, Isabelle Caillard, Florence Camarroque, Rémy Carpentier, Georges Conti, Gérard Cruchet, Jean Dautremay, Christian Drillaud, Richard Elbaz, Daniel Fondimare, Pierre Forget, Bernard Freyd, Patrick Guyonnaud, Jean Haas, Jean-Louis Jacopin, Yves Kerboul, Josseline Lacarte, Alain Margnat, Mohamed Mokhatafi.

A suicidal man, Paul (Allio), is placed in a mental home, where he refuses to eat or drink. When he is moved to an area of the hospital where more forceful methods of treatment are used, he submits. He will be compelled to continue his miserable existence in the asylum.

A revolutionary look at how society treats its mentally ill, this film was shot in 16 millimeter with a very small budget. The austere atmosphere, in part a result of economic not artistic restraint, helped to make this one of the best of the films from the 1970s that explored insanity. Director Féret used 19 actors professional, and rather than have them spend time in asylums, he made an intellectual exercise of their treatment. Philosopher Michel Foucault believed the film successfully proved how accepted asylum treatments can actually produce or exacerbate mental illness.

Critics found the film very realistic and depressing. Some faulted Féret for not taking a more obvious position on his findings. Others hailed it as a brilliant, modernized experiment in cinéma verité. It won the Prix Jean Vigo in 1975.

180 *Histoire de Wahari* 1975 Color   *Director* Jacques Monod and Vincent Blanchet; *Producer* Beauviala; *Screenplay* Jean Monod; *Photography* Vincent Blanchet; *Sound* Jean Monod and Vincent Blanchet; *Editing* Catherine Poitevin. Running time: 70 minutes.

A documentary that follows the daily life of the Indian natives of Venezuela. It is shockingly authentic in its simplicity and honesty. Its subjects are a mother and child, laughter, bodies, a tree falling in the jungle, the death of an animal, the joy of a man alone. It uses no voiceover, narration or music, but only the sounds of the Indian people and nature.

This film defies traditional definition. It is much more than a traditional documentary about Indian natives or a treatise by a student of the great anthropologist Claude Lévi-Strauss. By refusing to use traditional documentary methods to communicate history or culture, the filmmakers took a gamble on letting the audience respond to the Indian natives as they were filmed. This unadulterated vision brings an amazing power to the cinematic experience. The filmmakers hoped to introduce a higher level of truth-telling in cinema, which would simply bring one culture in extremis to another.

André Cornand of *Image et Son* declared this film to be "a turning point in the history of cinema . . . it opens the universal dialogue of the future." It has never been released in the United States. The film won the Prix Georges Sadoul in 1974.

181 *Hoa Binh (Hoa-Binh)* 1970 Color   *Director* Raoul Coutard; *Producer* Gilbert de Goldschmidt; *Screenplay* Raoul Coutard, based on Françoise Lorrain's novel *The Column of Ash*; *Photography* Raoul Coutard; *Music* Michel Portal; *Sound* Michel Laurent; *Editing* Victoria Mercanton. Running time: 93 minutes.

Cast: Phi Lan, Huynh Cazenas, Xuan Ha, Le Quynh, Bui Thi Than, Tran van Lich, Danièle Delorme, Lan Phuono, Ann Tuan, Kien Ahn.

A war film about an 11-year-old boy, Hung (Lan), growing up in the midst of the Vietnam war. After his father joins the Vietcong and his mother dies, he must care for his little sister. They beg and scavenge in the streets of Saigon until Hung is finally reunited with his father.

The first film by the cinematographer of many Godard and Truffaut New Wave classics, including *Breathless*. This is a very moving picture that looks at the children of war in an emotional, yet unsentimental way. Its title means "peace" in Vietnamese, which in 1969 when the film was released, was a heavily loaded word. Coutard, who went to Vietnam as a photojournalist when he was 20 and stayed for 11 years, manages to avoid coming out for one side of the war or the other. Instead, war is merely the horrible background that has fashioned these children's perception of everything. The film was quite controversial because at the time it was made not taking a stand was controversial.

French critics on both the Right and the Left criticized Coutard for not arguing for one side or other in his film, which is just what admiring critics praised as his genius and daring. When the film was released in the United States in 1971, Robert Hatch of *The Nation* exclaimed: "To make a gentle picture about South Vietnam today is an extraordinary ambition; *Hoa Binh* is an extraordinary picture." It won the Prix Jean Vigo in 1970, was nominated for an Oscar for Best Foreign Film and won Best Picture at the London Film Festival and Best First Film at Cannes 1970.

182 *L'Homme de Rio (That Man from Rio)* 1964 Color   *Director* Philippe de Broca; *Producer* Films Ariane, United Artists; *Screenplay* Philippe de Broca, Jean-Paul Rappeneau, Ariane Mnouchkine, Daniel Boulanger; *Photography* Edmond Séchan; *Music* Georges Delerue; *Set* Mauro Monteiro Filho; *Sound* Jacques Maumont; *Special Effects* Gil Delamare; *Editing* Laurence Méry and Françoise Javet. Running time: 120 minutes.

Cast: Jean-Paul Belmondo, Françoise Dorléac, Jean Servais, Simone Renant, Adolfo Celi, Roger Dumas, Daniel Ceccaldi, Milton Ribeiro, Ubiraci de Oliveira, Max Elloy, Nina Myral, Louise Chavalier, Marie Marc, Robert Blome, Lucien Raimbourg, Maurice Hartwig, Christian Bagot, Aubry, Piervil, André Tomasi.

A mystery, adventure film/farce about Adrien Dufourquet (Belmondo), a French Air Force pilot on leave, who returns to Paris to spend time with his fiancée (Dorléac). When she is kidnapped right in front of him, he pursues her and her

Un Homme et une femme (A Man and a Woman), 1966; directed by Claude Lelouch.

kidnappers to Brazil, where he finds himself caught up in an intrigue involving stolen statuettes.

Called an ode to Hitchcock or a cinematic cartoon strip, this wild chase film was a success and made Belmondo and de Broca world famous. Belmondo wanted to make the leap from serious dramatic actor to bankable comic superstar in this picture, and he did. The high-pace hijinx made this an international success. Belmondo's stunts are wild. At a time when thrillers were taking themselves oh-so-seriously, this was a fresh find.

Critics and the public loved this film. Bosley Crowther of *The New York Times* called this "a studiously overblown farce thriller that is as wild as a runaway train." *The Morning Telegraph* raved: "It is French, it is funny and it is deliciously foolish."

183 *Un Homme et une femme (A Man and a Woman)*   1966 Color *Director* Claude Lelouch; *Producer* Les Films 13; *Screenplay* Claude Lelouch, Pierre Uytterhoeven, based on a story by Claude Lelouch; *Photography* Claude Lelouch; *Music* Francis Lai; *Lyrics* Francis Lai, Pierre Barouh, Baden Powell, Vincius de Moraes; *Set* Robert Luchaire; *Editing* Claude Lelouch, G. Boisser, Claude Berri. Running time: 107 minutes.

Cast: Anouk Aimée, Jean-Louis Trintignant, Pierre Barouh, Valerie Lagrange, Simone Paris, Antoine Sire, Souad Amidou, Yane Barry, Paul Le Person, Henri Chemin, Gérard Sire.

The love story of a man (Trintignant) and a woman (Aimée) who meet while

L'Horloger de Saint-Paul (*The Clockmaker*), 1973; directed by Bertrand Tavernier.

visiting their children at boarding school. They learn about each other's lives on a ride back to Paris and a successive visit to the school. She is an actress and widow; he is a racecar driver whose wife committed suicide because of his dangerous lifestyle. They spend one night together and do not connect; then their affair is over and then it is not.

One of the most romantic love stories of the 1960s, with a sweet, sad score that will forever evoke nostalgia. *A Man and Woman* was Lelouch's sixth feature film, but it marked the commercial and international beginning of his career, as well as his greatest cinematic moment. He is still an auteur, despite those who may dismiss him as sentimental. The film has a distinctive style and tone that makes it a very original and special work.

A Man and a Woman was an enormous success in France and abroad. Some critics originally accused Lelouch of making an artsy film of little substance. *Cahiers du Cinéma*'s review claimed "there is not one centimeter of celluloid that supports" the lovers' passion. But with time the film has earned its place as a classic love story of great beauty that loses none of its magic over the years. An unsuccessful sequel was made called *A Man and A Woman Twenty Years Later*. The original film won an Oscar for Best Foreign Film and for Best Screenplay and the Grand Prize Palme d'Or at Cannes in 1966.

184 *L'Homme qui aimait les femmes (The Man Who Loved Women)*
1977 Color   *Director* François Truffaut; *Producer* Films du Carrosse, Artistes Associés; *Screenplay* François Truffaut, Michel Fermaud and Suzanne Schiffman; *Photography* Nestor Almendros; *Music* Maurice Jaubert; *Set* Jean-Pierre Kohut Svelko; *Editing* Martine Barraqué-Curie. Running time: 120 minutes.

Cast: Charles Denner, Brigitte Fossey, Nelly Borgeaud, Geneviève Fontanel, Nathalie Baye, Sabine Glaser, Leslie Caron, Jean Dasté, Roger Leenhardt, Valerie Bonnier, Martine Chassing, Roselyne Puyo, Anna Perrier, Monique Dury, Nella Barbier, Fréderique Jamet, M. J. Montfaion, Henri Agel, Jean Servat, Michel Marti.

The adventures of a bachelor, Bertrand (Denner), who cannot get enough of women and will go to incredible extremes to get a date with any woman who catches his fancy. This is not the story of a skirtchaser, but rather the intimate portrait of a connoisseur of women, who is charming and sincere and becomes more sympathetic with each of his new conquests.

This is an extraordinary film that plumbs the feelings of a man who loves many women. With Truffaut's characteristic light humor, this film was made at just the right moment in time, when sexual obsession could still be ironic and celebrated and not held up to scorn by political correctness and feminist righteousness. This was Truffaut's seventeenth feature and is probably drawn somewhat from Truffaut's own experiences, as he was known as a great lover of women. The black and white flashbacks of Bertrand's memories of his mother are very effective at suggesting that his desperate quest is to find the maternal love that he lacked.

Some American critics were offended by this film, believing it to be a simple ode to a philanderer; they were insulted by women's objectification. Others recognized that Truffaut intended to celebrate the fairer sex. Howard Kissel declared it "an exhilarating, droll portrait of a provincial Casanova."

185 *L'Horloger de Saint-Paul (The Clockmaker)*   1973 Color   *Director* Bertrand Tavernier; *Producer* Lira Films; *Screenplay* Jean Aurenche, Pierre

Bost, and Bertrand Tavernier, based on Georges Simenon's novel *L'Horloger d'Everton*; *Photography* Pierre William Glenn; *Music* Philippe Sarde; *Set* Jean Mandaroux; *Editing* Armand Psenny, Arianne Boeglin. Running time: 105 minutes.

Cast: Philippe Noiret, Jean Rochefort, Jacques Denis, Julien Bertheau, Yves Alfonso, Jacques Hilling, Clotilde Joano, William Sabatier, Sylvain Rougerie, Andrée Tainsy, Cécile Vassort, Hervé Morel, Christine Pascal, Jacqueline Corot, Liza Braconnier, André San Fratello, Sacha Bauer, Henri Vart, Louis Morard, Jean Marigny, Janine Berdin, Bernard Frangin, Papa Chauvin, Tiffany Tavernier, Henri Pasquale, Johnny Wesseler.

The clockmaker, Michel Descombes (Noiret), lives and works in the Saint-Paul quarter of Lyons. When his son (Rougerie), whom he raised on his own after his wife left him, disappears after having killed a security guard, Michel is questioned by the police. During the investigation, he realizes that he barely knows his son. He and a detective (Rochefort) set out to find the boy and learn the reasons for his crime. Once the son is arrested and sentenced to 20 years in prison, the relations between father and son begin on a new, stronger footing.

Tavernier's first film was hailed as not just a comment on the distance that separates the generations, but as an intelligent commentary on the pervasive problems of France in the late 1960s and the profound misunderstanding between youth and the established, older generation. Noiret was superb.

When it was released in the United States, *The Boston Globe*'s critic raved: "*The Clockmaker* is a masterpiece ... a great thriller and a journey of spiritual discovery .... An exciting and touching film." Vincent Canby of *The New York Times* declared the teaming up of Noiret and Tavernier "a startling combination of old and new talents." The film won the Prix Louis Delluc in 1973.

186 *Hotel Terminus (The Life and Times of Klaus Barbie)*   1988 Color *Director* Marcel Ophüls; *Producer* Memory Pictures Company; *Photography* Michael Davis, Pierre Boffety, Reuben Aaronson, Wilhelm Rosing, Lionel LeGros, Daniel Chabert, Paul Gonon; *Sound* Michel Trouillard and Anne Weil; *Editing* Albert Jurgenson, Catherine Zins. Running time: 267 minutes.

The film relates the life and times of Klaus Barbie, otherwise known as "the Butcher of Lyon," from his childhood through his Nazi career, his anti-communist spy work, and his celebrated trial as a war criminal.

This documentary is a fitting follow-up to Ophüls' *The Sorrow and the Pity*, the definitive film account of World War II. Ophüls interviewed hundreds of people who knew Barbie in all kinds of ways, from those he denounced to those to whom he reported. He wanted to remind the world of the horrors of extremism and to refute once and for all the notion that the concentration camps were a figment of the imagination. He introduced the film by saying: "As you know, this isn't a film about the holocaust, nor is it a biography of a mass criminal. It is a film about the individual's career: manifestations of rejection, of complicity, of calculated indifference." Ophüls conducted the majority of the interviews himself and was wounded while doing research in Brazil. He edited 120 hours of interviews down to four and one half hours.

Critics around the world hailed *Hotel Terminus* as another landmark film. One critic declared: "Ophüls' riveting chronicle elevates journalism to literature." *The New York Times* said, "*Hotel Terminus* emerges ultimately not as a study of one person, place or event, but as a contemplation of the human condition."

House of Pleasure *see* **Le Plaisir**

I as in Icarus *see* **I comme Icare**

187 *I comme Icare (I as in Icarus)* 1979 Color *Director* Henri Verneuil; *Producer* V. Films, SFP, Antenne 2; *Screenplay* Henri Verneuil and Didier Decoin; *Photography* Jean-Louis Picavet; *Music* Ennio Morricone; *Set* Jacques Saulnier; *Sound* Serge Deraison, Jacques Maumont; *Editing* Henri Lanoë. Running time: 120 minutes.

Cast: Yves Montand, Pierre Vernier, Jean-François Garraud, Roger Planchon, Jacques Sereys, Michel Etcheverry, Jean Lescot, Didier Sauvegrain, Jacques Denis, Roland Blanche, Gabriel Cattand, Jean Négroni, Michel Albertini, Henry Djanik, Jacqueline Staup, Jean Obé, Jean Leuvrais, Jean-Claude Jay, Robert Party, Erick Desmarestz, Jean-Pierre Bagot, Joséphine Fresson, Daniel Léger, Brigitte Lahaie, Michel Raskine, Michel Dussarat, Didier Obin-Labastrou, Christian Remer, Roland Amstutz, Georges Staquet, Georges Beller, Benoit Brione, Louis Navarre, Maurice Bénichou, Jacques Bryland, Françoise Bette, Gérard Lorin, Marcel Maréchal, Michel Pilorge, Edmond Bernard, Georges Trillat, Paco, Etienne Diran, Gérard Moison, Thierry de Wavrin, Alain Olivier, Henri Verneuil.

A suspense thriller about a dogged prosecutor, Henri Volny (Montand), who rejects the official explanation of a presidential assassination. He believes more than one person was involved. As he gets closer to discovering the truth, his investigation becomes ever more dangerous. The question is: Will his quest for the truth bring about his own fatal downfall, as in the myth of Icarus?

This is a fascinating and entertaining political-fiction film that examines how men accept and defy authority. The director conceded that the assassination resembles Kennedy's shooting, but he was not setting out to offer a new conspiracy theory, even if the CIA does seem to be behind the plan. In fact, he was inspired by the Yale University experiments on "Submission to Authority," undertaken by Stanley Milgram, which showed how a normal, non-aggressive person could be induced to hurt a stranger when under the instruction of an authority he or she respects. Yves Montand is brilliant in his portrayal of the passionate prosecutor.

The film was a great hit in France and performed reasonably well abroad. A Canadian critic called it "a master work ... a thriller that tops the Americans on their own ground." It won the Grand Prix du Cinéma Français in 1979.

I Don't Hear the Guitar Anymore *see* **J'entends plus la guitare**

I Love You Me No Longer *see* **Je t'aime, moi non plus**

I Married a Shadow *see* **J'ai épousé une ombre**

188 *L'Immortelle* 1963 B&W *Director* Alain Robbe-Grillet; *Producer* Tamara, Como Films; Cocinor, Dino de Laurentiis; *Screenplay* Alain Robbe-Grillet, based on one of his stories; *Photography* Maurice Barry; *Music* Georges Delerue; *Set* Konnell Melissos; *Sound* Jean Philippe; *Editing* Bob Wade. Running time: 95 minutes.

Cast: Françoise Brion, Jacques Doniol-Valcroze, Guido Celano, Ulvi Uraz, Catherine Robbe-Grillet, Catherine Blisson, Quinterio, Sezer Sezin, Ayfer Feray, Needet Majfi Ayral, Vahi Oz, Osman Olonyok, Guido Celano.

André Varrais, a professor known as N. (Doiniol-Valcrose), who has just arrived in Istanbul, meets a beautiful young woman (Brion), known as L., who becomes his mistress. One day, she disappears as suddenly as she had appeared. Knowing little about her, N. has a hard time pursuing her. When she reappears, she is terrified. The next night, she is killed in an automobile accident. In trying to uncover the mystery behind this woman, N. is killed as well.

The master of the *nouveau roman*'s first attempt at the cinéma-roman is, of course, a very literary film with no time or space. Robbe-Grillet shot the film entirely on location in Istanbul. It is supposed to feel like a dream, strange and familiar at the same time, and, in fact, the whole thing may just be the last thoughts of N. as he lays dying.

Some critics found the film colder, more disconcerting, and not as interesting as *Last Year at Marienbad*. Others hailed it as revolutionary narrative. It won the Prix Louis Delluc in 1963.

The Impudent Girl *see* **L'Effrontée**

189 *India Song* 1975 Color   *Director* Marguerite Duras; *Producer* Sunchild, Armorial; *Screenplay* Marguerite Duras, based on her novel *Le Vice Consul*; *Photography* Bruno Nuytten; *Music* Carlos d'Alessio; *Editing* Solange Leprince. Running time: 120 minutes.

Cast: Delphine Seyrig, Michel Lonsdale, Mathieu Carrière, Didier Flamand, Claude Mann, Vernon Dobtcheff, Claude Juan, Satasinh Manila, and the voices of Nicole Hiss, Monique Simonet, Viviane Forrester, Dionys Mascolo, Marguerite Duras, Françoise Lebrun, Benoit Jacquot, Nicole-Lise Bernheim, Kevork Kutudjan, Daniel Dobbels, Jean-Claude Biette, Pascal Kané, Marie-Odile Briot.

Set in India in the 1930s, this is the tale of Anne-Marie Stretter (Seyrig) and the Vice Consul (Lonsdale) who is in love with her. At an Embassy Ball, Anne-Marie is surrounded by admirers, many of whom she trifles with, but none of whom she really cares about. Insane with passion, the ignored Vice Consul runs out into the Calcutta night howling Anne-Marie's name. The next day, she disappears. Years later, she dies in the islands.

A cinematic essay by Duras, in which she proved that words can have a larger role in films, which had traditionally relied on images for the real power and drama. She saw the movie as a love story pieced together from the lovers' different remembrances. Different voices comment on the scenes; they complete, interpret and contradict what happens on the screen. Little of India or of the love story are actually seen. In the marvelous way of Duras, everything is suggested.

Critics at Cannes applauded *India Song* for its subtle, intelligent psychological exploration. Vincent Canby of *The New York Times*, however, dismissed it as simply a "four-hankie story."

190 *Indochine* 1991   *Director* Régis Wargnier; *Producer* Paradis Films, Bac Films, Orly Films, Ciné Cinq; *Screenplay* Erik Orsenna, Louis Gardel, Catherine Cohen, Régis Warner; *Photography* François Catonné; *Music* Patrick Doyle; *Set* Jacques Bufnoir; *Sound* Guillaume Sciama; *Costumes* Gabriella Pescucci, Pierre-Yves Gayraud; *Editing* Geneviève Winding. Running time: 160 minutes.

Cast: Catherine Deneuve, Vincent Perez, Linh Dan Pham, Jean Yanne,

Dominique Blanc, Henri Marteau, Carlo Brandt, Gérard Lartigau, Hubert Saint-Macary, Andrzej Seweryn, Mai Chau, Alain Fromager, Chu Hung, Jean-Baptiste Huynh, Thisbault De Montalembert, Eric Nguyen, Trinh van Thinh, Tien Tho, Tie Hoe, Tranh Huu Trieu, Nguyen Lan Trung, Nhu Quynh, Michel Voita, Martin Barre Astich, Lam Binh, Tat Binh, Nguyen Huu Bong, Jean-Pierre Debris, Clayton Dowty, Anoy Ew Lek Ee, Edgar Givry, Quang Hai, Ngo Hoa, Ba Hoang, Hong Khien, Gia Khoan, Hoang Kiem, M. Lap, Anna Lim, Van Quy, Dhevaakar Suppiah, Julie Ten, Ngoc Thoa, Nguyen Van Thoi, Trong Thuy, Jean de Tregomain, Dan Si Van, Hai Yen.

Set in French Indochina in the 1930s and 1940s, this is the story of the relationship between a French colonial woman, Eliane (Deneuve), who runs a rubber plantation in Indochina and the orphaned royal Indochinese daughter whom she raises. Fiercely independent, Eliane manages to indulge in love affairs and despotic business methods, until the country she has always known as home begins to strain against colonialism. Just as the country rebels against France, so does her daughter, Camille (Pham), defy her mother and break out on her own.

A glorious weaving of the personal and historical relationships of a French woman and her adopted daughter, and of the French empire and her colony Indochina, *Indochine* was the first fictional film to present an historically accurate account of events in Indochina in 1930, the events that set the stage for the disastrous relations between Indochina and France, and later Vietnam and the United States. The director had Deneuve in mind for the complex part of Eliane from the start, and it is one of the best performances of her career. The wonderful screenplay was written by novelist Erik Orsenna, who went on to win France's most prestigious literary award, the Prix Goncourt, for *Love and Empire*. This was one of the first films to be shot in Vietnam after the war, and it brought visions of the beautiful Indochinese landscape back to the West. In fact, a wave of tourism interest in Vietnam erupted in France and the United States after the movie was released.

French politicos on the left and the right were offended by the film, each believing it defended the other one's side, but critics on both sides of the Atlantic loved it. *Newsday*'s Jack Matthews lauded *Indochine* for blending "exotic settings, panoramic landscapes, historical heft—with the passion of French melodrama to make it the season's best buy in an import." It won the Oscar for Best Foreign Film in 1992.

The Inquisitor *see* **Garde à vue**

Inside Out *see* **La Vie à l'envers**

Intimate Relations *see* **Les Parents terribles**

It's My Life *see* **Vivre sa vie**

191 *J'ai épousé une ombre (I Married a Shadow)* 1983 Color *Director* Robin Davis; *Producer* Sara Films, TF1 Films Productions; *Screenplay* Patrick Laurent and Robin Davis, based on William Irish's novel *I Married a Dead Man*; *Photography* Bernard Zitztermann; *Music* Philippe Sarde; *Set* Yvan Maussion; *Sound* Michel Laurent; *Editing* Marie Castro Vasquez. Running time: 110 minutes.

Cast: Nathalie Baye, Francis Huster, Véronique Genest, Richard Bohringer, Madeleine Robinson, Guy Tréjean, Victoria Abril, Maurice Jacquemont, Solenn Janiou, Humbert Balsan, Marcel Roche, Arlette Gilbert, André Thorent, Christine Paolini, Jean-Henri Chambois.

Hélène (Baye), whose boyfriend has just abandoned her, meets a wealthy young couple on a train. Bernard and Patricia Meyrand, who are going to meet their family in Bordeaux, are amazed at how much Hélène resembles Patricia. When the train derails and the couple is killed, the Meyrand family is convinced that Hélène is really Patricia. Hélène does not disabuse them of this idea and falls in love with Pierre, the son. But when her former lover finds out and wants to profit from her deceit, she and Pierre must kill him.

This romantic suspense thriller was based on a novel by the author of such hits as *Rear Window* and *The Bride Wore Black*. It was Davis' fourth feature film. In trying to "avoid violence and penetrate a romantic and passionate universe," she masterfully blended all of the great elements of the genre thriller: mistaken identity, the missing lover, even the trademark encounter on a train. And yet, the film is highly original. Nathalie Baye gives a wonderful performance.

This film was a huge hit in France. *Le Matin* said of *I Married a Shadow*: "Distinguished and pure melodrama — we applaud it on every level." *Le Nouvel Observateur* raved: "Vive le suspense melodramatique — the cinema of Hitchcock and Lang is now joined by Robin Davis."

192 *Je t'aime, moi non plus (I Love You Me No Longer)*   1976 Color *Director* Serge Gainsbourg; *Producer* Claude Berri; *Screenplay* Serge Gainsbourg; *Photography* Willy Kurant and Yann Le Masson; *Music* Serge Gainsbourg; *Set* Théo Meurisse; *Sound* Antoine Bonfanti; *Editing* Willy Kurant. Running time: 90 minutes.

Cast: Jane Birkin, Joe Dallessandro, Hughues Quester, René Kolldehoff, Gérard Depardieu, Jimmy Loverman Davis.

A strange love story set in the United States about a homosexual truck-driving couple who are broken up by an androgynous waitress (Birkin) in a bar. She and one of the men (Dallesandro) manage to forge a temporary sexual and emotional relationship despite the many obstacles put in their way — not the least of which are motel owners, who are constantly throwing them out of their establishments for their nocturnal noises. Finally, the jilted lover gets his revenge on the happy couple.

This was singer-songwriter Serge Gainsbourg's first film, and as a quirky sexual quest, it is one of the most original films of its time. In many ways, however, Gainsbourg was both ahead of his time and behind it with this picture. It falls into the *Midnight Cowboy* and *My Own Private Idaho* school of filmmaking, with its unblinking look at down-and-out people and places, but the climate for Gainsbourg in the 1970s was less interested in this subject than audiences were a decade earlier and a decade later. All of the performances are solid.

Many critics dismissed the film as too offbeat and quirky. *Variety* called it "a quirky tale that is more a ballad than a truly poetic or dramatic pitch."

193 *Je vous salue, Marie (Hail Mary!)*   1984 Color   *Director* Jean-Luc Godard; *Producer* Pégase, Sara Films, SSR, JLG Films; *Screenplay* Jean-Luc Godard; *Photography* Jean-Bernard Menoud, Jacques Firmin; *Music* Bach,

Dvorak; *Sound* François Musy; *Editing* Jean-Luc Godard. Running time: 107 minutes.

Cast: Myriem Roussel, Thierry Rode, Philippe Lacoste, Manon Anderson, Juliette Binoche, Malachi Jara Kohan, Dick, Johann Leysen, Anne Gauthier.

The modernized story of the birth of Christ. Archangel Gabriel (Lacoste) flies into Geneva, landing at the airport, of course. He finds Mary (Roussel) pumping gas at her father's gas station and tells her of her sacred destiny. Her taxicab-driving boyfriend, Joseph (Rode), is not thrilled by the news, but accepts the inevitable birth. The child is born and is quite an uppity little tot.

Godard's metaphysical history of the immaculate conception is fascinating. It is easily the best of his later films. Not surprisingly, it stirred up quite a lot of opposition within the Catholic community, including condemnation by the pope, but it is actually less iconoclastic than one would think. Godard has merely transposed the Christian myth to modern times, he has not questioned it at all. Even his rebellious depiction of Jesus can be seen as a way of emphasizing His impact on the future. When *Hail Mary!* debuted in the United States at the New York Film Festival, over 3,000 Catholic demonstrators, who called the film blasphemous, protested outside Lincoln Center. Despite the fact that Godard's Mary marries Joseph after her immaculate conception and preaches chastity, the film received similar protests in other cities around the world.

Hail Mary! inspired passionate responses when it was released, with many denouncing it as heresy before ever hearing what it was about, and others defending it as a great evangelical gift to Catholicism, disguised as a movie. Armond White called *Hail Mary!* "an intellectual's Christmas pageant, a lyrical hypothesis on sex and love, faith and divinity."

194 *Jean de Florette* 1987 Color   *Director* Claude Berri; *Producer* Renn Productions, A2, RAI, 2DD; *Screenplay* Claude Berri and Gérard Brach, based on the novel *L'Eau des collines* by Marcel Pagnol; *Photography* Bruno Nuytten; *Music* Jean-Claude Petit; *Set* Bernard Vezat; *Sound* Pierre Gamet; *Costumes* Sylvie Gautrelet; *Editing* Arlette Langmann, Hervé de Luze, Noëlle Boisson, Sophie Coussein. Running time: 122 minutes.

Cast: Yves Montand, Gérard Depardieu, Daniel Auteuil, Elisabeth Depardieu, Armand Meffre, Pierre Nougaro, Marc Betton, Jean Maurel, Roger Souza, Margarita Lozano, André Dupon, Pierre-Jean Rippert, Didier Pain, Fransined, Chantal Liennel, Marcel Champel, Bertino Benedetto, Marcel Berbert, Hippolyte Girardot, Gabriel Bacquier, Ernestine Mazurowna, Christian Tamisier, Marcel Berbert, Jo Daumerg.

Set in the hills of Provence, this is an epic about a farmer, Le Papet (Montand), who covets a tract of land with a spring on it. When city-bred Jean de Florette (Depardieu) inherits the land and tries to farm it with his wife and young daughter, Le Papet and his nephew, Ugolin (Auteuil), do everything they can to frustrate their neighbor's efforts, including burying the spring. Jean de Florette literally kills himself bringing water from the hills to his land. After his funeral, Le Papet and Ugolin get the farm at a cheap price, but Jean de Florette's daughter Manon sees them when they dig up the source of the spring. The *Manon of the Source* sequel finishes the story.

Claude Berri spent six years pursuing the rights to Pagnol's novel and more money, $18 million, than had ever been spent on a French film to make this absolutely riveting tale of human meanness and kindness. Berri raised much of the money to make the film himself, and, by doing so, proved that big budgets in France could mean big profits. All the principal parts are played with extraordinary intelligence and depth. The natural landscape is as beautiful and harsh as the people who inhabit it.

Some French critics, who championed experimental filmmaking, complained that Berri was merely rehashing old tales and old ways. But the beauty of this epic on the big screen feels completely fresh. Of seeing *Jean de Florette*, one American critic wrote: "It is a complete achievement in itself, a towering yet completely approachable accomplishment of the contemporary cinema."

Jenny Lamour *see* **Le Quai des orfèvres**

195 *J'entends plus la guitare (I Don't Hear the Guitar Anymore)* 1991 Color   *Director* Philippe Garrel; *Producer* Les Films de l'Atlante; *Screenplay* Philippe Garrel and Marc Cholodenko; *Photography* Caroline Champetier; *Music* Faton Cahen; *Sound* René Levert; *Editing* Sophie Coussein, Yann Dedet. Running time: 98 minutes.

Cast: Benoît Régent, Johanna Ter Steeg, Yann Collette, Mireille Perrier, Brigitte Sy, Anouk Grinberg, Adélaïde Blasquez.

The story of two couples beginning with their vacation in a villa. Gérard (Régent) swears to his girlfriend, Marianne (Ter Steege), that he will love her forever and beyond; but over the years they go their separate ways. He marries someone else and has a child. But when he learns that Marianne has died, he is unbelievably upset.

This film was hailed as the ideal example of first-person cinema. It is another intensely autobiographical work, in which Garrel manages to capture moments in all their sensuality and emotion. He uses close-ups of faces to force an intimacy that evokes great feeling. He plays with concepts of fidelity and betrayal, vis-à-vis women and men and personal ideals. The film was an homage to his late wife, Nice.

When this film came out, the French critics loved it. *La Revue du Cinéma* hailed Garrel as "the last of the primitifs." *Positif* declared that he made films which seemed as natural as breathing. *Cahiers du Cinéma* said it was much more than a film: "It is a 'moment of being' as Virginia Woolf said . . . . Prose of existence equals uninterrupted poetry."

The Jerk *see* **Le Corniaud**

196 *La Jetée (The Pier)*   1963 B&W   *Director* Chris Marker; *Producer* Argos Films; *Screenplay* Chris Marker; *Photography* Chris Marker; *Music* Trevor Duncan and Russian liturgies; *Editing* Jean Ravel. Running time: 29 minutes.

Cast: Davos Hanich, Hélène Chatelain, Jean Négroni, Jacques Ledoux, André Heinrich, Philbert von Lifchitz.

A fantastical, "photo novel" set in Paris after World War III. Only a few people have survived the nuclear destruction. Living in tunnels underground, they decide that their only hope for survival is to send emissaries through time, to the past and to the future, in search of aid. A young man (Hanich) is picked because of his vivid memory of a woman he saw once on the jetway at Orly airport. His passage through time is a success, but he chooses not to save humanity and finds his death on the airport jetway.

Jeux interdits (Forbidden Games), 1952; directed by René Clement.

This is an extraordinary experiment and achievement in photo-montage by one of the least well known, but most influential New Wave directors, Chris Marker. A master of documentaries, Marker here uses a succession of still photographs and an anonymous voice to tell a futuristic story with an eerie reality. It was Marker's only fictional film.

Often compared to the work of Resnais and Varda, *The Pier* was one of Marker's most acclaimed films. *Le Monde* said: "Through anguish, insanity, and the hypothetical condemnation of the human race," the film becomes "a sad meditation on love and death, happiness and peace." The film won the Prix Jean Vigo in 1963.

197 *Les Jeux de l'amour (The Love Game* or *Playing at Love)* 1960 B&W *Director* Philippe De Broca; *Producer* Ajym Films; *Screenplay* Philippe de Broca, Daniel Boulanger, Geneviève Cluny, based on an idea by Geneviève Cluny; *Photography* Jean Penzer; *Music* Georges Delerue; *Set* Jacques Saulnier and Bernard Evein; *Sound* Jean Labussière; *Editing* Laurence Méry. Running time: 83 minutes.

Cast: Jean-Pierre Cassel, Geneviève Cluny, Jean-Louis Maury, Mario David, Claude Cerval, François Maistre, Alain Maury, Robert Vattier, Maria Pacôme, Pierre Repp, Lud Germain, Claude Chabrol, Georges Delerue, Jeanne Pérez, Daniel Boulanger, Philippe de Broca, Jean-Pierre Moulin, Jean-Paul Thomas, Jackie Rollin, Myriam Hannesco.

The story of a young couple who love each other, but want different things from the relationship. Suzanne (Cluny), an antique dealer, wants marriage and a baby;

her artist boyfriend, Victor (Cassel), does not. After numerous disagreements, the two finally seem to break up, and François (Maury), a mutual friend, proposes to Suzanne. When she accepts, Victor relents and Suzanne then accepts his proposal.

This is a great romantic comedy that makes masterful use of dialogue, settings, and characters and was hailed as the first comedy of the New Wave. Lovers' looney logic is played to great heights in the amorous arguments. Paris is shown in all its romantic glory as a great backdrop for love, and furniture plays a greater role than it ever has before in film. Cassell became known as the Danny Kaye of French films because of his delightful performance. On its way to the United States, the film was seized by custom officials, who feared its love scenes were immoral, but when it was shown in a Federal courtroom, officials found it tame and released it immediately.

French critics were thrilled that a New Wave film could have a happy ending. *The Observer* called it "the best sex-comedy for years." *Time* magazine declared it "a delightfully risky, frisky, upstairs-downstairs and in my lady's chamber sort of farce." It won the Golden Bear at the Berlin Film Festival in 1960.

198 *Jeux interdits (Forbidden Games)*   1952 B&W   *Director* René Clément; *Producer* Silver Films, Corona; *Screenplay* Jean Aurenche, Pierre Bost and René Clément, based on François Boyer's novel *Crois de bois, crois de fer*; *Photography* Robert Juillard; *Music* Narciso Yepes; *Set* Paul Bertrand; *Sound* Jacques Lebreton; *Editing* Roger Dwyre. Running time: 85 minutes.

Cast: Brigitte Fossey, Georges Poujouly, Louis Herbert, Suzanne Courtal, Laurence Badie, Denise Péronne, Madeleine Barbulée, Janine Zorelli, Maud Slover, Fernande Roy, Violette Meunier, Annie Ravel, Lucien Hubert, Jacques Marin, Amédée, André Wasley, Louis Saintève, Pierre Mérovée, Bernard Musicson, Georges Sauval, André Enard.

Set in the French countryside, during World War II, five-year-old Paulette (Fossey) witnesses the killing of her parents and her pet dog by a German bombardment. A peasant family takes her in, and she grows close to the youngest son Michel (Poujouly). Together they become fascinated with death and steal crosses from the town cemetery to adorn her pet dog's grave. Because of their crime, the children are separated, and Paulette is sent to an orphanage.

This is truly one of the most important films ever made on the horrors of war. Clément made it after already completing two other very important, but very different films on World War II — the docudrama, *Battle of the Rails*, and the submarine drama, *The Damned*. The children are treated as complicated human beings, neither "good" nor "bad," but certainly affected by the violence around them. Childhood is not paradisaical here; ~~Renoir~~ *Clément* wanted it to be a true portrait of childhood. None of the actors in the film had considerable experience. Fossey, whom Clément eventually chose to play Paulette, was vacationing with her family in Nice when Clément was testing children for the part, and her parents appear in the film as Paulette's parents.

When awarded the Grand Prix Independent at Cannes in 1952, it was heralded "for having known how to raise up, with a singular lyric purity and an exceptional force of expression, the innocence of childhood over the tragedy and desolation of war." It won the Oscar for Best Foreign Film in 1951, the Lion d'Or at the Venice Biennal and the New York Film Critics' Award for Best Foreign Film in 1952.

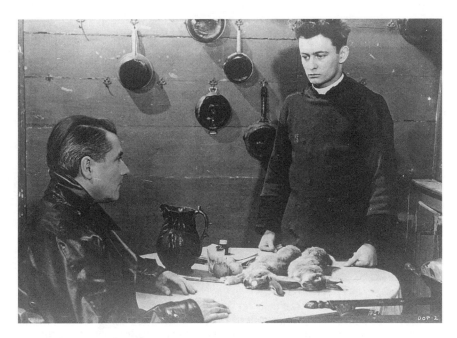

Journal d'un curé de campagne (*Diary of a Young Country Priest*), 1950; directed by Robert Bresson.

The Joker *see* **Le Farceur**

199 *Jour de fête* 1949 B&W   *Director* Jacques Tati; *Producer* Fred Orain and Cady Films; *Screenplay* Jacques Tati, Henri Marquet, and René Wheeler; *Adaptation* René Wheeler; *Dialogue* Jacques Tati and Henri Marquet; *Photography* Jacques Mercanton; *Music* Jean Yatove; *Set* René Moulaert; *Editing* Marcel Moreau. Running time: 70 minutes.

Cast: Jacques Tati, Santa Relli, Guy Decomble, Paul Frankeur, Delcassan, Robert Balpo, Maine Vallée, Jacques Beauvais, Roger Rafal, and the inhabitants of St.-Sevère.

A hilarious slapstick comedy about the postman of St.-Sevère, François (Tati), who happily delivers the mail by bicycle. He takes his time, stopping to chat, even lending a hand on the farm if he is needed. That is, until the carnival comes to town and shows a movie about the efficiency of the United States Postal System. François takes up the new mission of delivering the mail *à l'Amérique* and whips recklessly around town. His crazed delivery ends when he lands in a ditch, and he abandons his mission to resume his casual routine.

This is Jacques Tati's first feature film. He made the film based on a short film he made two years earlier called *School for Postmen* (*L'École des facteurs*). The Tati theme, which America's movie clown Charlie Chaplin also dealt with in his films, is man versus the machine, and traditional versus modern life. François is the early version of Tati's Hulot. He has some of the same comic qualities and certainly the same subtle blend of idiocy and sensitivity which audiences adore. The film was shot in a new color process called "Thomson-Color" which turned out horribly, and if a black and white back-up print had not been made, the movie would not exist at all. Few distributors wanted to touch the movie when it came out, because in the late 1940s movies about the war and the Occupation were what were selling in France, not rural mailman comedies.

The public loved the film when it came out. It was generally well received by critics. Some complained that the film was too long and only became truly funny in the last quarter, which may be the result of stretching a plot designed for a short film into a full-length feature. But the slapstick antics and François' character are certainly the film's greatest strengths. It won the Grand Prix du Cinéma Français in 1950 and Best Screenplay at the Venice Biennal in 1949.

200 *Journal d'un curé de campagne (Diary of a Young Country Priest)* 1950 B&W   *Director* Robert Bresson; *Producer* UGC; *Screenplay* Robert Bresson, based on the novel by Georges Bernanos; *Photography* Léonce-Henry Burel; *Music* Jean-Jacques Grünenwald; *Set* Pierre Charbonnier; *Sound* Jean Rieul; *Editing* Paulette Robert. Running time: 110 minutes.

Cast: Claude Laydu, Nicole Ladmiral, Nicole Maurey, Armand Guibert, Jean Riveryre, Rachel Berendt, Martine Lemaire, Antoine Balpêtre, Serge Benneteau, Jean Danet, Léon Arvel, Yvette Etiévan, Gaston Séverin, Bernard Hubrenne, Germaine Stainval, Gilberte Terbois, François Valorbe, Morange.

A young priest (Laydu), just out of the seminary is brimming with faith, but is completely unable to touch his country parishioners, whose concerns are more immediate and terrestrial than spiritual. While the priest leads a solitary struggle to spread faith within his northern French community, cancer spreads through his body and slowly kills him.

One of the finest religious films ever made, this is considered Bresson's great masterpiece. His fourth feature film made five years after his wonderfully successful *Ladies of the Park*, *The Diary of a Young Country Priest* is a very faithful adaptation of Bernanos' novel. Bresson adapted the novel himself, and the original producer found his screenplay too undramatic, so Bresson found another producer. The dialogue is taken almost word for word from the book. Bresson insisted that most of the actors be non-professionals and they all had to believe in God. Laydu, who had never acted before, actually lived in a monastery to master his saintliness. Even the clothes he wore in the film were lent to him by priests. The bareness of the narrative as told by diary entries builds a believable sadness, and Bresson's stark shots show real soul-searching.

This film brought a new credibility to "literary" films. One American critic exclaimed: "This film proves a work entirely of the interior life can pass to the screen." Pauline Kael of *The New Yorker* called it "surely the one great religious film of recent years." It won the Prix Louis Delluc in 1950 and the French Critics' Prix Méliès in 1951.

201 *Le Journal d'une femme de chambre (Diary of a Chambermaid)* 1963 B&W   *Director* Luis Buñuel; *Producer* Serge Silberman/Michel Safra; *Screenplay* Luis Buñuel and Jean-Claude Carrière, based on the novel by Octave Mirbeau; *Photography* Roger Fellous; *Set* Georges Wakhevitch; *Sound* Antoine Petitjean; *Costumes* Georges Wakhevitch; *Editing* Louisette Hautecoeur. Running time: 85 minutes.

Cast: Jeanne Moreau, Georges Geret, Michel Piccoli, Daniel Ivernel, Jean-Claude Carrière, Françoise Lugagne, Jean Ozenne, Gilberte Géniat, Muni, Bernard Musson, Dominique Sauvage, Claude Jaeger, Joëlle Bernard, Andrée Tainsy, Geymond Vital, Dominique Zardi, Madeleine Damien, Jeanne Pérez, Jean Franval, Marcel Rouzé, Pierre Collet, Françoise Bertin, Aline Bertrand, Marguerite Dubourg, Gabriel Gobin, Marc Eyraud, Michel Daquin, Marcel Le Foch.

The story of a young Parisian woman, Célestine (Moreau), who is employed as a chambermaid in Normandy for the Monteil family. Her boss, Mr. Monteil (Piccoli); the stepfather, Mr. Rabour (Ozenne); and a servant, Joseph (Geret); all make passes at her. When a little girl is found raped and murdered in the forest, Célestine suspects Joseph. She accepts his amorous advances and begins amassing evidence against him. When he is arrested, she marries an old army officer. Joseph is released because of insufficient evidence and opens a café in Cherbourg.

This is the first of Buñuel's last period of films, the ones he filmed in France, and always with Carrière. The novel took place at the end of the nineteenth century, but Buñuel set it instead in 1928 in France, a time of political and social upheaval. Another version of the novel was adapted by Jean Renoir with Paulette Goddard and Burgess Meredith in the United States in 1946 as *Diary of a Chambermaid*.

Some critics found Célestine's change from passive maid to sleuthing detective gave the film a schizophrenic feel. Others found its historical setting out of step with the New Wave experiments of the day. In a broader context, though, it is fascinating in how it resembles and differs from other Buñuel films. As always, he presents a complex look at society.

202 *Judex*   1964 B&W   *Director* Georges Franju; *Producer* Comptoir Français du Film; *Screenplay* Jacques Champreux and Franci Lacassin, based on the 1916 film by Louis Feuillade and Arthur Bernède; *Photography* Marcel Fradetal; *Music* Maurice Jarre; *Set* Robert Giordani; *Sound* Jean Labussière; *Costumes* Christiane Courcelles; *Editing* Gilbert Natot. Running time: 100 minutes.

Cast: Channing Pollock, Michel Vitold, Edith Scob, René Génin, Francine Bergé, Jacques Jouanneau, Théo Sarapo, Philippe Mareuil, Silva Koscina, Benjamin Boda, Roger Fradet, Luigi Cortese, Ketty France, Jean Degrave, Suzanne Gossen, Pierre Vernet, André Méliès, Luigi Cortèse, Jean-François Remi, Bernard Charlan, Edouard Francomme.

An action film–cum–morality tale in which a caped and masked hero, Judex (Pollock), first orders the banker, Favraux (Vitold), who has made his fortune by profiting from others' misery, to give half of his fortune to the poor. Favraux refuses. When his daughter, Jacqueline (Scob), is kidnapped by a former governess who wants her fortune, Judex saves her. Jacqueline marries her hero, who turns out to be none other than her father's assistant, Vallières. Good triumphs over evil, but not before lots of chases and masks and general superhero fare.

An homage to Louis Feuillade's 1916 12-part serial of the same name and substance, this movie is probably the best superhero movie ever made. The black and white photography does more for the world of good and evil than any Hollywood color or special effects could. Franju succeeds beautifully in evoking the past and the present and in fulfilling his aim of wanting to prove that nothing is more realistic than poetry—in this case, cinematic poetry.

Critic Marcel Allain called Franju's *Judex* a "miracle." Georges Sadoul credited the director with "supreme taste and an archaeologist's sense."

The Judge Fayard Called the Sheriff *see* **Le Juge Fayard dit "le Shérif"**

203 *Le Juge Fayard dit "le Shérif" (The Judge Fayard Called the Sheriff)*
1977 Color   *Director* Yves Boisset; *Producer* Yves Gasser, Yves Peyrot, CCFC, Action Films, Société Française de Productions; *Screenplay* Yves Boisset, Claude Veillot, Luc Béraud; *Photography* Jacques Loiseleur; *Music* Philippe Sarde; *Set* Maurice Sergent, Serge Sommier, Laurent Chamard; *Sound* Michel Chamard; *Editing* Albert Jurgenson, Laurence Leininger. Running time: 112 minutes.

Cast: Patrick Dewaere, Aurore Clément, Philippe Léotard, Michel Auclair, Jean Bouise, Jean-Marc Thibault, Daniel Ivernel, Jean-Marc Bory, Henri Garcin, Jacques Spiesser, Marcel Bozzuffi, Yves Alfonso, Roland Blanche, Lucky Blondo, François Dyrek, Maurice Dorléac, Luc Florian, Myriam Mézières, Bernard Giraudeau, Odile Poisson, René Boulac, Philippe Brizzard, Marie-Pierre de Gérando.

A thriller based on the killing of a district attorney by the Mafia in Lyon in the 1970s. Judge Fayard (Dewaere) is an honest man who will stop at nothing to do the right thing. After Commissioner Marcheron (Invernel) is assassinated, the Judge decides to uncover a connection between an underworld gang and some right-wing politicians. He is shot while delivering the incriminating documents to the Society of Civic Aid, but, of course, there is a copy of the documents in the right hands.

This was one of the better French political films that swept France in the 1970s after Costa-Gavras' hit, *Z*. It was inspired by the real murder of Judge Renaud. When the film came out, the government insisted that mentions of the Society of Civic Aid be bleeped over because they were defamatory. Patrick Dewaere's performance is superb.

The film was well received by critics and the public. It won the Prix Louis Delluc in 1976.

Jules and Jim *see* **Jules et Jim**

204 *Jules et Jim (Jules and Jim)* 1962 B&W   *Director* François Truffaut; *Producer* Films du Carrosse-SEDIF; *Screenplay* François Truffaut and Jean Gruault, based on the novel by Henri-Pierre Roché; *Photography* Raoul Coutard; *Music* Georges Delerue and Boris Bassiak; *Set* Bernard Evein; *Costumes* Fred Capel; *Editing* Claudine Bouché. Running time: 105 minutes.

Cast: Jeanne Moreau, Oskar Werner, Henri Serre, Vanna Urbino, Boris Bassiak, Sabine Haudepin, Marie Dubois, Bernard Largemains, Ellen Bober, Pierre Fabre, Kathe Noëlle, Annie Nelsen, Christiane Wagner, Danielle Bassiak, Jean-Louis Richard, Michel Varesano, and the voice of Michel Subor.

An introverted German Jew, Jules (Werner), and a garrulous Frenchman, Jim (Serre), are the best of friends. They find the girl of their dreams in Catherine (Moreau), but Jules marries her. After World War I, Catherine becomes Jim's lover. A few years later, when Jim decides to marry Gilberte (Urbino), Catherine invites him for a drive in the country and drives the car into the Seine, killing them both. Jules is left with a child to raise alone and the job of burying his two great loves.

Maybe the best love-triangle movie ever made. A moving story of a woman who is torn between loving two men and the men who love her and each other. The film was based on a little known, semi-autobiographical novel by a Parisian playboy-turned–art dealer, who died before he could adapt the novel himself. In Truffaut and Gruault's adaptation, they moved the action to take place from 1912 to 1933 and to end just when the Nazi menace was looming in the future. This is an astonishing work that thrilled some and angered others. It was probably Moreau and Truffaut's most popular film.

"The beauty, the real wisdom, of *Jules and Jim* is that the disillusionment of its characters — their painfully protracted awareness of failure — doesn't diminish the value of their moral experiment," wrote critic Terrence Rafferty. The film won the Prix de l'Académie du Cinéma for Best French Film, and Jeanne Moreau won Best Actress. When it came out in the United States, *New Yorker* critic Pauline Kael wrote: "I think it will rank among the great lyric achievements of the screen, right up there with the work of Griffith and Renoir."

Just Before Nightfall see **Juste avant la nuit**

205 *Juste avant la nuit (Just Before Nightfall)*   1970 Color   *Director* Claude Chabrol; *Producer* André Genovès, Columbia; *Screenplay* Claude Chabrol, based on Adward Atiyah's novel *L'Etau*; *Photography* Jean Rabier; *Music* Pierre Jansen; *Set* Guy Littaye; *Sound* Guy Chichignoud; *Editing* Jacques Gaillard. Running time: 106 minutes.

Cast: Stéphane Audran, Michel Bouquet, François Périer, Anna Douking, Jean Carmet, Dominique Zardi, Paul Temps, Henri Attal, Daniel Lecourtois, Pascal Gillot, Brigitte Perrin, Célia, Marina Ninchi, Marcel Gassouk, Clélia Matania, Roger Leumont, Dominique Marcas, Sylvie Lenoir, Jean-Marie Arnoux, Gilbert Servien.

In a rough love game, Charles (Bouquet) strangles his mistress Laura (Douking), who is also the wife of his best friend, François (Périer). The police do not suspect Charles, a good family man with a nice wife and kids, but he is tormented by his guilt. He confesses to his wife and François, both of whom react with surprisingly little emotion and console him. Eventually, though his wife does mete out her own form of justice.

This was the natural sequel to *The Unfaithful Wife*, because this time the man kills the mistress, instead of his wife's lover, and is undone by confession, rather than redeemed by his silence. In an interview, Chabrol summed up the plot as the reverse of the normal scenario with a man who wants to confess and cannot find anyone to listen.

Many critics did not find it as interesting as Chabrol's other works. They felt that rather than fleshing out a moral dilemma, Chabrol set out to preach a point, and therefore remained too distant from his subject matter to make it really compelling. But it is a fascinating complement to *The Unfaithful Wife*.

206 *Justice est faite (Justice Is Done)*   1950 B&W   *Director* André Cayette; *Producer* Silver Films, Robert Dorfmann; *Screenplay* André Cayatte and Charles Spaak; *Photography* Jean-Serge Bourgoin; *Music* Raymond Legrand; *Set* Jacques Colombier; *Sound* Antoine Archimbaud; *Editing* Christian Gaudin. Running time: 105 minutes.

Cast: Valentine Tessier, Claude Nollier, Antoine Balpêtré, Noël Roquevert, Raymond Bussières, Marcel Pérès, Juliette Faber, Nane Germon, Jean-Pierre Grenier, Jacques Castelot, Dita Parlo, Annette Poivre, Michel Auclair, Jean

Debucourt, Marce Mouloudji, Marguerite Garcya, Elisabeth Hardy, Agnès Delahaie, Anouk Ferjac, Jean d'Yd, Emile Drain, Paul Frankeur, Claude Nicot, Robert Moor, Geneviève Morel, Lucien Pascal, Jean Vilar, Paul Faivre, Marcelle Hainia, Cécile Didier, Léonce Corne, Albert Michel, Roger Vincent, Gustave Gallet, Frédéric Mariotti, Madeleine Gérôme, Nina Myral, Camille Guérini, Robert Rollis, Colette Régis, Marie-Louise Godard, Madeleine Suffel, Maurice Schutz, Fernand Gilbert, Henri Coutet, Albert Malbert, Emile Genevois, Maurice Marceau, Sylvain, André Numès Jr., Françoise Hornez, Benoite Lab, Nicolas Amato, Marcel Rouzé, René Pascal, Alain Raffaël, Jean-Claude Rameau, Renée Gardès, Dominique Marcas, Maryse Paillet.

Elsa Lundenstein (Nollier) is on trial in Versailles for the murder of her wealthy lover, whom she killed because he was dying of terminal cancer. As the members of the jury hear testimony, they also continue to go about their lives. Among the jurors are a waiter, a horse breeder, a printer, a retired officer, a merchant, an antique dealer and a farmer. Elsa's fate lies with them and their personal prejudices. Do they believe it was a mercy killing or a crime of greed?

This wonderful film noir, which allows the audience to learn the details of the murder as the jury does, was a very shocking idea for a movie at the time, because it shifted the focus away from the woman on trial to the jurors and their moral biases. Cayette successfully reveals how justice is done according to a random group of individuals' private moral codes and prejudices. Seven years after this film, Sidney Lumet made his name with the same concept in *Twelve Angry Men.*

Bosley Crowther of *The New York Times* hailed this film as proof of the revival of French film. He called it "a beautiful manifestation of the traditional candor and inquisitiveness of the French." It won the Grand Prix Internationale at the Venice Biennal in 1950.

Justice Is Done *see* **Justice est faite**

207 *Kashima Paradise* 1973 Color   *Director* Yann Le Masson and Benie Deswarte; *Producer* COFERC; *Screenplay* Yann Le Masson and Benie Deswarte; *Photography* Yann Le Masson; *Music* Hiroshi Hara; *Sound* Benie Deswarte. *Commentary* Chris Marker. Running time: XX minutes.

A documentary about daily life in a Japanese village as the construction of an industrial complex in the area brings changes. Within one year, the village life evolves from an almost medieval character to an advanced industrial pace.

This documentary could be seen as a microcosm of the history of Japan in the 50 years after World War II as the entire country rushed out of an ancient culture to rapidly embrace Western industrialism. The film began as sociologist Benie Deswarte's thesis on changes in rural communities, and it takes a Marxist perspective in examining the clash between traditional ways and modernization. The battle between the police defending the airport building and protesting peasants and students is shocking. While the individual characters are less important than the issues being explored, the film is quite moving.

Critics recognized both the film's faults and fortes. Margaret Tarratt in *Films and Filming* wrote: "For all its absorbing subject matter, it is stylistically an uneven film." Russell Davies of the *London Observer* concurred: "Like most of the other cinema's imports, *Kashima Paradise* is overlong and doctrinaire, but well worth the price of a ticket." It won the Prix Georges Sadoul in 1973.

Keep an Eye on Amelia *see* **Occupe-toi d'Amélie**

The Keepers *see* **La Tête contre les murs**

Killer *see* **Que la bête meure**

The King and Mr. Bird *see* **Le Roi et l'oiseau**

The King and the Bird *see* **Le Roi et l'oiseau**

The King and the Mockingbird *see* **Le Roi et l'oiseau**

The King of Hearts *see* **Le Roi de cœur**

A King Without Distractions *see* **Un Roi sans divertissement**

The Kite from Across the World *see* **Le Cerf-volant du bout du monde**

Knave of Hearts *see* **Monsieur Ripois**

The Lacemaker *see* **La Dentellière**

208 *Lacombe, Lucien* 1974 Color *Director* Louis Malle; *Producer* NEF-UPF-Vides Films and Hallelujah Films; *Screenplay* Louis Malle and Patrick Modiano; *Photography* Tonino Delli Colli; *Music* Django Reinhardt and songs of the era; *Set* Henri Vergnes; *Editing* Suzanne Baron. Running time: 135 minutes.

Cast: Pierre Blaise, Aurore Clément, Holger Lowenadler, Gilberte Rivet, Thérèse Ghiese, Stéphane Bouy, Loumi Jacobesco, René Bouloc, Pierre Decazes, Jean Rougerie, Cécile Ricard, Jacqueline Staup, Ave Ninchi, Pierre Saintons, Jean Bousquet, Jacques Rispal, Walter Sedlmayr, Roger Riffard.

Set in June 1944 in a tiny village in the southwest of France. A young boy, Lucien Lacombe (Blaise), by a series of coincidences more than by design, ends up working for a group of French collaborators. When he meets a Jewish tailor and falls in love with his daughter, France (Clément), he does not give up the easy lifestyle of the collaborators until France and her grandmother are taken away by the Gestapo. Lucien kills their German escort and tries to escape with them, but he is stopped by the Resistance.

When the film came out, there was a huge reaction against Malle for portraying the French Resistance in a poor light, and shortly after the French outcry Malle emigrated to America where he went on to make such American films as *Atlantic City* and *Pretty Baby*. What interested Malle was the idea of the role chance plays in historic events. As an indifferent survivor, Lucien could just as easily have joined the Resistance as the Gestapo. Malle wanted to tell the story without judging Lucien, and that objectivity was the root of the scandal. For in the 1970s, the issue in France was still a black and white one, with no room for gray interpretations: all collaborators were still bad and all Resistance fighters were good.

While many French critics could not forgive Malle for his patriotic indifference, American critics recognized the film as the work of a great filmmaker. Frank Rich in the *New Times* raved: "*Lacombe, Lucien* most profoundly fufills Santayana's dictate that we remember the past, and as it does so, Louis Malle also makes us remember just what great filmmaking is all about." Pauline Kael of *The New Yorker* said: "The picture is a knockout." It was nominated for an Oscar for Best Foreign Film and won the French Critics' Prix Méliès in 1974.

Ladies of the Park *see* **Les Dames du Bois de Boulogne**

The Lame Devil *see* **Le Diable boiteux**

209 *Landru (Bluebeard)* 1963 Color   *Director* Claude Chabrol; *Producer* Rome Paris Films, CCC; *Screenplay* Françoise Sagan; *Photography* Jean Rabier; *Music* Pierre Jansen; *Set* Jacques Saulnier; *Sound* Julien Coutellier; *Costumes* Maurice Albray; *Editing* Jacques Gaillard. Running time: 115 minutes.

Cast: Charles Denner, Danielle Darrieux, Michèle Morgan, Catherine Rouvel, Juliette Mayniel, Hildegarde Neff, Mary Marquet, Denise Provence, Stéphane Audran, Raymond Queneau, Jean-Pierre Melville, Jean-Louis Maury, Sacha Briquet, Robert Burnier, Françoise Lugagne, Claude Mansard, Giselle Sandré, Mario David, Serge Bento, Diana Lepvrier, Huguette Forge, Christian Lude, Dominique Zardi, Pierre Vernier, André Fouché, Alain Quercy, Charles Bayard, Louis Saintève, Roger Vincent, Philippe Castelli, Frank Maurice, Henri Attal, André Badin, Jacques Munier, Louis Lyonnet, Eric Muller, Jacques Robiolles, René Pannetrat, Pierre Lafont, Joseph Hendley, André Dino, Bernard Papineau, Robert Barre, Jean-Marie Arnoux.

A comedy based on the true story of the French mass murderer Henri-Désiré Landru, who killed at least ten women during World War I. Landru (Denner) lures wealthy women to his house, where he persuades them to sign their fortunes over to him and then kills them and disposes of their bodies. He pursues his psychotic passion purely for the money, until he is finally arrested and sent to the guillotine.

Suprisingly, this macabre tale makes for great comedy in the hands of Chabrol. Both he and novelist Françoise Sagan, who wrote the film's screenplay, were more interested in the bourgeois connection and the idea of murder for money than with understanding the psychology of a mass murderer. The art nouveau locations and glorious costumes set the time period and could well stand alone as an aesthetic documentary of the era.

Many critics faulted Chabrol's use of World War I newsreel footage. They found it undercut his humor and provided what was possibly a too facile explanation for Landru's heinous deeds. But still more found it delightful.

The Last Battle *see* **Le Dernier Combat**

The Last Holiday *see* **Les Dernières Vacances**

The Last Métro *see* **Le Dernier Métro**

Last Year at Marienbad *see* **L'Année dernière à Marienbad**

210 *La Lectrice (The Reader)* 1988 Color   *Director* Michel Deville; *Producer* AAA Productions, Eléfilm, TSF Productions, Ciné 5, Sofimage; *Screenplay*

Rosalinde and Michel Deville, based on a novel by Raymond Jean; *Photography* Dominique Le Rigoleur; *Music* Ludwig von Beethoven; *Set* Thierry Leproust; *Sound* Philippe Lioret; *Editing* Raymonde Guyot. Running time: 98 minutes.

Cast: Miou-Miou, Maria Casarès, Patrick Chesnais, Pierre Dux, Régis Royer, Brigitte Catillon, Christian Ruché, Sylvie Laporte, Marianne Denicourt, Clotilde de Bayser, Simon Eine, Jean-Luc Boutté, Christian Blanc, Michel Raskine, Bérangère Bonvoisin, André Wilms, Clotilde de Bayser, Léo Campion, Charlotte Farran, Hito Jaulmes, Maria de Medeiros, Isabelle Janier, Sylvie Jean.

Constance (Miou-Miou) is an avid reader who identifies with a heroine in the novel *The Reader*. Blessed with a lovely voice, she reads in bed to her lover and acts the part of Marie, who volunteers to read to people in a convalescent home. She befriends a young parapalegic, Eric (Royer), a sentimental general's wife (Casarès), and a mother and daughter. By reading Maupassant, Tolstoy and Lewis Carroll, Constance manages to transport these sad, broken people out of their lonely lives.

An intelligent film that succeeds in its literary underpinnings by matching classic texts with innovative images and is one of Deville's best works. It blends humor, poetry, sex and surrealism. Michel Deville worked with his wife Rosalinde for 15 years before she wrote this film, her first screenplay. They wanted to make a film about the joys of reading, which they do by connecting the characters with the stories they read. "In the film there are several inner universes which we wanted to render unusual, a bit unreal and out of sync," said Rosalinde Deville. The multiple layers are further emphasized, with actors playing multiple parts in the film. Miou-Miou, for whom the role of Constance/Marie was written, gives one of her best performances.

Critics called it sensual, poetic and elegant. Dave Kehr of the *Chicago Tribune* raved: "Michel Deville could be the last purveyor of what was once known to art house audiences as 'the French touch'—a little bit of irony for the intellect, and a little bit of naughtiness for the libido." The film was nominated for nine Césars and won the Prix Louis Delluc.

211 *Léon Morin, prêtre (Leon Morin, Priest)* 1961 B&W   *Director* Jean-Pierre Melville; *Producer* Rome Paris Films, C.C. Champion Rome; *Screenplay* Jean-Pierre Melville, based on the novel by Béatrice Beck; *Photography* Henri Decaë and Jean Rabier; *Music* Albert Raisner and Martial Solal; *Set* Daniel Guéret; *Sound* Guy Villette; *Editing* Jacqueline Meppiel, Nadine Marquand, and Marie-Josèphe Yoyotte. Running time: 130 minutes.

Cast: Jean-Paul Belmondo, Emmanuelle Riva, Irène Truc, Nicole Mirel, Marco Behar, Monique Hennessy, Monique Bertho, Patricia Gozzi, Edith Loria, Lucienne Lemarchand, Adeline Aucoc, Howard Vernon, Gérard Buhr, Volker Schlöndorff, Serge Vannier, Ernest Varial, Madeleine Ganne, Gisèle Grimme, Marielle Gozzi, Nelly Pittore, Nina Grégoire, Louis Saintève, Cedric Grant, Marc Eyraud, Georges Lambert, André Badin.

Set in occupied France, this psychological drama explores the love of a young atheist and Marxist war widow (Riva) for a handsome, but committed priest (Belmondo). A militant communist hiding out in the Alps enters a confessional to play head games with the priest. She returns again and again, moved not by religion, but by her passion for the priest. When he rejects her, she goes back to Paris to resume her political life.

Hailed as one of the only "genuine religious films in the history of cinema," this film is much more. With a masterful director schooled in handling intellectual and spiritual material and two superb actors, *Leon Morin, Priest* is a work of great art. The screenplay was based on a factual account about a woman during the war who was converted to Catholicism as she fell in love with a young priest. Belmondo and Riva are both beautiful, and the dialogue they toss back and forth is subtle and deep.

Critics admired the intelligence and reserve of this film. Gordon Gow exclaimed: "Although Jean-Pierre Melville has pointed out that he is not a Christian, his direction of *Leon Morin, Priest* has resulted in a film of Christian sentiments and one that should interest people of any religion."

Leon Morin, Priest *see* **Léon Morin, prêtre**

Let Joy Reign Supreme *see* **Que la fête commence**

212 *Le Lieu de crime (Scene of the Crime)* 1986 Color   *Director* André Téchiné; *Producer* T. Films, Films A2; *Screenplay* André Téchiné, Olivier Assayes and Pascal Bonitzer; *Photography* Pascal Marti; *Music* Philippe Sarde; *Set* Jean-Pierre Kohut Svelko; *Sound* Michel Klochendler; *Costumes* Caroline de Vivaise and Chirstain Gasc; *Editing* Martine Giordano. Running time: 90 minutes.

Cast: Catherine Deneuve, Victor Lanoux, Danielle Darrieux, Wadeck Stanczak, Nicolas Giraudi, Jacques Nolot, Claire Nebout, Jean-Claude Adelin, Jean Bousquet, Christine Paolini, Philippe Landoulsi, Michel Grimaud.

A romantic thriller about a nightclub owner, Lili (Deneuve), and her son, who get caught up in dangerous situations as they try to hide a criminal. Fourteen-year-old Thomas (Giraudi) meets an escaped convict, Martin (Stanczak). Martin saves Thomas' life — when his fellow escapee plans to kill the boy, Martin shoots him first. Martin then meets Thomas' mother, Lili, who is divorced and runs a nightclub on the river. They become passionately involved, but the other escaped convict's girlfriend wants revenge for her lover's murder.

Téchiné's best film, *Scene of the Crime* is full of romance, intrigue and personal histories — it is perfect auteur material. Téchiné he said of Deneuve's character, who propels the film: "She is a woman who rebels against herself and the life she has led up until now. We realize that this very sweet woman is possessed by a violence which will slowly turn into what others consider madness. The spectator must judge for himself." This is one of Deneuve's best roles. The first ten minutes of the film were inspired by the opening of Charles Dickens' *Great Expectations*.

French critics loved *The Scene of the Crime*. The film was chosen as the official selection at the Cannes Film Festival. American critics were less taken with it. They did not deny its beauty, but felt it was more of a series of lovely scenes than a full-fledged movie. David Denby of *New York* was in the minority when he exclaimed: "But while you're watching it, *Scene of the Crime* is completely absorbing, propelled as it is by the kind of innocent, unself-conscious storytelling energy that was once the staple of French and American filmmaking."

Life and Nothing But *see* **La Vie et rien d'autre**

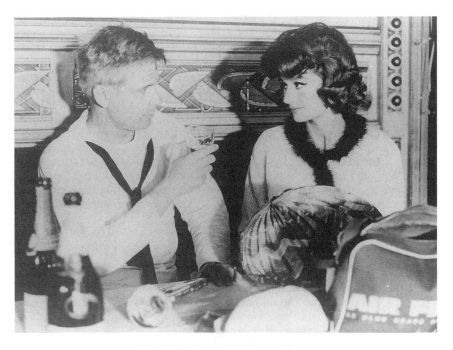

Lola, 1960; directed by Jacques Demy.

213 *Lola* 1960 B&W   *Director* Jacques Demy; *Producer* Rome Paris Films; *Screenplay* Jacques Demy; *Photography* Raoul Coutard; *Music* Michel Legrand with extracts by Bach, Beethoven, Mozart, Weber, and a song by

Marguerite Monnot; *Set* Bernard Evein; *Costumes* Bernard Evein; *Editing* Anne-Marie Cotret. Running time: 90 minutes.

Cast: Anouk Aimée, Marc Michel, Elina Labourdette, Jacques Harden, Allan Scott, Margo Lion, Annie Dupéroux, Catherine Lutz, Corinne Marchand, Dorothée Blank, Isabelle Lugghini, Annick Noël, Yvette Anziani, Anni Zamyre, Ginette Valton, Jacques Goasguen, Babette Bardin, Jacques Lebreton, Gérard Delaroche, Carlo Nell, Marie-Christine Maufrais, Raphaël Héry, Jean Porcher.

Lola (Aimée) is a cabaret dancer and single mother who patiently awaits the return of Michel (Harden), the father of her child and the only man she has ever loved. Neither Frankie (Scott), an American sailor, nor Roland (Michel), a long-lost school friend can make Lola forget the man who abandoned her seven years before. The story explores the power and sorrow of first love as all the characters in the film find themselves somehow connected to Lola and her idealized love, which proves worth waiting for when Michel drives up in a big American Cadillac and takes her off into the sunset.

This was Demy's first film and his New Wave style touched with realism, romanticism and neo-classicism makes it wonderfully fresh, even decades later. It is considered his best film because of the poetic symmetry of encounters and coincidences, though *Umbrellas of Cherbourg* is more well known. Demy turned his hometown of Nantes into an enchanted city of fairy tale romance. He dedicated the film to Max Ophüls, and he enriches the film with references to American symbols and other movies, including Ophüls' *Lola Montès* and *La Ronde*, which is evoked in the series of coincidences. Anouk Aimée is absolutely lovely.

When it was released at the height of New Wave experiments, some French critics complained that it was very sentimental and melodramatic in an old-fashioned way. One admiring critic saw it as an attempt to relate the story of one woman's life without using flashbacks. When it was rereleased in America in 1990, *The New York Post* critic called it: "Just sheer miracle as a first feature film or, for that matter, as any film about men, women, longing, chance, and love."

214 *Lola Montès (The Fall of Lola Montes)*   1955 Color   *Director* Max Ophüls; *Producer* Gamma Films, Florida Films, Union Films; *Screenplay* Max Ophüls, Annette Wademant, Frank Geiger, and Jacques Natanson, based on the novel by Cécil Saint-Laurent; *Photography* Christian Matras; *Music* Georges Auric; *Set* Jean d'Eaubonne; *Sound* Antoine Petitjean; *Costumes* Marcel Escoffier and Georges Annenkov; *Editing* Madeleine Gug. Running time: 100 minutes.

Cast: Martine Carol, Anton Walbrook, Peter Ustinov, Ivan Desny, Lise Delamare, Paulette Dubost, Henri Guisol, Oskar Werner, Will Quadflieg, Werner Finck, Gustav Waldau, Béatrice Arnac, Hélèna Manson, Friedrich Domin, Claude Pinoteau, Walter Kiaulehn, Willy Rösner, Pieral, Marcel Ophüls, Germaine Delbat, Edy Debray, Jean Filliez, Bernard Musson, Willy Eichberger, Jacques Fayet, Betty Philipsen, Hélène Iawkoff, Jeanine Fabre, Yvonne Dany.

The story of Maria Dolorès Porriz y Montez, known as Lola Montès (Carol). In 1880, she is the main attraction of the Mammouth Circus in New Orleans. Once the beauty of Europe, she was the lover of Liszt (Quadflieg) and the King of Bavaria (Walbrook), among others. After the story of her life is told each night, Lola performs a death-defying leap before she is locked in a golden cage where she is viewed by the audience, and people pay a dollar to kiss her hand.

This was Ophüls' last film and many believe it to be his greatest. He made it after the successful string of *La Ronde*, *Le Plaisir* and *The Earrings of Madame de*. . . . Apparently, Ophüls got the idea for *Lola Montès* after hearing about Judy Garland's nervous breakdown and Zsa Zsa Gabor's celebrated romances. It is a grand visual experience in color with Ophüls' creative choreography. He made it with a star-studded cast and an enormous budget.

Though it was expected to be an enormous success, the film bombed when it opened in Paris in 1955. Two years later, as Ophüls was dying, his producers cut it down by almost an hour and put it in chronological order, with Lola Montès' life told in order of events, which was a mistake because Ophüls' art lay in the narrative construction. It was not until 1969 when a reconstructed version was released that it was accorded critical accolades. While it was badly received by the public, the film did become a cult favorite of cinema buffs. It was either loved or hated by the critics, who dismissed it as long and boring or hailed it as a Baroque masterpiece. When it was finally released in the United States in 1969, Andrew Sarris declared the film a masterpiece, echoing France's New Wave critics who loved it.

The Long Absence *see* **Une Aussi Longue Absence**

Look at Madness *see* **Regard sur la folie**

215 *Loulou* 1980 Color *Director* Maurice Pialat; *Producer* Klaus Hellwig, Yves Gasser, Yves Peyrot; *Screenplay* Arlette Langmann and Maurice Pialat; *Photography* Pierre William Glenn; *Music* Philippe Sarde; *Set* Max Berto; *Sound* Dominique Dalmasso; *Editing* Yann Dedet. Running time: 110 minutes.

Cast: Gérard Depardieu, Isabelle Huppert, Guy Marchand, Humbert Balsan, Bernard Tronczyk, Xavier Saint Macary, Christian Bouchet, Frédérique Cerbonnet, Jacqueline Dufranne, Willy Safar, Agnès Rosier, Patricia Coulet, Patrick Playez, Jean-Claude Meilland, Gérald Garnier, Catherine de Guirchitch, Jean Van Herzeele, Patrick Poivey.

Nelly (Huppert), the wife of advertising executive André (Marchand) meets a handsome thug, Loulou (Depardieu), at a disco. Seduced by his rough ways and animal magnetism, she is abruptly brought out of her humdrum life. For a short time, she imagines she can maintain her bourgeois married life, while staying involved with Loulou and even having his baby. After meeting Loulou's gang, though, she realizes she has to choose.

This is one of Pialat's finest films and a fantastic example of modern social realism. The best scene is the family scene with its confrontation between the traditional values of the bourgeoisie and the freedom offered to bohemians. Like many great French films, such as *Breathless* and *The Keepers*, this film explores the allure of independence and liberty and the suffocation of bourgeois security. It captures the ambiguous anguish of the late 1970s very deftly.

Many French critics found Depardieu's character too unappealing to really inspire Huppert's character to abandon her social status, but others hailed the film's liberating erotic abandon. Andrew Sarris called *Loulou*'s Huppert and Depardieu "the sexiest couple in the history of the cinema."

The Love Game *see* **Les Jeux de l'amour**

Love on the Run *see* **L'Amour en fuite**

Loulou, **1980; directed by Maurice Pialat.**

Love Without Pity *see* **Un Monde sans pitié**

The Lover *see* **L'Amant**

The Lovers *see* **Les Amants**

Lovers and Thieves *see* **Assassins et voleurs**

Lovers, Happy Lovers! *see* **Monsieur Ripois**

The Lovers of Verona *see* **Les Amants de Vérone**

216 *Lumière (Light)* 1976 Color   *Director* Jeanne Moreau; *Producer* Orphé Arts, FR3; *Screenplay* Jeanne Moreau; *Photography* Ricardo Aronovitch; *Music* Astor Piazzola; *Set* Raoul Albert; *Sound* Harald Maury; *Costumes* Christian Gasc; *Editing* Albert Jurgenson. Running time: 95 minutes.

Cast: Jeanne Moreau, Francine Racette, Lucia Bosè, Caroline Cartier, Marie Henriau, Monique Tarbes, Keith Carradine, Bruno Ganz, François Simon, Francis Huster, Bruno Ganz, Jacques Spiesser, Niels Arestrup, Georges Wod, Alexsandre, René Feret, Anders Holmquist.

The reunion of four actresses, who are closer to each other than the men who are their romantic partners. They each recount their hopes and anguishes. When a friend of Laura's kills himself, they all take stock of their lives. Sarah (Moreau) is at the height of her career, but involved in a messy tangle of love affairs. Laura (Bosè) has sacrificed her career to become a mother living in a troubled marriage. Caroline (Cartier) devotes all to her career. Julienne (Racette) finds the answer to all her worries in running off with a new lover.

This was Moreau's directorial debut and one of the first female-friendship movies ever made. In discussing the film, she said, "It is about the life women lead when we are alone together. I didn't do this as an activist or a feminist, though I am for equality. But I thought it was necessary to show that intimacy that is only possible among women alone." At the time *Lumière* opened, the depth that female characters displayed in this film was revolutionary. Rarely had there been a film focusing on women's struggles with balancing love and friendship, family and career. The film sparked a number of female-bonding movies and has become a regular selection at women's film festivals.

The film received rave reviews when it opened in France and was well received in the United States. Applauding the worldy, intelligent women of Moreau's film, Dan Rottenberg wrote in *Chicago*: "I think I know the women in *Lumière*, but I have never seen them before on a movie screen."

Lust for Evil *see* **Plein Soleil**

The Mad Cage *see* **La Cage aux folles**

217 *Ma Nuit chez Maud (My Night at Maud's* or *My Night with Maud)* 1969 B&W   *Director* Eric Rohmer; *Producer* Films du Losange, La Guéville, Simar, Renn Productions, Films du Carrosse, Films des Deux Mondes; *Screenplay* Eric Rohmer; *Photography* Nestor Almendros; *Set* Nicole Rachline; *Sound* Jean-Pierre Ruh; *Editing* Cécile Decugis. Running time: 110 minutes.

Cast: Françoise Fabian, Jean-Louis Trintignant, Marie-Christine Barrault, Antoine Vitez, Léonide Kogan, Anne Dubot, Marie Becker, Guy Léger, Marie-Claude Rauzier.

Games of love are played at one's own risk in the provinces, where truth and falsehoods are not easy to distinguish. A young engineer, Jean-Louis (Trintignant),

Madame de ... (The Earrings of Madame de ...), 1953; directed by Max Ophüls.

learns the hard way when he is frustrated by his love for a girl (Barrault) he thinks is out of his reach and allows a friend to introduce him to a young divorcée, Maud (Fabian), who sets a "moral" trap.

This is the quintessential proof that a man and a woman talking can make for a great movie. It is the third film of Rohmer's six-part "Moral Tales." The idea that a Catholic man, a Marxist man and a liberated woman talking about religion and probability late into the night could make an exciting movie may seem absurd, but Rohmer pulls it off with great wit and grace. In fact, he makes male-female elevated banter sexier than most on-screen bedroom antics. Creating the right mood was so important for Rohmer that he waited a whole year to shoot the film on Christmas Eve. Trintignant does a fabulous job portraying the moral and intellectual anguish of a thinking man with physical urges.

The film was a great international success. In the United States, it was called a "gem" or "much ado about nothing." In defending his rave review against an angry reader letter, Roger Ebert said: "*My Night at Maud's* assumes that we are intelligent, perceptive adults who do not need to have everything spelled out. Being alive can be a tremendously subtle and exciting enterprise, and Eric Rohmer shares that delight with us." The film won the French Critics' Prix Méliès and the New York Film Critics' Award for Best Screenplay. It was nominated for Oscars for Best Foreign Film and Best Original Screenplay in 1969.

218 *Madame Bovary* 1991 Color   *Director* Claude Chabrol; *Producer* MK2 Productions, CED Productions, FR3 Films; *Screenplay* Claude Chabrol, based on the novel by Gustauve Flaubert; *Photography* Jean Rabier; *Music* Matthieu

Chabrol, Scarlatti, Donizetti, Johann Strauss and J.M. Tavernier; *Set* Michèle Abbe; *Sound* Jean-Bernard Thomasson; *Costumes* Corinne Jorry; *Editing* Monique Fardoulis. Running time: 140 minutes.

Cast: Isabelle Huppert, Jean Yanne, Jean-François Balmer, Christophe Malaboy, Lucas Belvaux, Christiane Minazzoli, Jean-Louis Maury, Florent Gibassier, Jean-Claude Bouillaud, Sabeline Campo, Yves Verhoeven, Marie Mergey, François Maistre, Dominique Clément, Etienne Draber, Jacques Dynam, Pierre-François, Christine Paolini, Thomas Chabrol, Henri Attal, André Thrent, Dominique Zardi, Gilette Barbier, and the voice of François Périer.

Gustauve Flaubert's classic about a farmer's daughter, Emma (Huppert), who marries her village's Doctor Bovary (Balmer). The country doctor's wife is carried away by fantasies of romance and passions for luxuries, which lead her down the tragic path of adultery, indebtedness and ultimately to suicide.

Chabrol beautifully adapted France's most read literary classic to the screen, proving that literary filmmaking is still a French art. This was Chabrol's forty-fourth film. Seven directors before him had adapted the novel, but he believed none were totally faithful. "I want this to be almost a film by Flaubert," he said. To achieve this, he used actual quotes from the novel throughout the film. The small-town social life is carefully wrought, as is Emma's emotional unraveling. Isabelle Huppert accomplishes the amazing feat of being at once familiar and fresh as Emma Bovary.

Not surprisingly *Madame Bovary* incited impassioned opinions in France, where just about every citizen has read the novel at least once. Some critics found Huppert miscast as Emma. Others adored the film. *Film Journal* said: "If, in the end, the film leads one back to the book for more, this in no way detracts from Chabrol's accomplishment. The director's tribute is our good fortune."

219 *Madame de* ... (*The Earrings of Madame de* ...) 1953

B&W   *Director* Max Ophüls; *Producer* Franco London Films, Indus Films, Rizzoli Films; *Screenplay* by Marcel Achard, Max Ophüls, and Annette Wademant, based on the novel by Louise de Vilmorin; *Photography* Christian Matras; *Music* Oscar Strauss; *Set* Jean d'Eaubonne; *Sound* Antoine Petitjean; *Costumes* Georges Annenkov and Rosine Delamare; *Editing* Boris Lewin. Running time: 100 minutes.

Cast: Danielle Darrieux, Charles Boyer, Vittorio de Sica, Mireille Perrey, Jean Debucourt, Jean Galland, Lia Di Leo, Germaine Stainval, Claire Duhamel, Michel Salina, Madeleine Barbulée, Paul Azaïs, Albert Michel, Colette Régis, Guy Favières, Léon Pauléon, Robert Moor, Emile Genevois, Léon Walther, Jacques Beauvais, Jean Degrave, Gérard Buhr, Georges Vitray, Jean Toulout, Roger Vincent, Josselin, Charles Bayard, René Worms, Max Mégy, Frank Maurice, Louis Saintève, Daniel Mendaille, Serge Lecointe.

A tragic love story set amongst the French aristocracy, in which a society wife's (Darrieux) flirtation with another man (de Sica) becomes a passionate obsession. When her husband (Boyer) gives her a pair of diamond earrings, they mean so little to her that she sells them to pay off debts and says that she has lost them. When her lover gives her the same earrings, they mean everything to her. Ultimately, she puts love before honor; the earrings become proof of her infidelity, and she destroys her life, her husband's and her lover's.

One of the most visually beautiful movies ever made, as the glittering world of crystal chandeliers, marble ballrooms and bejeweled and begowned women is

La Maman et la putain (The Mother and the Whore), 1973; Jean Eustache.

captured by the fluid, swirling camera style for which Ophüls is most famous. Because of his sensitive direction, the transformation of a society woman from shallow to sincere, from dilettantish to dying of love is harrowingly moving. Regarded by many as Ophüls' masterpiece, the film has fabulous performances by all three principal actors and probably Darrieux's best performance ever.

Some critics claimed that style overwhelmed Ophüls' film and left him with a trite representation of decadent lives. British critic Lindsay Anderson dismissed Ophüls and *The Earrings of Madame de ...* as "uncommitted, unconcerned with profundities." But others argue that the degree of sensibility expressed in the film could not exist in a less refined setting. Ophüls' style is about glitter and glamour. As Pauline Kael wrote: "By removing love from the real world of ugliness and incoherence and vulgarity, Ophüls was able to distill the essences of love."

Madame Rosa *see* **La Vie devant soi**

220 *Maine-Océan (Maine-Ocean Express)* 1985 Color *Director* Jacques Rozier; *Producer* Paolo Branco; *Screenplay* Jacques Rozier, Lydia Feld; *Photography* Acacio de Almeida; *Music* Chico Buarqure, Hubert Degex, Anne Frédérick; *Sound* Nicolas Lefebvre; *Editing* Jacques Rozier, Martine Brun. Running time: 131 minutes.

Cast: Bernard Menez, Yves Afonso, Luis Rego, Rosa-Maria Gomes, Lydia Feld, Pedro Armendariz Jr., Bernard Dumaine, Mike Marshall, Jean-Jacques Jelot-Blanc, Christian Bouillette.

The story of a number of odd characters who meet on a Brittany-bound train, the Maine-Océan Express from Paris. A Brazilian samba dancer, Dejanira (Gomes), meets two ticket inspectors: Le Garrec (Menez) and Pompiseau (Rego). Dejanira accompanies a young lawyer, Mimi de Saint-Marc (Feld), to the trial of a sailor whom she is defending against an assault charge. After the girl does a pathetic job of trying to help the sailor's defense, the group is reunited on an island off the Breton coast. They indulge in a samba rehearsal and one of the train inspectors fantasizes that he is a movie star, before some of them take off on a plane for the United States.

This zany film was the comeback film of obscure New Wave director Jacques Rozier, who after the success of *Adieu Philippine* only made two other films in 26 years. The film is a celebration of chaos, an emotional joyride and a cinematic holiday. Rozier was more interested in creating odd character studies than weaving a traditional plot line. The music and photography are wonderful. It has a rare quirky quality that works.

Some critics did not make the suspension of disbelief Rozier had hoped to effect. *Variety* said: "*Maine-Océan* goes nowhere, and takes well over two hours to get there." But *La Revue du Cinéma* hailed the work as "the anti-hip film par excellence" and applauded Rozier's "unbelievable daring." The film won the Prix Jean Vigo in 1986.

Maine-Ocean Express *see* **Maine-Océan**

Mama, There's a Man in Your Bed *see* **Romuald et Juliette**

221 *La Maman et la putain (The Mother and the Whore)* 1973 B&W *Director* Jean Eustache; *Producer* Flite, Losange, Simar, Ciné Qua Non, V.M.

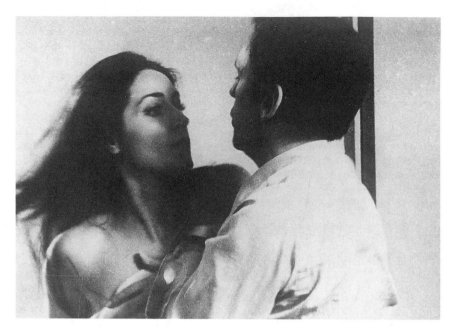

Ma Nuit chez Maud (My Night at Maud's), 1969; **Eric Rohmer.**

Films; *Screenplay* Jean Eustache; *Photography* Pierre Lhomme; *Music* Offenbach, Mozart with songs by Damia, Fréhel, Edith Piaf, Marlène Dietrich, Deep Purple, and Zarah Leander; *Set* Outdoors; *Costumes* Catherine; *Editing* Jean Eustache, Denise de Casabianca. Running time: 210 minutes.

Cast: Bernadette Laffont, Jean-Pierre Léaud, Françoise Lebrun, Isabelle Weingarten, Jacques Renard, Berthe Grandval, Jean-Noël Picq, Jessa Darrieux, Marinka Matuszewski, Geneviève Mnich, Jean Douchet, Noël Simsolo, Jean Eustache, Pierre Cottrell, Bernard Eisenschitz, Douchka, Jean-Claude Biette, André Téchiné.

Alexandre (Léaud) passes his days reading and hanging out in the cafés of Saint-Germain des Près. He lives comfortably with an older woman, Marie (Lafont), until he meets a young nurse, Veronika (Lebrun). The three manage to live together happily for a short while, but just when Marie and Alexandre begin to understand that Veronika is unstable, she announces that she is pregnant with Alexandre's baby and wants to keep it. Alexandre is caught between two women: a mother and trouble.

One of the most important French films of the decade, this work captured a great sense of the period. After working as an assistant director for New Wave directors such as Godard and making two feature length movies of his own, Eustache put himself on the cinematic map with this film, which captured perfectly the aimless anguish of a generation. Eustache was heavily influenced by Renoir, and this film and the way in which he made it reflect that debt. He wrote, directed and edited. It is very referential because he was interested in exploring the relationship between life and film.

Many have hailed it as the film that signaled the end to the New Wave era. Some critics found it too long and vulgar. Most, though, were thrilled by its intelligent freshness and applauded the young filmmaker's depth. Unfortunately, Eustache made only one more feature movie. He committed suicide in 1981, after he was permanently injured in an accident. The film won the Special Jury Prize, the Grand Prix and the International Critics Award at Cannes.

Man About Town *see* **Le Silence est d'or**

A Man and a Woman *see* **Un Homme et une femme**

A Man Escaped *see* **Un Condamné à mort s'est échappé**

The Man Who Loved Women *see* **L'Homme qui aimait les femmes**

222 *Manèges (The Cheat* or *The Riding School)* 1950 B&W *Director* Yves Allégret; *Producer* Discina; *Screenplay* Jacques Sigurd; *Photography* Jean-Serge Bourgoin; *Music* Real sounds; *Set* Auguste Capelier, based on designs by Alex Trauner; *Sound* Jean Calvet and Jacques Carrier; *Editing* Maurice Serein. Running time: 90 minutes.

Cast: Simone Signoret, Jane Marken, Bernard Blier, Frank Villard, Jean Ozenne, Jacques Baumer, Laure Diana, Gabriel Gobin, Fernand Rauzéna, Mona Doll, Jean Hébey, Yvonne Rozille, Pierre Naugier, Alain Debrus, Maurice Derville, Gisèle François, Diana Bel, Pierre Leproux, Jacques Harden, Monroy, Pierre Leproux.

Dora (Signoret) has been injured in an automobile accident. At her bedside, thinking she will certainly die, her mother (Marken) confesses to Dora's husband, Robert (Blier), that her daughter never loved him but only wanted to marry him for his money. She was actually on her way to see one of her lovers when she got in the accident. Horrified, Robert leaves the wretched mother and daughter. Dora remains paralyzed.

This film is a wonderfully intelligent tale of suspense as well as a biting social critique. It was one of the films that set the stylistic tone of postwar French filmmaking. The director builds suspense and emotion with flashbacks and character revelations to create a searing condemnation of materialism and greed. This was one of Simone Signoret's early roles, and her performance as the grasping wife is multi-faceted and enthralling. Bernard Blier does an equally wonderful job as her doting husband.

Critics and the public loved this film noir. *Variety* said: "The film is underlined with a bitter irony that makes it one of the most important social films to come out of France this year."

223 *Manon* 1948 B&W *Director* Henri-Georges Clouzot; *Producer* Alcina; *Screenplay* Henri-Georges Clouzot and Jean Ferry, based on Abbé Antoine-François Prévost's novel, *Manon Lescaut*; *Photography* Armand Thiard; *Music* Paul Misraki; *Set* Max Douy; *Sound* William Sivel; *Editing* Monique Kirsanoff. Running time: 90 minutes.

Cast: Cécile Aubry, Michel Auclair, Serge Reggiani, Gabrielle Dorziat, Raymond Souplex, Henry Vilbert, Simone Valère, Andrex, Hélène Manson, Daniel

Yvernel, Jean Despeaux, Gabrielle Fontant, Robert Dalban, Michel Bouquet, Max Elloy, Charles Camus, Jacques Dynam, Edmond Ardisson, Jean Termerson, François Joux, André Valmy, Jean Hebey, Charles Vissières, Genviève Morel, Frédéric Mariotti, Harry Niel, Frank Maurice, Jean Lagache, Marcel Pérez, Jean Marc Tennberg, Louis Vonelly, Georges Fabre, Pierre Trabaud, Robert Frétel, Rosy Varte, Dora Doll, Liliane Maigné, Max Doria, Wanda Ottoni, Hubert de Lapparent, Perette Souplex, Victor Tabournot.

A tragic love story that takes place at the end of the Occupation. While France celebrates liberation from the Nazis, two young lovers' troubles are just beginning. After Manon (Aubry), who is condemned by the people in her village for her amoral conduct during the war, falls in love with a Resistance fighter, Robert (Auclair), the two escape to Paris. Manon's brother, Léon (Reggiani), exploits her vulnerable situation and forces her into prostitution. Finally, the lovers set off for Israel, but both of them do not come out of the desert alive.

This is one of the greatest love stories made after the war. Its motto, "Nothing is dirty when you are in love," came out of a world where black markets and black hearts seemed to be the norm. It explored passionate love that could survive any hardship, any distance and any pain. The lovers who almost survived all of the obstacles put in their path were ultimately liberated by their love. It was the film that launched Cécile Aubry.

Many were offended by the film's apparent condoning of an amoral woman, but that attitude missed the point. One French critic dismissed Manon, the film and the character with, "this graceful, little creature's only aim in life is pleasure." But Clouzot was concerned not with pleasure, but passion. "With a total ignorance of evil and an instinctual disregard for sin, she desperately seeks to be a woman swept away by her crazy love for the one man she loves," wrote A. Kyrou. It won the International Grand Prize at the Venice Biennal and the French Critics' Prix Méliès in 1949.

224 *Manon des sources (Manon of the Spring)*   1987 Color   *Director* Claude Berri; *Producer* Renn Productions, A2, RAI, 2DD; *Screenplay* Claude Berri and Gérard Brach, based on Marcel Pagnol's novel, *L'Eau des collines*; *Photography* Bruno Nuytten; *Music* Jean-Claude Petit; *Set* Bernard Vezat; *Sound* Pierre Gamet; *Costumes* Sylvie Gautrelet; *Editing* Genviève Louveau, Hervé de Luze. Running time 113 minutes.

Cast: Yves Montand, Emmanuelle Béart, Daniel Auteil, Elisabeth Depardieu, Armand Meffre, Pierre Nougaro, Marc Betton, Jean Maurel, Roger Souza, Margarita Lozano, André Dupon, Pierre-Jean Rippert, Didier Pain, Fransined, Chantal Liennel, Hippolyte Girardot, Gabriel Bacquier, Lucien Damiani, Tiki Olgado, Jean Bouchaud, Yvonne Gamy, Eve Brenner.

The sequel to *Jean de Florette* begins about a dozen years after Jean died of exhaustion trying to farm his arid land in the Provençal hills. His daughter, Manon (Béart), lives wild in the hills. Ugolin (Auteil) falls desperately in love with her, but she rejects him. To revenge her father's death, she blocks the source of the town's water supply. In front of the entire town, she accuses Ugolin and Le Papet (Montand) of killing her father. Ugolin hangs himself and Manon marries the local school teacher. When Le Papet learns that Jean was his long-lost son, he dies of sorrow, bequeathing his sprawling, prosperous farm to Manon.

This beautiful film is a great drama and a visual masterpiece. It works both as a sequel and on its own. The two films were made for $17 million in the south of France. They brought majestic drama and beauty to Pagnol's Provençal tale. This film launched the splendid careers of Emmanuele Béart and Daniel Auteil, who are lovers in real life and have worked together in other films, such as *A Heart in Winter*.

Like *Jean de Florette*, this film received rave reviews from critics in France and abroad. Roger Ebert of the *Chicago Sun-Times* said, "*Manon* announces the arrival of a strong and beautiful new actress from France in Emmanuelle Béart." The two films won eight Césars and were co-winners of the National Board of Review's Best Foreign Language Film Award.

Manon of the Spring *see* **Manon des sources**

Man's Hope *see* **L'Espoir**

225 *Le Mari de la coiffeuse (The Hairdresser's Husband)*   1990 Color *Director* Patrice Leconte; *Producer* Lambert Productions, TF1 Films Productions; *Screenplay* Patrice Leconte; *Adapatation* Patrice Leconte and Claude Klotz; *Photography* Eduardo Serra; *Music* Michael Nyman; *Set* Yvan Maussion; *Sound* Pierre Lenoir; *Editing* Joëlle Hache. Running time: 84 minutes.

Cast: Jean Rochefort, Anna Galiena, Roland Bertin, Maurice Chévit, Philippe Clévnot, Jacques Mathou, Anne-Marie Pisani, Claude Aufaure, Albert Delpy, Henry Hocking, Ticky Holgado, Michèle Laroque, Pierre Meyrand, Youssef Hamid, Laurence Ragon, Yveline Ailhaud, Thomas Rochefort.

A romantic and erotic obsession that began when 12-year-old Antoine fell in love with the woman who cut his hair. As an adolescent, he lived between haircuts and fantasies about the hairdresser. Determined to marry a hairdresser, grown-up Antoine (Rochefort) achieves his goal. Her name is Mathilde (Galiena), and he proposes while she cuts his hair for the first time. When he comes back for a second cut, she accepts and their sexual and emotional adventure begins.

This is a wonderful mix of art, eroticism and humor that grew out of the director's own adolescent obsession with his hairdresser. "I loved the way this woman tended to me. She smelled good, she was gentle and her voice was very calm. I figured that whoever lived with her must be the happiest man in the world," said Leconte. He did not marry a hairdresser, so instead he wrote a love story about what "ought to have been." His light touch plays just above a surface of darkness and perversity to make this an interesting and amusing film in the tradition of Truffaut's *The Man Who Loved Women*.

Critics generally liked this film. *Film Review* said: "The art of such playfulness is never to outstay your welcome or delve into artschool boorishness. Leconte does neither, and produces what is probably the greatest film about hairdressers ever made."

226 *Marianne de ma jeunesse (Marianne of My Youth)*   1955 B&W   *Director* Julien Duvivier; *Producer* Filmsonor, Regina, Royal Film, Allfram; *Screenplay* Julien Duvivier, based on Peter Mendelssohn's novel *Douloureuse Arcadie*; *Photography* Léonce-Henri Burel; *Music* Jacques Ibert; *Set* Jean d'Eaubonne; *Sound* Antoine Archimbaud, Maurice Laroche; *Editing* Marthe Poncin. Running time: 105 minutes.

Cast: Marianne Hold, Pierre Vaneck, Gil Vidal, Jean Galland, Isabelle Pia, Jean Yonnel, Gérard Fallec, Jacques de Féraudy, Adi Berber, Serge Delmas, Fredrich Domin, Michel Ande, Jean-François Bailly.

A schoolboy, Vincent (Vaneck), arrives at a Bavarian castle, where the children of wealthy families go to school. As an amusement, he leads his new friends into the country to discover a magical new world. By a lake, Vincent, who has a poetical nature, meets a beautiful young magician, Marianne (Hold). He is captivated, but when she disappears, he never knows if she was real or just a dream.

A poetic fantasy, this film creates a wonderful cinematic dreamworld, where ogres, haunted castles and vanishing beauties exist. Duvivier had played with fantasy on film before, but this is easily his greatest success. He evokes familiar fairy tale sights and subtly suggests Freudian themes. The performances of the boys are wonderful. The photography is lovely.

This was an enormous critical and commercial success in France. American critics were less enamoured. *Cue* said, "Duvivier presents an overlong and rather disjointed mood piece."

Marianne of My Youth *see* **Marianne de ma jeunesse**

The Mark of the Day *see* **Le Point du jour**

227 *Masculin féminin (Masculine-Feminine)* 1966 B&W   *Director* Jean-Luc Godard; *Producer* Anouchka, Argos Films, Svensk Filmindustri; *Screenplay* Jean-Luc Godard, based on the Guy de Maupassant stories *The Signal* and *Paul's Mistress*; *Photography* Willy Kurant; *Music* Francis Lai; *Sound* René Levert; *Editing* Agnès Guillemot, Marguerite Renoir. Running time: 103 minutes.

Cast: Jean-Pierre Léaud, Chantal Goya, Marlène Jobert, Michel Debord, Birger Malmsten, Eva Britt Strandberg, Catherine Duport, Elsa Leroy, Françoise Hardy, Brigitte Bardot, Antoine Bourseiller, Chantal Darget, Dominique Zardi, Henri Attal.

Paul (Léaud) is a 1960s dreamer in search of the perfect love. He thinks he finds it when he meets Madeleine (Goya) at a café. They move in together and she pursues a singing career while he goes to work for a market research company. Soon after Madeleine becomes pregnant, Paul falls from scaffolding. Not knowing whether it was suicide or an accident, she wonders whether to have their baby.

This is one of Godard's best movies and Léaud's finest adult role. Godard has said that this was his exploration of the generation of the "children of Marx and Coca-Cola." The film contains full interviews, which he felt made the movie as much a documentary of youth culture as a love story about disappointment. Unfortunately, when people under the age of 18 were banned from seeing the film in France, Godard was cut off from the main audience whom he had hoped to reach.

Godard said, "I wanted to show the moments of these kids. One is always reproached in film for not tackling the whole issue. But that is it, cinema is life and life is full of different things .... I have fifteen sequences in the film, I subtitled them 'Fifteen precise facts'." Critics found that the film vacillated between the poignant and the painful, but most hailed it as extremely intelligent, if ideological.

Masculine-Feminine *see* **Masculin féminin**

228 *Les Maudits (The Damned)*   1947 B&W   *Director* René Clément; *Producer* Spéva Films; *Screenplay* Jacques Companeez and Alexandroff, based on Jacques Companeez's story idea; *Adaptation* Jacques Rémy and René Clément; *Dialogue* Henri Jeanson; *Photography* Henri Alekan; *Music* Yves Baudrier; *Set* Paul Bertrand; *Sound* Joseph de Bretagne and Robert Teisseire; *Editing* Roger Dwyre. Running time: 105 minutes.

Cast: Florence Marly, Anne Campion, Paul Bernard, Henri Vidal, Michel Auclair, Marcel Dalio, Fosco Giacchetti, Jo Dest, Lucien Hector, Carl Munch, Kronefeld, Jean Didier, Paul Sabas, Claude Vernier, George Niemann, Andreas von Halberstadt, Max Hermann, Pierre Fuchs, Jean Lozach, Carrère, Michel Thierry.

At the end of World War II, a group of Nazis and Nazi sympathizers try to flee to South America by submarine. When the sub is attacked and one of the passengers is wounded, they stop on the French coast and force young Dr. Guilbert (Vidal) to come with them. For all of the passengers, from the German general to a rich Italian couple, the voyage ends badly. The doctor is the only one left when the Americans meet the submarine.

One of the first great war films by the master of them all, this fictionalized film has documentary aspects similar to his classic *Battle of the Rail*. Clément's intent was to recreate a microcosm of France's tensions and struggles during the war within the confines of the submarine. In a submarine that was reconstructed on a movie set, Clément creates the literal and metaphorical sense of Sartre's *No Exit*. He brings out the extreme personalities very well.

The Damned was a huge success in France and did well in the United States. Critics found it gripping and masterfully wrought. *PM* raved: "A cross-section of moral and sexual corruption seldom treated by the popular films!" The film won the Prize for Best Adventure Film at Cannes in 1947.

229 *Mauvais Sang (Bad Blood* or *The Night Is Young)*   1986 Color *Director* Leos Carax; *Producer* Les Films Plain Chant, Soprofilms, FR3 Films; *Screenplay* Leos Carax; *Photography* Jean-Yves Escoffier; *Music* Benjamin Britten, Prokofiev, Charlie Chaplin; *Set* Michel Vandestien, Thomas Peckre, Jack Dubus; *Sound* Harrick Maury; *Costumes* Robert Nardonne; *Editing* Nelly Quettier, Hélène Muller. Running time: 125 minutes.

Cast: Denis Lavant, Juliette Binoche, Michel Piccoli, Hans Meyer, Julie Delpy, Carroll Brooks, Hugo Pratt, Serge Reggiani, Mireille Perrier, Jérôme Zucca, Charles Schmitt, Philippe Fretin.

Alex (Lavant) was a petty thief until his father died suspiciously on the Métro. He goes into hiding and two former associates of his father, Hans (Meyer) and Marc (Piccoli), convince him to help them steal the only known cure to a horrible new disease that ravages false lovers. Another gang, who is also after the drug and had a hand in his father's death, tries to woo Alex to their side, but he only has eyes for Marc's girlfriend (Binoche).

Leos Carax's second film is another brilliant exercise in modern expressionist filmmaking. It confirmed his auspicious debut and some even dubbed him Godard's heir apparent. He exhibited a great flair for creating a new look and feel to cinema, in the same way that Beineix did in *Diva* and the New Wave directors did 20 years earlier. He pays tribute to cartoons, Buster Keaton, and even his own film, *Boy Meets Girl*, which also starred Lavant as Alex.

French critics applauded Carax's cinematic sense of daring. The film has not yet been distributed in the United States. *La Revue du Cinéma* exclaimed "Brilliantly acted, fascinating because of its feverish passion for film and its intelligent distance from romantic archetypes, *Bad Blood* is a sure thing, an event in our cinema." The film won two awards at the Berlin Film Festival.

230 *Les Mauvaises Rencontres (The Bad Liaisons)* 1955 B&W *Director* Alexandre Astruc; *Producer* Films Marceau; *Screenplay* Alexandre Astruc and Roland Laudenbach, based on Cecil Saint-Laurent's novel *Une sacrée salade*; *Photography* Robert Lefebvre; *Music* Maurice Leroux; *Set* Max Douy; *Sound* Antoine Archimbaud; *Editing* Maurice Serein. Running time: 84 minutes.

Cast: Jean-Claude Pascal, Anouk Aimée, Philippe Lemaire, Gaby Sylvia, Claude Dauphin, Yves Robert, Giani Esposito, Madeleine Ganne, Michel Piccoli, Jean Ozenne, Charles Bayard.

Told in flashbacks, this is the story of an ambitious young woman, Catherine Racan (Aimée), who comes to Paris with her lover, Pierre (Esposito), but he leaves her to return to the provinces soon after they arrive. Blaise Walter (Pascal), a big newspaperman, launches her career as a journalist. Catherine, in turn, helps her new lover, Alain (Lemaire), get his photographs published. Her meeting with Dr. Danieli (Dauphin), whom she visits to get an abortion, proves to be her most important encounter, and she finally does become famous, though not in the way she had intended.

This early New Wave film explores the moral and intellectual incertitude of young modern people. It is quite literary, with voiceovers and flashbacks and very little camera movement. Astruc himself, who was heavily influenced by Orson Welles, believed it marked a very important point in French filmmaking, from which there was no going back. "I was working against the overuse of camera movements, overly studied framing, all embellishments. In all of that there is something old-fashioned and juvenile," he said.

Some critics compared *Bad Liaisons* to Hitchcock's films. They rejoiced that a filmmaker was interested in young intellectuals' concerns and in showing Paris an ambition in new, flattering lights. Others deemed it too intellectual, pretentious, and unpolished. Of course, the people who loved it most were those under the age of 30.

Max *see* **Max et les ferrailleurs**

Max and the Junkmen *see* **Max et les ferrailleurs**

231 *Max et les ferrailleurs (Max or Max and the Junkmen)* 1970 Color *Director* Claude Sautet; *Producer* Lira Films, Sonocam; *Screenplay* Claude Sautet, Claude Néron and Jean-Loup Dabadie, based on the novel by Claude Néron; *Photography* René Mathelin; *Music* Philippe Sarde; *Set* Pierre Guffroy; *Sound* René Longuet; *Editing* Jacqueline Thiédot. Running time: 110 minutes.

Cast: Michel Piccoli, Romy Schneider, Bernard Fresson, François Périer, Georges Wilson, Boby Lapointe, Michel Creton, Henri-Jacques Huet, Jacques Canselier, Alain Grellier, Maurice Auzel, Philippe Léotard, Robert Favart, Léa Gray, Dany Jacquet, Danielle Durou, Betty Beckers, Dominique Zardi, Jacques Cottin, Bernard Musson, Henri Coutet, Albert Augier, Michel Dupleix, Jean-Paul Blonday, Gaston Meunier, Jack Lenoir, Alain Belard, Muriel Delumaux.

Le Mépris (Contempt), **1963; directed by Jean-Luc Godard.**

A police story about Max (Piccoli), an officer who takes his job very seriously. When he meets up with his old friend, Abel (Fresson), who has gone bad, Max decides to set the perfect trap. When the commissioner wants to arrest Lily (Schneider) for complicity, Max, who has fallen in love with her, kills him, and he is arrested while she goes free.

This film is more of a portrait of paranoia than a police drama. Sautet was interested in the idea of personal obsessions playing out to their destructive extreme. His depiction of society's shady characters is authentic and instructive. The film has traces of his earlier Lino Venturi thrillers and old Fritz Lang films. Piccoli and Schneider are both wonderful. The screenwriter went on to collaborate with Sautet throughout the 1970s.

The film was a great success. Critics applauded Sautet's ability to bring a natural romanticism to a police thriller. *Film and Filming* called it a "minor Sautet gem."

May Fools *see* **Milou en mai**

232 *La Meilleur Façon de marcher (The Best Way to Get Along)* 1975
Director Claude Miller; *Producer* Filmobic/Mag Bodard, J.F. Davy; *Screenplay* Claude Miller; *Photography* Bruno Nuytten; *Music* Alain Jomy; *Set* Hilton McConnico; *Costumes* Hilton McConnico; *Editing* Jean-Bernard Bonis. Running time: 90 minutes.

Cast: Patricke Dewaere, Patrick Bouchitey, Christine Pascal, Claude Piéplu, Michel Blanc, Marc Chapiteau, Michel Such, Frank D'Ascanio, Nathan Miller.

Set in 1960 in a summer camp in the Auvergne region, this is the story of two young men. Marc (Dewaere) is a virile outdoorsman. Philippe (Bouchitey) teaches drama to the children at the camp. One night Marc spies Philippe dressed in women's clothing, a revelation that profoundly changes their relationship. Even though Philippe is involved with a woman (Pascal), a dangerous mistrust and hostility arises between the two men.

Claude Miller's film is a brilliantly balanced work that navigates uncharted territory with subtlety, humor and intelligence. It explores a man's confusion about his sexuality without resorting to any pat answers or conclusions. In fact, its examination of intolerance goes beyond homosexuality and relates to any form of prejudice. Both Dewaere and Bouchitey handle their roles masterfully.

The film was warmly received by French critics when it came out. François Truffaut in *L'Avant-Scène du Cinéma* applauded Miller's film for its depth and control. He exclaimed, "The words racism, sexism, fascism, homosexuality, virility are never said and they don't need to be in this dance of death."

Ménage *see* **Tenue de soirée**

Ménage à trois *see* **Tenue de soirée**

233 *Le Mépris (Contempt)* 1963 Color   *Director* Jean-Luc Godard; *Producer* Rome Paris Films, Concordia, Compania Champion; *Screenplay* based on Alberto Moravia's novel, *Il Diprezzo*; *Adaptation* Jean-Luc Godard; *Photography* Raoul Coutard; *Music* Georges Delerue; *Sound* William Sivel; *Editing* Agnès Guillemot. Running time: 100 minutes.

Cast: Brigitte Bardot, Michel Piccoli, Jack Palance, Fritz Lang, Georgia Moll, Linda Véras, Jean-Luc Godard.

While filming a movie of *The Odyssey* in Italy, Camille (Bardot), who is married to the film's screenwriter, Paul (Piccoli), finds the magic of their marital love broken in one decisive moment. No longer able to love him, she decides to run off with the film's American producer (Palance). Her decision proves to be irreversible.

One of the best, most beautiful and certainly easiest to follow of Godard's films. Godard described the film as "the story of a misunderstanding between a man and a woman." Despite a major display of Bardot's buttocks, there is something very sad and realistic in this story of how true love can seem to vanish in one moment when one lover becomes in some way contemptible in the other lover's eyes. It is also a fabulous homage to cinema, including a great scene in which Fritz Lang discusses film with Godard.

Critics generally lauded *The Contempt*. American critic Armond White described the film's depth: "Each character represents a level of inquiry on sex, love, power and creativity. Because he is more poet than pedant, Godard counters the verbal emphasis with nearly overwhelming visual and sensual beauty."

Midnight Meeting *see* **Le Rendez-vous de minuit**

234 *Milou en mai (May Fools)* 1990 Color   *Director* Louis Malle; *Producer* Nouvelles Editions de Films, TF1, Ellepi Films; *Screenplay* Louis Malle; *Photography* Renato Berta; *Music* Stéphane Grappelli; *Set* Willy Holt; *Sound* Jean-Claude Laureux; *Editing* Emmanuelle Castro. Running time: 105 minutes.

Cast: Michel Piccoli, Miou-Miou, Michel Duchaussoy, Dominique Blanc, Harriet Walter, Paulette Dubost, Bruno Carette, François Berléand, Martine Gautier, Rozenn Le Tallec, Renaud Danner, Jeanne Herry-Leclerc, Benjamin and Nicolas Prieur, Marcel Bories, Etienne Draber, Valérie Lemercier, Hubert Saint-Macary, Bernard Brocas, Georges Vaur, Jacqueline Staup, Anne-Marie Bonange, Denise Juskiewenski.

The death of a family matriarch brings a family together to a great estate in May 1968. The woman's 60-year-old son, Milou (Piccoli), who lived with her, gathers his brother and his wife, his niece and his daughter together with the family lawyer for the burial. Fights erupt over the inheritance. When a nephew arrives fresh from the riots in Paris, the world's larger social problems complicate things even further.

This provocative film is another masterful work by Malle, who once again integrates the personal and public perspectives of an important event in French history. He said that he wanted "to do a portrait of a family and a country estate in ruins that represents a privileged way of life that is about to end." As a child of privilege, Malle identified very strongly with the central character of Milou, who recognizes the lost lifestyle and mourns its passing. All of the performances are very good.

Some French critics complained that *Milou en Mai* was a poor shadow of Malle's *Murmur of the Heart*. Many others recognized its unique bittersweet charm. Lewis Archibald said, "This tale of some giddy goings on in the Spring goes down like May wine, bright, invigorating and with the lightest of sharp aftertastes."

Mr. Hulot's Holiday *see* **Les Vacances de Monsieur Hulot**

Mr. Klein *see* **Monsieur Klein**

235 *Moi, un noir* 1958 Color *Director* Jean Rouch; *Producer* Pierre Braunberger, Films de la Pléiade; *Screenplay* Jean Rouch; *Photography* Jean Rouch; *Music* Yapi Joseph Degre; *Sound* André Lubin and Radio Abidjan; *Editing* Marie-Josèphe Yoyotte and Catherine Dourgnon. Running time: 70 minutes.

Cast: Oumarou Ganda, Petit Touré, Alassane Maiga, Amadou Demba, Karidyo Faoudou, Seydou Guede, Madamoiselle Gambi.

The story of four Nigerians, three men and a woman, living in a shantytown in the Ivory Coast. The men go by the nicknames of Edward G. Robinson, Eddie Constantine and Tarzan. They have left their villages to make it in Abidjan, where malnutrition and destitution are the norm. During the week they search for menial jobs; but on the weekends they laugh, dance, get drunk, and dream.

This film blurred the lines between documentary and fiction in a significant way. It also presented a revolutionary perspective on Africa and its inhabitants. The director wanted to show daily lives in the most realistic fashion possible. He turned his camera on and the men went about living their lives. The magic he created was through showing the organic beauty in reality. This film was a major turning point in breaking the bonds of what cinéma vérité once had to be and was also a major influence on the work of many New Wave directors.

The film was a hit with critics, who compared Rouch to Rosselini, but it was

Mon Oncle (My Uncle), 1958; directed by Jacques Tati.

not a huge success at the box office. In *Arts*, Jean-Luc Godard wrote: "The director doesn't track the truth because it is scandalous, but because it is amusing, tragic, gracious, loony. What is important is that the truth is there . . . . His film offers us the open Sesame to poetry." It won the Prix Louis Dellluc in 1958.

236/7 *Mon Oncle (My Uncle)* 1958 Color   *Director* Jacques Tati; *Producer* Spectre Films, Gray Film, Alter Films, Films del Centauro; *Screenplay* Jacques Tati, Jacques Lagrange and Jean L'Hote; *Photography* Jean-Serge Bourgoin; *Music* Norbert Glanzberg, Alain Romans, Franck Barcellini; *Set* Henri Schmitt; *Editing* Suzanne Baron. Running time: 116 minutes.

Cast: Jacques Tati, Jean-Pierre Zola, Alain Becourt, Adrienne Servantie, Lucien Frégis, Jean-François Martial, Dominique Marie, André Dino, Betty Schneider, Max Martel, Yvonne Arnaud, Claude Badolle, Denise Péronne, Nicole Batailler, Dominique Derly, Régis Fontenay, Claire Rocca, Michel Goyot, Nicole Regnault, Edouard Francomme, Jean Rémoleux, Mancini, Suzanne Franck, René Lord, Marguerite Grillières, Loriot, Jean Meyet.

Hulot (Tati) lives happily in his old-fashioned way in an old neighborhood; but his ultra-modern, urbane family wants to help him out. His wealthy brother-in-law, Monsieur Arpel (Zola), wants to find him a job, while his sister wants to get him married to a fine lady. Their noble, middle-class ambitions reap hilarious results when pinned on the non-conformist Hulot.

Jacques Tati's first color film is one of his best. Its subject is the clashing of values, with Tati representing old traditions and his sister representing ultra-modern progress. Hulot is no longer the odd-ball, but he has a larger social and cultural significance as a member of the Old World. Tati finds unlimited possibility for humor and mishap in the modern world. After the film was shot, Tati spent a year editing and dubbing it. He also used a much larger film crew than he had ever worked with before.

Critics disagreed about how much of a message Tati intended. Some believed his film was similar to Italian neorealism because it explored larger social issues by examining small everyday events. Others disagreed, arguing that *Mon Oncle* may have been his best, most humorous and polished film to date, but that it still carried no coherent social message. When the movie was released in 1958, it became the most financially successful of all French films that year. French critics believed one of the reasons that Tati's films were so successful was that comedy had become so rare in French filmmaking at the time. It won the Special Jury Prize at Cannes and the French Critics' Prix Méliès in 1958. In 1959, it won the Oscar for Best Foreign Film and the New York Film Critics' Award.

238 *Mon Oncle d'Amérique (Les Somnambules)* 1980 Color   *Director* Alain Resnais; *Producer* Pierre Dussart, Andréa Films, TF1; *Screenplay* Jean Gruault, based on the works of Henri Laborit; *Photography* Sacha Vierny; *Music* Arié Dzierlatka; *Set* Jacques Saulnier; *Sound* Jean-Pierre Ruh, Jacques Maumont, Georges Prat; *Editing* Albert Jurgenson. Running time: 123 minutes.

Cast: Gérard Depardieu, Nicole Garcia, Roger Pierre, Nelly Borgeaud, Pierre Arditi, Marie Dubois, Gérard Darrieu, Philippe Laudenbach, Laurence Roy, Bernard Malaterre, Alexandre Rignault, Véronique Silver, Jean Lescot, Geneviève Mnich, Maurice Gautier, Ina Bédard, Stéphanie Lousteau, Guillaume Boisseau, Damien Boisseau, Jean-Philippe Puymartin, Ludovic Salis, François Calvez, Catherine Frot, Valérie Dréville, Gaston Vacchia, Monique Mauclair, Bertrand Lepage, Max Vialle, Yves Peneau, Jean-Bernard Guillard, Jean Dasté, Laurence Février, Charlotte Bonnet, Sébastien Drai, Anne Christine Joinneau, Marjorie Godin, Liliane Gaudet, Maria Laborit, Isabelle Ganz, Albert Médina, Laurence Badie, Carenne Ferrey, Sabine Thomas, Catherine Serre, Jacques Rispal, Hélène Manson, Serge Feuillard, Gilette Barbier, Dominique Rozan, Michel Muller, Martine Armand.

Midway through their lives, two men, Jean (Pierre) and René (Depardieu), and a woman, Janine (Garcia), are disappointed by their lots. Each dreams of an American uncle, a guardian angel, who will make their dreams come true. Their lives are examined against French scientist Henri Laborit's findings that human behavior is determined by unconscious impulses that give way to fight, flight, suicide, suffering and love, rather than by a magical muse. The three act and react, creating their own destinies.

This was Resnais' greatest commercial success and one of his best movies. It has a documentary feel with Henri Laborit explaining his findings directly to the camera. There are many film references as each character has a film hero that inspires him: for René it is Gabin, for Jean it is Marais, and for Janine it is Darrieux. What interested Resnais most was the structure, blending theoretical discourse with the unfolding of the individual lives.

Some critics complained that the film vacillated between drama and documentary and did not deliver enough of either. *L'Avant-Scène du Cinéma* said, "*Mon Oncle d'Amérique* is the merging of the genetic and the episodic charade, it is Treasure Island fed into the computer, it is Lewis Carroll's electric brain swelling." The film won the Special Jury Prize at Cannes, the Grand Prix du Cinéma Français, the French Critics' Prix Méliès, and the New York Film Critics' Award for Best Foreign Film in 1980. It was nominated for six Césars and an Oscar for Best Original Screenplay.

239 *Le Monde du silence (The Silent World)* 1956 Color *Director* Jacques Yves Cousteau and Louis Malle; *Producer* Filmad, FSJYC; *Photography* Edmond Séchan; *Underwater shots* taken by Louis Malle, Jacques Yves Cousteau, Albert Falco, Frédéric Dumas; *Music* Yves Baudrier; *Sound* Jacques Carrère; *Editing* Georges Alépée. Running time: 86 minutes.

An expedition with Jacques Cousteau in the Red Sea, the Indian Ocean and the Persian Gulf, which was filmed both underwater and above and captures, among other subjects, the activities of sponge fishers, an encounter with a troop of dolphins, a ship wrecked on the bottom of the Gulf of Suez, a feeding frenzy of sharks attacking a whale carcass, the deepest dive ever photographed, and an explanation of the customs of sea turtles.

The inventor of the self-contained underwater breathing apparatus, Jacques Cousteau, teamed up with a young director, Louis Malle, destined to become one of the world's great filmmakers, to make much more than the average documentary. After the enormous success of Cousteau's book by the same name, which chronicled a similar expedition, he decided to make this film. His crew travelled thousands of miles on his boat, the *Calypso*, filming sea discoveries as they went. The film was the most comprehensive look at the waterworld ever made.

Critics loved *The Silent World*'s view on the magical world under the sea. *The New Yorker* exclaimed: "By the time the film has run its course, he has succeeded in making us feel as if we were, in truth, taking part in this expedition." The film won the Palme d'Or at Cannes and was the co-winner of the French Critics' Prix Méliès in 1956.

240 *Un Monde sans pitié (Love Without Pity)* 1989 Color *Director* Eric Rochant; *Producer* Alain Rocca; *Screenplay* Eric Rochant; *Photography* Pierre Novion; *Music* Gérard Torikian; *Set* Thierry François; *Sound* Jean-Jacques Ferran; *Costumes* Zelia Van Den Bulke; *Editing* Michèle Darmon. Running time: 84 minutes.

Cast: Hippolyte Giradot, Mireille Perrier, Yvan Attal, Jean-Marie Rollin, Cécile Mazan, Aline Still, Paul Pavel, Anne Kessler, Patrick Blondel, Yves Boonen, Jean-Luc Porraz, Vincent Vallier, Patrick Pineau, Pierre Trabuy, Marc Behin, Biana, Hervé Falloux, Bernard Mazzinghi, Maryse Meryl, Gérard Dauzat, Claude Segarel, Olivier Destrez, Paul Bisciglia, Jean Clément, Marc Belini.

Set at the end of the 1980s and the beginning of the 1990s, on Paris' Left Bank, this is a love story about two young people who have very different approaches to life. A bachelor, Hippo (Giradot), lives with his younger drug-dealing brother, Xavier (Rollin), and despite his youth has already given up on the world. That is, until he meets Nathalie (Perrier), a brilliant young college student who is determined to succeed in whatever she does. The two fall passionately in love, but then Nathalie wins a scholarship to study in the United States When she returns a year later, she discovers that things change and remain the same.

This film beautifully captures the angst and anguish of teens and young adults in the 1980s. In France, the "generation X" apathy and angst was called the "j'm'en foutisme" or "I couldn't care less" spirit. Like many films of the late 1980s, the director found a poetry in the bleakness of the city. The film offers one of the most fresh and authentic views of contemporary Paris. This was Rochant's first film. He made it at age 28, and it announced an exciting new talent. It was one of the most successful debut movies in years.

Some critics hailed *Love Without Pity* as the *Breathless* of the 1990s. *Présence du Cinéma Français* exclaimed: "The passionless character in *Love Without Pity* might quickly have become irritating, even insipid, if it weren't for his disarming sincerity, his lucidity, and his sense of humor, which cause the viewer to quickly side with him." It won the Critics Prize at the Venice Biennal and two Césars.

241 *Le Monde sans soleil (World Without Sun)*   1964 Color   *Director* Jacques Yves Cousteau; *Producer* Requin Associés, CEIAP, Arsay Films; *Photography* Pierre Goupil; *Music* Serge Baudo; *Editing* Georges Alépée. Running time: 90 minutes.

Another underwater documentary about the adventures of Jacques Cousteau and his crew. It chronicles the experiences of seven ocean scientists who live for a full month 40 to 80 feet below the surface of the Red Sea. Their mission was to establish the first man-made underwater colony and prove that not only was life underwater possible, but it could be enjoyable.

Made after the great success of *The Silent World*, this film was hailed for boldly charting new cinematic territory as it further plumbed the depths of life underwater. The movie was released just as space exploration was capturing the world's fascination. It served as a wake-up call to the world that mysterious terrain exists below as well as above. The color photography brought a new perspective to the underworld, as did an expanded focus on Cousteau's team, the oceanauts and their mission.

The Christian Science Monitor called the film "luminous and lovely." *The Washington Post* raved, "*World Without Sun* is a record of endless fascination. Don't miss it." It won the Grand Prix du Cinéma Français in 1964 and was nominated for an Oscar.

242 *Monsieur Hire*   1989 Color   *Director* Patrice Leconte; *Producer* Carcassonne, Hachette Première, Europe 1 Communications; FR3 Films, CNC, Soficas; *Screenplay* Patrick Dewolf, Patrice Leconte, based on the novel by Georges Simenon, *Les Fiancelles de Monsieur Hire*; *Photography* Denis Lenoir; *Music* Michael Nyman; *Set* Ivan Maussion; *Sound* Pierre Lenoir; *Editing* Joëlle Hache. Running time: 88 minutes.

Cast: Michel Blanc, Sandrine Bonnaire, Luc Thuillier, André Wilms, Eric Béranger, Manuelle Berton, Philippe Dormoy.

Monsieur Hire (Blanc) is a lonely man, who lives without friends or activities, except for peeping on his lovely young neighbor, Alice (Bonnaire). When a murder is committed in the neighborhood, the odd Monsieur Hire, of course, becomes a suspect. Alice catches on to his peeping on her, and she befriends him in order to frame him for the murder that he knows she is involved in.

A modern film noir mystery with erotic overtones, *Monsieur Hire* is a fascinating and compelling film. Michel Blanc, who had worked on many films with Leconte, is wonderful as this strange character who is at once repulsive and intriguing. Leconte adapted the film from the same Simenon novel as Julien Duvivier's 1946 *Panic*, but set it in a modern, urban setting. His psychological portrait is gripping, suspenseful, and masterfully directed. It was the work that established Leconte as a serious filmmaker.

The film received rave reviews when it debuted at the Cannes Film Festival. American critics hailed the film as an astoundingly intelligent mystery. Roger Ebert raved in the *Chicago Sun Times*, "*Monsieur Hire* is a film about conversations that never are held, desires that never are expressed, fantasies that never are realized, and murder."

243 *Monsieur Klein (Mr. Klein)* 1976 Color   *Director* Joseph Losey; *Producer Screenplay* Franco Solinas, Fernando Morandi; *Photography* Gerry Fischer; *Music* Egisto Macchi and Pierre Porte; *Set* Pierre Duquesne; *Sound* Jean Labussière; *Editing* Henri Lanoë. Running time: 122 minutes.

Cast: Alain Delon, Jeanne Moreau, Juliet Berto, Suzanne Flon, Jean Bouise, Michel Lonsdale, Francine Bergé, Louis Seigner, Michel Aumont, Massimo Girotti, Francine Racette, Roland Bertin, Etienne Chicot, Pierre Vernier, Jacques Maury, Gérard Jugnot, Jean Champion, Pierre Frag, Fred Personne, Isabelle Sadoyan, Maurice Vallier, Christian de Tilière, Rosine Rochette, François Viaur, Magali Clément, Hermine Karagheuz, Dany Kogan, Mireille Franchino, Maurice Jany, Michel Delahaye, Alain David, Stéphane Quatrehomme, Maurice Baquet.

Robert Klein (Delon) is an art dealer, who makes a particularly good living during the Occupation by buying paintings from Jews in desperate straits. Then one day, his name appears in a Jewish paper, even though he is not Jewish. His life, livelihood and social status are all at stake. To save himself, he must uncover the person who is using his name as a cover to fool the Nazis.

A Kafkaesque story from one of the world's most esteemed filmmakers, *Monsieur Klein* was Losey's first French-language film. He created it out of the various trials that many people in France experienced during the Occupation. On a deeper level, Losey explores human identity in general, and what it means to be a Jew in particular. This is certainly one of Alain Delon's greatest roles and performances. Losey's views of Paris from the Gare d'Austerlitz and St.-Eustache to La Coupole are familiar and haunting.

The film debuted as France's official selection at the Cannes Film Festival and was an immediate critical success. Rex Reed in *The Daily News* raved: "A gloomy, haunting tale of conscience in the style of a thriller, it is Losey's *North by Northwest* re-mounted in Nazi-occupied Paris.... *Mr. Klein* is one of the more fascinating films this year." It won three Césars, including one for Best Director and one for Best Film in 1976.

244 *Monsieur Ripois (Lovers, Happy Lovers!* or *Knave of Hearts)*
1954 B&W   *Director* René Clément; *Producer* Graetz, Transcontinental; *Screenplay* Hugh Mills, René Clément, and Raymond Queneau, based on Louis Hémon's novel, *Monsieur Ripois et la némésis*; *Photography* Oswald Morris and Freddy Francis; *Music* Roman Vlad; *Set* Ralph Brinton; *Sound* Cecil Mason; *Costumes* Pierre Balmain and Freda Pearson; *Editing* Françoise Javet and Vera Campbell. Running time: 100 minutes.

Cast: Gérard Philipe, Germaine Montéro, Valérie Hobson, Margaret Johnston, Joan Greenwood, Diana Decker, Natasha Parry, Eric Pohlmann, Eileen

Monsieur Ripois (*Lovers, Happy Lovers!*), 1954; directed by René Clément.

Way, Bill Shine, Monica McLeod, Richard Hart, Arthur Howard, Beryl Cook, Margot Field, Mai Bacon, Julie Anslow, Bette Vivian, David Coste, Martin Benson, Gérard Camplan, John Boston.

Monsieur Ripois (Philipe) is an incurable French ladies' man living in London. When his English wife, Catherine (Hobson), gets fed up with his wayward ways and goes to Scotland to arrange a divorce, he sets his sights on her best friend, Patricia (Parry). To win her attention and sympathy, he tries recounting all of his sad love affairs. When that does not work, he plans to stage his suicide; but the plan backfires, and he ends up falling and paralyzing himself.

This is René Clément's best film and a fabulous moral tale. Sketching a complicated, but believable psychological portrait was so important to Clément that he hired a psychoanalyst as a consultant to advise him on the film. Ripois is a born seducer, who is unable to mend his ways or to be conscious of how he hurts others. The fabulous Gérard Philipe is at his very best. The scenes of London as seen through the eyes of a young Frenchman are memorable.

Some critics were unhappy with Clément's adaptation of Hémon's novel. Originally, Jean Aurenche, who adapted such great works as *Diary of a Young Country Priest*, was going to write the screenplay, but instead Clément did it himself with Raymond Queneau and Hugh Mills. That they changed Monsieur Ripois' first name from Amédée to André was seen as just the first of their transgressions. But others hailed the film as a work that is in and of itself, a masterpiece. It won the Special Jury Prize at Cannes for direction in 1954.

245 *Monsieur Vincent* 1947 B&W   *Director* Maurice Cloche; *Producer* UGC, EDIC. *Screenplay* Jean Bernard-Luc and Jean Anouilh; *Adaptation* Jean Anouilh, Maurice Cloche and Jean Bernard-Luc; *Dialogue* Jean Anouilh; *Photography* Claude Renoir; *Music* Jean-Jacques Grünenwald; *Set* René Renoux; *Sound* Jean Rieul; *Costumes* Rosine Delamare; *Editing* Jean Feyte. Running time: 110 minutes.

Cast: Pierre Fresnay, Aimé Clariond, Lise Delamare, Jean Debucourt, Gabrielle Dorziat, Robert Murzeau, Marcel Pérès, Jean Carmet, Yvonne Gaudeau, Véra Norman, Germaine Dermoz, Ginette Gaubert, Renée Thorel, Georges Vitray, Pierre Dux, Marcel Vallée, Michel Bouquet, Paul Faivre, Paul Demange, Guy Favières, Claude Nicot, Maurice Marceau, René Stern, Tony Taffin, Francette Vernillat, Gabrielle Fonton, Maximilienne, Geneviève Morel, Marthe Mellot, Nicole Riche, Alice Reichen, Yvonne Claudie, Joëlle Janin, Paul Renoir, Jean-Marc Tennberg, Georges Cerf, Max Rogerys, Max Harry, Jean Favre-Bertin, Gabert, Victor Vina, Andé Dumas, Jeanne Hardeyn.

A biographical picture about the life of Saint Vincent de Paul (Fresnay), a man who spent his entire life trying to help the unfortunate in France in the early 1600s. The parishioners whom he worked to save were victims of great ignorance, fear and misery. Vincent was later canonized by the Catholic Church for his good works with children and the sick.

This is a wonderful biographical and religious picture, which postwar France found extremely inspirational. Cloche began the film before the Occupation, but could not finish it until after the war. He funded the production of the film by selling subscriptions for profit shares through local churches. The dialogue by playwright Jean Anouilh is brilliant. Pierre Fresnay's skill in rendering the spiritual mission of a devoted religious man relaunched his film career.

The film was a great success in France and enjoyed an arthouse run in the United States. *The New York Herald Tribune* declared, "With Pierre Fresnay giving a strong and touching portrayal of the title role, the work has sweep, religious fervor and pictorial beauty." It won the Oscar for "Most outstanding foreign language film released in United States during 1948" before there was a category for Best Foreign Film. Pierre Fresnay won Best Actor at the Venice Biennal 1947.

246 *La Mort en ce jardin, cela s'appelle l'Aurora (Death in the Garden* **or** *Evil Eden)*   1956 Color   *Director* Luis Buñuel; *Producer* Dismage, Producciones Tepayac; *Screenplay* Luis Alcoriza, Luis Buñuel, Raymond Queneau, and Gabriel Arout, based on the novel by José André Lacour; *Photography* Jorge Stahl Junior; *Music* Paul Misraki; *Set* Edouard Fitzgerald; *Sound* José de Perez; *Editing* Marguerite Renoir. Running time: 104 minutes.

Cast: Georges Marchal, Simone Signoret, Charles Vanel, Michèle Girardon, Michel Piccoli, Tito Junco, Raul Ramirez, Stéfani, Luis Aceves Castanedas, Jorge Martinez de Hoyos, Alberto Pedret, J.M. Lambert, Alicia del Lago.

A motley group on the run from a brutal regime takes to the Brazilian jungle. An ex-convict, a prostitute, a priest, a trader, an adventurer, and a miner and his deaf daughter travel from selfishness to selflessness and then return to their old nasty ways. They bury the dead of an airline crash and dress up in their clothes before one goes mad and starts killing the others.

Believed to be one of Buñuel's most accessible films, this movie was made in 1956, but not released in the United States until 1977. The references to *The Wages of Fear* are obvious and the differences between Buñuel's surreal approach and Clouzot's realistic one exemplify the differences between these two auteurs and the changes in French cinema in 20 years.

Though few critics hailed this as a perfect work, most recognized it as a revolutionary comment on Christianity versus human nature.

247 *Mort en fraude (Fugitive in Saigon* **or** *Fraudulent Death)*   1957 B&W   *Director* Marcel Camus; *Producer* Intermondia; *Screenplay* Marcel Camus, based on the novel by Jean Hougron; *Dialogue* Michel Audiard; *Photography* Edmond Séchan; *Music* Vietnamese music arranged by N'Guyen Hum Bâ; *Lyrics* Henri Crolla; *Set* Paul-Louis Boutié; *Sound* Jean-Claude Marchetti; *Editing* Jacqueline Thiédot. Running time: 105 minutes.

Cast: Daniel Gélin, Anne Méchard, Lucien Callamand, Jean Combal, Jacques Chancerel, Vietnamese peasants.

Set in Indochina during the beginning of the national struggle against the French empire, Paul Horcier (Gélin) takes refuge in a tiny Vietnamese village when he is wrongly sought by the police for drug trafficking. He falls in love with a lovely Eurasian woman (Méchard). Eventually, he is killed by the police, when he tries to confront the traffickers.

This was Camus' first film, and it proved to be a surprisingly true and rare evocation of Indochina as it was in the last days of French colonialism. Camus manages to capture very well the heady atmosphere of a country on the brink of falling apart. Daniel Gélin is wonderful as an innocent and a daring do-gooder.

Some French critics applauded the mix of documentary glimpses and suspense. Others faulted it. The film ran in England, but was never released in the

United States. *Variety* said: "Film starts out as a taut thriller and segues into one of the first French filmic looks at the Indochinese debacle of 1950."

248 *La Morte en direct (Death Watch or Death in Full View)*   1980 Color   *Director* Bertrand Tavernier; *Producer* Selta Films, Little Bear, Antenne 2, Sara Films, Gaumont, SFP, Les Films 13, Planfilm; *Screenplay* David Rayfield and Bertrand Tavernier, based on David Compton's novel, *The Continuous Katherine Mortenhoe*; *Photography* Pierre William Glenn; *Music* Antoine Duhamel; *Set* Tony Pratt; *Sound* Michel Desrois; *Editing* Armand Psenny and Michael Ellis. Running time: 128 minutes.

Cast: Romy Schneider, Harvey Keitel, Harry Dean Stanton, Thérèse Liotard, Max von Sydow, William Russel, Carolyn Langrishe, Vadim Glowna, Bernard Wicki, Eva Maria Meineke, Paul Young, Derek Royle, Carey Wilson, John Sheddon, Peter Kelly, Freddie Boardley, Julian Hough, Ida Schuster, Maureen Jack, Vari Sylvester, Boyd Nelson, Jake d'Arcy, Bill Riddoch.

Set in Scotland in the not-too-distant future, Katherine (Schneider) is considered exceptional because she is dying in a world that has virtually eliminated mortality with scientific advances. After signing a contract allowing a television producer to shoot her story, Catherine runs off to the country to be with her husband, Gerald (Von Sydow). A reporter (Keitel) with a camera hidden in his head follows her.

This science fiction movie is more intelligent than most. It was a real departure for Tavernier in genre, language and locale. Tavernier made the film in English and shot most of it in Scotland. One of most interesting ideas explored is the media "vulturedom" that preys on personal tragedy. The international cast worked well to complement one another and create a sense of the global village.

Some critics complained that this was evidence of why a humanist filmmaker should not try to make a science-fiction picture. Others loved Tavernier's leaps of imagination brought to big screen life. Kevin Thomas of the *Los Angeles Times* called it "a major film in every way."

Mortelle Randonée [sic]   *see*   **Mortelle randonnée**

249 *Mortelle randonnée (Deadly Circuit or Mortelle Randonée* [sic]*)* 1982 Color   *Director* Claude Miller; *Producer* Téléma, TF1; *Screenplay* Michel Audiard, Jacques Audiard, based on the novel by Marc Behm; *Dialogue* Michel Audiard; *Photography* Pierre Lhomme; *Music* Carla Bley; *Set* Jean-Pierre Kohut Svelko; *Sound* Paul Lainé, Alex Pront; *Editing* Albert Jurgenson. Running time: 120 minutes.

Cast: Michel Serrault, Isabelle Adjani, Guy Marchand, Stéphane Audran, Sami Frey, Geneviève Page, Jean-Claude Brialy, Macha Méril, Dominique Frot, Etienne Chicot, Philippe Lelièvre, Isabelle Ho, Jeanne Herviale, Michel Such, Luc Béraud.

This is the story of a private detective known as the Eye (Serrault) assigned to a pretty young woman (Adjani), who reminds him of his long-lost daughter. He tracks her as she commits a series of murders. When he finally decides to stop her killing, it is too late. Rather than be apprehended, she kills herself.

A modern film noir, this film is a dark study of obsession that is beautifully presented. It is a gripping tale that spirals ever deeper into danger and deception. The screenplay is not only a strong adaptation from the novel, it is a witty and wise work as well. Serrault and Adjani circle each other like fascinated animals, desperately drawn to one another and yet always aware of the danger the other presents.

The film was hailed by critics in France, but it was never distributed in the United States. Pascal Mérigeau in *La Revue du Cinéma* exclaimed, "*Mortelle Randonnée*, a veritable voyage to the end of the night, evokes trouble, a vertigo of which there are few comparable works."

The Mother and the Whore *see* **La Maman et la putain**

250 *Mouchette* 1967 B&W *Director* Robert Bresson; *Producer* Argos Films, Parc Films; *Screenplay* Robert Bresson, based on Georges Bernanos' novel, *Nouvelle Histoire de Mouchette*; *Photography* Ghislain Cloquet; *Music* Montevardi; *Set* Pierre Guffroy; *Sound* Séverin Frankiel and Jacques Carrière; *Costumes* Odette LeBarbenchon; *Editing* Raymond Lamy. Running time: 90 minutes.

Cast: Nadine Mortier, Jean-Claude Guilbert, Marie Cardinal, Paul Hébert, Jean Viment, Marie Susini, Liliane Princet, Raymonde Chabrun, Suzanne Hugeunin, Marine Trichet, Robert Bresson.

The last day in the life of Mouchette (Nortier), a 14-year-old girl abandoned by her alcoholic parents. On her way home, Mouchette performs an act of kindness for a villager, who then brutally rapes her. She goes to her mother to tell her, but her mother dies before she can tell. Full of despair, the girl drowns herself.

Certainly, the saddest of Bresson's films, but also one of the most beautiful. In Bresson's second adaptation of a Bernanos novel, the first being the *Diary of a Young Country Priest*, his aim was to show that misery and cruelty were everywhere, not just in the obvious realms of war and murder. By showing the lonely, terrorized life of a young girl in search of affection and kindness, who meets only brutality and sorrow, he succeeds brilliantly. As in many of his other films, Bresson used a non-professional cast and wrung great performances from them.

American critic Henry Sheehan wrote of *Mouchette*: "For all the austerity, the stylistic provocations of acting and detail, what Bresson leaves you with at the end of his films is a profound sense of humanity, a sense that is more acute because of his appreciation for something greater that invests it." *Mouchette* was the co-winner of the French Critics' Prix Méliès in 1967.

Mountain Pass *see* **Passe-montagne**

251 *Mourir d'aimer* (*To Die of Love* or *Dying of Love* or *Mourir d'Aimer*) 1970 Color *Director* André Cayatte; *Producer* Franco London Films, Cobra Films; *Screenplay* André Cayatte, Albert Naud, and Pierre Dumayet; *Photography* Maurice Fellous; *Music* Louiguy; *Set* Robert Clavel; *Sound* René C. Forget; *Editing* Boris Lewin. Running time: 117 minutes.

Cast: Annie Giradot, Bruno Pradal, François Simon, Monique Mélinand, Nathalie Neil, Claude Cerval, Nicolas Dumayet, Bernard Jeantet, Marcelle Ranson, Hélène Dieudonné, Edith Loria, Marianick Révillon, Marie-Hélène Breillat, Jean Marconi, Jean Bouise, Jean-Paul Moulinot, Marcel Pérès, Claudine Berg, André Reybaz, Jacques Marin, Madeleine Damien, Martine Simon, Roger Trapp, Marthe Villalonga, Charles Millot, Maurice Nazil, Bernard Musson, Raymond Meunier, Yves Barsacq, Daniel Bellus, Clément Thierry, Marius Laurey, Marcel Gassouk, Jacky Blanchot, Jean Minisini, Marius Balbinot, Léo Peltier, Frank Combeau, Jean Bolo, Pipo Merisi, Guy Davout.

In the spring of 1968 in Rouen, a 30-year-old professor, Danièle (Giradot), and a student, Gérard (Pradal), who is 13 years her junior, have a passionate love affair. When his parents vow to put an end to it and to ruin Danièle, Gérard flees his new school. When Danièle refuses to reveal where he is, she is thrown in prison for two months while awaiting trial. She is tried, sentenced to a year in prison and then pardoned, only to face the threat of the prosecutor's appeal. When a letter asking Gérard to meet her never reaches him, tragedy follows.

This love story was taken from the true story of Gabrielle Russier. It wrestles with the issue of society determining where love can and cannot exist. The Russier trial and suicide divided French society so severely that it drew comparisons to the Dreyfus case. It resulted in challenges to the moral code and law in France by the press, intellectuals and famous writers. Intellectuals asked why French culture condones the initiation of young men into the ways of love by older women and then punishes them in society. When the film came out, the real-life parents, who pressed charges against Russier and put their son in a mental clinic, sued for defamation damages and seizure of all prints of the film. Their son left his parents on his eighteenth birthday. Annie Giradot is superb as Danièle.

The film was a huge success, with over 700,000 people seeing it in the first week it opened. *Le Canard Enchaîné* exclaimed: "This very beautiful film of André Cayatte's is an overwhelmingly damning document .... The world right now is filled with 'love stories.' This one should affect France a lot .... It should also anger and disturb a lot of comfortable, 'right-thinking' French people." It won the Grand Prix du Cinéma Français in 1970.

252 ***Le Mouton à cinq pattes (The Five-Legged Sheep)*** 1954 B&W *Director* Henri Verneuil; *Producer* Films Raoul Ploquin; *Screenplay* Albert Valentin, Jean Manse, Jean Marsan, Jacques Perret, Henri Troyat, René Barjavel; *Photography* Armand Thirard; *Music* Georges Van Parys; *Set* Robert Clavel; *Sound* William Sivel; *Editing* Christian Gaudin. Running time: 100 minutes.

Cast: Fernandel, Françoise Arnoul, Andrex, Georges Chamarat, Paulette Dubost, Noël Roquevert, Louis de Funès, Edouard Delmont, Denise Grey, René Génin, Nina Myral, Yvette Lucas, Léopoldo Frances, Tony Jacquot, Lolita Lopez, Micheline Gary, Dario Moréno, Ky Duyen, Michel Ardan, Edmond Ardisson, Paquerette, Yannick Malloire, José Casa, Manuel Gary, Jean Diener, René Havard, Albert-Michel, Rapaël Patorni, Philippe Richard, Frank Maurice, Gil Delamare, Alinda Kristensen, Jocelyne Bressy, Max Desrau, Loche.

The mayor of Trézignam decides to reunite the St.-Forget quintuplets on the anniversary of their fortieth birthday. The quintuplets, named A to E, have not spoken to their crotchety old father for years. The mayor sees a great publicity opportunity in a surprise family reunion. The town doctor rounds up all of the brothers. What he brings back are a successful beautician; a poor, but happy window washer with four daughters; a sea captain; a priest; and a "Miss Lonelyhearts" columnist.

This is the funniest of Fernandel's postwar movies. He plays six different roles. He plays the father and all five sons, which offers a great range for his comedic talents. His sea captain role is particularly hysterical, perhaps one of his best characters ever. Verneuil used Fernandel and a strong supporting cast to great effect.

As expected, this film was a huge hit in France where Fernandel was adored.

Some complained that this was a thinly veiled vehicle for Fernandel to get maximum screen time. But that was just what appealed to many others.

Muriel or the Time of Return *see* **Muriel ou le Temps d'un retour**

253 *Muriel ou le Temps d'un retour (Muriel or the Time of Return)*
1963 Color *Director* Alain Resnais; *Producer* Argos Films, Alpha Productions, Eclair, La Pléiade, Dear Films; *Screenplay* Jean Cayrol; *Photography* Sacha Vierny; *Music* Hans-Werner Henze; *Set* Jacques Saulnier; *Sound* Antoine Bonfanti; *Editing* Kenout Peltier, Eric Pluet. Running time: 117 minutes.

Cast: Delphine Seyrig, Jean-Pierre Kérien, Nita Klein, Jean-Baptiste Thierrée, Claude Sainval, Laurence Badie, Jean Champion, Jean Dasté, Martine Vatel, Yves Vincent, Nelly Borgeaud, Philippe Laudenbach, Robert Bordenave, Catherine de Seynes, Gaston Joly, Julien Verdier, Paul Chevalier, Wanda Kérien, Laure Paillette, François Bertin, Eliane Chevet, Jean-Jacques Lagarde.

Set in 1962 in Boulogne. Hélène (Seyrig) is a widow who lives with her stepson, Bernard (Thierrée). While Hélène tries to rekindle a romance with an old lover, Alphonse (Kérien), Bernard is haunted by the memory of torturing and killing a young woman named Muriel, when he was a soldier in Algeria.

Resnais' third film, which as usual explores the role of memory in present action, is one of his best. The extremely complicated plot was, Resnais said, a way to explore how love depends on memories, both sentimental and horrific. Against the intense emotions of absolute fear and passion, Resnais contrasts the machinations of daily life. The beautiful score and photography magnify Resnais' themes.

Many critics dismissed *Muriel* when it came out. They found it so avant-garde as to be incomprehensible. Others, like Truffaut in *Cahiers du Cinéma*, defended *Muriel*'s daring innovation. Critic Georges Sadoul, who found the film "profoundly moving," wrote: "It is less a film to see than to re-see," for he found the second viewing much more illuminating than the first. Delphine Seyrig won the Volpi Cup for Best Actress at the Venice Biennal in 1963.

Murmur of the Heart *see* **Le Souffle au cœur**

My Life to Live *see* **Vivre sa vie**

My Mother's Castle *see* **Le Château de ma mère**

My New Partner *see* **Les Ripoux**

My Night at Maud's *see* **Ma Nuit chez Maud**

My Night with Maud *see* **Ma Nuit chez Maud**

My Uncle *see* **Mon Oncle**

254 *Le Mystère Picasso (The Mystery of Picasso)* 1956 *Director* Henri-Georges Clouzot; *Producer* Filmsonor; *Screenplay* Henri-Georges Clouzot; *Photography* Claude Renoir; *Music* Georges Auric; *Sound* Joseph de Bretagne; *Editing* Henri-Georges Clouzot (images) and Henri Colpi (sound). Running time: 78 minutes.

Cast: Pablo Picasso.

A documentary on Pablo Picasso at work. The only accompaniment to the painter's brushstrokes is the music of Georges Auric. The film begins in black and white, then switches to color, and finally the finished canvases are shown in cinemascope.

This is one of the finest documentaries or studies of the artist at work in any medium. For many years, Clouzot had wanted to make a film of his friend Picasso, but he did not undertake the project until he found a special ink that allowed him to put the camera behind Picasso's canvas, so viewers actually see a picture emerging on the screen as if Picasso were behind it drawing. Intended to only last ten minutes, the film ended up being closer to an hour and a half long.

The critics only complaint about the film was that it did not include a short survey of some of Picasso's finished works. But Truffaut spoke for the majority when he hailed the film as not only a great cinematic experience, but also proof to anyone who had heretofore failed to appreciate the genius and talent of Picasso. "A Picasso work executed before our eyes, here is a miracle which, if it were necessary, would be enough to justify the magic of moviemaking. What surety of hand, what perpetual ingenuity, what verve, what good humor, and how great our pleasure is to watch Picasso erase, start over, transform, enrich!" The film won the Special Jury Prize at Cannes in 1956.

The Mystery of Picasso *see* **Le Mystère Picasso**

Naked Childhood *see* **L'Enfance nue**

The Nark *see* **La Balance**

255 *La Neige était sale (The Snow Was Dirty)* 1953 B&W *Director* Luis Saslavsky; *Producer* Tellus Films; *Screenplay* André Tabet, Luis Saslavsky, based on the novel by Georges Simenon; *Photography* André Bac; *Music* René Cloërec; *Set* René Moulaërt; *Sound* Robert Biard; *Editing* Isabelle Elman. Running time: 104 minutes.

Cast: Daniel Gélin, Marie Mansart, Valentine Tessier, Antoine Balpêtré, Daniel Ivernel, Vera Norman, Nadine Basile, Jo Dest, Joëlle Bernard, Paul Faivre, Camille Guérini, Jean-Pierre Mocky, Robert Moor, Claude Vernier, Georges Tabet, Pierre Duncan, Micheline Gary, Frédéric Valmain, Denyse Réal, Georges Scey, Andrée Tainsy, Jean Verner, Henri San-Juan, Jimmy Urbain.

A psychological drama about a tortured young man, Frank (Gélin), who has been scarred emotionally by his mother's (Tessier) work as a prostitute. He lives in a brothel that she runs during the German Occupation. He kills a German officer for kicks. He gets into trouble with a local gangster and seduces a sweet, innocent young girl (Mansart), who he then gives as a gift to his unsavory friend. The Gestapo finally catches up with him.

This haunting film noir was adapted from Georges Simenon's novel and its hit play adaptation. It is a dark, depressing and disturbingly believable look at how despair can drive an aimless soul to destruction. Saslavsky manages to blend drama with literary depth. The always-on-the-edge atmosphere of the Occupation is evoked very well. Gélin and Mansart are both superb. In fact, it was Gélin's favorite film of his career.

The film did well in France, where critics appreciated it as a moody meditation on moral demise. It was never released in the United States.

Night and Fog *see* **Nuit et bruillard**

The Night Is Young *see* **Mauvais Sang**

256 *Noce blanche* 1989 Color   *Director* Jean-Claude Brisseau; *Producer* Films du Losange, La Sorcière Rouge; *Screenplay* Jean-Claude Brisseau; *Photography* Romain Winding; *Music* Jean Musy; *Set* Margaret Menegoz; *Sound* Georges Prat; *Costumes* Maria-Luisa Garcia; *Editing* Lisa Garcia. Running time: 90 minutes.

Cast: Vanessa Paradis, Bruno Cremer, Ludmilla Mikaël, François Negret, Véronique Silver, Jean Dasté, Catherine Soullard, Françoise Henri, Philippe Tuin, and the students of Portail Rouge Lycée in Saint-Etienne.

Philosophy teacher François Hainaut (Cremer) is happily married. He becomes interested in one of his students, Mathilde (Paradis), when she is threatened with being held back a grade. She is brilliant, but troubled. He gives her extra help, and she seduces him. When his wife finds out that he is cheating on her, he still cannot break it off with Mathilde. When they are caught making in love in a classroom, all hell breaks loose.

This passionate love story is surprisingly serene. Jean-Claude Brisseau wanted to create a very realistic, authentic portrait of how wild, destructive love could flourish in the most unlikely place between sane, well intentioned people who are weak. The issues of parental irresponsibility and a flawed educational system were concerns that Brisseau had also explored in *The Sound and the Fury*. Vanessa Paradis proved a bewitching woman-child.

Critics lauded this highly philosophical love story. Alain Masson of *Positif* exclaimed: "The beauty of *Noce Blanche* lies in its multitude of diverse tones which are held together with an overarching purity."

257 *Nous ne vieillirons pas ensemble (We Will Not Grow Old Together)* 1972 Color   *Director* Maurice Pialat; *Producer* Lido Films, Empire Films; *Screenplay* Maurice Pialat; *Photography* Luciano Tovoli; *Music* Jean-Claude Vannier; *Set* Outdoors; *Sound* Claude Jauvert; *Editing* Arlette Langmann. Running time: 106 minutes.

Cast: Marlène Jobert, Jean Yanne, Macha Méril, Jacques Galland, Christine Fabrega, Muse Dalbray, Maurice Rich, Harry Max, Patricia Pierangeli.

The story of a married couple caught in a disastrous cycle of love, betrayal, break-up and make-up. Jean (Yanne) is a 40-year-old filmmaker who is married to Françoise (Méril), but is having an affair with Catherine (Jobert). When he brings her on location with him in the south of France, he treats her so badly that she runs away. They reconcile only to break up again.

This is an important feminist film by a male director. The woman triumphs by recognizing her own self-worth and using her strength to leave an abusive lover. Pialat was very open about this being an autobiographical film, with Jean Yanne's part being Pialat. It is an intelligent, rigorous look at the complicated nature of relationships. Considering Pialat's connection to the film, it is a brutally honest self-analysis. Jean Yanne is superb as a loving and destructive man.

Critics hailed this as a remarkably important and understated film. They applauded Pialat's austerity and sensitivity. Jean Yanne won the award for Best Actor at Cannes in 1972, though as a comment on his break with Pialat, he refused to appear to accept it.

258 *Nous sommes tous des assassins (We Are All Murderers)* 1952 B&W *Director* André Cayatte; *Producer* UGC; *Screenplay* André Cayatte and Charles Spaak; *Photography* Jean-Serge Bourgoin; *Music* Raymond Legrand; *Set* Jacques Colombier; *Sound* Antoine Petitjean; *Editing* Paul Cayatte. Running time: 115 minutes.

Cast: Marcel Mouloudji, Antoine Balpêtré, Raymond Pellegrin, Claude Laydu, Louis Seigner, Amedeo Nazzari, Georges Poujouly, Henri Vilbert, Yvonne Sanson, Julien Verdier, Lucien Nat, Henri Crémieux, Paul Faivre, Daniel Mendaille, André Reybas, Jacques Morel, Paul Frankeur, Marcel Pérès, Jean-Pierre Grenier, Jean-Marc Tennberg, François Joux, Jérome Goulven, Jean-Paul Moulinot, Pierre Sergeol, Line Noro, Charles Lemontier, Solange Sicard, Anouk Frejac, Monette Dinay, Yvette Etiévant, Yvonne de Bray, Jacqueline Pierreux, Sylvie, Juliette Faber, Lise Berthier, Andrée Le Dantec, Elisabeth Hardy, François Vibert, Marie France, Renée Gardes, Alinda Kristensen, Henri Coutet, Roland Lesaffre, Julien Verdier Faivre, Alexandre Rignault, René Blancard, Leonce Corne, Jean Daurand, André Valmy, Charles Bouillaud, Gabriel Gobin, Fernand René, Maurice Dorléac, Rémy Clary, Jacques Denoël, Kronefeld, Roger Vincent, René Lacourt, Léon Larive, René Berthier, Jean Clarieux, Joe Davray, Victor Vina, Paul Barge, Max Fromm, Philippe Kellerson, Louis Saintève, Pierre Morin, Guy Mairesse, Frank Maurice, Doudou Babet, Emile Morel, Pierre Fromont, Gaston Garchery, Marius David, Claude Cernay, Marcel Rouzé, Jean Brunel, Jacques Muller, Francomme, Jacques Morice, Pierre Duncan, Henri Cote, Philippe Chauveau, Lucien Raimbourg, Bernard Musson, Maurice Juniot, Jean-Jacques Steen.

The stories of five people awaiting the death penalty: a doctor (Balpêtré) convicted of poisoning his wife; a young Corsican (Pellegrin), who avenged the honor of his wife; a peasant (Verdier), who killed his baby daughter because she cried too much; another man (Pérès), who turned violent after brain surgery; and René Le Guen (Mouloudji), who, after a brutal childhood, sold arms and killed for the Resistance during World War II.

Cayette, who was educated as a lawyer, made this film when capital punishment was still legal and practiced in France. Cayette made a series of films that attacked the death penalty, this being only one of four. His aim was not to penetrate the emotional lives of those condemned to death, but to show the condemned as victims of society's abuses. The movie was very well received by the public. In Britain the title was followed by a question mark.

Some critics found its heavy handed sermonizing on the evils of execution overbearing and ultimately boring. Others hailed the details Cayette chose to focus on, and thereby argue his position, brilliant — for instance, the guards sneaking into the cells of the condemned to tie them up and lead them to the guillotine with no warning. It won the Special Jury Prize at Cannes in 1952.

Nude Childhood *see* **L'Enfance nue**

La Nuit américaine (Day for Night), **1973; directed by François Truffaut.**

Nude in a White Car *see* Toi, le venin

259 *La Nuit américaine (Day for Night)* 1973 Color *Director* François Truffaut; *Producer* Films du Carrosse-PECF; *Screenplay* François Truffaut, Jean-Louis Richard, and Suzanne Schiffman; *Photography* Pierre William Glenn; *Music* Georges Delerue; *Set* Damien Lanfranchi; *Sound* Michel Laurent; *Costumes* Lisèle Roos; *Editing* Yann Dedet, Martine Barraqué. Running time: 115 minutes.

Cast: Jacqueline Bisset, Valentina Cortese, Jean-Pierre Amumont, Alexandra Stewart, Jean-Pierre Léaud, François Truffaut, Jean Champion, Nathalie Baye, Dani, Bernard Menez, Nike Arrighi, Gaston Joly, David Markham, Maurice Seveno, Zénaïde Rossi, Christopher Vesque, Henri Graham, Marcel Berbert.

A drama about the people involved in making a film. From the stars to the script girls, love lives, dirty secrets, and even the tragic death of one of the actors are intertwined with the daily machinations of "the show must go on" philosophy that drives film production.

A sort of magical mystery tour of life behind the scenes of a movie with a true master of film as the guide. Truffaut wanted the film to address the question of film's importance in the world. "Is Film better than life?" He made *Day for Night* after directing 12 features and drew all the material for this film from real incidents that he had experienced as a filmmaker

Day for Night was a great international success. Film critic and professor Annette Insdorf called it "one of the most lyrical biographies of a film." It won the Oscar for Best Foreign Film, the New York Film Critics' Award for Best Motion Picture, Best Director and Best Supporting Actress for Valentina Cortese's performance in 1973.

260 *Nuit et bruillard (Night and Fog)*   1955 B&W and Color   *Director* Alain Resnais; *Producer* Argos Films, Como Films, Cocinor; *Screenplay* Alain Resnais, based on Olga Wormers and Henry Michel's *The Tragedy of the Deportations*; *Text* by Jean Cayrol, spoken by Michel Bouquet; *Photography* Ghislain Cloquet, Sacha Vierny; *Music* Hans Eisler; *Historic counsel* André Michel and Olga Wormser. Running time: 31 minutes.

A documentary that intersperses color photographs of Nazi concentration camps ten years after World War II with black and white photographs taken during the war. As the pictures flash on the screen, the horrors of the war are told in detail.

One of the most important documentaries on the Holocaust ever made. Though many credit Resnais' cinematic breakthroughs *Last Year at Marienbad* and *Hiroshima, mon amour* with changing art movie history, this documentary may be his most important and universally respected work. His accomplishment was, in critic Kevin Thomas' words, "to wrest a work of art from the most terrible instance of man's inhumanity to man in history." He creates a devastatingly beautiful and sad montage of photographs, video, music, voices, facts and feelings into 31 minutes. His title refers to the expression Hitler used to describe his solution for "the Jewish problem"; they were to vanish into the "night and fog."

When *Night and Fog* came out in Paris, Truffaut wrote in *Cahiers du Cinéma* that "Resnais has given us a history lesson, cruel no doubt, but needed." He said it was neither a film, a documentary, nor a poem, "but a meditation on the most important event of the 20th century." It won the Prix Jean Vigo and the Gold Medal from the Grand Prix du Cinéma Français in 1956. The following year it won the Documentary Grand Prize in Karlovy-Vary.

261 *Les Nuits de la pleine lune (Full Moon Over Paris)*   1984 Color *Director* Eric Rohmer; *Producer* Films du Losange, Films Ariane; *Screenplay* Eric Rohmer; *Photography* Renato Berta; *Music* Elli and Jacno; *Set* Pascale Ogier; *Sound* Georges Prat, Gérard Lecas; *Editing* Cécile Degugis. Running time: 102 minutes.

Cast: Pascale Ogier, Tcheky Karyo, Fabrice Lucchini, Virginie Thévenet, Anne-Séverine Liotard, Christian Vadim, Laszlo Szabo, Lisa Garneri, Mathieu Schiffman, Hervé Grandsart, Noel Coffman.

Louise (Ogier) and Rémi (Karyo) are lovers, who despite different temperaments, live together happily in the suburbs of Paris. She plays hard and works hard. He prefers a quieter life. When she gets a studio in Paris, the trouble begins. She spends more and more time going out with a journalist friend, but by the time that she finally decides she no longer needs more space, but wants to be with Rémi, he has had enough. He has fallen in love with someone else. Louise is left a victim of her own doing.

This look at the life and times of young adults in the 1980s focuses on the costs of raw ambition, and it spoke to many of the yuppie generation. With his trademark dialogue of wit and intelligence, Rohmer cast a cold eye on some of the common ways of young people of the era in this, the fourth of his "Comedies and Proverbs" series. He said he was not judging them, rather bearing witness. The cast and setting were extremely believable. Pascale Ogier, who is the daughter of actress Bulle Ogier, in particular, was wonderful. Sadly, she died of a heart attack not long after the film came out.

Critics hailed this as further testament to Rohmer's reign as the king of talk cinema. *The Aquarian* said, "In past sense Eric Rohmer is an especially welcome, always invigorating Fall tonic and *Full Moon in Paris* is pretty much of a vintage offering." Pascale Ogier won the award for Best Actress at the Venice Biennal.

262 *Les Nuits fauves (Savage Nights)*   1992 Color   *Director* Cyril Collard; *Producer* Banfilm Ter, Erre Produzioni; *Screenplay* Cyril Collard, based on his book; *Photography* Manuel Teran; *Music* Cyril Collard, René-Marc Bini, Damia, Noir Désir; *Set* Jacky Macchi; *Sound* Michel Brethez, Dominique Hennequin; *Editing* Lise Beaulieu. Running time: 125 minutes.

    Cast: Cyril Collard, Romane Bohringer, Carlos Lopez, Corinne Blue, Maria Schneider, Clémentine Célarié, René-Marc Bini, Clementine Celaire, Maria Schneider, Claude Winter, Laura Favali, Francisco Gimenez, Diego Porres, Samir Guesmi, Jean-Jacques, Aissa Jabri, Dominique Figaro, Stéphan Lakatos, Christophe Chantre, Marine Delterme, Anna-Lopez Villanua, Yannick Tolila, Regine Arniaud, Michel Voletti, Olivier Pajot, Olivier Chavarot, Claudio Zaccai, Denis D'Arcangelo, Rosa Castro, Nella Banfi, Luc Palun, Fabrice Bagni, Nicolas Davy, Laurent Laguerre, Paco Gimenez, Pavlouska, Martine Breheret, Olivier Ramon, Benjamin Lubet, Emmaneul Bosc, Magali Noaro, Ben Farouk.

    Thirty-year-old Jean (Collard) is intelligent and attractive. The world is his for the taking. A filmmaker and musician with a boyfriend, Samy (Lopez), and a girlfriend, Laura (Bohringer), Jean has it all—until he finds out that he is HIV positive. When life is short, choices have to be made.

    This autobiographical film, which Collard, wrote, directed and starred in, inspired hundreds of French to get tested for HIV, stirred up much controversy, and heralded the brief but brilliant career of Collard. He died of AIDS just before his film swept the Césars. The controversy was over the fact that although the character Jean knows he has the virus, he sleeps with Laura and does not tell her. It shows the HIV character as complex, sympathetic and morally irresponsible. Unfortunately, the film signaled the tragic end to an exciting filmmaker. But it also announced the emergence of a great young actress, Bohringer, and inspired a new view of modern, rough filmmaking. The film shows a gritty side of Paris rarely depicted.

    When it opened in France, some critics called it brilliant; others called it morally reprehensible. The film received similar responses in England and the United States. *Paris Libération* said: "*Savage Nights* is not a well-mannered movie. It's a bit cruddy, even. But how much better is its speed, with its risks and its multiple pile-ups, to most contemporary cinema, which merely slithers across a polished parquet floor."

263 *Numéros zéro*   1981 Color   *Director* Raymond Depardon; *Producer* Agence Gamma, Raymond Depardon; *Photography* Raymond Depardon; *Sound* Raymond Depardon; *Editing* Olivier Froux. Running time: 90 minutes

    A documentary about the making of the daily newspaper *Le Matin de Paris*, which begins with the start-up efforts and follows through to the printing of the first issue. It focuses on the hectic pace and high-pitched spirits of the newspaper world and the role of the press in a free society.

    This was one of the best documentaries made in the 1980s. It was hailed as a prime example of cinéma direct, which used little commentary and editing but relied instead on the power of images and a neutral tone in relating events. It captures a remarkable group of talented and ambitious professionals at a crucial period in their career. At a time when publishing industries around the world faced more newspaper closings than openings, and even established independents were being gobbled up by multi-national conglomerates, this film also captured the last vestige of the old-fashioned newspaper business. Ironically, when the film was selected to be shown at the International Documentary Film Festival in Lilles the president of *Le Matin* tried to stop its screening.

La Revue du Cinéma exclaimed, "The polemics and publicity aside, *Numéros Zéro* is first and foremost remarkable because of its documentary approach, which is reminiscent of Fred Wiseman's work: brutal images, no commentary, without effect or intervention apparent in its point of view." The film won the Prix Georges Sadoul in 1979.

The Nun *see* **La Religieuse**

Obsession *see* **Pierrot le fou**

264 *Occupe-toi d'Amélie (Oh, Amelia!* or *Keep an Eye on Amelia)*
1949 B&W *Director* Claude Autant-Lara; *Producer* Lux Films; *Screenplay* Jean Aurenche and Pierre Bost, based on the play by Georges Feydeau; *Photography* André Bac; *Music* René Cloërec; *Set* Max Douy; *Sound* William Sivel; *Costumes* Monique Dunan; *Editing* Madeleine Gug. Running time: 92 minutes.

Cast: Jean Desailly, Danielle Darrieux, Julien Carette, Louise Conte, André Bervil, Grégoire Aslan, Roland Armontel, Victor Guyau, Charles Deschamps, Lucienne Granier, Marcelle Arnold, Paul Demange, Colette Ripert, Primerose Perret, Albert-Michel Francoeur, Richard Francoeur, Palmyre Levasseur, Robert Auboyneau, Valentine Camax, Eugène Yvernès, Robert Le Béal, Jean Pignol, Henry Laverne, René Brun, Alain Stume, Georges Forster, Françoise Morens, Etienne Decroux.

A romantic comedy about Amélie Pochet (Darrieux), the lovely mistress of Lieutenant Milledieu. When the lieutenant's friend, Marcel (Desailly), needs money and asks Milledieu if he can borrow Amélie, so he can marry her to get a twelve-thousand-franc wedding gift from his uncle, Milledieu obliges. Of course, when the big day finally arrives the bride and groom do not have to fake their feelings.

Claude Autant-Lara considered this wonderful comedy to be his best movie. "*Amélie* has an astonishing youthfulness, a rhythm, an allure, a tempo...," said the director. He adapted it from Feydeau's hit play, but made it into a work all its own. It critiques social customs in a lighthearted, but effective way. The sets, costumes and performances are all delicious. Darrieux brings new meaning to the word lively.

The French public and critics enjoyed this film more than Americans did. Though *The New York Times* did remark: "The French, who not only have a profound appreciation of l'amour but also have been known to take it lightly, are ribbing that divine sentiment with a vengeance in *Oh, Amelia!*"

Oh, Amelia! *see* **Occupe-toi d'Amélie**

On Pain of Love *see* **Le Grand Chemin**

On the Track *see* **Un Étrange Voyage**

One Deadly Summer *see* **L'Été meurtrier**

One Life *see* **Une Vie**

An Only Son *see* **Un Fils unique**

265 *Orfeu Negro (Black Orpheus)* 1959 Color *Director* Marcel Camus; *Producer* Dispat Films, Gemma Cinematografica, Turpan Films; *Screenplay* Jean Viot, Marcel Camus, based on Vinicius de Moraes' play *Orfeu da Conceição*; *Photography* Jean-Serge Bourgoin; *Music* Antonio Carlos Jobim and Luis Bona; *Sound* Amaury Leenhardt; *Editing* Andrée Feix. Running time: 105 minutes.

Cast: Marpessa Dawn, Bruno Higeno-Mello, Lourdes de Oliveira, Léa Garcia, Adhemar de Silva, Waldemar de Souza, Alexandro Constantino, Jorge dos Santos, Aurino Cassanio.

The myth of Orpheus (Mello) and Eurydice (Dawn) set in Rio de Janiero during carnival. In this reinterpretation Orpheus is a tramway conductor and Eurydice is a peasant. When the two fall in love, Eurydice's old love hunts her down and kills her. Orpheus goes to her in the morgue to revive her.

Camus' one great film is a cinematic carnival. With pulsing samba music and the backdrop of Rio, the mythic tragedy is once more thrilling. Instead of professional actors, Camus chose a soccer player and a dancer to star in his modern myth. The film was in many ways an adieu to an historic period in French filmmaking. It was made on a shoe-string budget, with the director only able to afford a one-way ticket to Rio and barely able to pay for the soundtrack. It won the Palme d'Or in competition with *Breathless*, but the New Wave would soon reign supreme.

The French unanimously adored this film. Americans either dismissed it as long and touristy or hailed it as a beautiful and interesting update of the myth. *The New Yorker* exclaimed: "The seduction of his film is its naive quality, emanating from its untrained Negro actors, who are like local shadows repeating the motions of a great civilized myth." The film won the Palme d'Or at Cannes and the Oscar for Best Foreign Film in 1959.

266 *Les Orgueilleux (The Proud and the Beautiful)* 1953 B&W *Director* Yves Allégret; *Producer* CICC Reforma, Chrysaor; *Screenplay* Jean Aurenche and Yves Allégret, based on Sartre's novel *Typhus*; *Dialogue* Jean Aurenche, Jean Clouzot, Pierre Bost; *Photography* Alexandre Philipps; *Music* Paul Misraki; *Set* Auguste Capelier and Gunther Geizo; *Sound* William Sivel, Luis Fernandez; *Editing* Claude Nicole. Running time: 103 minutes.

Cast: Michèle Morgan, Gérard Philippe, Carlos Lopez Moctezuma, Victor Manuel Mendoza, Michèle Cordoue, Adrien Toffel, Carla Lopez, Arturo Soto Rangel, Jaime Fernandez.

A very unlikely love story set in a port town in Mexico. A young woman, Nellie (Morgan), who has lost her husband to spinal meningitis, and an old, alcoholic doctor, Georges (Philipe), fall in love and give each other a new reason to live. When an epidemic threatens to ravage the area, Georges, with the help and support of his new love, pulls himself together to care for the sick.

This is one of the most famous French films. A love story set amidst the ruins, it blends misery and hope, death and eros. Michèle Morgan is at her most luminous in the role of Nellie. Adapted from a Sartre novel, it was one of many films of the early postwar period, such as *The Cheat* and *Dedée*, that presented a very pessimistic view of human nature. In fact, it went so far in presenting an unglamorous human portrait as to show someone vomiting, which outraged many and provoked threats of censorship — for at the time, bodily functions were not acceptable movie fare.

Critics hailed *The Proud and the Beautiful* for its unblinking look at human nature. Bosley Crowther of *The New York Times* exclaimed: "Call it insidiously hypnotic. Say it is shrewdly done to shock. Allow that it runs against reason and violates the rules of etiquette. It still grabs you at the beginning and carries you along into a tale that is as off-beat and spiritually mysterious as was that former French film, *Forbidden Games.*"

267 *Orphée (Orpheus)*   1950 B&W   *Director* Jean Cocteau; *Producer* Les Films du Palais Royal; *Screenplay* Jean Cocteau; *Photography* Nicolas Hayer; *Music* Georges Auric; *Set* Christian Bérard and Jean d'Eaubonne; *Sound* Pierre Calvet; *Costumes* Marcel Escoffer; *Editing* Jacqueline Sadoul. Running time: 112 minutes.

Cast: Jean Marais, Maria Casarès, François Périer, Marie Dea, Edouard Dhermit, Henri Crémieux, Jacques Varennes, André Carnège, Juliette Greco, Renée Cosima, Roger Blin, Pierre Bertin, Jean-Pierre Melville, René Lacourt, Julien Maffre, André Carnège, René Worms, Henri San Juan, Claude Borelli, Jean-Pierre Mocky, Victor Tabournot, Jacques Doniol-Valcroze, Claude Mauriac, Philippe Bordier.

The modern adaptation of the myth of Eurydice and Orpheus. Set in Paris in 1950, the movie opens with the famous poet Orphée (Marais) in the Poets Café. When a young poet is killed in front of the café, Orpheus accompanies the princess (Casarès) back to her chalet with the body. The princess and the dead poet disappear through a mirror and Orpheus wakes up the next day in the mountains alone. The princess' chauffeur, Heurtebise (Périer), brings Orpheus home to his wife, Eurydice (Dea). Love between the living and the dead follows.

This film is probably the supreme example of poetry in cinematic motion. Cocteau first explored the Orpheus myth in his one-act play of the same name in 1926, and he picked it up again with his last film, *Testament d'Orphée* (1960), but this is his movie masterpiece. The special effects are wonderful, with Orpheus diving through a mirror and being blown through the limbo between life and death, and a Rolls Royce spouting cryptic poetry. Jean Marais broods beautifully as the tortured artistic soul. Cocteau could not get backing for the film, because it was viewed as too unconventional and risky commercially; so the cast worked on credit. Cocteau described *Orpheus* as "a detective film, bathed on one side in myth, and on the other in the supernatural." He considered Greta Garbo and Marlene Dietrich for Casarès' role.

Orpheus was a huge success. *The New York Herald Tribune* declared it "sheer cinematic magic . . . . Employing a camera with vaulting imagination and studding his work with sparse and provocative dialogue, the French poet and screen artist has fashioned an arresting and evocative blend of realism." *Newsweek* raved, "For sheer dramatic intensity and brilliance of execution it ranks among the best efforts of one of the few men who have yet succeeded in writing poetry with a moving-picture camera." The film won the Critics' Prize at the Venice Biennal in 1950.

Les Orgueilleux (The Proud and the Beautiful), 1953; directed by Yves Allégret.

Orpheus *see* **Orphée**

Other People's Money *see* **L'Argent des autres**

268 *L'Ours (The Bear)* 1988 Color   *Director* Jean-Jacques Annaud; *Producer* Renn Productions; *Screenplay* Gérard Brach, based on Jeams Oliver Curwood's novel *The Grizzly King*; *Photography* Philippe Rousselot; *Music* Philippe Sarde; *Set* Toni Ludi; *Sound* Laurent Quaglio; *Costumes* François Disle; *Editing* Noëlle Boisson. Running time: 96 minutes.

Cast: Tcheky Karyo, Jack Wallace, André Lacombe, the bear Douce, the bear Bart, and the bear Doc.

A nature adventure about an orphaned bear cub pursued by a small band of hunters. To survive the cub faces all sorts of danger, including a hungry puma, but is taken under the proverbial wing of an adult male bear who protects him. When the big bear is wounded by the hunters, he attacks their camp. He corners one of the hunters, but after frightening him, leaves him unharmed.

The animal picture of the decade, Jean-Jacques Annaud's *The Bear* was a big-budget film that paid off big. It was set and shot entirely outdoors in the Pyrenées, with multiple bears playing the roles and with only six minutes of dialogue. Annaud said his aim was to teach people that animals have intelligence and feelings too and that "the greatest thrill is not to kill but to let live." With so little dialogue, the film made an easy international transition. *The Bear* was the most popular movie of the year in France and was very popular in the United States as well, grossing over $120 million. On both sides of the Atlantic, adults and children lined up to get in and wiped away tears on the way out.

What thrilled audiences—the way in which Annaud captured dramatic moments in nature to build his plot—was just what angered some critics, who felt the film had a sensationalistic, false reenactment quality. They accused Annaud of treating a melodramatic saga like a nature movie. They were outraged that Annaud used bear trainers to teach his subjects to limp. *Cahiers du Cinéma* called it an "adventure in marketing ... with the bears singing 'We Are the World, We Are the Bears.'" Other critics called it genius. *The Philadelphia Inquirer* exclaimed: "With a simple stroke of genius, Jean-Jacques Annaud has taken some humble narrative ingredients and fashioned them into a fable of elemental power that will mesmerize children and captivate adults with its sophisticated subtext."

269 *Outremer (Overseas)* 1990 Color   *Director* Brigitte Roüan; *Producer* Paradise Productions; *Screenplay* Brigitte Roüan, Philippe Le Guay, Christian Rullier, Cedric Khan, based on a story by Brigitte Roüan; *Photography* Dominique Chapuis; *Music* Pierre and Mathieu Foldes; *Set* Roland Deville; *Sound* Dominique Vieillard, Dominique Hennequin; *Costumes* Florence Emir; *Editing* Yann Dedet. Running time: 100 minutes.

Cast: Nicole Garcia, Brigitte Roüan, Marianne Basler, Philippe Galland, Yann Dedet, Bruno Todeschini, Pierre Doris, Monique Mélinarnad, Zappy Max, Coralie Seyrig, Jean-Claude de Goros, Jean-Louis Ribes, Georges Fricker, Jean-Marie Marion, Silvana de Faria.

A family saga about three *pied noirs* sisters; they are of French descent but born and raised in Algeria. Living in colonial Algeria on the verge of the war for indepence, all three sisters dream of knights in shining armor, but the men in their lives do not measure up. Zon (Garcia) is married to a naval officer (Galland), who has little time to indulge her restive, romantic nature. Malene (Roüan) marries a plantation owner (Dedet), who turns out to be a weaker man than what she wanted. Gritte (Basler) resists marrying like her sisters and becomes involved with an Algerian rebel.

The directorial debut of Brigitte Roüan, who plays one of the sisters in the film as well, presents a very interesting look at the life and dreams of women in the French colonies. Based on some of Roüan's own experiences growing up in French-ruled Algeria, the film is told in flashback through each sister's point of view, so the memories build on each other. Roüan counterbalances the women's personal struggles with the growing political tension of Algeria in the 1950s.

Critics welcomed this highly personal look at a crucial period in French history. They lauded Roüan's subtle and intelligent observation.

The Outsiders *see* **Bande à part**

Overseas *see* **Outremer**

Panic *see* **Panique**

270 *Panique (Panic)* 1947 B&W   *Director* Julien Duvivier; *Producer* Filmsonor; *Screenplay* Charles Spaak, Julien Duvivier, based on Georges Simenon's novel, *Mr. Hire's Engagement*; *Photography* Nicolas Hayer; *Music* Jacques Ibert; *Set* Serge Piménoff; *Editing* Marthe Poncin. Running time: 100 minutes.

Cast: Viviane Romance, Michel Simon, Paul Bernard, Charles Dorat, Lucas Gridoux, Max Dalban, Emile Drain, Guy Favières, Louis Florencie, Marcel Pérès, Lita Recio, Louis Lions, Jenny Leduc, Michel Ardan, Michèle Auvray, Jean-François Martial, Robert Balpo, Josian Dorée, Lucien Paris, Magdeleine Gidon, Olivier Darrieux, Germaine Géranne, Sylvain, Suzanne Després, Lucien Carol, Emma Lyonel, Paul Franck, Fernand Dally.

When a murder is committed in a Parisian suburb, the police and his neighbors suspect Monsieur Hire (Simon), a strange, solitary man. The murderer is really the lover of Alice (Romance), the woman Monsieur Hire loves from afar. Alice frames Hire; and while trying to escape an enraged mob pursuing him, he falls from a rooftop and dies. In his pocket is a photo that proves his innocence.

A film noir of the highest possible order. *Panic* was the first film that Duvivier made after returning to France from Hollywood after World War II. Based on a Simenon novel, it explores mob psychology and how society is quick to condemn and execute a loner. "It says that people are not nice, that the crowd is imbecilic, that outsiders are always harmed," said Duvivier of this film, which he believed was the most significant of his career.

The film was the subject of much critical acclaim in France and the United States. Bosley Crowther of *The New York Times* lauded the picture as a "vivid and disturbing melodrama" and a "thoroughly fascinating and sardonic social comment."

271 *Un Papillon sur l'épaule (A Butterfly on the Shoulder)* 1978 Color *Director* Jacques Deray; *Producer* Actions Films, Citel Films, Gaumont; *Screenplay* Jean-Claude Carrière, Tonino Guerra, Jacques Deray, based on John

Les Parapluies de Cherbourg (The Umbrellas of Cherbourg), **1963; directed by Jacques Demy.**

Gearon's novel, *The Velvet Wall*; *Photography* Jean Boffety and Jean Charvein; *Set* François de Lamothe and José Antonio de la Guerra de la Pas; *Sound* Pierre Lenoir; *Editing* Henri Lanoë. Running time: 95 minutes.

Cast: Lino Venturi, Claudine Auger, Paul Crauchet, Jean Bouise, Nicole Garcia, Laura Betti, Xavier Depraz, Roland Bertin, Dominique Lavanant, Jacques Maruy, Jose Luis Lifante.

A Hitchcockian thriller à la français. Soon after Roland (Venturi) jumps ship in Barcelona, he gets caught up in murders and kidnappings. When he is arrested only one man can prove his innocence. When Roland narrowly escapes all sorts of danger to reach the man, he learns that his savior cannot help him.

This suspenseful thriller about mistaken identity and government persecution is one of Deray's best films. It manages to merge gripping entertainment and existential meditations. Deray obviously had in mind the works of such masters of the American film noir as Howard Hawks. The terror he evokes is palpable. Lino Venturi's performance is very good.

French critics lauded this film comparing it to Hitchcock and Kafka. It was never distributed in the United States. The film won the Grand Prix du Cinéma Français in 1978.

272 *Paradiso* 1977 Color   *Director* Christian Bricout; *Producer* Z Productions and Rush; *Screenplay* Christian Bricout; *Photography* Philippe Rousselot; *Music* Ariel Kalma, Klaus Doldirger, Martin Factory; *Sound* Michel Brethez; *Editing* Youcef Tobni, Manoela Ferreira, Christine Ayat.

Cast: Didier Sauvegrain, Gérard Darrieu, Annie Savarin, Bernadette Le Saché, Brigitte Roüan, Poussine Mercanton, Jeanne Allard, Coralie Seyrig.

One night in the life of a desperate, unemployed young man (Sauvegrain) searching for love on the fringes of society. He is chased from his home by his father, who despairs over the aimless lives of his children. He talks to a woman who works in the public bathrooms, drives a girl around the city, and befriends a drug addict, before finally spending the night with the woman from the bathrooms.

A startling film by one of France's great socially conscious filmmakers. Bricout was among a number of French filmmakers in the 1970s and 1980s, who hoped to affect social awareness and perhaps affect change through realistic and moving depictions of large social problems. The view of the nocturnal urban underworld is fascinating, if amazingly bleak.

Critics hailed the film as announcing the important arrival of a new talent. They lauded Bricout's raw look at the underbelly of society and his poetic filming. The film won the Prix Jean Vigo in 1977.

273 *Les Parapluies de Cherbourg (The Umbrellas of Cherbourg)* 1963 Color *Director* Jacques Demy; *Producer* Parc-Madeleine-Beta Films; *Screenplay* Jacques Demy; *Photography* Jean Rabier; *Music* Michel Legrand; *Set* Bernard Evein and Claude Pignot; *Costumes* Jacqueline Moreau; *Editing* Anne-Marie Cotret. Running time: 90 minutes.

Cast: Catherine Deneuve, Nino Castelnuovo, Anne Vernon, Marc Michel, Ellen Farner, Mireille Perrey, Harald Wolff, Jean Champion, Pierre Caden, Jean-Pierre Dorat, Bernard Fradet, Michel Benoist, Philippe Dumat, Dorothée Blank, Jeanne Carat, Jean-Paul Chizat, Patrick Bricard, Bernard Garnier, François Charet, Jacques Camelinat, Roger Perrinoz, Paul Pavel, Rosalie Varda, Hervé Legrand.

A bittersweet musical about Geneviève (Deneuve), the daughter of a woman (Vernon) who runs an umbrella shop. Geneviève is in love with a mechanic, Guy (Castelnuovo), of whom her mother does not approve. Instead, she makes Geneviève marry a jeweler (Michel) to legitimize her baby, while Guy is off at war in Algeria. When he gets back he marries somebody else, and when Geneviève bumps into him pumping gas one day years later, he refuses to meet their daughter.

This is Jacques Demy's most well known and beloved movie. It was a hit from the day it opened. He played up the romance and the music beautifully. He painted the houses of Cherbourg glorious pastel colors and had all of the dialogue set to music and used the dubbed voices of real singers. It is so light and witty that it is no wonder many of the songs have become popular classics. This very charming vehicle is the movie that made Deneuve a star.

Though some critics said it was not as vibrant as American musical classics, it is certainly the best French musical since René Clair's early films. Critic Georges Sadoul wrote in *Les Lettres Françaises*: "This ciné-opera brings a new style to poetic realism and should enjoy enough success to allow Jacques Demy to make a sequel to *Umbrellas*, as it is a sequel to *Lola*." It won the Prix Louis Delluc in 1963. The next year it won the Grand Prize at Cannes and the French Critics' Prix Méliès. In 1965, it was nominated for Oscars for the Best Story and Screenplay and Best Song for "I Will Wait for You." It went on to be staged Off Broadway.

274 *Les Parents terribles (Intimate Relations* or *The Storm Within)* 1948 B&W *Director* Jean Cocteau; *Producer* Films Ariane; *Screenplay* Jean

Cocteau, based on his play; *Photography* Michel Keller; *Music* Georges Auric; *Set* Guy de Gastyne; *Sound* Antoine Petitjean; *Editing* Jacqueline Sadoul. Running time: 105 minutes.

Cast: Jean Marais, Yvonne de Bray, Gabrielle Dorziat, Marcel André, Josette Day, Jean Cocteau.

The dramatic family story about an obsessively possessive mother (de Bray), who does not want her handsome son, Michel (Marais), to marry Madeleine (Day), the girl he loves. Eventually, secret love affairs are exposed, including a relationship between Michel's father and Madeleine. Their discovery drives the mother to suicide.

Many, including Cocteau, believe that this is his finest cinematic work. He adapted it from his play, which a decade earlier included almost exactly the same cast. He restricted himself to two sets to create a *No Exit* atmosphere of hellish claustrophobia. Cocteau said of his aim: "Only on film could the theatrical project fully express itself and could *The Terrible Parents* clearly become an apartment tragedy, where the cracking open of a door could mean more than a monologue delivered in bed." In fact, *Cahiers du Cinéma* editor André Bazin used the work as the definitive ideal of theatrical filming.

When the film first came out, some dismissed it as simply filmed theater. Others, like André Bazin, hailed it as "pure" cinema.

Paris Belongs to Us *see* **Paris nous appartient**

Paris Does Strange Things *see* **Eléna et les hommes**

Paris Frills *see* **Falbalas**

Paris Is Ours *see* **Paris nous appartient**

275 *Paris 1900* 1947 B&W   *Director* Nicole Védrès; *Producer* Pierre Braunberger; *Screenplay* Nicole Védrès and Pierre Braunberg; *Music* Guy Bernard; *Editing* Myriam Borsoutzky, Yannick Bellon, and Alain Resnais; *Commentary* Nicole Védrès. Running time: 90 minutes.

A film about Paris in the year 1900, made up entirely of photos from that year. It is a sweet tribute to a former time of music-halls and Maxim's, dinner jackets, wasp waists and plumed boas. But it is also the last hurrah before the two world wars ravaged Europe.

The film was the first important montage documentary made in France. Such exercises in cinéma vérité were popular in Russia in the 1920s, but Védrès' nostalgic look at the City of Lights at the turn of the century was very original when it came out in France in 1947. She proved that modern film could be used to explore the past. The photos she chose emphasized the lost era more than the changed city. She alternated images of Monet painting waterlilies with images of the great workers' riots. In the joy and in the struggle, she revealed the tension about to explode on the temporal horizon.

Paris 1900 enjoyed a strong following when it was released. Critic Georges Sadoul lauded the sensitive selection by which Védrès brought life to the film's still images: "by this her film avoids being one-dimensional, superficial. It acquires a blood, a soul, a heart." *Paris 1900* won the Prix Louis Delluc and the French Critics' Prix Méliès in 1947.

276 *Paris nous appartient (Paris Belongs to Us* or *Paris Is Ours)* 1960 B&W   *Director* Jacques Rivette; *Producer* Ajym Films, Films du Carrosse; *Screenplay* Jean Gruault; *Photography* Charles Bitsch; *Music* Philippe Arthuys; *Set* Outdoors; *Sound* Christian Hackspill; *Editing* Denise de Casabianca. Running time: 137 minutes.

Cast: Betty Schneider, Gianni Esposito, Françoise Prévost, Daniel Crohem, François Maistre, Jean-Claude Brialy, Birgitta Juslin, Noëlle Leiris, Monique Le Porrier, Louis Roblin, Malka Ribowska, Anne Zambire, Paul Bisciglia, Jean-Pierre Delage, Jean Martin, Henri Poirier, Jean-Marie Robain, André Thorent, Jacques Demy, Jean-Luc Godard, Claude Chabrol.

A New Wave thriller about a Sorbonne student, Anne (Schneider), who by becoming involved with a theater group putting on a production of Shakespeare's *Pericles* penetrates a mysterious world of intellectuals, actors, political refugees and conspirators plotting world destruction. She sets about solving the murder of a guitarist, Juan, then saves her brother from a dangerous conspiracy. After a shooting and a suicide, Anne realizes the conspiracy was never real.

An early New Wave film, Jacques Rivette's first feature was not met with much enthusiasm when it was released in France, but it has since become an art house classic. He started the film in 1958 with money borrowed from *Cahiers du Cinéma*, where he worked as a critic. The film was finished in 1961 on a shoe-string budget with friends like Godard, Chabrol and Truffaut lending a hand. It helped establish much of the New Wave sensibility. For example, it was the first of the New Wave films to make cinema references with its inclusion of a few minutes of Fritz Lang's *Metropolis*.

Some critics found its evocation of bohemian Paris life in the 1950s very skillfully done, but only a few found it as avant-garde as its New Wave predecessors. Critic Pierre Marcabru of *Combat* wrote: "The life of Paris, in a cinematic sense, is put in a new light. For the first time, the stones and the streets have a secret grace which is that of the imaginary." Others complained that the film was weighted down with a sense of impending doom not supported by dramatic tension.

277 *Une Partie de campagne (A Day in the Country)*   1946 B&W   *Director* Jean Renoir; *Producer* Pierre Braunberger; *Screenplay* Jean Renoir, based on Guy de Maupassant's story, known in English as "A Country Excursion"; *Photography* Claude Renoir, Serge Bourgoin, Albert Viguier, and Eli Lotar; *Music* Joseph Kosma; *Set* Robert Gys; *Editing* Marguerite Renoir. Running time: 41 minutes.

Cast: Sylvia Bataille, Gabriello, Jane Marken, Georges Darnoux, Jacques Bernard Brunius, Paul Temps, Gabrielle Fontan, Jean Renoir, Marguerite Renoir, Pierre Lestringuez, Jacques Becker, Alain Renoir.

A Sunday in the country with the Dufour family, merchants from Paris, with their daughter, Henriette (Bataille), and her intended, Anatole (Temps). While Mr. Dufour and Anatole take a boat fishing, two young men join the ladies for the afternoon. Henriette spends a brief, but passionate time with one of the young men (Darnoux). Years later, after she has married Anatole, she meets the man again. They had never stopped thinking of each other.

One of Renoir's most important works, this film is full of his love of life. His fascination with man's relationship to nature is beautifully expressed in his cinematography. The whole is a simple celebration of love and heartbreak, sunshine playing on water, dancing in the grass, nature and humanity working together to express immense happiness and utter sorrow. Filmed in 1936, it was not released until 1946 because of production problems and the intervention of World War II. The film evokes the spirit of impressionism, which Renoir undoubtedly picked up from his father, the painter Auguste Renoir; and, in fact, the film was shot in an area where Renoir's father often painted. There is a wonderful rhythm to the film, which focuses on the idea that one moment in life can be seized or not—and, perhaps, forever imprison people with their choice.

Cahiers du Cinéma editor André Bazin called the love scene between Henri and Henriette "One of the most beautiful sequences in all of cinema. . . . I can think of no other director, except perhaps Chaplin, who is capable of evoking such a wrenching bit of truth from a face, from an expression." Another critic Pierre Leprohon spoke for many when he wrote: "*A Day in the Country* may not be Renoir's greatest film, but it may be most dear to those who admire him, because it seems the one closest to his heart, and to ours."

278 *Le Passage du Rhin (Tomorrow Is My Turn)*   1960 B&W   *Director* André Cayatte; *Producer* Franco London Films, Gibé, UFA; *Screenplay* André Cayatte, Armand Jammot and Pascal Jardin, based on the novel by Armand Jammot; *Photography* Roger Fellous; *Music* Louiguy; *Set* Jacques Colombier; *Sound* Georges Mardiguian; *Editing* Boris Lewin. Running time: 124 minutes.

Cast: Georges Rivière, Charles Aznavour, Nicole Courcel, Cordula Trantow, Jean Marchat, Betty Schneider, Lotte Ledl, Bernardi, Georges Chamarat, Michel Etchevery, Benno Hoffmann, Colette Régis, David Tonnelli, Alfred Schieske, Ruth Hansmeister, Albert Dinan, Albert Rémy, Yves Barsacq, Henri Lambert, Bernard Musson, Jean Verner, Christian Brocard, Serge Frédéric, Louis Lalanne, Michel Arène.

Set during World War II, two French soldiers, Roger (Aznavour) and Jean (Rivière), are taken captive and forced to work on a German farm. The farmer's daughter, Helga (Trantow), is tricked into helping Jean escape and catches the fancy of Roger, who refuses to leave her. When the war ends, the two soldiers find that they cannot return to their lives or their loves as they were before the war.

By showing the effects of the war on German citizens, this film presented a novel perspective. What interested Cayatte was the struggle beyond the front, the personal and moral struggle for liberty and peace and how extreme circumstances bring out the best and worst in people. It is a war movie without battles, focusing rather on the issues of the homefront.

Tomorrow Is My Turn was the most popular of Cayatte's later works. Paul V. Beckley of the *New York Herald Tribune* said: "Such films as this add to man's stock of conscientious, sincere probing into the dilemmas of our century, and while it is difficult to predict what will live longest, it seems likely that *Tomorrow Is My Turn* will be among those social documents that will prove most useful to future historians."

279 *Passe-montagne (Mountain Pass)*   1978 Color   *Director* Jean-François Stévenin; *Producer* Les Films du Losange, FR3; *Screenplay* Jean-

François Stévenin, Babou Rappeneau, Stéphanie Granel, Michel Delahaye; *Photography* Lionel Legros, Jean-Yves Escoffier; *Music* Philippe Sarde; *Set* Geoffroy Larcher, Roger Stévenin and Marc Sergent; *Sound* Yves Zlotnicka; *Editing* Yann Dedet. Running time: 110 minutes.

Cast: Jacques Villeret, Jean-François Stévenin, Texandre Barberat, Yves Lemoigne, Denise Gremion, André Riva, Christine Paris, Stéphanie Granel, Brigitte Levoyet, Henri Paris, Pierre Facinetti, Raymond Benoit, Jean-Paul Charton, Bernard Chemarin, Kampf, the Tournier twins, Charlot Epailly, Micky Bonnefoy, Yvette Baroudelle, Fred Piard, Dominique Piard, Pascal Piard, Cob Piard, Georges-Henri Piard, Clément Vincent, Jean-Yves Metraux, Gaby Auger, Louis Benoit.

A divorced mechanic, Serge (Stévenin), who lives in a small town in the Jura mountains, stops to help a Parisian architect, Georges (Villeret), whose car has broken down on the highway. The two become friends fast and Georges accompanies Serge on a journey through the forest. They end up meeting some villagers, with whom they spend an evening drinking and dancing.

This was the first film by Stévenin, and it announced a great new talent. He both directed and acted in the film, playing the part of Serge. He plays with secrets and things not being what they appear. In a way, the film is about two middle-aged men on a quest. It was seen as a metaphor for men's mid-life crises and their ways of reacting to them.

French critics hailed the film as an auspicious debut. *Positif* exclaimed: "It is impossible to classify *Mountain Pass* within French cinema. It is very much an auteur film. . . . From the point of view of the spectator, *Mountain Pass* can function as a trap: after the first five minutes, it can open strange doors." The film won the Prix Georges Sadoul in 1978.

280 *Pauline à la plage (Pauline at the Beach)* 1983 Color *Director* Eric Rohmer; *Producer* Films du Losange; *Screenplay* Eric Rohmer; *Photography* Nestor Almendros; *Music* Jean-Louis Valéro; *Sound* Georges Prat; *Editing* Cécile Decugis. Running time: 94 minutes.

Cast: Amanda Langlet, Arielle Dombasle, Pascal Gregory, Fedor Atkine, Simon de la Brosse, Rosette, Michel Ferry, Marie Boulteloup.

Two cousins, 15-year-old Pauline (Langlet) and divorced Marion (Dombasle), take a seaside vacation. The two of them become involved romantically with three men. Henri (Atkine) wants to live free of attachments and sees no emotional ties to physical encounters. Pierre (Gregory) seeks an ideal love. Sylvain (de la Brosse) is just finding his amorous way. Marion believes in passion. Pauline does not believe in love at first sight. Everybody loses and hurts others. They learn about love and betrayal in the process, with Pauline gaining true wisdom.

In this, the third film in Rohmer's "Comedies and Proverbs" series, he once again gives good talk by exploring different attitudes toward love. Rohmer looks at love with a blend of cynicism and compassion, wryness and warmth. As usual, he manages to capture a realism in human relations and human nature.

French and American critics loved this film. It was Rohmer's biggest hit to date in the United States. Vincent Canby exclaimed in *The New York Times*, "The next best thing to a day at the seashore is this effervescent, sunlit comedy of romantic manners about several intensely self-absorbed, articulate adults and one pretty, clear-eyed teenager." It won the French Critics' Prix Méliès in 1983.

Pauline at the Beach *see* **Pauline à la plage**

281 *Le Peau et les os (Skin and Bones)* 1961 B&W   *Director* Jean-Paul Sassy; *Producer* Contact Organisations, Société Nouvelle Pathé Cinéma, Standard Films, Films Raoul Ploquin; *Screenplay* Jean-Paul Sassy, Jacques Panigel; *Photography* Georges Leclerc; *Music* Louiguy; *Set* Sydney Bettex; *Sound* Séverin Frankiel; *Editing* Pierre Gilette. Running time: 92 minutes.

Cast: Gérard Blain, Juliette Mayniel, André Oumansky, René Dary, Julien Verdier, Jean-Pierre Jaubert, Etienne Bierry, Pierre Richard, Robert Party, Jean Besnard, Yves Barsacq, Georges Adet, Henri Lambert, Georges Lycan, Michel Ferrand, Henri Coutet, Charles Bouillard, Claude Castaing, Gilles Léger, Jean Barrez, Rodolphe Marcilly, Sam Endel, Yvon Sarray, Hubert Deschamps, Emile Genevois, Roger Trécan, Pierre Peloux, Marie Donneaud.

The story about the machinations of life in prison. Charly (Oumansky) is the prisoner who has the most power inside. When a young man named Mazur (Blain) arrives, Charly becomes irritated by the boy's introspective nature. Mazur spends his time thinking about the girl he loved, and whom he was convicted of killing, despite his arguments to the contrary. Another prisoner takes his side to oppose Charly and in the end, they manage to prove Mazur's innocence.

This is an interesting prison movie that blends a documentary-like look at prison life and a drama about human nature. Sassy was interested in the idea of how people react in extreme situations: the natural-born leader who strives for more and more power and the generous spirit, who despite a hard life will reach out to help the underdog. He evokes the hard prison life effectively. Gérard Blain and André Oumansky both succeed well at portraying their characters' evolutions.

Many French critics liked the film. It was never distributed in the United States. The film won the Prix Jean Vigo in 1961.

282 *Le Père Noël est une ordure (Santa Claus Is a Louse)* 1982 Color *Director* Jean-Marie Poiré; *Producer* Trinacra, Les Films du Splendid; *Screenplay* the team from Splendid; *Photography* Robert Alazraki; *Music* Vladimir Cosma; *Set* Willy Holt; *Editing* Catherine Kelber. Running time: 105 minutes.

Cast: Anémone, Thierry Lhermitte, Marie-Anne Chazel, Gérard Jugnot, Christian Clavier, Josiane Balasko, Bruno Moynot, Martin Lamotte, Claire Magnin, Jacques François.

Set in a social service office that answers calls from people in crisis around Christmastime, this farce focuses on three social workers who have to deal with an assortment of nuts that surprise even them. One visitor is a Santa Claus searching for his pregnant wife, another is a depressed transvestite, and a third is a greasy immigrant who hands out bad chocolates. Aptly, they all end up at the zoo.

This hilarious comedy mixes social satire and modern angst to generate great laughs. Adapted from a farce produced by France's leading café-theater company, this film was well directed and blessed with great performances by a troupe of talented young actors.

This was a huge hit in France, but was never distributed in the United States. Some critics lauded the film as ribald comedy. Others, such as *Cinéma*, found it "insulting both to the viewer and to cinema."

Péril *see* **Péril en la demeure**

283 *Péril en la demeure (Péril)* 1984 Color   *Director* Michel Deville; *Producer* Gaumont, Eléfilm, TF1; *Screenplay* Michel Deville, based on René Belletto's novel, *Sur la terre comme au ciel*; *Photography* Martial Thury; *Music* Brahms, Granados, Schubert; *Set* Philippe Combastel; *Sound* André Hervée, Alain Sempé, Claude Villand, Joël Beldent; *Costumes* Cécile Balme; *Editing* Raymonde Guyot. Running time: 100 minutes.

Cast: Anémone, Richard Bohringer, Nicole Garcia, Christophe Malavoy, Michel Piccoli, Anaïs Jeanneret, Jean-Claude Jay, Hélène Roussel, Elisabeth Vitali, Daniel Vérité, Frank Lapersonne, Olivier Foneau.

A thriller about a handsome young guitar teacher, David (Malavoy), who agrees to give lessons to the teenage daughter (Jeanneret) of an industrialist (Piccoli) and his wife, Julia (Garcia). Not long after he and Julia start having an affair, David is mugged. A hired killer, David (Bohringer), comes to his rescue and the two become friends. Compromising videotapes, robberies, break-ins and murder follow.

This gripping psychological thriller is one of Deville's best pictures. Deville, who is one of France's most cerebral directors, was interested in the revelation of character through the complicated nature of human relationships. By keeping the picture always from David's point of view, Miller is able to make the most of the double crossing and deception. This was Deville's twenty-third film. Malavoy and Bohringer are particularly good.

Critics found the film either pretentious or sophisticated. *The Aquarian* said *Péril* is "one of those cool, sophisticated outwardly stylish thrillers where appearance is everything but nothing is really what it seems, especially to a protagonist who generally becomes more and more of an innocent as various webs immerse him." It was the co-winner of the French Critics' Prix Méliès in 1985.

284 *Le Petit Criminel (The Little Gangster* or *The Little Criminal)* 1990 Color   *Director* Jacques Doillon; *Producer* Sara Films; *Screenplay* Jacques Doillon; *Photography* William Lubtchansky; *Music* Philippe Sarde; *Sound* Jean-Claude Laureux; *Editing* Catherine Quesemand. Running time: 100 minutes.

Cast: Richard Anconina, Gérald Thomassin, Clotilde Courau, Jocelyne Perhirin, Cécile Reigher, Daniel Villanova, Dominique Huchede, Dominique Soler, Amanda Regi.

The story of a 12-year-old boy (Thomassin) who does not know his father and is neglected by his mother. One day the phone rings and he discovers he has an older sister somewhere. He sets out to meet her, but misses the meeting. He robs a pharmacy and takes a policeman (Anconina) hostage. His sister (Courau) comes to his aid and the two forge a relationship while running from the police with their hostage.

This picture of kids on the run is a simple story on the surface but has complex undertones and was hailed as the most moving social picture in years. Doillon masterfully balances the high drama of the crime scenes with the poignant relationship scenes. To create greater emotional credibility, he used non-actors to play the children's roles. The film is beautifully photographed by veteran cinematographer Lubtchansky, who brings a haunting quality to the provincial landscapes. The dialogue is superb and a fear that its intelligence would be lost in translation may be why the film was never released in the United States. The little boy, played by Thomassin, is a sweet, sad portrait.

The Little Gangster did very well in France, where critics received it warmly. The film won the Prix Louis Delluc, received special mention at the Berlin Film Festival and was nominated for five Césars.

The Phantom of Liberty *see* **Le Fantôme de la liberté**

285 *Pickpocket* 1959 B&W   *Director* Robert Bresson; *Producer* Agnès Delahaie, Lux Films; *Screenplay* Robert Bresson; *Photography* Léonce Henri Burel; *Music* Lulli; *Set* Pierre Charbonnier; *Sound* Antoine Archimbaud; *Editing* Raymond Lamy. Running time: 75 minutes.

Cast: Martin Lassalle, Marika Green, Pierre Leymairé, Jean Pélegri, Kassagi, Pierre Etaix, Sophie de Saint-Just, Dolly Scal, César Gattegno.

Michel (Lassalle) does not know what to do with himself, so he becomes the apprentice to a professional pickpocket (Kassagi), who teaches him all of the tricks of the trade. Despite the fact that he is being followed by a police officer and has a lovely girlfriend, he cannot stop stealing.

This is one of Bresson's best and most accessible films; it explores themes of destiny and how certain acts determine the individual. It was a very influential movie for young directors. In fact, screenwriter-director Paul Schrader was so affected by Bresson that he wrote a book about him. As in his other films, Bresson manages to seamlessly interweave his protagonist's inner thoughts, their dialogue and actions to depict a gripping psychological portrait. The film was inspired by Dostoevsky's *Crime and Punishment*. Bresson, always a zealot for authenticity, wanted to shoot the entire picture out on the streets. With the aid of special lights rigged to car batteries, he was able to and the results are strikingly candid street shots of Paris. The train station pickpocketing scene is wonderful. Bresson hired a "professional" pickpocket to teach Lassalle.

When it was first released in Paris, this film did not do well commercially or critically. The British, however, lauded it. The film was not released in the United States until 1963, and it received raves. *Newsweek* hailed it as "lawless and flawless." "Director Robert Bresson is a kind of Flaubert of the movies," the reviewer continued. "The Frenchman's work has a precision, a purity, a clarity which is almost chilling." *Films and Filming* entreated: "But do see this gripping film: it's as true, and as powerful, as the best literature can offer, and is the ideal film through which to enter Bresson's world."

The Pier *see* **La Jetée**

286 *Pierrot le fou (Obsession)* 1965 Color   *Director* Jean-Luc Godard; *Producer* Rome Paris Films, De Laurentiis, SNC, Cinematografica; *Screenplay* Jean-Luc Godard, based on Lionel White's novel, *Le Demon de Onze Heures*; *Photography* Raoul Coutard; *Music* Antoine Duhamel and Boris Bassiak; *Set* Pierre Guffroy; *Sound* René Levert; *Editing* Françoise Colin. Running time: 112 minutes.

Cast: Jean-Paul Belmondo, Anna Karina, Dirk Sanders, Roger Dutoit, Raymond Devos, Graziella Galvani, Hans Meyer, Jimmy Karoubi, Pascal Aubier, Alexis Poliakoff, Laszlo Szabo, Jean-Pierre Léaud, Princess Aïcha Abadie, Samuel Fuller, Christa Nell, Pierre Hanin.

A thriller about Ferdinand, a.k.a. Pierrot (Belmondo), who, after running off with his child's babysitter, Marianne (Karina), finds brutally murdered bodies everywhere he turns. Gangsters and double crossing are involved, as Marianne betrays Pierrot for love and money. He kills her in a shootout. When Pierrot finally considers returning to his family, it is too late. He has painted his face blue, wrapped explosives to his head and cannot extinguish the lit fuse.

One of Godard's great successes, *Pierrot* is full of artistic and literary references that range from Renoir and Rimbaud to Picasso, but it is also a perfect blend of action, drama, romance and adventure. Louis Aragon wrote of Godard: "The disorder of our world is his raw material—all this shantytown of our lives without which we couldn't live, but which we manage not to see. And of this, as of accidents and murder, he creates beauty." Richard Burton was originally considered for the Belmondo role.

French critics saw the film as a cinematic poem and a call to arms against commercialized civilization. Critic Georges Sadoul wrote that he was "transported by this new work, carried away by its lyric folly, its abundant sobriety, its sweet bitterness, its grand gaiety on the verge of tears, its rigorous casualness."

Pig Across Paris *see* **La Traversée de Paris**

Pirate's Fiancée *see* **La Fiancée du pirate**

287 *La Piscine (The Pool)* 1969 Color   *Director* Jacques Deray; *Producer* SNC; *Screenplay* Jean-Emmanuel Conil; *Dialogue* Jean-Claude Carrière; *Photography* Jean-Pierre Tardes; *Music* Michel Legrand; *Sound* René Longuet; *Editing* Paul Cayatte. Running time: 100 minutes.

Cast: Alain Delon, Romy Schneider, Maurice Ronet, Jane Birkin, Paul Crauchet, Steve Eckardt, Suzy Jaspar, Madly Bramy, Thierry Chabert, Stéphanie Fugain.

Jean-Paul (Delon) and Marianne (Schneider) are a happy couple living in a villa on the Côte d'Azur. But when Harry (Ronet) and his daughter Penelope (Birkin) arrive, trouble in paradise begins. The two men hide their feelings of intense dislike and competition behind fake friendliness. Harry tries to seduce Marianne, who was once his lover, while Jean-Paul sets out to seduce Penelope. Jean-Paul ends up drowning Harry. Marianne keeps the secret and Penelope leaves. The happy couple resume their life.

A gripping tale of building tension that results in violence, this brilliantly controlled film was the breakthrough work that put Deray on the cinematic map as an auteur. It was also the beginning of a long and productive relationship between Deray and Delon, who went on to make six other movies together, including *Borsalino*. This remains one of Deray's best films, with fluidity, grace, precision of direction and a fine mixture of aesthetic and emotional sense.

Deray has been compared to the great Otto Preminger, and critics hailed this film as his *Laura*. Unfortunately, it was never released in the United States.

288 *Le Plaisir (House of Pleasure)* 1952 B&W   *Director* Max Ophüls; *Producer* CCFC; *Screenplay* Jacques Natanson, Max Ophüls, based on three stories by Guy de Maupassant; *Photography* Christian Matras, Philippe Agostini; *Music* Joe Hajos, Maurice Yvain, based on works by Jacques Offenbach; *Set* Jean d'Eaubonne; *Sound* Jean Renoul; *Costumes* Annenkov; *Editing* Léonide Azar. Running time: 95 minutes.

Cast: Claude Dauphin, Jean Galland, Gaby Morlay, Daniel Gélin, Simone Simon, Jean Servais, Jean Gabin, Madeleine Renaud, Danielle Darrieux, Ginette Leclerc, Mila Parely, Pierre Brasseur, Paulette Dubost, Mathilde Casadesus, Hélèna Manson, René Blancard, Louis Seigner, Gaby Bruyère, Henri Crémieux, Marcel Pérès, Antoine Balpêtré, Georges Baconnet, Michel Vadet, Robert Lombard, Arthur Devère, Paul Azaïs, Emile Genevois, Jocelyne Jany, Janine Viénot, Yzelle, Claire Olivier, Yvonne Dany, Jean Meyer, Charles Vissières, Amédée, Jo Dest, René Hell, Georges Vitray, Rognoni, René Pascal, Marcel Rouzé, Palau, Pierre-Louis Calvet, François Harispuru.

Three Maupassant stories, "Le Masque," "La Maison Tellier" and "Le Modèle," were adapted to make this film. "The Mask" is about an old man (Galland) who wears a mask to dance in a music hall as a young man. When he collapses and is brought home to his elderly wife (Morlay), she tells the doctor (Dauphin) the story of a ladies man unable to grow old. The longest and most substantial of the three stories is "The Tellier House," which is about a brothel in Normandy and the journey of the brothel's girls for a day in the country to celebrate the Communion of the Madame's niece. "The Model" is the story of an artist (Gélin), who falls in love with his nude model (Simon), then falls out of love with her but cannot escape her.

The film was made after the success of *La Ronde*. Maupassant's fascination with women and happiness are the themes that connect these stories. Ophüls' fanciful, fluid direction brings a wonderful contrast to the underlying sadness of these stories, all of which explore people searching desperately and vainly for happiness. The sets and costumes, as usual, are wonderful, and Ophüls uses his acrobatic camera style to make the most of them.

French critics were disappointed with *Le Plaisir* when it opened. Perhaps, it was not what they anticipated after *La Ronde*, but one critic accused Ophüls of making a movie that was merely "useless games with the camera." American critics were much kinder. Even those who claimed that the stories were just a pretext for Ophüls' direction, called this film brilliant. The English version of this film is narrated by Peter Ustinov, which is a bit off-putting, because he narrates in English and the film follows with French subtitles.

Playing at Love *see* **Les Jeux de l'amour**

289 *Playtime* 1967 Color   *Director* Jacques Tati; *Producer* Spectra Films; *Screenplay* Jacques Tati; *Adaptation* Jacques Lagrange; *Photography* Paul Rodier and Marcel Manchi; *Music* Francis Lemarque, with songs by David Stein and James Campbell; *Sound* Jacques Maumont; *Editing* Gérard Pollicand. Running time: 152 minutes.

Cast: Jacques Tati, Barbara Denneck, Jacqueline Lecomte, Valérie Camille, France Rumilly, France Delahalle, Laure Paillette, Colette Proust, Erika Dentzler, Yvette Ducreux, Rita Maiden, Nicole Ray, Luce Bonifassy, Evy Cacallaro, Alice Field, Eliane Firmin-Didot, Ketty France, Nathalie Jeam, Oliva Poli, Sophie Wennek, Jack Gauthier, Henri Piccoli, Léon Doyen, Georges Montant, John Abbey, Reinhart Kolldehoff, Grégory Katz, Marc Monjou, Yves Barsacq, Tony Andal, André Fouché, Georges Faye, Michel Fancini, Billy Kearns, Bob Harley, Jacques Chauveau, Douglas Reard, François Viaur, Gilbert Reeb, Billy Bourbon.

More adventures of Monsieur Hulot (Tati). This time he is in Paris to keep

Plein Soleil (Purple Noon), 1959; directed by René Clément.

an appointment with a Monsieur Giffard (Montant). Though he gets lost in the hallways and offices of the hotel, he does meet a young American woman (Dennek), who is part of a tour group staying in the same hotel. After various non-traditional tourist adventures, the two cannot seem to say good-bye.

Many consider this wonderful slapstick comedy from the great Jacques Tati to be his most polished and fully realized work. This was his second to last movie made for the big screen. Tati once again puts Hulot up against the modern world to great comic effect. He spent three years and over a million dollars on the film. Who could have thought such laughter could be wrought from neon, plastic and skyscrapers? The gags are wonderful as is Tati's intelligent, light touch. Despite the huge budget, the film has a very personal, small film feel to it, with every scene rendered with the utmost care and for a highly observant audience.

Playtime was warmly received by the French critics and public; they declared it one more Tati masterpiece. When it was released five years later in the United States, American critics were divided. Some, such as the *New Leader*, accused Tati of becoming "a crashing bore." Kenneth Tyman, however, declared, "Jacques Tati is the supreme inventor and exponent of physical gags. He is the Nabokov of movie farce, and *Playtime* is his subtlest masterpiece." Vincent Canby of *The New York Times* simply said it was one "of the greatest screen comedies of all time."

290 *Plein Soleil (Purple Noon* or *Lust for Evil)* 1959 B&W *Director* René Clément; *Producer* Paris Film Productions; *Screenplay* René Clément, Paul Gégauff, based on Patricia Highsmith's novel *Mr. Ripley*; *Photography* Henri Decaë; *Music* Nino Rota; *Set* Paul Bertrand; *Editing* Françoise Javet. Running time: 119 minutes.

Cast: Alain Delon, Marie Laforêt, Maurice Ronet, Elvire Popesco, Erno Crisa, Franck Latimore, Billy Kearns, Ave Ninchi, Romy Schneider, Vivianne Chantel, Nerio Bernardi, Lili Romanelli, Nicolas Petrov.

Set in Italy in 1959, Ripley (Delon) is hired by a rich American to find his son and persuade him to come home. As Ripley's charge is the spoiled Philip Greenleaf (Ronet), who has no desire to return to the United States, his task is impossible. His anger and frustration build as Greenleaf constantly makes fun of him in front of Greenleaf's attractive girlfriend (Laforêt). During an argument, Ripley kills Greenleaf and then assumes his identity. He makes Greenleaf's death look like a suicide and succeeds in seducing the girl, but in the end, of course, he is discovered.

Considered one of the great films of the 1950s, *Purple Noon* is high art and high entertainment. *Purple Noon* came out just when the New Wave directors were emerging on the cinema scene, which did not stop this more traditional thriller from becoming a huge hit, but it was the last of an era. It announced an amazing talent, who would be one of the biggest and most prolific leading men of the next 30 years: Alain Delon, in one of his greatest roles. When it came out, the color photography was so extraordinary as to be called mind-blowing. The wonderful music was written by Nino Rota, who worked on most of Fellini's films.

Some French critics declared this national treasure better than all of Hitchcocks' films combined.

291 *Le Point du jour (The Mark of the Day)*   1947 B&W   *Director* Louis Daquin; *Producer* Ciné France; *Screenplay* Vladimir Pozner; *Adaptation* Vladimir Pozner and Louis Daquin; *Dialogue* Vladimir Pozner; *Photography* André Bac; *Music* Jean Wiener; *Set* Paul Bertrand; *Sound* Tony Leenhardt; *Editing* Claude Nicole. Running time: 101 minutes.

Cast: Jean Dasailly, René Lefèvre, Loleh Bellon, Michel Piccoli, Gaston Modot, Paul Frankeur, Jean-Pierre Grenier, Hélène Gerber, Lise Graf, Suzanne Demars, Marie-Hélène Dasté, Catherine Monot, Serge Grave, Guy Sargis, Léon Larive, Pierre Latour, Pierre Françasi, Julien Lacroiz, Guy Favières, Yvette Etiévant, Louis Daquin, Julien Verdier.

Set in northern France just before World War II, this is the story of the life of mine workers. One woman wants to get married and continue to work in the mines. Another fears she will have to follow her fiancé to Poland. A young boy wants to follow in his father's footsteps and become a miner.

Daquin's great masterpiece was the realization of this — his wish to make "the first French film devoted to the working man." While it now seems less realistic than it did at the time, the film did become the benchmark for socialist realism. He shot the entire film on location. The occasional stiff scene and awkward dialogue do not undermine the film's greatest strength — its honest look at the mining life. The photography is superb, as are the actors.

Unfortunately, the public did not respond to Daquin's work. His realism was a sharp contrast to the extravagant epics that were popular just after the war. Critic Georges Sadoul despaired over the public's indifference to *Le Point du Jour*, which he considered to be "the real artistic happening of the year."

292 *La Pointe courte*   1955 B&W   *Director* Agnès Varda; *Producer* Tamaris Films; *Screenplay* Agnès Varda; *Photography* Louis Stein; *Music* Pierre

Barbaud; *Sound* Georges Mardiguian; *Editing* Alain Resnais. Running time: 75 minutes.

Cast: Philippe Noiret, Sylvie Montfort, and the inhabitants of La Pointe Courte.

The story of a nameless couple living in the fishing village, La Pointe Courte. The man has returned home. He and his wife do not get along. They have a hard time adjusting to life as a couple. Caught up in their own concerns, they are not involved in the goings-on of the village just outside their window.

Agnès Varda's first film is one of the precursors of the New Wave. The couple's loveless relationship is delicately balanced against an almost documentary treatment of the life of the fishing village. Their selfish egotism is emphasized by the complex larger world, to which they are completely oblivious. While the film's overly literary quality grates, Varda's great talent is easily glimpsed in this work, which was inspired by William Faulkner's *The Wild Palms*. The part of the man was also the great Philippe Noiret's first film role.

While the critics who called this film jumbled and overly intellectual had valid criticisms, the original Varda voice made it an exciting debut all the same. In *Cahiers du Cinéma*, Truffaut called it an "ambitious, probing, intelligent, experimental work."

Poison *see* **La Poison**

293 *La Poison (Poison)* 1951 B&W *Director* Sacha Guitry; *Producer* SNEG, Paul Wagner, Gaumont; *Screenplay* Sacha Guitry; *Photography* Jean Bachelet; *Music* Louiguy; *Set* Robert Dumesnil; *Sound* Fernard Janisse; *Editing* Raymond Lamy. Running time: 82 minutes.

Cast: Michel Simon, Germaine Reuver, Jean Debucourt, Nicolas Amato, Pauline Carton, Jeanne Fusier-Gir, Duvalleix, Louis de Funès, Jacques Varennes, Marcelle Arnold, Georges Bever, Léon Walther, Luce Fabiole, Henri Laverne, Marthe Sarbel, Jacques Derives, Yvonne Hébert, Michel Nastorg, Marie Fromet, André Dalibert, Max Dejean, Jacques de Féraudy, Harry Max, Roger Poirier, Nicolas Amato, Louis Eymond, Henri Belly, Thérèse Quantin, Robert Mercier, Yannick Malloire, Jacomet, P. Paillet, Jimmy Urabain, Allain Malloire, N. Malloire, Lenoir.

A tale of the perfect murder. A husband (Simon) visits his lawyer (Debucourt) to explain how he has just killed his wife (Reuver) by accident. In the course of their conversation, he learns all of the intricacies of involuntary homicide and then returns home and poisons his alcoholic wife. Of course, when he goes to trial, the jury pities the poor man's loss, and he is acquitted.

One of Guitry's great films and certainly one of the two best films he made after World War II. He made the film in only nine days, and said it was one of the most fun films he had ever worked on. To make his star Michel Simon happy, Guitry promised to shoot every scene only once, and he did this by preparing every detail in advance. Simon and Reuver deliver great performances as a married couple full of rage and disgust for one another. The courtroom scenes are extremely witty and entertaining. In Guitry's last films, he was credited with "an almost diabolic aptitude for describing thieves and rogues," which is in strong evidence in *Poison*. Guitry's aim was to have his grotesque murderer seduce viewers so completely that they are thrilled when he gets away with his crime.

Porte des Lilas (Gates of Paris), 1957; directed by René Clair.

The critics all loved Simon's performance. People flocked to what they considered a great thriller, though few remarked on how subtly Guitry had subverted common beliefs about justice and the law.

The Pool *see* **La Piscine**

294 *Porte des Lilas (Gates of Paris* or *Gates of Lilacs)* 1957 B&W *Director* René Clair; *Producer* Filmsonor, Rizzoli Films, Cinétel, Séca; *Screenplay* René Clair, based on René Fallet's novel *La Grande Ceinture*; *Photography* Robert Lefebvre and Albert Militon; *Music* Georges Brassens; *Set* Léon Barsacq; *Sound* Antoine Petitjean; *Costumes* Rosine Delamare; *Editing* Louisette Hautecoeur. Running time: 96 minutes.

Cast: Pierre Brasseur, Georges Brassens, Henri Vidal, Dany Carrel, Raymond Bussières, Amédée, Alain Bouvette, Louis Bougette, Annette Poivre, Gabrielle Fontan, Alice Tissot, Albert Michel, Gérard Buhr, Paul Faivre, Teddy Bilis, Georges Bever, Charles Bouillard, Sylvain, Jacques Marin, José Montheilet, Philippe Houy, Jean Rieubon, Michel Lucas, Christian Denhez, Georgette Peyron, Joël Monteilhet, Edouard Francomme, Balpo, Paul Préboist, Georges Aminel, Annie Gardel.

A heavy-drinking neighborhood guy, Juju (Brasseur), lives in the Lilas section of Paris. He does not do much but hang around with his musician friend (Brassens). When he meets a man named Barbier (Vidal) hiding out from the police in his friend's place, he initially likes him. When he learns that Barbier intends to seduce young Maria (Carrel), whom Juju has always loved, he kills Barbier.

Clair, who always thought of himself as a writer who made films, made a masterpiece with this film. Many consider it to be the finest film of his long career. His evocation of the dark suburban underworld, the haunts of criminals and ne'er-do-wells is truly poetic. He examines human failings and miseries with bravery and beauty. Pierre Brasseur delivers the best performance of his career in this film. The music is wonderful.

Gates of Paris was hailed as a masterpiece by some. Others deemed it only a fair Clair work. *The Saturday Review* exclaimed: "In *Gates of Paris* René Clair reveals that he is still one of the world's great directors." The film won the Grand Prix du Cinéma Français in 1957.

295 *Les Portes de la nuit (Gates of the Night)* 1945 B&W *Director* Marcel Carné; *Producer* Pathé Cinéma; *Screenplay* Jacques Prévert, based on his ballet *Le Rendez-vous*; *Dialogue* Jacques Prévert; *Photography* Philippe Agostini; *Music* Joseph Kosma; *Set* Alexandre Trauner; *Costumes* Mayo; *Sound* Antoine Archimbaud; *Editing* Jean Feyte. Running time: 120 minutes.

Cast: Pierre Brasseur, Yves Montand, Nathalie Nattier, Serge Reggiani, Saturnin Fabre, Jean Vilar, Dany Robin, Raymond Bussières, Sylvia Bataille, Julien Carette, Mady Berry, Fabien Loris, Jane Marken, Jean Maxime, René Blancard, Michel Salina, Christian Simon.

One night after the liberation of Paris, Jean (Montand) is reunited with the most beautiful girl he has ever laid eyes on—Malou (Nattier). The backdrop to their fateful meeting is a city in tumultuous transition as angry husbands return, collaborators and black-marketers flee, and Resistance heroes rule. The two forget their personal tragedies as they find happiness together, but the effects of the war are not entirely over and, tragically, the couple is torn apart.

This was the final collaboration of the dynamic duo of Marcel Carné and Jacques Prévert. It is a beautiful movie with extraordinary music, including Kosma's famous song "Autumn Leaves," exquisite photography and Carné's favorite theme — destiny. The young Yves Montand is great.

Gates of the Night did not meet critics' expectations when it was released because Marlene Dietrich and Jean Gabin were originally slated to play the two lead roles, but they backed out. In fact, the movie bombed. Critics declared it dated and melodramatic. Over the years, it has grown enormously in esteem.

296 *Pourquoi pas! (Why Not!)* 1977 Color   *Director* Coline Serreau; *Producer* Dimage, SND; *Screenplay* Coline Serreau; *Photography* Jean-François Robin; *Music* Jean-Pierre Mas; *Set* Outdoors; *Sound* Alain Lachassagne; *Editing* Sophie Tatischeff. Running time: 93 minutes.

Cast: Samy Frey, Christine Murillo, Mario Gonzalès, Nicole Jamet, Michel Aumont, Mathé Souverbie, Marie-Thérèse Saussure, Alain Salomon, Bernard Crombe, Xavier Saint Macary, Nicolas Serreau, Dorothy Marchini, Louise Chevalier, Ghislaine Péan, André Marcon, Geneviève Mnich, Luce Fabiole, Véronique Vitale.

A tender ménage à trois tale about Fernand (Frey), Louis (Gonzalès) and Alexa (Murillo). Alexa and Fernand are both recently divorced and find new comfort and excitement in a relationship with the bisexual Louis. After a few problems, the threesome finds harmony when Fernand introduces another woman and four makes for happiness.

Serreau's first feature film explores an unusual lifestyle, but her point was to open people's minds. She made the film at age 30, and it announced the arrival of an exciting new director, who was immediately compared to the subversive Blier. By mixing her characters' past lives with their present ones, Serreau gives deeper meaning to their search for happiness and makes their decisions more believable. Serreau said of her intentions: "The moral of this film is that the old repressive world is collapsing and an absurd moral system is giving its last gasp, so it's time to live."

Critics admired this film, which they saw as a charming feminist argument for a more liberal society. *The Boston Globe* said, "It's a dry, wry, droll, witty and sophisticated taste of the kind of French pastry that perhaps only the French can make out of love and sex." The film won the Prix Georges Sadoul in 1977.

Practice Makes Perfect *see* **Le Cavaleur**

297 *Préparez vos mouchoirs (Get Out Your Handkerchiefs)* 1978 Color   *Director* Bertrand Blier; *Producer* Ariane, Capac, Sodec; *Screenplay* Bertrand Blier, Philippe Dumarçay; *Photography* Jean Penzer; *Music* Georges Delerue; *Set* Jean André; *Sound* Jean-Pierre Ruh; *Editing* Claudine Merlin. Running time: 108 minutes

Cast: Gérard Depardieu, Patrick Dewaere, Carole Laure, Michel Serrault, Riton, Eleonore Hirt, Sylvie Joly, Jean Rougerie, Michel Beaune, Liliane Rovere, André Thorent, Roger Riffard, Phillipe Brigaud.

A sex comedy about a devoted husband, Raoul (Depardieu), who worries that his wife, Solange (Laure), is depressed. He asks another man, Stéphane (Dewaere), to try to satisfy her, but he has no more luck than her husband. Finally, Solange finds love when the three go off to supervise kids at a summer camp. She meets a 13-year-old boy, Christian (Riton), who gets her pregnant.

In this hilarious film, Blier tackles modern issues that confront men and women in their relationships. Depardieu and Dewaere are a lovable duo of dunces who are unable to please their damsel in distress. They can be vulgar one minute and sensitively rapt in Mozart the next, but they never cease to charm. And yet something subversive is just under the surface, always saving the film from sappy sentiment. This captures a wonderful post-women's liberation era and shows just how complicated liberation can be.

Just as Blier's early film, *Going Places*, did, *Get Out Your Handkerchiefs* raised outraged cries of sexism from some. Critic David Denby wrote of its strengths: "*Handkerchiefs* holds in balance the two moods of buoyant comedy and heart-piercing sadness right to the end. It's one of the screen's rare lyric triumphs in recent years." It won the Oscar for Best Foreign Film and the Best Picture award from the National Society of Film Critics in 1978. George Delerue's music won a César for Best Score.

The Pretty Miller Girl *see* **La Belle Meunière**

Private Projection *see* **Projection privée**

298 *Le Procès de Jeanne d'Arc (The Trial of Joan of Arc)*   1961 B&W
Director Robert Bresson; *Producer* Agnès Delahaie, Pathé; *Screenplay* Robert Bresson, based on the transcripts of the trial; *Photography* Léonce Henri Burel; *Music* Francis Seyrig; *Set* Pierre Charbonnier; *Sound* Antoine Archimbaud; *Costumes* Lucilla Mussini; *Editing* Germaine Artus. Running time: 65 minutes.

Cast: Florence Delay, Jean-Claude Fourneau, Marc Jacquier, Roger Honorat, Jean Gillibert, André Brunet, Richard Pratt, Philippe Dreux, Gérard Zing, Paul-Robert Nimet, Michel Hérubel, Marcel Darbaud, André Régnier, André Maurice, Harry Sommers, Donald O'Brien, Arthur Le Bau, Robert Minet, Yves Le Prince, Pierre Duboucheron, Henri Collin-Delavaud, Claude Perrone, Guy-Louis Duboucheron, Alain Blaisy, Eric Siroux, Jean Collombier, Pierre Gauthier, Samners, Jean Payen, Nicolas Bang.

A fascinating historical adaptation of the trial, sentencing and execution of Joan of Arc. A young French peasant girl (Delay) was tried by the government and the church for heresy because of her visions and her arrogance. After the English court found her guilty, she was burned at the stake as a witch. The Catholic church later canonized her.

Bresson did not turn the legend into a soaring epic, but rather, by basing the screenplay entirely on the actual transcripts of the trial, he created a realistic portrait of how a smart, brazen girl can be turned by popular imagination into a witch and then a saint. His aim was "to make real a marvelous young girl." Once again, he used non-actors to ensure a realistic quality. His talents at turning literature and history into great cinema were put to good use here. He weaves theology, psychology, drama and history beautifully.

Joan of Arc had already been the subject of over twenty films, when Bresson made this one, but that did not stop viewers or critics from appreciating his angle. When it was released in France, few could fail to be moved by the significance of national resistance in response to an occupied country. The film won the Special Jury Prize at Cannes.

299 *Le Professionel (The Professional)* 1981 Color   *Director* Georges Lautner; *Producer* Cerito/ Films Ariane; *Screenplay* Michel Audiard; *Photography* Henri Decaë; *Music* Ennio Morricone; *Sound* Alain Sempé; *Editing* Michèle David. Running time: 105 minutes

Cast: Jean-Paul Belmondo, Jean Desailly, Robert Hossein, Cyrielle Claire, Michel Beaune, Jean-Louis Richard, Sidiki Bakaba, Marie-Christine Descouard, Bernard-Pierre Donnadieu, Pierre Vernier, Elisabeth Margoni, Gérard Darrieu, André Weber, Jacques Canselier, Beate Kopp, Cheik Doukouré.

A thriller about a special agent, Beaumont (Belmondo), who is ordered to assassinate the president of Malawy, a small African country. Though he is held in an African prison for a while, when he gets out he goes about finishing his assignment. His target comes to Paris on an official state visit, but there has been a change of plans. His government no longer wants the dictator killed, so they hunt Beaumont to prevent him from completing his mission. Shots are fired in the end with fatal errors made.

This film was one of the top ten biggest hits of the 1980s in France and it is an important cultural document because Belmondo is such a huge star in France. Lautner and Belmondo teamed up many times to make stunt-filled action pictures, and this is one of their better collaborations.

Some critics complained that the film was just another Belmondo vehicle, but that did not keep the crowds away. They loved it, and even a few critics conceded that Lautner and Belmondo are professional thrill makers.

The Professional *see* **Le Professionel**

300 *Projection privée (Private Projection)* 1974 Color   *Director* François Leterrier; *Producer* Albina du Boisrouvray; *Screenplay* François Leterrier; *Photography* Jean Badal; *Music* Serge Gainsbourg and Jean-Claude Vannier; *Editing* M. J. Yoyotte. Running time: 90 minutes.

Cast: Françoise Fabian, Jean-Luc Bideau, Jane Birkin, Bulle Ogier, Jacques Weber, Barbara Laage, Françoise Laurent, Jean Gobbi, Sabine Glaser, Yan Brina, Jean-Louis Fortuit, Elisabeth Huppert, Simono.

Filmmaker Denis Mallet (Bideau) has decided to make a movie based on his past, but the project dredges up more than just memories. Years before, Mallet left his wife, Marthe (Fabian), to marry a younger woman, Camille (Ogier). Marthe died in a car accident soon after. When Mallet decides to film a similar scene, Camille confesses that she told Marthe of the love affair and did not stop her from killing herself when maybe she could have.

This is a great thriller that plays with a film within a film. Leterrier was interested in the idea of life imitating art and art imitating life. He carried out that concept to an extreme degree with exciting results that became a sort of textbook case of filmmaking experiments that has since been used in film schools. The play on the first wife, the second wife and then the woman who plays the first wife and what they all signify to the director proves an interesting example of how to manipulate narrative structures and symbols and maintain a somewhat mainstream, traditional work.

Private Projection was a success in France, with critics and the public admiring it. It was never released in the United States. *Variety* said, "It works on various levels of the past, creating present difficulties and does have some stylish observation but gets fastidious at times in perhaps forcing the style on its characters." The film won the Grand Prix du Cinéma Français in 1973.

The Proud and the Beautiful *see* **Les Orgueilleux**

Purple Noon *see* **Plein Soleil**

301 *Le Quai des orfèvres (Jenny Lamour)* 1947 B&W   *Director* Henri-Georges Clouzot; *Producer* Majestic Films; *Screenplay* Henri-Georges Clouzot, Jean Ferry, based on the novel by Stanislas-André Steeman; *Dialogue* Henri-Georges Clouzot; *Photography* Armand Thirard; *Music* Francis Lopez and Albert Lasry; *Set* Max Douy; *Sound* William Sivel; *Costumes* Jacques Fath; *Editing* Charles Breoneiche. Running time: 105 minutes.

Cast: Louis Jouvet, Suzy Delair, Simone Renant, Bernard Blier, Charles Dullin, Claudine Dupuis, Pierre Larquey, Raymond Bussières, René Blancard, Jean Daurand, Robert Dalban, Gilberte Géniat, Jeanne Fusier Gir, Paul Demange, Charles Blavette, François Joux, Léo Lapara, Jean Sinöel, Dora Doll, Annette Poivre, Henri Arius, Jacques Grétillat, Jean Dunot, Jean Hebey, Gabriel Gobin, Fernand René, Georges Pally, Charles Vissières, Joëlle Bernard, Paul Temps, Bob Ingarao, Henry Niel, Franck Maurice, Raphaël Patorni, André Numès, Palmyre Levasseur, Yvonne Ménard, Claire Olivier, René Lacourt, Joe Davray, Claude Péran, Jean Sylvère, Marcel Rouzé, Sacha Tarride, Maurice Juniot, Michel Seldow, François Gilbert Moreau.

Inspector Antoine (Jouvet) investigates the murder of a vicious old man, Brignon (Dullin). He enters a dark world of music halls and cabarets, where he comes across the singer Jenny Lamour (Delair) and her protective husband, Maurice (Blier), who is his first suspect. Antoine uncovers the truth eventually and his encounters with this sordid side of Paris cause him to reflect on the vicissitudes of life.

This magnificent film noir was one of the works that earned Clouzot the title of France's master of suspense. It was his second feature and his return to the screen after *The Raven* was denounced as enemy propaganda after the war because of its negative portrayal of a French village. His stunning set and camera movement, which work together to create the quintessential French film noir atmosphere, helped set the standard for the decade's filmmakers. Clouzot looks at his characters and their world with a mixture of hard-boiled pessimism and romanticism. He reveals them as down-and-out, even corrupt, souls and then redeems them as they fall in love.

Critics everywhere loved the character of Jenny Lamour. *Time* magazine called the film "the best movie treatment of show business since 1925" and dubbed Delair "a Mae West who really means it." *Look* raved: "Songs, sex, and subtle wit enliven an adult French whodunit." The film won the international prize for direction at the Venice Biennal in 1947.

A Quarter to Two Before Jesus Christ *see* **Deux Heures moins le quart avant Jésus Christ**

302 *Les Quatre Cent Coups (The 400 Blows)* 1958 B&W *Director* François Truffaut; *Producer* SEDIF, Films du Carrosse; *Screenplay* François Truffaut and Marcel Moussy; *Photography* Henri Decaë; *Music* Jean Constantin; *Set* Bernard Evein; *Sound* Jean-Claude Marchetti; *Editing* Marie-Josèphe Yoyotte. Running time: 93 minutes.

Cast: Jean-Pierre Léaud, Patrick Auffay, Claire Maurier, Albert Rémy, Yvonne Claudie, Georges Flamant, Guy Decomble, Pierre Rep, Jacques Monod, Richard Kanayan, Jeanne Moreau, Jean-Claude Brialy, Christian Brocard, Robert Beauvais, Marius Laurey, Luc Andrieux, Henri Vilojeux, Claude Mansard, Bouchon, Jacques Demy.

The boyhood misadventures of a very troubled and troublesome 14-year-old boy, Antoine Doinel (Léaud). Neglected by his parents and uninterested in school, Antoine, along with his friend, René (Auffay), plays hooky from school one day, an adventure that starts a chain of delinquent events. When he is caught stealing a typewriter, he is sent to reform school and into psychoanalysis. He runs away from the school and heads for the seashore, which has become his fantasy-land.

One of the films, along with Chabrol's *Handsome Serge* and *The Cousins* and Godard's *Breathless*, that marked the beginning of the New Wave. The first of the Antoine Dionel series, this bears all the marks of Truffaut the auteur, his obsessions with childhood, education and the psychology of his characters. Though not structurally innovative or very shocking, its originality lies in its sensibility, the evenness of the tone and the realism of the characters and the lyricism of the direction. It is a real first-person film, in part, because it is very autobiographical. Originally, Truffaut planned to make it 20 minutes long. It was shot in only two and a half months and was dedicated to André Bazin, one of the founders of *Cahiers du Cinéma* and Truffaut's mentor and sort-of adopted father. In what would become a defining characteristic of the New Wave, Truffaut included visual homages to Jean Vigo's *Zero for Conduct* and *L'Atlante*.

The 400 Blows was an instant hit, thanks partly to the fact that it won Best Director at Cannes before it opened. When it opened in the United States, John Russell compared the film to William Wordsworth's work, and wrote that *The 400 Blows* was "a cinematic equivalent of *The Prelude*, vividly chronicling the 'growth of a poet's mind'." In addition to winning Best Director at Cannes in 1959, it was also co-winner of the French Critics' Prix Méliès. It also won the New York Film Critics' Award for Best Foreign Film and was nominated for an Oscar for Best Original Screenplay.

303 *Que la bête meure (This Man Must Die* or *Killer)* 1969 Color *Director* Claude Chabrol; *Producer* Films la Boëtie; *Screenplay* Paul Gégauff, based on the novel by Niklauss Blake; *Photography* Jean Rabier; *Music* Pierre Jansen; *Set* Guy Littaye; *Sound* Guy Chichignoud; *Editing* Jacques Gaillard. Running time: 113 minutes.

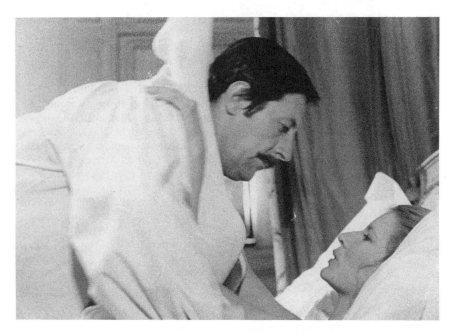

Que la fête commence (Let Joy Reign Supreme), 1975; directed by **Bertrand Tavernier.**

Cast: Michel Duchaussoy, Jeanne Yanne, Caroline Cellier, Maurice Pialat, Anouk Ferjac, Marc di Napoli, Lorraine Rainer, Stéphane di Napoli, Guy Marly, Louise Chevalier, Dominique Zardi, Jean-Louis Maury, Raymone, Michel Charrel, Robert Rondo, Georges Charrier, Jacques Masson.

When Charles Thénier's (Duchaussoy) son is killed by a hit-and-run driver, he decides to hunt down the driver and kill him. What he finds is Paul Decourt (Yanne), a brutal mechanic who terrorizes his own family, particularly his 12-year-old son Philippe (di Napoli). When Charles befriends the son, he learns that the boy wants to kill his father. When Paul is poisoned, Philippe and Charles are alternately accused and then confess.

This gripping thriller is arguably one of Chabrol's best films and certainly one of his most entertaining. Chabrol wanted to make a film in the style of Fritz Lang that questioned the place of blame. To this end, he never reveals who killed Paul. All of his favorite themes, ignorance, bourgeois posturing and revenge are worked seamlessly into this film, as he plays the thoughtless murderer against the cunning one. Jean Yanne finds one of the best roles of his career in the beastly character of Paul.

This Man Must Die was one of Chabrol's great commercial successes. Critics applauded the seductive way in which Chabrol made murder so attractive.

304 *Que la fête commence (Let Joy Reign Supreme)* 1975 Color *Director* Bertrand Tavernier; *Producer* Lira Films; *Screenplay* Jean Aurenche and Bertrand Tavernier; *Photography* Pierre William Glenn; *Music* Antoine Duhamel, based on the music of Philippe d'Orléans; *Set* Pierre Guffroy; *Sound* Michel

Desrois and Auguste Galli; *Costumes* Jacqueline Moreau; *Editing* Armand Psenny. Running time: 120 minutes

Cast: Philippe Noiret, Jean Rochefort, Jean-Pierre Marielle, Christine Pascal, Marina Vlady, Monique Lejeune, Nicole Garcia, Gérard Desarthe, Alfred Adam, Thierry Lhermitte, Stéphane Bouy, Jean-Roger Caussimon, Hélène Vincent, François Dyrek, Jean Rougerie, Monique Chaumette, Bernard Lajarrige, Bernadette Le Saché, Daniel Duval, Blanche Rayne, Colette Proust, Jacques Hilling, Andrée Tainsy, Pierre Moncorbier, Jean-Paul Farre, Michel Berto, Brigitte Rouen, Raymond Girard, Georges Riquier, Jean Amos, Michel Beaune, Anthony Stewart, François Valorbe, Sophie Jany, Maurice Jacquemont, Bruno Balp, Michel Blanc, Liza Braconnier, Pierre Forget, Gilles Guillot, Marie-Jo Simenon, Jean Turlier, Guy Gerbeaud, Yves Elliot, Yvon Lec, Jean Le Mouel, René Morard, Jacques Lelut, Bertrand Migeat, Jacques Van Dooren, Christian Clavier, Roland Amstutz, Gilbert Bahon, Jacky Pratoussy, Patrice Raynal, Richard Bigotini, Agnès Chateau, Philippe Chaveau, Claude Furlan, Erice Lorvoire, Gérard Pichon, Jean-Jacques Moreau, Bernard Pierrot, Jean-Paul Poirier.

Set in 1719 when Philippe d'Orléans (Noiret) was regent of France. A liberal and a reformer, Philippe d'Orléans allows himself to be advised by the Abbé Dubois (Rochefort), who convinces him that the only way to appease England and put an end to rebellious stirrings in France is to execute the Marquis de Pontcallec (Marielle).

This colorful epic brought to life, in an exciting and very realistic way, a turbulent period of French history. Tavernier's great gift to French filmmaking was helping to revive the art of quality filmmaking and this film, his second, was a great tool in that effort. It proved that historical, beautiful pictures could be art and could attract audiences in modern time. Tavernier packed it with wonderful costumes, scenery and fascinating historical details. The music that accompanies the film was actually written by Philippe d'Orléans, illustrating just how cultured and refined the regent was in real life.

Let Joy Reign Supreme was a great success in France. One French critic called it "a fresco full of humor, vitality and modernity." Vincent Canby of *The New York Times* raved, "*Let Joy Reign Supreme* is a witty, provocative, visually dazzling re-creation of French political and social life during the crucial last years of Philippe d'Orléans." The film won the French Critics' Prix Méliès in 1975.

Quest for Fire *see* **La Guerre du feu**

Ramparts of Clay *see* **Les Remparts d'Argile**

The Reader *see* **La Lectrice**

The Red and the Black *see* **Le Rouge et le noir**

The Red Balloon *see* **Le Ballon rouge**

The Red Circle *see* **Le Cercle rouge**

The Red Inn *see* **L'Auberge rouge**

305 *Regard sur la folie (Look at Madness)* 1962 B&W *Director* Mario Ruspoli; *Producer* Anatole Dauman; *Photography* Michel Brault; *Editing* Henri Lanoë. Running time: 53 minutes.

A documentary about mental illness that was shot in a psychiatric hospital in Saint-Alban with the cooperation of the hospital's doctors. Patients range from obsessives to catatonics, but all have their moments of pain and joy.

This was one of the most important documentaries of the 1960s. It made use of innovative technology to capture candid moments, which before would have been impossible to film unobtrusively. This kind of filmmaking was the bridge between cinéma vérité and "direct" filming, and in fact, the film was at the center of a documentary debate about film intervention. Ruspoli strove for pure documentary. He wanted to show only what was before his eyes. To make this film, he used the innovative, lightweight equipment of the time to minimize staging, editing and the subject's awareness of the camera.

Jean Paul Sartre said "the film by Mario Ruspoli is not a documentary; it invites us by admirable images, for the first time to experience mental illness... [I]t makes us understand that men are not crazy, but all crazies are men."

306 *La Religieuse (The Nun* or *Suzanne Simonin, la religieuse de Diderot)* 1966 Color *Director* Jacques Rivette; *Producer* Rome Paris Films, SNC; *Screenplay* Jean Gruault, based on the novel by Diderot; *Photography* Alain Levent; *Music* Jean-Claude Joly; *Set* Jean-Jacques Fabre; *Sound* Guy Villette; *Costumes* Gitt Magrini; *Editing* Denise de Casabianca. Running time: 100 minutes.

Cast: Anna Karina, Liselotte Pulver, Micheline Presle, Francine Bergé, Christiane Lenier, Francisco Rabal, Catherine Diamant, Yori Bertin, Annick Morice, Jean Martin, Wolfgang Reichmann, Danielle Palmero, Marc Eyraud, Françoise Godde, Michel Delahye, Charles Millot, Pierre Meyrand, Gilette Berbier.

A religious story set in the eighteenth century about a young woman, Suzanne Simonin (Karina), who is shut away in a convent against her will. She struggles against the cold sisters at first, but is gradually subdued by the Mother Superior (Presle) and takes her religious vows. After her legal attempts at escape fail, one of her confessors tells her he was forced to enter the church as well and tries to seduce her. She ends up in a brothel, then throws herself out of a window.

The most successful film of Jacques Rivette, the New Waves' most literary director, *The Nun* is an historical and moral exploration of what a too strict moral code costs society's non-conformists. Rivette first adapted the Diderot work as a play, then adapted the play for the screen. He has said that what interested him about the work, is: "It is extremely written, because it came out of the experience of working on the stage, and finally because the subject deals with Catholicism, which is the absolute peak of theater." He found the story relevant because the rigid Catholic order of the eighteenth century paralleled in many ways, the intolerant atmosphere of France just before the riots of 1968. He made the film on a very small budget and took a gamble on Karina that paid off, as she had only been in a few of her husband Godard's movies.

Banned in France when it was released in 1966, *The Nun* was only shown in theaters after a two-year legal battle, official selection at the Cannes Film Festival, and a name change from *La Religieuse* to *Suzanne Simonin, la religieuse de Diderot*. When the movie came out in the United States in 1971, *Village Voice* critic Molly Haskell wrote of *The Nun* and Karina's portrayal of her: "Diderot's nun, like very few women in life and fewer in literature (some of Ibsen and Shaw's heroines maybe) desires freedom, not for love of a man or for God, but for its own sake .... She is, to use Simone de Beauvoir's distinction, transcendental rather than immanent, but she is also feminine."

307 *Les Remparts d'Argile (Ramparts of Clay)*   1970 Color   *Director* Jean-Louis Bertucelli; *Producer* Jean-Louis Bertucelli; *Screenplay* Jean Duvignaud, based on his novel *Chekika*; *Photography* Andréas Winding; *Sound* Oumi; *Editing* François Ceppi. Running time: 87 minutes.

Cast: Leila Schenna, the inhabitants of Téhouda, Algeria.

This is the story of life in a village on the edge of the desert in Tunisia. The men of the village work in a quarry. The women do chores. One young woman, Rima (Schenna), spends her day fetching water from a well and eavesdropping on the children's classes. When the men go on strike and the troops are sent in, Rima cuts off the soldiers' water supply. But her motives are misunderstood and the village treats her as if she has gone mad.

This beautiful film exposes the hardship of desert life through a series of small rebellions, triumphs and defeats. It combines the era's fascination with social filmmaking, cultural discovery and a documentary style. The director used only one actor and had her interact with the inhabitants of Téhouda and real Algerian soldiers for the filming. He was interested in making a film that showed the danger in both modern and old-fashioned ways, without ever becoming didactic. There is no dialogue, only Berber songs.

French critics lauded the film's austere beauty. *Variety* said, "Fine mood, atmosphere and a classical rigidity give this tale of an event in a backward part of a newly independent North African country a telling force and a transcendent theme on old ways in conflict with the new." The film won the Prix Jean Vigo in 1971.

308 *Rendez-Vous*   1985 Color   *Director* André Techiné; *Producer* Alain Terzian; *Screenplay* André Techiné, Olivier Asayas; *Photography* Renato Berta; *Music* Philippe Sarde; *Set* Jean-Pierre Kohut Svelko; *Sound* Jean-Louis Ughetto, Dominique Hennequin; *Editing* Martine Giordano. Running time: 87 minutes.

Cast: Juliette Binoche, Lambert Wilson, Wadeck Stanczak, Jean-Louis Trintignant, Dominique Lavanant, Anne Wiazemsky, Jean-Louis Vitrac, Philippe Landoulsi, Caroline Faro, Jacques Nolot, Arlette Gordon, Michèle Moretti, Olympia Carlisi, Serge Martina.

The story of a young woman, Nina (Binoche), who comes to Paris to become an actress. Paulot (Stanczak) falls in love with her, but she is more interested in his suicidal roommate, Quentin (Wilson). They become lovers, but then Quentin does kill himself. Nina is offered the part in a play that was to be performed by a girl who killed herself years earlier as part of a suicide pact she made with Quentin, who has now, much later, kept his end of the deal.

This film, which could be seen as a simple morality tale about overcoming fear and self-destructive impulses, is a very complicated pyschological film that announced a great director at the height of his career and the emergence of two great young actors, Binoche and Wilson. Téchiné is known as one of the great modern auteur filmmakers, and this film reveals much of his personal vision and style. He manages to blend violence with visual poetry.

This film was a great success at Cannes, where it was the official selection, and at the box-office. Critics compared it to an S&M Romeo and Juliet and an updated *Last Tango in Paris*. It won the award for Best Director at Cannes in 1985.

Rendez-Vous at Midnight *see* **Le Rendez-vous de minuit**

309 *Rendez-vous de juillet (Appointment with Life)* 1949 B&W *Director* Jacques Becker; *Producer* UGC and SNEG; *Screenplay* Jacques Becker and Maurice Griffe; *Dialogue* Jacques Becker; *Photography* Claude Renoir; *Music* Jean Wiener and Mezz Mezzrow; *Set* Robert-Jules Garnier; *Sound* Antoine Archimbaud; *Editing* Marguerite Renoir. Running time: 112 minutes.

Cast: Daniel Gélin, Nicole Courcel, Pierre Trabaud, Maurice Ronet, Brigitte Auber, Louisa Colpeyn, Yvonne Yma, Bernard La Jarrige, Louis Seigner, Philippe Mareuil, Francis Mazières, Gaston Modott, Capucine, Maria Riquelme, Annie Noël, Robert Lombard, Charles CaMusic, Emile Ronet, Claude Luter, Alain Quercy, Jacques Fabbri, Léon Larive, Paul Barge, Pierre Mondy, Albert Malbert, Gérard Le Moro, Robert Le Béal, Léon Bary, René Stern, Colette Régis, Yvette Lucas, Julienne Paroli, Cécilia Paroli, Jacques Hilling, Paul Villé, Henri Belly, Jean Pommier, Michel Barbey, Jean Valmence, René Berthier.

Young boys and girls spend the summer of 1948 together in the Left Bank jazz clubs, where they share their hopes, dreams and anguish. One wants to be an ethnologist, the others want to act, but all love jazz. Couples form and break up and reform, but they all remain friends, and at the end of the summer the ethnologist leads them off to Africa.

This is a fresh, lyrical look at the new youth of the postwar period and their hopes and dreams. It was one of many films that tried to capture Paris as it was swept up in Sartre's existentialism. But to his credit, Becker did not get too carried away. His portraits of the many different young characters are well drawn. While he satirizes some of their bourgeois families, Becker's angle is essentially one of affectionate appreciation for the intense pain, pleasure and passion of youth.

Some critics claimed that the film was not tightly plotted and that, while its young characters represented the concerns of the period, they lacked a depth of emotion. Others were thrilled by the film's lighthearted tone and breezy style. It won the Prix Louis Delluc in 1949 and the French Critics' Prix Méliès in 1950.

310 *Le Rendez-vous de minuit (Midnight Meeting or Rendez-Vous at Midnight)* 1962 B&W *Director* Roger Leenhardt; *Producer* Argos Films, Films du Compas; *Screenplay* Roger Leenhardt; *Photography* Jean Badal; *Music* Georges Auric; *Set* Bernard Evein; *Sound* André Hervé; *Editing* Henri Lanoë. Running time: 90 minutes.

Cast: Lili Palmer, Michel Auclair, Robert Lombard, Lucienne Lemarchand, Michel de Ré, France Anglade, José Luis de Villalonga, Jean Galland, Alvaro Ghéri, Michèle Méritz, Daniel Emilfork, Marcel Charvey, Alexandra Stewart, Maurice Ronet, Bruno Balp, Alvaro Gheri, Max Montavon, Christian Brocard, Irène Sologoub, Olga Wassily.

In the middle of watching a film, a woman (Palmer) becomes hysterical and walks out of the theater. A film critic, who had been Jacques (Auclair), sitting near her, offers to walk her home. She tells him that what upset her was that the heroine in the movie decided to kill herself at exactly the same time that she decided to do the same. Jacques falls in love with her and brings her back to the theater, but she disappears. Is it the heroine in the movie or Eva who throws herself in the Seine?

This complex cinematic exercise has been called Leenhardt's fine farewell to cinema. Leenhardt was a film critic and a major philosophical influence on the New Wave directors. He took a high-art stand, and rejected cinema for cinema's sake, but rather encouraged experimentation. In this, his second and last film, he deftly alternates between the couple's story and the film they were watching as a means to tell this story. He obviously had the earlier work of Resnais and other New Wave and Nouvelle Roman artists in mind.

Critics declared this film to be the work of a critic, which from some was a compliment to its challenging narrative structure and from others was a way of saying it was too boringly intellectual.

311 *Le Retour de Martin Guerre (The Return of Martin Guerre)* 1982 Color *Director* Daniel Vigne; *Producer* SFPC, SPFMD, FR3; *Screenplay* Jean-Claude Carrière; *Photography* André Neau; *Music* Michel Portal; *Set* Alain Nègre; *Sound* Michel Chamard; *Costumes* Anne-Marie Marchand; *Editing* Denise de Casabianca. Running time: 123 minutes.

Cast: Gérard Depardieu, Nathalie Baye, Roger Planchon, Bernard-Pierre Donnadieu, Maurice Barrier, Isabelle Sadoyan, Rose Thiéry, Maurice Jacquemont, André Chaumeau, Stéphane Péan, Sylvie Méda, Chantal Deruaz, Dominique Pinon, Valérie Chassigneux, Tcheky Karyo, René Bouloc, Adrien Dequesne, Francis Arnaud, Philippe Babin, Jean-Claude Perrin, Neige Dolsky, Axel Bogousslavsky, Gilbert Gilles, Alain Recoing, René Bouloc, Alain Frerot, André Delon, Daniele Loo, Marcel Champel, Yvette Petit, Jean Julliac, Jean-Paul Barathieu, Guy Bertrand, Bruno Bentegeac, Pierre Bouchet, André d'Avant-Cour, Daniel Giraud, Christian Fiter, Francis Chevillon, Guy Jacquet, Roger Payrot.

Based on a real sixteenth century trial, this is the story of Martin Guerre (Depardieu), a peasant who left his village to fight for the king and returns nine years later a different man. His wife, Bertrande (Baye), loves the new man he has become more than she ever thought she could. But when Martin has a financial dispute with his uncle, the town becomes divided about whether he is really Martin Guerre or an imposter. Finally, a trial is called and a magistrate decides Martin and Bertrande's fate.

This is a wonderful historical romance with two of France's greatest modern stars in one of their best performances. Despite its medieval setting, the film deals with issues of identity and deception, the individual's role in society, and love and greed, all of which have a remarkable relevance to modern society, which was Vigne's aim. "In my film, I tell a very modern story that happened to take place in the sixteenth century," he explained.

The Return of Martin Guerre did well in France, but it did better in the United States. In fact, by foreign film standards, it was an American blockbuster. At one movie theater, it ran for more than seven months. Roger Ebert of *The Chicago Sun Times* wrote, "*The Return of Martin Guerre* is compassionate, perceptive about human nature . . . it's the most moving love story in a long time." Hollywood made a mediocre American adaptation, which set the story in the post–Civil War South with Richard Gere and Jodie Foster, called *Sommersby*. The film won three Césars.

The Return of Martin Guerre *see* **Le Retour de Martin Guerre**

Le Revenant *see* **Un Revenant**

312 *Un Revenant (The Ghost* or *Le Revenant)* 1946 B&W   *Director* Christian-Jacque; *Producer* Compagnie franco-coloniale; *Screenplay* Henri Jeanson, Christian-Jacque, Louis Chavance; *Photography* Louis Page; *Music* Arthur Honegger; *Set* Pierre Marquet; *Sound* Jean Rieul; *Editing* Jacques Desagneux. Running time: 100 minutes.

Cast: Louis Jouvet, Louis Seigner, Jean Brochard, François Périer, Gaby Morlay, Marguerite Moreno, Ludmilla Tcherina, Maurice Nazil, Léo Lapara, Arthur Honegger, Armand Lurville, Hélène Ronsard, Max Bozzoni, Julienne Paroli, Albert-Michel, Germaine Stainval, Anouk Ferjac, Lucien Geuervil, Frank Maurice, Arthur Hoérée.

Two bourgeois families in Lyons, the Nisards and Gonins, unite to prevent an unsuitable marriage. Jean-Jacques Sauvage (Jouvet) is the unwanted suitor and Genviève Gonin (Morlay) is the fair lady, whom he jilts at the last. The men of the Gonin and Nisard families put their differences aside to work together in thwarting the union.

This delightful film was one of the few holdovers of the old romantic school to come out after World War II. Vaudevillian filmmaker extraordinaire Christian-Jaque had the perfect light touch for this charming comedy. It was the last vestige of the spirit of French filmmaking from the 1930s and 1940s. Ludmilla Tcherina and François Périer are both wonderful in their roles. Morlay gives one of the finest performances of her career.

Un Revenant was hailed as a wonderful romantic work by French critics, but the film was never released in the United States. This film was one of the four films chosen to represent France at the first Cannes Film Festival in 1946.

313 *Le Rideau cramoisi (The Crimson Curtain)* 1952 B&W   *Director* Alexandre Astruc; *Producer* Argos Films, Como Films; *Screenplay* Alexandre Astruc, based on Barbey d'Aurevilly's novel *Les Diaboliques*; *Photography* Eugen Shuftan; *Music* Jean-Jacques Grunenwald; *Set* Antoine Mayo; *Editing* Jean Mitry. Running time: 44 minutes.

Cast: Anouk Aimée, Jean-Claude Pascal, Jim Gérald, Marguerite Garcia, Yves Furet, Jean Servais, Jean Valroy.

Set during the first empire, this is an impossible love story about a young officer staying in the home of a bourgeois couple who have a beautiful, aloof daughter, Albertine (Aimée). He loves her from afar until one night she comes to his room and becomes his lover. But true love cannot blossom in such close and closeted quarters.

Hailed as one of the important precursors of the New Wave, this was the first film by critic and author Alexandre Astruc. Based on a mystery by Barbey d'Aurevilly, this film offered Astruc a great chance to experiment with style and narrative. Astruc was very influenced by such twentieth century writers as Faulkner, Malraux, Camus and Sartre. To give the film a more literary feel, he chose to tell the story without any dialogue, but rather used a voice over spoken by the officer years later. Astruc described his film style in a famous 1948 essay as using the camera as a pen and coined the cinema expression "camera-stylo."

French critics compared the film to the works of Renoir. *The New Yorker* declared, "The lyric quality of the photography and of certain speechless scenes equals the horrifying beauty of the old German film classic, *The Cabinet of Dr. Caligari*." The film won the Prix Louis Delluc, the Prix Femina and the Special Jury Prize at Cannes in 1952.

The Riding School *see* **Manèges**

Rififi *see* **Du Rififi chez les hommes**

The Riflemen *see* **Les Carabiniers**

314/5 *Les Ripoux (My New Partner)* 1984 Color *Director* Claude Zidi; *Producer* Film 7; *Screenplay* Claude Zidi; *Photography* Jean-Jacques Tarbes; *Music* Francis Lai; *Set* Françoise Deleu; *Sound* Jean-Louis Ughetto; *Costumes* Olga Pelletier; *Editing* Nicole Saunier. Running time: 107 minutes.

Cast: Philippe Noiret, Thierry Lhermitte, Grace de Capitani, Régine, Julien Guiomar, Claude Brosset, Albert Simono, Bernard Bijaoui, Pierre Frag, Jacques Santi, Olivier Granier, Louise Chevalier, Jean-Claude Bouillaud, François Cadet, Jacques Frantz, Guy Kerner, Jean Lanier, Simon Mickael, Jean Cherlian, Henri Atal, Salah Cheurfi, Gérard Couderc, Alain David, Cheikh Doukouré.

René (Noiret) is a detective who plays by his own rules. He lives with a prostitute and takes bribes. When a new partner threatens to disrupt his habits, he gets him hooked on a prostitute girlfriend and teaches him how easily extra cash can come to policemen. But his rookie partner learns very quickly and his appetite soon outpaces René's.

From a comic director, who is generally dismissed for making sloppy, commercial successes, this is a film that manages to artfully mix humor with social sleuthing. Zidi set out to make a more ambitious picture than usual. He was interested in exploring the corruption that exists within police departments. The title comes from the Verlan slang word, *pourris*, which means the rotten ones. Noiret is great.

This was the second biggest box-office success in France in the 1980s, after *Three Men and a Cradle*. Zidi surprised French critics, who were used to his less crafted, more commercial works; they liked it. Americans were evenly divided between those who found it to be a painful rip-off of American television cop shows and fans who loved Noiret as a cop. It won the César for Best Film and Best Director in 1984.

Riptide *see* **Une si jolie petite plage**

316 *Le Roi de cœur (The King of Hearts)* 1967 Color *Director* Philippe de Broca; *Producer* Société de Fildebroc, Les Productions Artistes Associés, Compania Cinematografica Montoro; *Screenplay* Daniel Boulanger; *Photography* Pierre Lhomme; *Music* Georges Delerue; *Costumes* Jacques Fonteray; *Editing* Françoise Javet. Running time: 102 minutes.

Cast: Alan Bates, Pierre Brasseur, Jean-Claude Brialy, Geneviève Bujold, Adolfo Celi, Françoise Christophe, Julien Guiomar, Micheline Presle, Michel Serrault, Marc Dudicourt, Daniel Boulanger, Pierre Palau, Jacques Balutin, Madeleine Clervanne, Jean Sylvain, Jacky Blanchot, Louis Jojot, Pier Paolo Capponi.

A comedy, supposedly based on a true story, about a World War I soldier

(Bates), who is ordered by his commanding general to find and defuse a bomb in a small French village. After he is knocked unconscious, Private Plumpick awakes to find that the formerly abandoned town is fully populated and functioning. The inhabitants, though, are inmates who have escaped from the local insane asylum. They believe Plumpick is their "King of Hearts." Love, danger and the horrors of war follow.

This wonderful lyric portrait of lunacy is one of the finest films of de Broca's career. It is an antiwar film that is full of fun and fantasy, which makes its arguments against militarism with laughs not guns. De Broca's idea was to show what happened if the lunatics really did take over the asylum, and his conclusion is that the world would be a better place if they did. The setting, costumes and photography are wonderful, as is Alan Bates.

The French critics ripped this film apart. It did not do well with the French public either. But when it was released a second time in 1973 in the United States, during the height of Vietnam War protests, it inspired a cult following among students. Part of its enormous collegiate appeal can probably be attributed to the fact that it poked fun at the ridiculousness of war and of established authority. It played at a movie theater at Harvard for over nine months. *The New Yorker* said, "De Broca must have real sweetness and force of character to turn the film into what it often is: a dream of carnival respite from caution and death."

317 *Le Roi et l'oiseau (The King and Mr. Bird* or *The King and the Bird* or *The King and the Mockingbird)* 1980 Color *Director* Paul Grimault; *Producer* Les Films Paul Grimault, Les Films Gibé, Antenne 2; *Screenplay* Jacques Prévert and Paul Grimault, based on Hans Christian Andersen's story *The Shepherdess and the Chimney Sweep*; *Dialogue* Jacques Prévert; *Set* Paul Grimault; *Music* Wojciech Kilar; *Sound* Henri Gruel; *Editing* Paul Grimault. Running time: 87 minutes.

Voices of Jean Martin, Pascal Mazzoit, Raymond Bussières, Agnès Viala, Renaud Marx, Roger Blin, Claude Piéplu, Hubert Deschamps, Philippe Derrez, Albert Médina.

An animated movie about King Charles, tyrannical ruler of Takycardie. When the King falls in love with a lovely peasant girl who loves a simple chimney sweep, a bird helps them run away from the King's men. They are caught, but the bird talks a den of lions out of eating the chimney sweep. In fact, he incites the lions to popular revolt. Like all good fairy tales, the lovers face struggles, but with the help of their feathered friend, good triumphs over evil.

This is an absolutely enchanting film from two of France's most important avant-garde artists. It was more than thirty years in the making and is, in part, a literal remake of France's first animated film. When graphic artist Paul Grimault made the first animated French film, *The Shepherdess and the Chimney Sweep*, with the poet Jacques Prévert in the late 1940s, they were so upset with the producers' changes that they disowned the film as their work when it was released in 1953. Ten years later, they bought back the film's negative and set about salvaging their work. They kept half of the first film and added footage to it to produce *The King and Mr. Bird*. And it is probably the best animated French film ever made. Everything works beautifully, the music, voices, scenes, and colors.

The King and Mr. Bird was hailed as France's great animated masterpiece by critics. They compared it to every great, from Disney and Arthur Rackham to Cocteau, Anouilh, Piranesi, Carné and Tati. It won the Prix Louis Delluc in 1979.

318 *Un Roi sans divertissement (A King Without Distractions)*   1963
Color   *Director* François Leterrier; *Producer* Films Jean Giono; *Screenplay* Jean Giono; *Photography* Jean Badal; *Music* Maurice Jarre and Jacques Brel; *Set* Philippe Ancellin; *Sound* Jacques Bompunt; *Editing* Françoise Javet. Running time: 85 minutes.
   Cast: Charles Vanel, Claude Giraud, Colette Renard, Albert Rémy, René Blancard, Pierre Repp.
   In the Alps in 1840, a young police officer, Langlois (Giraud), is sent to investigate the disappearance of a young girl. While he is making his inquiries, another girl disappears. He follows the murderer's trail and finds the bodies of the two girls, who have been strangled to death. He tracks the man to his house, where he kills him. Langlois' first killing of the murderer whets his appetite for more blood. To indulge his new passion and spare others, he kills himself.
   Hailed as a great literary film, full of poetic images and dialogue, this is Leterrier's greatest work. Giono began the screenplay with Pascal's phrase "A king without the ability to get beyond himself is a man full of misery," but a real-life trial about a Doctor Petiot, who killed 27 people in the 1940s, became the center of the story. Despite the gruesome subject matter, the sets and scenes of the film resemble great paintings.
   Unfortunately, after this film met a mixed reception, Leterrier turned to making less artistically ambitious, more commercial works. Some critics lauded its moody meditation on the blurred lines between outlaw and law man. Other critics found it awkwardly literary, with language ill-suited for the screen. It won the Grand Prix du Cinéma Français in 1963.

319 *Romuald et Juliette (Mama, There's a Man in Your Bed)*   1989
Color   *Director* Coline Serreau; *Producer* Carcassonne, Cinéa, Eniloc Films, FR3; *Screenplay* Coline Serreau; *Photography* Jean-Noël Ferragut; *Music* Jérôme Reese; *Set* Jean-Marc Stehle; *Sound* Philippe Lioret, Gérard Lamps; *Editing* Catherine Renault. Running time: 108 minutes.
   Cast: Daniel Auteil, Firmine Richard, Pierre Vernier, Maxime Leroux, Gilles Privat, Muriel Combeau, Catherine Salviat, Sambou Tati, Jacques Poitrenaud, Nicolas Serreau, Alain Trétout, Alain Fromager, Caroline Jaquin, Gilles Cohen, Alexandre Basse, Aissatou and Mamdou Bah, Marina M'Boa Ngong.
   A white man, Romuald (Auteil), who is an executive at a yogurt company falls in love with Juliette (Richard), the black woman who cleans his office. She has five children, all by different husbands, and does not have enough money to pay the rent. He has a beautiful wife, a beautiful girlfriend, and children who are driven to school by a chauffeur. Together, the two solve a nasty office politics intrigue; and despite the coincidence of their names, these two lovers do not end up committing suicide side by side.
   This is another wonderful comedy that tackles serious social issues with laughter by one of France's great modern filmmakers. Serreau, who came out of the 1968 protest tradition, uses the same light touch that she perfected in her smash hit, *Three Men and a Cradle*, to get her concerns about the racism and social injustice

across with subtlety. Daniel Auteil and Firmine Richard, who made her movie debut in this role, are both charming.

The film was a huge hit in France, though critics complained that Serreau's social protest was too warm and fuzzy. Some American critics liked it. Others, echoing the French criticism, felt it glossed glibly over racial and economic realities. Disney hired Serreau to do an American remake. *Time* magazine said, "By film's end any skeptic will believe that natural combatants — rich and poor, white and black, man and woman can be made gracious allies. It takes just a little goodwill and a very good film."

320 *La Ronde* 1950 B&W *Director* Max Ophüls; *Producer* Sacha Gordine; *Screenplay* Jacques Natanson, Max Ophüls, based on the play *Der Reigen* by Arthur Schnitzler; *Dialogue* Jacques Natanson; *Photography* Christian Matras; *Music* Oscar Strauss; *Set* Jean d'Eaubonne; *Sound* Pierre Calvet; *Costumes* Georges Annenkov; *Editing* Léonide Azar. Running time: 92 minutes.

Cast: Simone Sigornet, Danielle Darrieux, Anton Walbrook, Serge Regianni, Simone Simone, Daniel Gélin, Odette Joyeux, Fernand Gravey, Jean-Louis Barrault, Isa Miranda, Gérard Philipe, Robert Vattier, Charles Vissières, Jean Clarieux, Marcel Mérovée, Jean Ozenne, René Marjac, Jacques Vertan.

A satirical look is cast upon the intertwining relationships of ten men and women, whose lives are ultimately joined as they pass a venereal disease from one to another. From a prostitute (Signoret) to a soldier (Reggiani), from the soldier to a maid (Simon), from the maid to the son of the family (Gélin) she works for, from the son to a married woman (Darrieux), from the wife to her husband (Gravey), from him to a working girl (Joyeux), from the girl to her poet lover (Barrault), from the poet to an actress (Miranda), from her to a count (Philipe) and from him back to the prostitute.

This elegantly filmed social satire was the first film Ophüls directed upon his return from Hollywood after World War II. It is one of his best. With irony and wit, Ophüls turns the deceivers and deceived into a personified vicious circle. All the stars in the cast delivered great performances. The elegant direction Ophüls evidenced in *La Ronde* became one of his trademarks.

This was one of the most successful films of the postwar decade. It was banned in New York State as "immoral" before the case went to the Supreme Court, and it was allowed to be shown after some editing was done in 1954. The full version was shown two years later. It won Best Screenplay and Best Decor at the Venice Film Festival in 1950, and received two Oscar nominations in 1951 for Screenplay and Decor. In 1951, the British Film Academy voted it Best Film. Roger Vadim's version, *Circle of Love*, had none of the wit and intelligence of the original.

A Room in Town *see* **Une Chambre en ville**

321 *Le Rose et le blanc (Les Aventures de Holly and Wood)* 1980 Color *Director* Robert Pansard-Besson; *Producer* Les Productions Berthemont; *Screenplay* Robert Pansard-Besson; *Photography* Sacha Vierny and Jean-Paul Meurisse; *Music* Antoine Duhamel; *Set* Jean-Claude Galloin; *Sound* Antoine Bonfanti; *Editing* Françoise Belleville. Running time: 100 minutes.

Cast: Raymond Pellegrin, Bulle Ogier, Michel Lonsdale, Yves Afonso, Vittorio Caprioli, Valérie Lagrange, Yves Robert, Claude Mekli, Mathieu Gain, Marcel Gassouk, Roger Trapp, Jean-Pierre Elga, Frédéric Veille, Michel Francini.

A modern fairy tale set in Paris' slums, where, despite the grim surroundings, dreams still do come true. Arthur writes a book about his favorite bandit and it becomes a best seller, thanks to the promotion work of his friend Luigi, who was formerly a peddler.

A post-modern mix of Lewis Carroll, comic books and Jean-Luc Godard make this film a thoroughly modern fantasyland. Pansard-Besson plays with literary and mythical allusions, but ultimately his point is the discovery of eternal childhood and what a magical mystery place the world can be. If a child identifies strongly enough with his hero, he will become him. The direction is sophisticated, and yet the film maintains a charming freshness.

French critics applauded its daring, but found the film fell short of attaining its ambitions. The film has never been distributed in the United States. It was co-winner of the Prix Georges Sadoul in 1980.

Roselyne and the Lions *see* **Roselyne et les lions**

322 *Roselyne et les lions (Roselyne and the Lions)*   1989 Color   *Director* Jean-Jacques Beineix; *Producer* Cargo Film, Gaumont; *Screenplay* Jean-Jacques Beineix; *Adaptation and Dialogue* Jean-Jacques Beineix and Jacques Forgeas; *Photography* Jean-François Robin; *Music* Reinhardt Wagner; *Set* Carlos Conti; *Sound* Pierre Befve; *Costumes* Valentine Breton des Loys; *Editing* Annick Baly, Marie Castro-Brechignac, Danielle Fillios. Running time: 134 minutes.

Cast: Isabelle Pasco, Gérard Sandoz, Philippe Clévenot, Günter Meisner, Wolf Harnisch, Gabriel Monnet, Jacques Le Carpentier, Dimitri Furdui, Melhi Duzenli, Carlos Pavlidis, Jaroslav Vizner, Carole Fredericks, Hakim Ghanem, Laurence Semonin.

A love story about two teenagers, Roselyne (Pasco) and Thierry (Sandoz), who decide they want to join the circus. They hope to become lion trainers and set out in search of the big-top big time. After running away and joining a second-rate show, they get the chance to work with the world's greatest circus, the Koenig in Munich.

Beineix's fourth film is another wonderful love story that pushes the cinematic envelope. He demanded that the actors prepare rigorously for the physical challenges, as he did with the diving scenes in *The Big Blue*. The actors worked with the animals for nine months so they would be comfortable doing the scenes with them — and the work paid off. The film beautifully explores the relationship between man and beast, as it has rarely been done on film. The lion scenes are breathtaking. Pasco and Sandoz's fine performances announced two great new French talents to watch.

Oddly, *Roselyne and the Lions* suffered exactly the same fate as *Diva*, except that it has yet to be resurrected with cult status. Like *Diva*, the film was eagerly awaited in France, but the French critics declared that it proved Beineix was prematurely washed up. They found the lovers' quest for beast training completely unbelievable. The film did miserably at the box office. The foreign critics, however, loved it. It has yet to be distributed in the United States, but when it is, it may receive enough acclaim to encourage the French to take another look.

323 *Le Rouge et le noir (The Red and the Black* or *Scarlet and Black)*
1954 Color   *Director* Claude Autant-Lara; *Producer* Franco London Documento Film, Gaumont; *Screenplay* Jean Aurenche, Pierre Bost and Claude Autant-

Le Rouge et le noir (The Red and the Black), 1954; directed by Claude Autant-Lara.

Lara, based on the novel by Stendahl; *Photography* Michel Kelber and Jacques Natteau; *Music* René Cloërec; *Set* Max Douy; *Costumes* Rosine Delamare; *Editing* Madeleine Gug. Running time: 198 minutes.

Cast: Gérard Philipe, Danielle Darrieux, Antonella Lualdi, Jean Martinelli, Jean Mercure, Antoine Balpétré, André Brunot, Anna Maria Sandri, Mirko Ellis, Georges Descrières, Robert Berri, Alexandre Rignault, Gérard Séty, Jacques Varennes, Albert Michel, Pierre Jourdan, Sylvain, Georges Wilson, Jean-Marie Amato, Raphaël Patorni, Paul Faivre, Thomy Bourdelle, Jean-Pierre Grenier, Hubert Noël, Beauvais, Marcel Loche, Lucien Guervil, Henri Hercé, Guy Régent, Jean-Michel Rouzière, Jacques Clancy, Suzanne Nivette, Claude Sylvain, Georgina.

Set in 1830, Julien Sorel (Philipe), the son of a carpenter, becomes the tutor to the children of M. and Mme. de Renal. A very ambitious young man, he seduces Mme. de Renal (Darrieux) and compromises the young daughter of the Marquise de la Mole, to whom he has become secretary, thanks to the help of Mme. de Renal. Mme. de Renal denounces him to the Marquise, and Julien shoots her in a violent rage, an act which, of course, separates him forever from his beloved.

One of the most representative films of French filmmaking in the 1950s, this is another wonderful literary adaptation by the master team of Aurenche, Bost and Autant-Lara with beautiful costumes and sets. Like the novel, this is a beautifully wrought look at social ambition and hypocrisy. Autant-Lara actually signed three contracts to bring this Stendahl classic to the big screen. Finally, when Gérard Philipe could not find a script that interested him, and Autant-Lara suggested *The Red and the Black*, the project moved forward.

Truffaut and other New Wave critics accused Autant-Lara of butchering a classic, but others who had a taste and appreciation for literary adaptations loved this. It won the French Critics' Prix Méliès in 1954.

Rough Day for the Queen *see* **Rude Journée pour la reine**

324 *Rude Journée pour la reine (Rough Day for the Queen)* 1973 Color   *Director* René Allio; *Producer* Polsim Productions, Citel Films, ORTF; *Screenplay* René Allio; *Photography* Denys Clerval; *Music* Philippe Arthuys; *Set* Christine Laurent, François Darne; *Sound* Paul Laine; *Editing* Sylvie Blanc. Running time: 104 minutes.

Cast: Simone Signoret, Jacques Debary, Olivier Perrier, Orane Demazis, Alice Reichen, Gérard Depardieu, Tanya Lopert, Christine Rorato, André Valtier, Michel Pereylon, Arlette Chosson, Denise Bonal, Pierre Léomy, Abdellah Badis, Giancarlo Pannese, Jean-Pierre Duperray, Thomas Vincent, Dominique Degoetje, Jenny Bellay, Gabriel Cattand.

Jeanne (Signoret) is a not-so-happily married second wife, who spends her days waiting on her family hand and foot and wishing she were elsewhere. When her handsome, but dilettantish stepson, Julien (Perrier), asks her to help him conduct a love affair, she not only delivers a letter to his loved one, but seeing herself as aiding in a noble cause, she helps the two of them run off together.

This touching film captured an anguish rarely documented, but quite pervasive in 1970s society—that of the unfulfilled housewife. It was Allio's fifth film, and he was interested in juxtaposing a passive dreamer with a young man of action in order to draw out certain ideological and political themes. What he accomplished was the ultimate protest on behalf of miserable housewives. Signoret is fabulous as the maladjusted housewife.

French critics compared this film as social commentary to the brilliance of Beaumarchais and Brecht. *Le Monde* declared it a "great political film." It was never distributed in the United States.

325 *La Salaire de la peur (The Wages of Fear)* 1953 B&W   *Director* Henri-Georges Clouzot; *Producer* CICC, Silver Films, Vera Films, Fono Roma Productions; *Screenplay* Henri-Georges Clouzot and Jérome Géronimi, based on the novel by Georges Arnaud; *Photography* Armand Thirard; *Music* Georges Auric; *Set* René Renoux; *Sound* William Sivel; *Editing* Henri Rust, Madeleine Gug, and Etiennette Muse. Running time: 131 minutes.

Cast: Yves Montand, Charles Vanel, Peter van Eyck, Folco Lulli, Jo Dest, Vera Clouzot, Dario Moreno, Pat Hurst, William Tubbs, Miss Darling, René Baranger, Rico Zermeno, Paul Centa, François Valorbe, Faustini, Joseph Palau Fabre, Luis de Limo, Grégoire Gromoff, Jeronimo Mitchell, Seguna, Evelio Larenagas.

A thrilling suspense story about four laborers, one Italian (Lulli), one German (van Eyck) and two French (Montand and Vanel), who are hired by an American company in South America to drive two trucks carrying highly explosive nitroglycerine across rugged and dangerous terrain. The pay promised is as high as the chances of dying on the job.

Regarded as Clouzot's greatest work, this is one of the most famous of all French films. Clouzot said of the suspenseful work: "A significant setting, complex human material, and the gripping accessory of a truck loaded with nitroglycerin allowed me to develop not the picturesque story, but the epic qualities; yes, this is an epic whose main theme is courage. And the opposite." The film gave a great boost to Vanel's career and established Montand as one of the best French actors of the century.

The critics and public were riveted by this film. *The New York Times* described the movie's power: "You sit there waiting for the theater to explode." The French version of 155 minutes was cut to 106 for United States release. The film won the Grand Prize at Cannes, and Vanel won Best Actor. It also won the Best Picture at the British Academy Awards and the French Critics' Prix Méliès in 1953.

326 *Sale comme un ange (Dirty Like an Angel)* 1991 Color *Director* Catherine Breillat; *Producer* CB Films, Veranfilms; *Screenplay* Catherine Breillat; *Photography* Laurent Dailland; *Music* Olivier Manoury; *Set* Olivier Paultre; *Sound* Georges Prat; *Costumes* Malika Brahim; *Editing* Anges Guillemaut. Running time: 103 minutes.

Cast: Claude Brasseur, Lio, Nils Tavernier, C.J. Philippe, Léa Gabrielle, Lorella Di Cicco.

A film about the sexual relationship between 50-year-old Debalchc (Brasseur), who is a misogynistic police officer, and a sweet young woman from the provinces. The little intimate contact that Debalche has had in the past was with prostitutes. But when his partner (Tavernier) marries a lovely woman (Gabrielle) and continues to sleep with the shady women he meets while working the streets, Debalche decides to move in on his wife. Debalche assigns his partner to a stakeout and uses the time when he knows his partner is working to spend time with the wife. He virtually rapes her, but she comes to him for more the next day.

This, Breillat's second feature after *36 filette*, is another brutal look at sex. Breillat is a filmmaker who looks at the dark side of sex as no other director has before. She examines in brutally honest and disturbing ways what people want and what they will submit to. She takes the secrets of bedrooms and of perverse minds and brings them together on film. She said of her aim: "I have always thought that desire was the taboo passage and that you mustn't suppress the taboo, but bring it out, because it can be very beautiful." Tavernier, who is the son of the director Bertrand Tavernier, and Brasseur are both very good, as is Gabrielle in the role of fallen woman.

Dirty Like an Angel provoked quite a controversy when it came out in France. Some critics found it shocking and needlessly vulgar. Others applauded Breillat's courage and hailed her as a pioneer in documenting sexual truths. The film has never been distributed in the United States.

O Salto *see* **Le Saut**

327 *Le Samourai (The Samourai or The Samurai)* 1967 Color *Director* Jean-Pierre Melville; *Producer* Filmel, CICC, Fida Ciné, Lépicier; *Screenplay* Jean-Pierre Melville, based on the novel by Gian McLeod; *Photography* Henri Decaë; *Music* François de Roubaix; *Set* Lamothe and Meurisse; *Sound* Longuet; *Editing* Monique Bonnot and Yo Maurette. Running time: 95 minutes.

Cast: Alain Delon, François Périer, Nathalie Delon, Jacques Leroy, Cathy Rosier, Jean-Pierre Rosier, Michel Boisrond, Robert Favart, Claude Nell, André

Thorent, Catherine Jourdan, Paul Vander, Georges Casati, Roger Fradet, Carl Lechner, Robert Rondo, André Salgues, Jack Leonard, Carlo Nell, Gaston Meunier, Ari Aricardi, Pierre Vaudier, Jacques Deschamps, Guy Bonnafous, Maurice Magalon, Roland Catalano, André Garret, Jean Gold, Georges Billy, Adrien Cayla-Legrand, Raymond Pierson, Gilbert Servien, Tony Roedel, Edouard Francomme.

A paid killer, Jeff Costello (Delon), is hired to assassinate the owner of a nightclub. Despite his very strong alibi, the police suspect him, and the man who hired him wants him dead. In the middle of this deadly mess, the samurai begins to realize the wrongs of his actions, but he has to kill to stay alive.

This is another one of Melville's great thrillers. Melville has always glorified the solitary man in his Resistance films and police films, such as *Bob the Gambler* and *The Stoolie*, but this is very close to an American film noir and set the standard for French police movies of the next decade. He said of his intention: "I liked the idea of beginning my story with a sort of meticulous, almost clinical, description of the behavior of a hired killer, who is by definition a schizophrenic. Jeff Costello is neither a crook nor a gangster; he is an innocent in the sense that a schizophrenic doesn't know he's criminal, although he is criminal in his logic and his way of thinking." It features Alain Delon in one of his finest performances.

Critics hailed this as the quintessential police thriller and the 1960s film noir extraordinaire that mixed modern bad guys with a touch of romance.

The Samourai / The Samurai *see* **Le Samourai**

328 *Le Sang des bêtes (Blood of the Beasts)* 1948 B&W *Director* Georges Franju; *Producer* Paul Legros; *Screenplay* Georges Franju; *Photography* Marcel Fradetal; *Music* Joseph Kosma. Running time: 22 minutes.

A film that shows all of the blood (and there is a lot) and brutality of the slaughterhouse. In a slaughterhouse on the outskirts of Paris, horses are shot in the head, sheep killed and cattle carved, all with their pleading eyes shown before their execution. Their slaughterers, meanwhile, whistle while they work.

This is one of the most shocking documentaries ever made. Franju's point was to use cinema to show people a daily facet of their life with which they rarely came in direct contact and to film an allegory for the horrors of the German concentration camp. His commentary was subtle enough that some viewers have missed his historical references. The unblinking look at slaughter so soon after the war offended some of those who did catch his inferences. Meat eaters cannot fail to flinch in recognizing the film's most obvious brutality. Franju set the bloody shots to a lyrical score by Joseph Kosma which magnifies the horror.

The British critic Raymond Durgnat said wild horses couldn't drag him to another viewing of *Le Sang des bêtes*. Some dismissed it as vegetarian propaganda. Others lauded it as poetry wrought from the most unlikely subject. When Cocteau saw this film, he wrote, "Every now and then, courageous filmmakers prove to us that cinema is the apparatus of realism and lyricism; it all depends on the angle that people take on life's events." Others criticized Franju for being more concerned with provoking a reaction than creating an honest, accurate documentary.

329 *Sans toit ni loi (Vagabond)* 1985 Color *Director* Agnès Varda; *Producer* Ciné Tamaris, A2; *Screenplay* Agnès Varda; *Photography* Patrick

Blossier; *Music* Joanna Bruzdowicz; *Sound* Jean-Paul Mugel; *Editing* Agnès Varda and Patricia Mazuy. Running time: 105 minutes.

Cast: Sandrine Bonnaire, Macha Méryl, Stéphane Freiss, Laurence Corta-delles, Marthe Jarnias, Yolande Moreau, Joel Fausse, Patrick Lepczynski, Yahiaoui Assouna, Christain Chessa, Setti Ramdane.

For Mona (Bonnaire), the freedom that she gains as she wanders through the French countryside in wintertime has its moments of glory and its troubled times. She lives with David for a few days in an abandoned chateau, then is picked up hitch-hiking by a professor, then stays with an old lady and her maid, and finally with a Tunisian migrant grape picker. After her dead body is found in a ditch, her story is told in flashback and in interviews with the people who met her along the road.

This is one of Varda's best films, if not her masterpiece. *Vagabond* is a portrait of a very untraditional young woman. Filmed in part by pseudo-realistic inter-views, Mona is a woman, who, like the director, wants to see and to experience, but refuses to judge. She is charting the outer edges of society; and in exposing her life on the road, Varda brought attention to the lifestyles of those society tends to ignore. This was one of the first films to look at the growing problem of homeless-ness, which hit Western nations in the 1980s.

Critics admired this film and the public slowly heeded their advice to see it. "Mona isn't set up to be a hero or a victim, nor are the people who make up 'society' monolithic in their response to her . . . . They are human. And, through this tough, memorable film, Ms. Varda reaches for our humanity with a force that very few movies can muster," wrote Julie Salamon in *The Wall Street Journal*. It was co-winner of the French Critics' Prix Méliès in 1985 and winner of the Golden Lion at the Venice Biennal. Sandrine Bonnaire won the César for Best Actress.

Santa Claus Is a Louse *see* **Le Père Noël est une ordure**

330 *Le Saut (Voyage of Silence* **or** *O Salto)* 1968 B&W   *Director* Christian de Chalonge; *Producer* Fildebroc, Artistes Associés; *Screenplay* Christian de Chalonge and Roberto Bodegas; *Photography* Alain Derobe; *Music* Luis Cilia; *Set* Claude Pignot; *Sound* Guy Villette; *Editing* Hélène Arnal. Running time: 92 minutes.

Cast: Marc Pico, Antonio Passalia, Ludmilla Mikaël, Henrique de Sousa, Americo Trindade, Heitor Fernandes, Joao Neto, Antonio Gonzalves, José Belchior, José Borges, Antonio Lopez, Luis Oliveira, Alfredo Neto and non-professionals (immigrant Portuguese workers).

The hard-luck tale of a young man, Antonio (Pico), who sets out from his poor Portuguese village to travel to Paris, where he hopes to find fortune. He makes an arduous journey across Spain and much of France only to arrive in Paris to find himself in a worse situation than he was in at home. The victim of constant racism and hostility, he returns home to a difficult and depressing existence.

This film was de Chalonge's first and one of the first French films to deal with the immigrant issue. De Chalonge spent a year researching the hard-luck life of im-migrants. He wanted to show the physical and emotional struggles they faced. He created a harsh condemnation of how society treats its immigrant or inferior classes. His vision is not restricted to the Portuguese experience. Americans watch-ing the huddled masses sneaking across borders in the night are sure to draw com-parisons to illegal Mexican and South and Central American immigrants.

A few critics did not like the film. *Newsday* found it a "tedious ... staged documentary." Most hailed it as an epic documentary, along the lines of *Grapes of Wrath. Time* magazine raved: "The movie is a small masterpiece of compassionate observation and emotional restraint." The film won the Prix Jean Vigo in 1968.

331 *Sauve qui peut, la vie (Every Man for Himself* or *Slow Motion)*
1980 Color   *Director* Jean-Luc Godard; *Producer* Sonimage, Sara Films, MK2 Films, Saga Productions, CNC, SSR, ORF, ZDF; *Screenplay* Jean-Claude Carrière and Anne-Marie Miéville; *Photography* William Lubtchansky, Renato Berta, and Jean-Bernard Menoud; *Music* Gabriel Yared; *Set* Romain Goupil; *Sound* Luc Yersin, Jacques Maumont, Oscar Stellavox; *Editing* Anne-Marie Miéville. Running time: 88 minutes.

Cast: Isabelle Huppert, Jacques Dutronc, Nathalie Baye, Roland Amstutz, Fred Personne, Anna Baldaccini, Cécile Tanner, Monique Barscha, Dore de Rosa, Michel Cassagne, Paul Muret, Catherine Freiburghaus, Claude Champion, Gérard Battaz, Serge Maillard, Angelo Napoli, Marie Luce Felber, Guy Lavoro, Michelle Gleiser, Maurice Buffat, Nicole Jacquet, Bernard Cazassus, Nicole Wicht, Roger Jendly, Eric Desfosses, Irène Floershiem, Giorgiana Eaton, Serge Desarnault.

Denise (Baye) quits her job and moves to the mountains. Her boyfriend Paul (Dutronc) does not want to lose her, but cannot bear to leave the city. Isabelle (Huppert) comes from the country to the city to earn money as a prostitute and wants to rent Denise's apartment. When Paul finds himself caught between the two women, he does lose Denise. A couple is torn apart by their long-distance relationship between Geneva and Paris, but for reasons of apathy or misgivings they do nothing to change their situation.

This was Godard's first commercial film in a decade, and it was called "a perfect reflection of the times in which we live: chaotic, pessimistic, fragmentary." In his first non-militantly avant-garde film in years, he returned to his favorite subjects of money, prostitution and human souls. Denise represents the imaginary, Isabelle commerce, and Paul (Godard's alter-ego in the film) represents fear. Of the film's whore-heroine, he said in typical Godardian fashion: "The whore's trade brings more money to dried-up scriptwriters than it does to pimps. I myself am only a whore fighting the pimps of cinema." While the film is more commercial than some of his previous films, Godard still plays liberally with narrative and a special slow-motion photography. It is extremely beautiful and funny.

The film opened at the Cannes Film Festival and was well received by French critics. Robert Hatch of the *Nation* wrote, "*Every Man for Himself* is repeatedly surprising, often of startling beauty, hard to keep in focus, enticing and evasive."

Scarlet and Black *see* **Le Rouge et le noir**

Scene of the Crime *see* **Le Lieu de crime**

332 *Shoah*   1985 Color   *Director* Claude Lanzmann; *Producer* Les Films Aleph, Historia Films; *Photography* Dominique Chapuis, Jimmy Glasberg, William Lubtchanski; *Sound* Bernard Aubouy, Michel Vionnet; *Editing* Ziva Glasberg. Running time: 570 minutes.

Le Saut (Voyage of Silence), 1968; directed by **Christian de Chalonge.**

Une si jolie petite plage (Riptide), **1949; directed by Yves Allégret.**

A nine-and-a-half-hour documentary on the Holocaust as seen through the eyes of the survivors. With no newsreels or old film footage, the horrors are told by the voices of the witnesses set against pictures from the present. Among those featured are concentration camp survivors and their Nazi commanding officers, as well as Holocaust scholars.

This is one of the most powerful documents ever made about World War II. "Shoah" means "annihiliation" in Hebrew. The film was ten years in the making, with Lanzmann, who fought in the Resistance during the war, filming over 350 hours of interviews in 14 countries. He said of the film: "It is an inquiry on the present of the Holocaust, or at the very least on a past whose scars are still so fresh and so inscribed in places and on minds that it appears with hallucinatory timelessness."

The film was a critical sensation in Paris where it was immediately declared "a monument against forgetting." Simone de Beauvoir in *Le Monde* raved, "...seeing today the extraordinary film of Claude Lanzmann, we realize that we knew nothing. Despite all our knowledge, the awful experience remained at a distance from us. For the first time, we live it in our heads, in our hearts, and in our flesh." The film has been shown around the world in theaters and on television.

Shoot the Pianist *see* **Tirez sur le pianiste**

Shoot the Piano Player *see* **Tirez sur le pianiste**

333 *Une si jolie petite plage (Riptide)* 1949 B&W *Director* Yves Allégret; *Producer* CICC, Emile Darbon and Dutch European; *Screenplay, Adaptation and Dialogue* Jacques Sigurd; *Photography* Henri Alekan; *Music* Maurice Thiriet; *Lyrics* Jacques Sigurd; *Set* Maurice Colasson; *Sound* Pierre Calvet and Jacques Carrère; *Editing* Léonide Azar. Running time: 91 minutes.

Cast: Gérard Philipe, Madeleine Robinson, Jean Servais, Julien Carette, Jane Marken, Mona Doll, Paul Villé, André Valmy, Christian Ferry, Gabriel Gobin, Gabrielle Fontan, Charles Vissières, Robert Le Fort, Yves Martel.

Set in a northern beach town during the winter. Pierre (Philipe) checks into a hotel staffed by public-aid adolescents. He has come back to the place where he grew up after having just killed an older singer, who was once his lover. The police and her former lover are after him. An orphan girl, Marthe (Robinson), who works in the hotel, as Pierre did in his youth, tries to save him, but her kindness comes too late; he kills himself.

This was one of the best films of the 1940s, and it contains one of Philipe's best performances. A dark and gloomy atmosphere permeates the film, which examines the psychological cost of committing a crime. The photography and the bleak seaside setting are superb. Philipe is devastatingly beautiful as the man degraded before his time.

French critics hailed this as one of France's great film noirs. American critics found it too heavy and long. *The New York Times* said, "*Riptide* shows signs of careful workmanship, but the film is burdened by an unhappy appearance of having been studiously contrived."

Sierra de Teruel *see* **L'Espoir**

334 *Le Silence de la mer (Silence of the Sea)* 1947 B&W *Director* Jean-Pierre Melville; *Producer* Melville Productions; *Screenplay* Jean-Pierre Melville, based on the novel by Vercors; *Photography* Henri Decaë; *Music* Edgar Bischoff; *Editing* Jean-Pierre Melville and Henri Decaë. Running time: 86 minutes.

Cast: Nicole Stéphane, Jean-Marie Robain, Howard Vernon, Ami Aaroe, Denis Sadier, Georges Patrix, Dietrich Kandler, Max Hermann, Henri Cavalier, Heim, Fromm, Rudel, Vernier.

A strict adapation of Vercours' novel about the impossible collaboration between France and Germany during the war. In the Jura Mountains, a German officer stays in the house of a French man and his niece. Against their silence, he speaks in beautiful French of his love for France, his favorite French authors and of the horrors of the war. They do not respond to his monologue, but they do grow to care for him.

This wonderful example of France's great literary filmmaking was Jean-Pierre Melville's first feature film. Taken from one of the great literary works that circulated secretly during World War II about the silent, anonymous French who risked their lives to resist the Nazis, it also marked the debut of the great cinematographer Henri Decaë. It is one of the films that most influenced the New Wave directors, because the dialogue was not traditional film dialogue, but really one man talking and others listening. Melville made it with a very small budget and without Vercours' permission.

French critics hailed this film as a masterpiece. It was never released in the United States. *Variety* missed the beauty of it when it said: "Jean-Pierre Melville has turned *Silence of the Sea* into a still photography rather than a moving picture."

335 *Le Silence est d'or (Man About Town* or *Silence Is Golden)* 1947 B&W *Director* René Clair; *Producer* Pathé and RKO; *Screenplay and Dialogue* René Clair; *Photography* Armand Thiarard; *Music* Georges Van Parys; *Set* Léon Barsacq and Guy de Gastyne; *Sound* Antoine Archimbaud; *Editing* Louisette Hautecoeur and Henri Taverna. Running time: 90 minutes.

Cast: Maurice Chevalier, François Périer, Marcelle Derrien, Dany Robin, Robert Pizani, Christiane Sertilange, Paul Ollivier, Roland Armontel, Raymond Cordy, Gaston Modot, Paul Demange, Bernard La Jarrige, Jean Daurand, Jane Pierson, Max Dalban, Albert Michel, Paul Francomme, Paul Faivre, Fernarnd Gilbert, Philippe Olive, Yvonne Yma, Cécile Didier, Tristan Sévere, Bruno Balp, Jean Berton, Maud Lamy, Fernand Blot, Frédéric Mariotti, Sylvain, Robert Berri, Eugene Yvernes, Albert Broquin, Georges Bever, Georges Sauval, Duncan, Simone Michels, Colette Georges, Marcel Charvey, Pierre Duncan, Léon Pauléon, Jean-Jacques Lécot, René Pascal, Victor Vina, Edouard Francomme, Tristan Sévère, Maurice Derville.

Set in the world of silent movie-making in the early 1900s, a young woman, Madeleine (Derrien), from the provinces is taken in by a 50-year-old movie director (Chevalier), at first he treats her like a daughter, but gradually he falls in love with her. But his adopted son Jacques (Périer), falls in love with her, too. After some romantic intrigue, as the older man witnesses the passionate vagaries of love, all ends well, and he graciously gives the younger two his blessing.

This romantic comedy, Clair's first film after returning to France after World War II, marked the endurance of French "quality" in films as well as the first joint

United States–French production (RKO and Pathé). Inspired by Molières' *The School for Wives*, this was Maurice Chevalier's first postwar film appearance, but instead of singing, he was cast in a dramatic role. The delightful story is marked by nostalgia for life before the two wars and the early days of cinema.

Man About Town was a great critical and popular success. Georges Sadoul lauded its "human warmth." The film won the French Critics' Prix Méliès in 1947 and the Grand Prize at the World Film Festival in Belgium.

Silence Is Golden *see* **Le Silence est d'or**

Silence of the Sea *see* **Le Silence de la mer**

The Silent World *see* **Le Monde du silence**

Skin and Bones *see* **Le Peau et les os**

The Slap *see* **La Gifle**

Slow Motion *see* **Sauve qui peut, la vie**

Small Change *see* **L'Argent du poche**

336 *Smoking/No Smoking* 1993 Color *Director* Alain Resnais; *Screenplay* Jean-Pierre Bacri, Agnese Jaoui, based on Alan Ayckbourn's play "Intimate Exchanges"; *Photography* Renato Berta; *Music* John Pattion; *Set* Jacques Qunternet and Marc Piniquier; *Sound* Bernard Bats and Gérald Lamps; *Costumes* Jackie Budin; *Editing* Albert Jurgenson. Running time: 140 minutes.

Cast: Sabine Azéma, Pierre Ardeti.

Two companion films about a British schoolteacher, Toby (Ardeti), and his wife, Celia (Azéma), and their relationships, romantic and otherwise, with their gardener Lionel (Ardeti), their maid, Sylvie (Azéma) and various friends. There are many story lines each with different endings depending on different small actions of the characters.

These two films take the idea of how small actions determine destiny to the furthest extreme, by actually showing many different scenarios when the characters do one thing differently. Resnais kept the feeling of viewing a play in the film by using only a few sets. The films were based on a series of short theatrical scenes by British playwright Alan Ayckbourn. Azéma and Ardeti play all of the different characters themselves and they do it so well that it could probably go unnoticed by many viewers.

The film was an enormous critical success in France. Both films showed at the same time, and Resnais forced the public to take the idea of chance even one step further by refusing to say which film to see first, though the order of viewing affects how the films are seen. They won five Césars in 1993, including Best Picture, Best Director, Best Actor and Best Screenplay.

The Snow Was Dirty *see* **La Neige était sale**

So Long Stooge *see* **Tchao-Pantin**

The Soldiers *see* **Les Carabiniers**

337 *Solo* 1969 Color   *Director* Jean-Pierre Mocky; *Producer* Balzac Films, Eclair, Cinevog; *Screenplay* Jean-Pierre Mocky; *Photography* Marcel Weiss; *Music* Georges Moustaki; *Set* Jacques Flamand, Françoise Hardy; *Sound* Séverin Frankiel, Lucien Yvonnet; *Editing* Marguerite Renoir. Running time: 89 minutes.

Cast: Jean-Pierre Mocky, Denis Le Guillou, Anne Deleuze, Sylvie Bréal, René-Jacques Chauffard, Marcel Pérès, Eric Burnelli, Alain Fourez, Ruddy Lenoir, Thérès Aspar, Jacques Flamand, Françoise Duroch, Jean-Pierre Renaud, Lorraine Santoni, Roger Lumont, Luc Andrieu, Yves Lefrançois, Jo Labarrère, Guy Denancy, Alexandre Randall, Jean Aron, Dominique Zardi, Vasco.

Virgile (Le Guillou) is an anarchist who is driven to mass murder by the upheaval of the May 1968 student riots that shook Paris. His brother, Vincent (Mocky), a violinist and thief, tries to track Virgile down; but instead of finding him, he gets into trouble with the police. By trying to save his brother, he ends up aiding his getaway and getting killed himself.

Mocky, who began his film career as an actor, both acts and directs here. The film is an interesting examination of the effects of France's political and social upheaval on two brothers. Mocky was hoping to show contemporary, anarchistic students that both the Establishment and revolutionaries use violence and destruction that harms innocent people.

This was the only political film to come out just after the 1968 riots and while some responded to Mocky's virulent message, others rejected it.

Les Somnambules *see* **Mon Oncle d'Amérique**

The Sorrow and the Pity *see* **Le Chagrin et la pitié**

338 *Le Souffle au cœur (Murmur of the Heart)* 1970 Color   *Director* Louis Malle; *Producer* Nouvelles Editions de Films, Marianne Productions, Vidès Productions, Franz Seitz Filmproduction; *Screenplay* Louis Malle; *Photography* Ricardo Aronovitch; *Set* Jean-Jacques Caziot; *Sound* Jean-Claude Laureux; *Editing* Suzanne Baron. Running time: 120 minutes.

Cast: Léa Massari, Daniel Gélin, Benoit Ferreux, Michel Lonsdale, Marc Winocourt, Fabien Ferreux, Gila Von Weitershausen, Ave Ninchi, Micheline Bona, Henri Poirier, Jacques Sereys, Jacques Gheusi, René Bouloc, François Werner, Yvon Lec, Annie Savarin, Michel Charrel, Jacqueline Chauveau, Corinne Kersten, Liliane Sorval, Eric Burnelli, Jean-Pierre Pessez, Nicole Carrière, Andrzej Zulawski, Eric Walter, Jean-Louis Blum, Lia Wanjtal, Hugette Faget, Isabelle Kloucowsky, Roland Demongeot, Bernadette Robert, Christophe Nollier, Jean-Micel Colle.

Set in Dijon in the 1950s, this is a sexual and intellectual coming-of-age story about a young boy, Laurent (Ferreux). His home life with a father who is a gynecologist and two brothers who take him to a prostitute to lose his virginity, is bourgeois family fare handled with a light humor. When it is discovered that Laurent has a heart murmur, he and his mother (Massari) go off for a cure. Their intimacy increases at the spa and they have an incestual interlude.

This is a Louis Malle masterpiece, which tackled serious generational and social issues with a wonderfully complex, yet comic, touch. Children questioned their parents' authority and pushed society's boundaries, but Malle remains an observer, not a propagandist. The incidents are revealed through the child's eyes and are thus rendered to be no more than tender rites of passage.

Because Malle seemed to pass no moral judgement on the mother-son incest scene, the film was viewed as scandalous when it first came out. It has since been reconsidered as a tender, sweet movie that works because of its characters.

The Sound and the Fury *see* **De bruit et de fureur**

339 *Le Soupirant (The Suitor)* 1962 B&W   *Director* Pierre Etaix; *Producer* CAPAC, Cocinor-Marceau; *Screenplay* Pierre Etaix; *Photography* Pierre Levent; *Music* Jean Paillaud; *Set* Raymond Tournon; *Sound* Jean Bertrand; *Editing* Pierre Gillette. Running time: 85 minutes.

Cast: Pierre Etaix, France Arnell, Karin Vesely, Laurence Lignières, Denise Pérronne, Claude Massot, Charles Bayard, Anna Abigaël, Lucien Frégis, Brigitte Juslin, Robert Blome, Kim Lohay, Edouard Francomme, Petit Bobo, Dominique Clément, Patrice Laffont, Loriot, Gilles Rosset, Roger Trapp, Pierre Vernet, Guy Pierauld.

A comedy about a nice young man (Etaix), who spends his days shut in his room absorbed by his scientific studies until his parents encourage him to get married. Convinced by their reasoning, he sets out to find the perfect wife. Stella (Arnell), a music-hall singer, becomes the object of his marital desire until he realizes that she is not what she seems. Finally, the woman he has been looking for turns out to be the lovely Swedish au pair (Vesely), who had been living under the same roof all along.

This wonderful burlesque was comedian/illusionist Etaix's first feature film. He had previously worked as a clown in the circus and as an assistant on Tati's *My Uncle*; and his short film *Happy Anniversary* won an Oscar in 1962 for Best Live Action Short Subject. The film is of the Tati and Chaplin school of comedy with wonderfully timed gags supplying the laughs.

Critics hailed this debut as the announcement of a great new comic talent. *Variety* said, "there is a timing, comedic flair and inventiveness about this that could make it a worthy art...." The film won the Prix Louis Delluc in 1962.

340 *Sous le soleil de satan (Under Satan's Sun)* 1987 Color   *Director* Maurice Pialat; *Producer* Daniel Toscan du Plantier; *Screenplay* Sylvie Danton, based on the novel by Georges Bernanos; *Photography* Willy Kurant; *Music* Henri Dutilleux; *Set* Katia Vischkof; *Sound* Louis Gimel; *Costumes* Gil Noir; *Editing* Yann Dedet. Running time: 98 minutes.

Cast: Gérard Depardieu, Sandrine Bonnaire, Maurice Pialat, Alain Artur, Yann Dedet, Brigitte Legendre, Jean-Claude Bourlat, Jean-Christophe Bouvet, Philippe Pallut, Marcel Anselin, Yvette Lavogez, Pierre d'Hoffelize, Corinne Bourdon, Thierry Der'ven, Marie-Antoinette Lorge, Bernard and Yolène de Gouy, Claudine Gauthier, Thierry Artur, Ghislain Boitrelle, Raymonde Jacquot, Frédéric Auburtin, Edith Colnel, Delphine Westrelin, Vincent Peignaux, Françoise Disle, Fabienne Deleforge, Yolain de Gelas, Anne Duquennoy, Karine Lambert, Carole Loth, Nathalie Lourtil, Sabrina Vervacke, Marie-Paul Vienne, Claudy Widszinski, Anne Cassaggnou, Guillaume, Jérôme, Franck and David Dohoye.

Father Donissan (Depardieu) is a priest obsessed with knowing whether he is a true follower of God or an unwitting instrument of the Devil. When a young girl in his parish goes to him for guidance after she kills the Marquise with whom she has been having an affair, Father Donissan tries to help her, but she kills herself. He punishes himself for his sins and for not leading his parishioners as well as he thinks he should. When he becomes the priest of another town, the villagers believe he is a saint, but even a miracle does not save him from his self-doubt.

A wonderful film that dares take on spiritual issues of good and evil in a somber, naturalistic style in the 1980s, *Under Satan's Sun* is a modern-day tribute to Bresson's *Diary of a Young Country Priest*. Depardieu is at the height of his career and still looking for a new challenge. His performance as a troubled, well meaning, but awkward priest proves that he can be as intellectual an actor as he can be a physical one. The tension between whether or not God exists in the beautiful and brutal rural life of the 1920s is revealed just as much through the cinematography, as through the struggles of the priest and his villagers.

Under Satan's Sun had the dubious honor of winning Grand Prize at Cannes by unanimous jury vote in 1987, but of being booed by the festival audience when the announcement was made. Many critics found its spiritual subject boring and out of date, but others hailed it as a truly great film.

341 *Souvenirs d'en France (French Provincial)*   1975 Color   *Director* André Téchiné; *Producer* Stephan, Simar, Renn Productions, Belstar; *Screenplay* André Téchiné and Marilyn Goldin; *Photography* Bruno Nuytten; *Music* Philippe Sarde; *Set* Philippe Galland; *Sound* Pierre Befve; *Costumes* Christian Gasc; *Editing* Anne-Marie Deshayes. Running time: 90 minutes.

Cast: Jeanne Moreau, Michel Auclair, Marie-France Pisier, Claude Mann, Orane Demazis, Aram Stephan, Hélène Surgère, Julien Guiomar, Michèle Moretti, Pierre Baillot, Marc Chapiteau, Jean Rougeul, Alan Scott, Zilouka, Caroline Cartier, Frédérique Bredin, Pierre Gautard, Jean-Claude Delsol, Louis Bihi.

A 40-year saga about a Spanish immigrant family who makes a life for themselves in the southwest of France. The father and his three sons establish a factory in a little village. When one son, Hector (Auclair), falls in love with the local laundress, Berthe (Moreau), the father tries to prevent the match, but they marry. During the war, Berthe virtually takes over the factory and the family, while she helps the Resistance. After the war, the family and factory face modernization issues.

This was Téchiné's second film, and it established him as a brilliant critic-turned-filmmaker with a talent for sweeping romantic films about family lives and struggles in France. In this film, what begins as a family dynasty tale turns into one woman's social and political odyssey. Téchiné masterfully blends a rich painterly visual flair with deep historical, sociological issues. Moreau's performance is monumental.

When *French Provincial* came out, critics compared Téchiné to everyone from Cocteau and Godard to Hitchcock and Welles. Pauline Kael of *The New Yorker* said: "It's gorgeous, heady stuff, and throughout, Téchiné invests the images with so much dramatic beauty that you're busy just taking it in."

The Specter of Freedom *see* **Le Fantôme de la liberté**

The Spice of Life *see* Les Casse-pieds

Stairway C *see* Escalier C

Stars at Noon *see* Les Étoiles de midi

State of Siege *see* État de siège

Statues Also Die *see* Les Statues meurent aussi

342 *Les Statues meurent aussi (Statues Also Die)* 1954 B&W *Director* Alain Resnais and Chris Marker; *Producer* Tadié Cinéma, Présence Africaine; *Screenplay* Alain Resnais and Chris Marker; *Photography* Chislain Cloquet; *Music* Guy Bernard; Commentary spoken by Jean Negroni. Running time: 29 minutes.

A documentary or visual essay on African Art. It focuses on the traditions and myths that the artwork springs from and explains how it is being turned into a cottage-industry by the West's cultural imperialism.

One of the decade's most important documentaries by one of France's most important documentary filmmakers, this was Marker's directorial debut. It was an amazing collaboration between a great documentarist to be and the New Wave director Resnais, who would go on to make such groundbreaking films as *Hiroshima, Mon Amour* and *Last Year at Marienbad*. The journalist, writer, photographer Marker said of his reason for wanting to make the film: "We put stones on our dead to keep them from leaving, the blacks keep them close to them to honor them and profit from their power with a simple basket of bones." This film set the standard for aesthetic analysis in films, which was a subject Resnais had already explored in his films *Van Gogh* and *Guernica*.

Though the French government did try to censor the film as an anti-colonial work, *Statues Also Die* was hailed as liberating the documentary genre, in much the same way the New Wave directors a few years later were hailed as revolutionizing fictional films. It won the Prix Jean Vigo in 1954.

343 *Stavisky* 1974 Color *Director* Alain Resnais; *Producer* Cérito, Euro International Films, Arianne Films; *Screenplay* Jorge Semprun; *Photography* Sacha Vierny; *Music* Stephen Sondheim; *Set* Jacques Saulnier; *Sound* Jean-Luc Ruh; *Costumes* Jacqueline Moreau; *Editing* Albert Jurgenson. Running time: 115 minutes.

Cast: Jean-Paul Belmondo, François Périer, Annie Duperey, Michel Lonsdale, Roberto Bisacco, Claude Rich, Charles Boyer, Pierre Vernier, Marcel Cuvelier, Van Doude, Jacques Spiesser, Michel Beaune, Sylvia Badesco, Maurice Jacquemont, Jacques Eyser, Fernand Guiot, Daniel Lecourtois, Gérard Depardieu, Mike Arrighi, Samson Fainsilber, Raymond Girard, Gigi Ballista, Guido Cerniglia, Yves Brainville, Yves Peneau, Jean Michaux, Niels Arestrup, Ismelda Marani, Dominique Rollin, Catherine Sellers, François Leterrier, Jean-Michel Charlier, Lucienne Legrand, Gabriel Cattand, Roland Bertin, Guy Pierauld, Paul Villé, Vicky Messica, Lionel Vtrant, Georges Yacoubian.

A historical film about the Stavisky Affair, one of the greatest money schemes ever, which was the biggest scandal to hit Paris in the 1930s, because the "affair"

Subway, 1985; directed by Luc Besson.

almost brought about the collapse of the French government. Serge Alexandre Stavisky (Belmondo) was a hustler who used phony investment schemes to gain both political clout and hundreds of investors who trusted him with millions. The police and the government actually helped protect Stavisky, so when the truth started to emerge, riots erupted. Stavisky took the suicide exit.

Resnais did not want to make a movie about the social and political implications of the affair, but preferred to make a portrait of the crook, about his happiness and his loss. Not the usual Resnais fare, coming after *Hiroshima, mon amour* and *Last Year at Marienbad*, but Resnais weaves a wonderful traditional drama. It was the first film that he made in the 1970s, after a six-year hiatus, and it brought him before a wide, popular audience. Stavisky is one of Belmondo's best roles.

Stavisky came out in France at a time when historical sagas were very popular. It was quite well received, but some critics said that the fact that one of the New Wave's most experimental filmmakers had chosen an historical drama and filmed it conventionally signalled the passing of the torch to the next generation of young talents.

Stolen Kisses *see* **Baisers volés**

The Stoolie *see* **Le Doulos**

The Storm Within *see* **Les Parents terribles**

The Story of Adèle H. *see* **L'Histoire d'Adèle H.**

The Story of Women *see* **Une Affaire de femmes**

A Strange Affair *see* **Une Étrange Affaire**

The Strange Ones *see* **Les Enfants terribles**

344 *Subway* 1985 Color   *Director* Luc Besson; *Producer* Films du Loup, Gaumont, TF1 Productions; *Screenplay* Luc Besson, Pierre Jolivet, Alain Le Henry, Sophie Schmit and Marc Perrier; *Photography* Ricardo Aronovitch and Carlo Varini; *Music* Paul Misraki; *Set* Frédéric Astich Barre; *Sound* Harald Maury, Harrick Maury; *Editing* Sophie Schmit. Running time: 104 minutes.

Cast: Isabelle Adjani, Christophe Lambert, Michel Galabru, Richard Bohringer, Jean-Hughes Anglade, Jean-Pierre Bacri, Jean Bouise, P.-A. Le Pogan, Jean Reno, Arthur Simms, Constantin Alexandrov, Jean-Claude Lecas, Eric Serra, Benoit Régent, Isabelle Sadoyan, Brigitte Chamarande, François Ruggiéri, Dominique Hennequin, Christian Gomba, Jimmy Blanche, Jean-Luc Miesch, Michel d'Oz, Alain Guillard, Jean-Michel Castanié, Catherine Luton, Guy Laporte, Marie Vincent, Pierre Garrive, Michel Montanary.

A beautiful young wife, Hélèna (Adjani), becomes involved with a mysterious street tough, Fred (Lambert). He introduces her to the hidden life of the Paris Métro, where musicians and pickpockets form their own society. As Helena falls in love with Fred, she learns that he is hunted by the police and killers hired by her husband. Love and trouble follow.

Subway proved that *Diva* was not an aberration. Besson's second film, which he made at age 25, firmly established the young director as one of the most exciting new talents in French film and set the style and agenda for French filmmaking in the next decade. As in *Diva*, Besson focused on a modern urban underworld and set it reeling with a thriller plot, hip music and great visuals. He filmed most of the movie underground in the tunnels of Paris' Métro.

Some critics dismissed *Subway* as a long music video with violence. Others made it a cult hit. Christopher Lambert won the César for Best Actor in 1985.

The Sucker *see* **Le Corniaud**

The Suitor *see* **Le Soupirant**

Summer Manœuvres *see* **Les Grandes Manœuvres**

A Sunday in the Country *see* **Un Dimanche à la campagne**

Sundays and Cybele *see* **Les Dimanches de ville d'Avray**

Suzanne Simonin, La Religieuse de Diderot *see* **La Religieuse**

Sylvia and the Ghost *see* **Sylvie et le fantôme**

Sylvia and the Phantom *see* **Sylvie et le fantôme**

345 *Sylvie et le fantôme (Sylvia and the Phantom* or *Sylvia and the Ghost)*   1945 B&W   *Director* Claude Autant-Lara; *Producer* Discina; *Screenplay* based on a play by Alfred Adam; *Adaptation and Dialogue* Jean Aurenche; *Photography* Philippe Agostini; *Music* René Cloérec; *Set* Lucien Carré and Jacques Krauss; *Costumes* Claude Autant-Lara and Christian Dior; *Sound* Jacques Lebreton; *Editing* Madeleine Gug. Running time: 102 minutes.

Cast: Odette Joyeux, François Périer, Jean Desailly, Louis Salou, Julien Carette, Jacques Tati, Pierre Larquey, Pierre Palau, Gabrielle Fontan, Claude Marcy, Lise Topart, Paul Demange, Raymond Rognoni, Colette Ripert, Albert-Michel, Gabert, Marguerite Cassan.

A fantastical love comedy about a dreamy adolescent, Sylvie (Joyeux), who falls in love with the man in a portrait that hangs in her family's chateau. First, her father pays someone to impersonate the man as a surprise for Sylvie's birthday. Next a number of young men take advantage of her romantic ideas by posing as the dead nobleman, and then his ghost appears — complicating things even further.

This was Autant-Lara's first postwar film and it offered just the light entertainment needed by people who went to the movies to escape from the hardship of their daily lives for a little while. It is a romance that plays with the supernatural and a young girl's fertile imagination. The score has been called one of the most beautiful ever composed for a movie. Odette Joyeux, who had worked with Autant-Lara before, is delightful. Jacques Tati has a small part as the ghost.

A hit in Paris, where critics called it a whimsical, comedy delight, *Sylvie and the Phantom* did not open in the United States until 1950. American critics were less taken with it. *The New York Times* called it "an excruciatingly coy and whimsical little pastry."

Symphonie Pastorale *see* **La Symphonie pastorale**

346 *La Symphonie pastorale (Symphonie Pastorale)*   1946 B&W *Director* Jean Delannoy; *Producer* Films Gibé; *Screenplay* based on André Gide's novel *Two Symphonies*; *Adaptation* Jean Aurenche and Jean Delannoy; *Dialogue* Jean Aurenche and Pierre Bost; *Photography* Armand Thirard; *Music* Georges Auric; *Set* René Renoux; *Sound* Albert Leblond; *Costumes* Georges Annenkov; *Editing* Suzanne Fauvel. Running time: 95 minutes.

Cast: Michèle Morgan, Pierre Blanchar, Jean Desailly, Line Noro, Jacques Louvigny, Andrée Clément, Rosine Luguet, Mona Dol, Germaine Michel, Robert Demorget, Albert Glado, Hélène Dassonville, Marius David, Florence Brière, Renée Bouzy.

A Swiss pastor (Blanchar) finds a blind and confused girl (Morgan). Despite the protests of his wife, he takes her in, cares for her and raises her with his own children. When she grows up and regains her vision through an operation, she chooses to die rather than decide between her love for the pastor's son Jacques (Desailly), and her feelings of gratitude to the pastor, who is jealous of the young couple's love.

To many, the sensitivity and intelligence of *Symphonie Pastorale* were the epitome of quality French filmmaking. It is certainly Jean Delannoy's masterpiece. Even Gide was pleased with the film adaptation of his novel, which is a superb example of France's literary tradition in film. Morgan, who is exceedingly beautiful and innocent, researched her role by spending time in a home for the blind. It turned out to be the film that revived her career in France after World War II, and is probably her best performance ever. The wonderful, very moving music works beautifully.

Symphonie Pastorale was a great success in France. American critics either found it melodramatic or an example of very distinguished filmmaking. It was one of the four films chosen to represent France at the first Cannes Film Festival in 1946. It won the Grand Prize and Michèle Morgan won Best Actress.

347 *Tatie Danielle* 1990 Color   *Director* Etienne Chatiliez; *Producer* Téléma, FR3 Films, Les Productions du Champ Poirier; *Screenplay* Florence Quentin; *Photography* Philippe Welt; *Music* Gabriel Yared; *Set* Geoffroy Larcher; *Sound* Guillaume Sciama, Dominique Dlamasso; *Editing* Catherine Renault. Running time: 110 minutes.

Cast: Tsilla Chelton, Catherine Jacob, Eric Prat, Neige Dolsky, Isabelle Nanty, Laurence Février, Virginie Pradal, Mathieu Foulon, Gary Ledoux, André Wilms, Patrick Bouchitey, Christine Pignet, Evelyne Didi, Frédéric Rossif.

Eighty-two-year-old Tatie Danielle (Chelton) is everyone's worst nightmare of a relative rolled into one, and she makes everyone around her miserable. Her grandnephew takes her in only to have her turn his family's life inside out; she loses one of the children and goes to the bathroom in her bed. When the family goes to Greece for a vacation, they leave Tatie with Sandrine (Nanty). A battle of wills follows, which, of course, turns into a great friendship.

Chatiliez's second feature is just as wild, smart and nasty as his first, *Life Is a Long Quiet River*, which shocked and seduced the movie world. The subject of his searing scrutiny is once again the middle-class French and all their faults and foibles, and his instrument of cruelty is a nasty old lady. It is biting and hilarious. The actors are relatively unknown, but fresh and funny.

Some critics were offended by Chatiliez's vulgar humor. Others found it extremely refreshing. *The Daily News* exclaimed, "*Tatie Danielle*, a cheeky social satire by French director Etienne Chatiliez, bravely challenges the notion that old ladies are merely sweet and respectable."

Taxi for Tobruk *see* Un Taxi pour Tobrouk

348 *Un Taxi pour Tobrouk (Taxi for Tobruk)* 1960 B&W   *Director*
Denys de la Patellière; *Producer* Franco-London Films, SNEG, Procura;
Screenplay René Havard; *Adaptation* René Havard, Denys de la Patellière and
Michel Audiard; *Photography* Marcel Grignon; *Music* Georges Garvareventz; *Set*
Paul-Louis Boutié; *Sound* Georges Mardiguian; *Editing* Jacqueline Thiédot. Running time: 132 minutes.
     Cast: Lino Ventura, Charles Aznavour, Maurice Biraud, Hardy Krüger, Ger-
man Cobos.
     Four men survive a battle in North Africa in the winter of 1942. Coming from
different social backgrounds, they get to know each other in their desperate circumstances. They take a German officer prisoner and unite to survive, but as they
approach their battalion, their comrades think they are the enemy attacking and
fire on them. Only one survives.
     This entertaining war movie is one of France's best battle pictures. Full of
suspense and twists, de la Pattalière keeps the tension and interest high. Aznavour
as a quiet Jewish doctor, Krüger as the cocksure German, and Ventura as a
frustrated professional boxer are all wonderful. They create real character portraits, which are the power of the movie.
     French and American critics either admired the movie or found it unoriginal.
The New York Herald Tribune called it "a taut war drama that is immeasurably
heightened by crack performances and crisp direction." *Taxi for Tobruk* was
released in the United States three years after its French debut. The film won the
Grand Prix du Cinéma Français in 1961.

349 *Tchao-Pantin (Tchao Pantin* or *So Long Stooge)* 1983 Color
Director Claude Berri; *Producer* Renn Productions, AMLF; *Screenplay* Claude
Berri and Alain Page, based on the novel by Alain Page; *Photography* Bruno
Nyutten; *Music* Charles Elie Couture; *Set* Alexandre Trauner; *Sound* Jean
Labussière; *Editing* Hervé de Luze. Running time: 100 minutes.
     Cast: Michel Coluche, Richard Anconina, Agnès Soral, Philippe Léotard,
Mahmoud Zemmouri, Ahmed Ben Ismael, Mickael Pichet, Michel Paul, Annie
Kerani, Pierrick Mescam, Vincent Martin, Albert Dray.
     Lambert (Coluche), an alcoholic who pumps gas at a filling station, becomes
friends; with Bensoussan (Anconina), a street kid and small-time drug dealer. The
two become friends; and when Lambert finds Bensoussan dead, he believes it was
not an overdose but murder. With the help of Bensoussan's young punk girlfriend
(Soral) and a police inspector (Léotard), he uncovers Bensoussan's killers, but his
sleuthing has its dangers.
     This is one of Claude Berri's most interesting works, as well as one of the 1980s
best movies focusing on Paris' underbelly. Berri, who later created magnificently
beautiful pastoral atmospheres in such films as *Jean de Florette*, here demonstrated
just as great a gift for evoking the seedy side of life. Coluche, who was known as
a comedy actor, proved that he is a fine dramatic actor.
     Some critics complained that what started out as a masterpiece quickly evolved
into a run-of-the-mill shoot-'em-up. Others loved it. David Denby of *Cue* said:
"See it for the enjoyably squalid atmosphere and the neo-Gabin tough guy

performance by Coluche." The film won five Césars, including ones for both Coluche and Anconina's performances.

350 *Tenue de soirée (Ménage or Ménage à trois)* 1986 Color *Director* Bertrand Blier; *Producer* Hachette Première, DD Productions, Ciné Valse; *Screenplay* Bertrand Blier; *Photography* Jean Penzer; *Music* Serge Gainsbourg; *Set* Théobald Meurisse; *Sound* Bernard Bats, Dominique Hennequin; *Editing* Claudine Merlin. Running time: 84 minutes.

Cast: Gérard Depardieu, Michel Blanc, Miou-Miou, Bruno Cremer, Jean-Pierre Marielle, Michel Creton, Jean-François Stévenin, Mylène Demongeot, Caroline Sihol, Jean-Yves Bertloot, Maurice Travail, Michel Pilorgé, Michel Such.

Antoine (Blanc) and Monique (Miou-Miou) are a down-and-out married couple. When they meet an immensely rich thief, Bob (Depardieu), the three seem to get along perfectly, until Bob becomes more interested in Antoine than Monique. While Monique is dazzled by Bob's money, Bob seduces Antoine. Ultimately, the trio ends up on the street dreaming of a child.

This is a quintessential Blier film, a picaresque view on the wild life and times of three fringe members of society. It is, therefore, the quintessential French film of the 1970s. During this decade, Blier's style and subjects were the most important new influence in film. While his humor and taste seemed to some over the top, Blier pushed the boundaries of cinema in a new and important way. In *Going Places* and *Ménage*, he not only brought some of the greatest new dramatic talent in France to the screen, but he brought before millions of viewers themes and subjects that had never before been thought fit for the movies. Of course, there were those who called it feminist farce, and others who declared it a misogynistic mess.

French critics either loved this or hated it. Americans compared it to David Lynch's *Blue Velvet.* David Kerr of *The Chicago Tribune* said: "Like *Blue Velvet*, it is profoundly unsettling in the way it shakes up our assumptions about the world and the roles of the men and women who inhabit it." Most found it unsettling, but interesting. Michel Blanc won Best Actor at Cannes in 1986.

351 *Le Testament d'Orphée (The Testament of Orpheus)* 1959 B&W *Director* Jean Cocteau; *Producer* Thuiller; *Screenplay* Jean Cocteau; *Photography* Roland Pontioseau and Raichi; *Music* Jacques Metehen; *Set* Pierre Guffroy; *Costumes* Janine Janet; *Editing* Marie-Josèphe Yoyotte. Running time: 80 minutes.

Cast: Jean Cocteau, Jean-Pierre Léaud, Nicole Courcel, Henri Crémieux, Daniel Gélin, Henri Torrès, Maria Casarès, Edouard Dhermite, Yul Brynner, Jean Marais, François Périer, Charles Aznavour, Pablo Picasso, Françoise Christophe, Claudine Auger, Luis-Miguel Dominguin, Henri Torrès, Alice Sapritch, Serge Lifar, Francine Weisweiler, Daniel Moosmann, Marie-Josèphe Yoyotte, Philippe Juzan, Brigitte Morissan, Georges Chretelain, Michèle Lemoigne, Guy Dute, Michèle Comte, Jean-Claude Petit, Alice Heyliger, Philippe, Michèle Lemoig, Gérard Chatelain, Lucia Bose, Françoise Arnoul, Françoise Sagan, Roger Vadim, Annette Stroyberg, Brigitte Bardot, Philippe Juzau.

The literary, autobiographical, philosophical, artistic and mythical odyssey of the Poet (Cocteau) through time and space. He journeys to meet the Sphinx, Oedipus, the Princess of Death, Isolde, Minerva, Picasso, a famous bullfighter and many others, before he finally arrives at his death.

This was Cocteau's last film, and it brought together all of his great talents as poet, surrealist artist and filmmaker, as well as many of the greats of French film and the arts. He plays the poet who dies, actually foretelling his own death by three years. The backing for the film came from Truffaut, who had just made a small fortune with *The 400 Blows*. When he began the project, Cocteau wanted to make a reflective triptych on his life's works. As was his method of working, though, once he got started his imagination ran wild. He produced magical special effects and an historic personal ode.

The Testament of Orpheus was not a great commercial success, despite great expectations and long lines on the day it opened. Some critics dismissed Cocteau's last endeavor as a chaotic rehash of his former stars and former themes. Others found that Cocteau's sense of the film's screen spectacle completely overcame the film's flaws and hailed this as one of his and cinema's greats.

The Testament of Orpheus *see* **Le Testament d'Orphée**

352/3 *La Tête contre les murs (The Keepers)* 1958 B&W   *Director* Georges Franju; *Producer* Sirius, Atica, Elphénor; *Screenplay* Jean-Pierre Mocky and Jean-Charles Pichon, based on the novel by Hervé Bazin; *Photography* Eugen Schufftan; *Music* Maurice Jarre; *Set* Louis Le Barbenchon; *Sound* René Sarrazin; *Editing* Suzanne Sandberg. Running time: 92 minutes.

Cast: Jean-Pierre Mocky, Anouk Aimée, Pierre Brasseur, Paul Meurisse, Charles Aznavour, Jean Galland, Edith Scob, Thomy Bourdelle, Jean Ozenne, Rudy Lenoir, Louis Masson, Roger Legris, Henri San-Juan, Doudou Babet, Max Montavon, Pierre Mirat, Luc Andrieu, Jacques Seiler, Raoul Marco, Véronique Nordey, Paul Demange, Sophie Poncin, René Alié, Sophie Saint-Just, Alexandre Randall, Monique Ardoin, Claude Castaing, Jacques Mancier, Claude Badolle, Jean Henry, André Thorent, Claude Mansard, Balpo, Pierre Koplitchev, Jean Labarrère, Georges Pally, Diego Masson, Jean Rougerie, Lucian Camiret.

François Gérane (Mocky) is a young man who is committed to an insane asylum by his father, because he views the son's insubordination as dangerous. Just before his girlfriend (Aimée) is about to arrange his release, François escapes. He tries to prove his sanity, only to be returned to the asylum.

Franju was a documentary filmmaker for two decades before he began making feature films, and the portrayal of asylum life is amazingly realistic. As in his documentaries, he finds great poetry in real life. Though some find the ambiguous treatment of the boy's sanity frustrating, the film remains a bold and poetic cry for freedom and a condemnation of society's restraints. Anouk Aimée, Edith Scob and Charles Aznavour are all fantastic.

When it debuted in Paris, the critic for *Le Monde* wrote: "Where does the real, the solid end, and the fantastic, the imaginary begin in this unusual world we find ourselves plunged into?" Jean-Luc Godard in *Cahiers du Cinéma* declared: "*The Keepers* is a film by crazies about crazies. It is thus a film of a crazy beauty...."

That Man from Rio *see* **L'Homme de Rio**

That Obscure Object of Desire *see* **Cet Obscur Objet du désir**

354 *Thérèse* 1986 Color   *Director* Alain Cavalier; *Producer* AFC, Films A2, CNC; *Screenplay* Alain Cavalier and Camille de Casabianca; *Photography* Philippe Rousselot; *Set* Bernard Evein; *Sound* Alin Lachassagne and Dominique Dalmasso; *Editing* Isabelle Dedieu. Running time: 90 minutes.

Cast: Catherine Mouchet, Aurore Prieto; Ghislaine Mona, Sylvie Habault, Hélène Alexandridis; Clémence Massart, Nathalie Bernart, Jean Pelegri, Michel Rivelin, Guy Faucon, Pierre Baillot, Jean Pieuchot, Armand Meppiel, Joël Le François, Pierre Maintigneux, Béatrice de Vigan, Noëlle Chantre, Anna Bernelat.

The story of Saint Thérèse of Lisieux, a 15-year-old girl (Mouchet) who wanted to enter the Church just like her older sisters. She finds life inside the convent very difficult. She falls sick with tuberculosis, but makes peace with her decision and her life just before she dies.

Using the true story of Thérèse Martin, Cavalier brought his talents as a classical filmmaker of the highest order to a new level. He was interested in juxtaposing the drudgery and dullness of a nun's daily life with the passion of her spirituality, and he uses the smallest, telling details to reveal this contrast. To prepare for the film, he read many religious documents and researched the Carmelites' lifestyle and their relationship with Jesus Christ as bridegroom.

Thérèse was a remarkably big success in France, where it debuted at the Cannes Film Festival. American critic Andrew Sarris said: "It is the closest thing to an unexpected epiphany I have experienced at this year's carnival." The film won six Césars, including Best Picture and Best Director. It also won the French Critics' Prix Méliès and the Jury Prize at Cannes.

355 *Thérèse Desqueyroux* 1962 B&W   *Director* Georges Franju; *Producer* Fimel; *Screenplay* Claude Mauriac, Georges Franju and François Mauriac, based on the novel by François Mauriac; *Photography* Christian Matras; *Music* Maurice Jarre; *Set* Jacques Chalvet; *Sound* Jeanne Labussière; *Editing* Gilbert Natot. Running time: 109 minutes.

Cast: Emmanuelle Riva, Philippe Noiret, Edith Scob, Sami Frey, Renée Devillers, Richard Saint Bris, Lucien Nat, Hélène Dieudonné, Jeanne Pérez, Jacques Monod, Renée Divillers, Jean-Jacques Rémy, Harry Vardier, Kléber Harpin.

Thérèse (Riva) is married to a man (Noiret) whom she hates. She is accused of trying to kill him, but her husband refuses to press charges against her. When he gets her home, though, he keeps her locked in her bedroom. Finally, he decides to let her go, never understanding why she wanted to kill him. She is freed to live an independent life in Paris.

This is a wonderful adaptation of Mauriac's novel and probably Franju's greatest fictional work. Franju saw Thérèse as "a Bovary who strikes back." She is not evil, but rather a victim of too large a spirit locked into too small a provincial life. She wants liberty, not revenge. Franju's delicate direction and Riva's poignant portrayal make this a fabulous film.

Possibly the severest critic of this film, François Mauriac wrote in a letter to Franju: "It is a very pretty work and I am happy and proud to have furnished you with the material, but it all belongs to you." Emmanuelle Riva won Best Actress at the Venice Film Festival in 1962.

356 *Thérèse Raquin (The Adultress)* 1953 B&W   *Director* Marcel Carné; *Producer* Paris Films, Lux Films; *Screenplay* Charles Spaak and Marcel Carné, based on the novel by Emile Zola; *Photography* Roger Hubert; *Music* Maurice Thiriet; *Set* Paul Bertrand; *Sound* Antoine Archimbaud; *Editing* Henri Rust. Running time: 105 minutes.

Cast: Simone Signoret, Raf Vallone, Jacques Duby, Sylvie, Roland Lesaffre, Marcel André, Maria Pia Casilio, Martial Rèbe, Nério Bernardi, Paul Frankeur, Madeleine Barbulée, Lucien Hubert, Francette Vernillat, Paul Frankeur, Nerio Bernardi, Alain Terrane, Bernard Véron, Jacques Hilling, Jean Sylvère, Danielle Dumont, Jean Rozenberg, Chantal Retz, Jean-Jacques Lecot, Claude Naudès.

Thérèse Raquin (Signoret), who is married to a man she abhors, and Laurent (Vallone), an Italian truck driver, are lovers who kill Thérèse's husband. Thérèse's mother-in-law, who is paralyzed, figures out their guilt; and there exists a witness. They do not escape their crime.

Many believe this to be Carné's greatest postwar film. Invested with the poetic realism of the period, Carné was more interested in explaining Thérèse through the concept of destiny than what some believe was Zola's explanation of how society shapes individuals. Simone Signoret brings Thérèse, in all her passion and self-centeredness, to great life.

The film was lauded by critics for its sombre intelligence. *Cue* said it had "the drive of doom characteristic of the Greek classic tragedy form."

The Thief of Paris *see* **Le Voleur**

The Things of Life *see* **Les Choses de la vie**

This Man Must Die *see* **Que la bête meure**

357 *Thomas l'imposteur (Thomas the Imposter)* 1965 B&W *Director* Georges Franju; *Producer* Filmel; *Screenplay* Michel Worms, Georges Franju, Raphaël Cluzel, and Jean Cocteau, based on the novel by Jean Cocteau; *Photography* Marcel Fradétal; *Music* Georges Auric; *Set* Claude Pignot; *Sound* André Hervé; *Editing* Gilbert Natot. Running time: 100 minutes.

Cast: Fabrice Rouleau, Emmanuelle Riva, Sophie Darès, Jean Servais, Rosy Varte, Michel Vitold, Bernard Lavalette, Edouard Dhermitte, Hélène Dieudonné, Jean-Roger Caussimon, Gabrielle Dorziat, Edith Scob, Michel Laclos, Rosy Varte, André Méliès, Jean Ozenne, Ramond Jourdan, Bob Lerick, Antone Marin, Gaston Meunier, Georges Casati, Jean Magis, Jean Degrave, Henri Coutet, Serge Rousseau, Robert Burnier, Pierre Mirat, Tristan Sévère, J. Henry, Michel Laclos, Claude Delmas, Roger Fradet, Jacques Jeannet, and the voice of Jean Marais.

During the confusing time after World War I, a young man, Thomas (Rouleau), passes himself off as the nephew of a general and a war hero. He helps the Princess de Bormes (Riva), who has started a hospital in her home to care for the wounded from the front. He falls in love with her daughter, Henriette (Darès), but is then sent off to the front. The lovers meet once again before Thomas is sent on a final mission.

Franju beautifully combined his talents as documentarist and a literary film-maker to make a fascinating adaptation of Cocteau's novel. He explored the ideas of a man's fantasy life and reality inexorably and disastrously colliding, while at the same time exposing the horrors of war, to which he was opposed. Of the title character, Franju said: "He is a dream adventurer who lives in a world which is the opposite of his dream."

Some criticized Franju for remaining too faithful to Cocteau's work and not putting his own imprint on the film. Others congratulated him for merging his style with Cocteau's. *The New York Post* said: "It almost becomes a fantasy, then clatters into front-line realism, and gets nowhere, except that you can watch it. And Cocteau addicts will."

Thomas the Imposter *see* **Thomas l'imposteur**

Three Fugitives *see* **Les Fugitifs**

Three Makes a Pair *see* **Les Trois font la paire**

Three Men and a Cradle *see* **Trois Hommes et un couffin**

Three Rooms in Manhattan *see* **Trois Chambres à Manhattan**

A Time to Live and a Time to Die *see* **Le Feu follet**

358 *Tirez sur le pianiste (Shoot the Piano Player* or *Shoot the Pianist)*
1960 B&W   *Director* François Truffaut; *Producer* Braunberger Pierre; *Screenplay* François Truffaut and Marcel Moussy, based on David Goodis' novel *Down There*; *Photography* Raoul Coutard; *Music* Georges Delerue; *Songs* of Félix Leclerc and Boby Lapointe; *Set* Jacques Mély; *Sound* Jacques Gallois; *Editing* Cécile Decugis. Running time: 80 minutes.

Cast: Charles Aznavour, Albert Rémy, Jacques Aslanian, Richard Kanayan, Marie Dubois, Nicole Berger, Michèle Mercier, Daniel Boulanger, Claude Mansard, Serge Davri, Alex Joffé, Claude Heyman, Boby Lapointe, Catherine Lutz, Alice Sapritch, Laure Paillette.

A drama about a nightclub piano player, Charlie Koller played by Aznavour, who in real life is a well known, popular singer in France. Koller has abandoned his life as a concert pianist after a romantic disaster. But when his brother, Richard (Aslanian), needs his help, Charlie finds himself embroiled with gangsters and a new lover (Dubois). Rather than starting fresh, he is on the road to more serious trouble.

Truffaut was a great fan of Hitchcock and Hawks, and this film was in many ways his tribute to them. He said of the film: "The idea behind *Shoot the Piano Player* was to make a film without a subject, to express all I wanted to say about glory, success, downfall, failure, women and love by means of a detective story. It's a grab bag." That it is. Part crime, part love story, part slapstick, this film turned out to be a wonderful forum for Truffaut's trademark touches. The photography and dialogue add up to much more than the parts of the plot. This was his second feature, made after the great success of *The 400 Blows* and before *Jules and Jim*.

French and American critics generally admired the film. *The New York Herald Tribune* ranked *Shoot the Piano Player* "among the best examples of the new French picture making," referring to the early stirrings of the New Wave.

To Our Loves *see* **À nos amours**

359 *Toi, le venin (Nude in a White Car* or *Blonde in a White Car)* 1959
B&W *Director* Robert Hossein; *Producer* Jules Borkon, Champs-Elysées Productions, Filmaur; *Screenplay* Robert Hossein, based on Frédéric Dard's novel
C'est toi le venin; *Photography* Robert Hossein; *Music* André Gosselain; *Set* Jean
André; *Sound* Jacques Lebreton; *Costumes* Jacques Heim, Pierre Balmain;
Editing Gilbert Natot. Running time: 92 minutes.

Cast: Robert Hossein, Henri Crémieux, Marina Vlady, Odile Versois, Pascal
Mazzotti, Hélèna Manson, Henri Arius, Charles Blavette, Isola Blondie, Paul
Coppel, Lucien Callamand, Jean Combal, Bréols.

Victor (Hossein) is a young, unemployed man who is seduced by a beautiful
nude in a white car. When he follows her home, he finds that she lives with her
equally beautiful sister. One of the sisters is paralyzed; the other sister takes care
of her. At first Victor cannot figure out which one seduced him, but soon they are
both in love with him. After he pays attention to the paralyzed Eva (Vlady), the
able sister, Hélène (Versois), runs off. But the secrets continue.

Hossein, who wrote, directed and starred in this film, sent shock waves
through the New Wave with this sexual thriller. He was interested in exploring
strange, erotic situations, which he certainly created with this tale of a nymphomaniac's mistaken identity. He establishes a strange, sexy tone and the women are
lovely to behold. This film, in many ways, signals a direction that the New Wave
did not follow, but it did foretell the popular "porno period" that would obsess
French filmmaking in a decade.

Critics either hailed Hossein's experimentation and courage or were offended
by what they believed was cheap sensationalism. *The Saturday Review* dismissed
the film by saying, "Certainly, few pictures in recent years have been so deliberately
designed to shock and titillate."

Tomorrow Is My Turn *see* **Le Passage du Rhin**

360 *Les Tontons flingueurs (The Great Spy Chase)* 1963 B&W *Director* Georges Lautner; *Producer* Gaumont, Corona Filmproduktion, Ultra Films;
Screenplay Georges Lautner and Albert Simonin, based on the novel by Albert
Simonin; *Photography* Maurice Fellous; *Music* Michel Magne; *Set* Jean Mandaroux; *Sound* Antoine Archimbaud; *Editing* Michèle David. Running time: 92
minutes.

Cast: Lino Ventura, Bernard Blier, Francis Blanche, Sabine Sinfen, Claude
Rich, Jean Lefebvre, Jacques Dumesnil, Horst Franck, Venantino Venantini,
Robert Dalban, Dominique Davray, Claude Régnier, Mac Rooney, Henri Cogan,
Pierre Bertin, Georges Nogaroff, Philippe Castelli, Paul Mercey, Yves Arcanel,
Anne Marescot, Charles Lavialle, Jean-Michel Derot, Paul Meurisse.

A film noir parody about Fernand (Ventura), who makes a death-bed promise
to a friend to take care of his widow (Sinfen). He also has to deal with four
nefarious spies from various European countries, who are trying to get their hands
on important weaponry innovations. The spies try to seduce the widow, but in the
end Fernand keeps his promise.

This hilarious comedy is one of Lautner's best. He takes on film noir and
thriller fare and hams it up with great force. Madness and murder makes for light
satire and good entertainment, as the spies vie for the voluptuous rich widow's attentions. Ventura and Blier work their magic as a spy and priest.

The film was such a success in France that it inspired a number of sequels and remakes. *The New York Post* called it "a hip James Bond spoof," though the dubbed version lost a lot in translation.

Too Beautiful for You *see* **Trop belle pour toi**

361 *Touchez pas au Grisbi (Grisbi* **or** *Honor Among Thieves)* 1954 B&W   *Director* Jacques Becker; *Producer* Del Duca, Antanès; *Screenplay* Jacques Becker, Maurice Griffe and Albert Simonin, based on the novel by Albert Simonin; *Photography* Pierre Montazel; *Music* Jean Wiener; *Set* Jean d'Eaubonne; *Sound* Jacques Lebreton; *Editing* Marguerite Renoir. Running time: 94 minutes.

Cast: Jean Gabin, René Dary, Jeanne Moreau, Lino Ventura, Paul Frankeur, Paul Oettly, Dora Doll, Gaby Basset, Daniel Cauchy, Michel Jourdan, Marilyn Befferd, Della Scala, Flavia Solivani, Jean Riveyre, Vittorio Sanipoli, Angelo Dessy, Denise Clair, Paul Barge, Robert Le Fort, Dominique Davray, René Hell, Jean Daurand, Jean Clarieux, Alain Bouvette.

Max (Gabin) and Riton (Dary) are two gangsters who have managed a fantastic hold-up. Riton talks about the job with his girlfriend, who tells Angelo (Ventura), a member of another gang. Angelo then kidnaps Riton and demands the gold from Max to save him. The hand-off does not go smoothly, and both Riton and Angelo are killed.

A great film noir about loyalty and betrayal that perfectly inspired the cult of gangster films that arose in the 1950s. Becker said the characters interested him more than the social issues or the plot, but he created a film noir with three-dimensional gangsters, who have their own laws and customs just like the bourgeoisie. He established a style and tone that the slew of thriller imitations that followed could not replicate. It was the first of many roles Gabin would play as a crook, and the film launched his postwar career.

Grisbi was a great commercial success, which appealed to critics and the public alike. François Truffaut wrote: "*Grisbi* is, in my eyes, a sort of settling of accounts between two fat cats — but fancy cats." He admired its subtlety, grace and power. *The New York Times* called it "a brilliantly atmospheric underworld drama."

362 *Tout le monde il est beau, tout le monde il est gentil (Everybody He Is Nice, Everybody He Is Beautiful)* 1972 Color   *Director* Jean Yanne; *Producer* Ciné Qua Non; *Screenplay* Jean Yanne and Gérard Sire; *Photography* Jean Boffety; *Music* Michel Magne; *Set* Jacques Dugied; *Sound* Jean-Pierre Ruh; *Editing* Anne-Marie Cottret. Running time: 106 minutes.

Cast: Jean Yanne, Bernard Blier, Marina Vlady, Michel Serrault, Jacques François, Jacqueline Danno, Daniel Prévost, Roger Lumont, Jean-Marie Proslier, Paul Préboist, Jean-Roger Caussimon, Henri Vibert.

In the name of truth, justice and honesty, a lone radio-reporter (Yanne) takes the groundbreaking action of telling the truth on the air. He is first fired for his honesty, then rehired to run the station. He uses his sharp tongue and quick wit to skewer the world's biggest public phonies as well as jeopardize some of the station's accounts.

For his first film as director, as well as actor (he had already won an award at Cannes for his role in *We Will Not Grow Old Together*), Jean Yanne drew on his own experience working as a journalist for a radio station. With a spirited satirical tone, he attacked the hierarchy and established order of the media world as well as Christian evangelicals. The film announced a new auteur with a sharp, biting and funny tone.

Some critics found Yanne's humor too mean-spirited and vulgar. *Variety* called it "a jaunty, perky, anarchistic comedy." It was never released in the United States.

363 *Tout va bien* 1972 Color *Director* Jean-Luc Godard; *Producer* Godard, Empire Films, Vicco Films; *Screenplay* Jean-Luc Godard and Jean-Pierre Gorin; *Photography* Armand Marco; *Set* Jacques Dugied; *Sound* B. Ortion, A. Bonfanti; *Editing* Kenout Peltier. Running time: 96 minutes.

Cast: Jane Fonda, Yves Montand, Vittorio Cappriolan Pignol, Pierre Oudry, Eric Chartier, Yves Gabrielli, Elizabeth Chauvin, Huguette Miéville, Anne Wiazemski, Marcel Gassouk, Bugette, Castel Casti, Michel Marot.

An American journalist (Fonda) and her French husband (Montand), who was once an avant-garde film director but who now shoots commercials, go to a sausage factory. A strike starts while they are there, and they are trapped in a socialist worker frenzy.

Another cinematic political manifesto by Godard, but this one, thanks to a star-studded cast, made it into movie theaters, where most of his other films never did. The plot is not the point here, but everything behind it is, including the fact that his two big stars both have left-wing political pasts. It was an interesting attempt by Godard to successfully marry his political and artistic agenda with an awareness of the economics of the star system. His behind-the-scenes look at the mechanics of a strike, which were common occurrences in France at the time, is fascinating.

As was to be expected, *Tout va bien* stirred up heated debate. Godard fans fawned over it, while some others found the film too didactic and abstract. American critics generally disliked it. *The New York Times*, however, declared, "*Tout va bien* is a film of true political importance, whether you believe its politics or not."

Traffic *see* **Trafic**

364 *Trafic (Traffic)* 1971 Color *Director* Jacques Tati; *Producer* Robert Dorfmann, Corona, Gébé Films, Océania Films; *Screenplay* Jacques Tati; *Photography* Edouard Van den Endern and Marcel Weiss; *Music* Charles Dumont; *Set* Adrien de Rooy; *Sound* Edouard Pelster; *Editing* Maurice Laumain, Sophie Tatischeff. Running time: 105 minutes.

Cast: Jacques Tati, Honoré Bostel, Maria Kimberly, Marcel Favel, Tony Kneppers, François Maisongrosse, Mario Zannelli, Franco Ressel.

Another hilarious Monsieur Hulot (Tati) comedy. This time Hulot fancies himself an inventor. When the Amsterdam Auto Salon opens, he decides that he wants to exhibit his new camper. He drives it to Holland with mishaps and disasters at every turn. By the time he gets there, of course, the Salon has closed.

Tati's talent is getting good-humored laughs out of everyday life, and *Traffic* is full of them. In this film, his fifth, he satirizes modern car culture. As usual, his visual antics provide the cinematic pleasure, the dialogue and plot are virtually insignificant. Tati makes hilarious comments on people, the cars they drive, and how they drive. There is even a section on the phenomenon of people picking their noses while sitting in traffic.

A huge hit in France, *Traffic* received both raves and pans in the United States. *The New York Times* exclaimed: "Tati's concern genuinely is human nature, which promotes a kind of naturalism — better than humanism — that enlivens and relaxes and extends the brilliant discipline of this great and very beautiful film."

365 *Trans-Europ Express* 1967 B&W   *Director* Alain Robbe-Grillet; *Producer* Como Films, Urbain; *Screenplay* Alain Robbe-Grillet; *Photography* Willy Kurant; *Music* Verdi and arrangements by Michel Fano; *Sound* Raymond Saint Martin; *Editing* Robert Wade. Running time: 90 minutes.

Cast: Jean-Louis Trintignant, Marie-France Pisier, Alain Robbe-Grillet, Catherine Robbe-Grillet, Charles Millot, Christian Barbier, Daniel Emilfork, Nadine Verdier, Henri Lambert, Raoul Guylad, Virginie Vignon, Paul Louyet, Prima Symphony, Gérard Pelaprat, Clo Vanesco, Salkin, Ariane Sapriel, Samy Helfon, Rézy Norbert.

A film within a film about a producer, director and script-supervisor who take the Trans-Europ Express from Paris to Antwerp. A drug smuggler (Trintignant) is also on board the train, though he travels in another time; he also plays himself — an actor in a movie called *Trans-Europ Express* made by Robbe-Grillet.

As to be expected from the man who made a legend out of narrative dissonance, Robbe-Grillet's second film has a plot that defies easy explanation. Robbe-Grillet explained his chaotic plots by saying: "Why make something simple, when it can be complicated?" He achieved many of the film's great moments by improvising. He asked his actors to go as far as they could with their characters.

Like so many highly experimental films of the time, *Trans-Europ Express* had its defenders and detractors both at home and abroad. *The Daily News* called it "a clever French travesty on crime, eroticism, spies, violence and death . . . unique in conception and presentation."

366 *La Traversée de Paris (Pig Across Paris)* 1956 B&W   *Director* Claude Autant-Lara; *Producer* Franco London Films, Continental Produzione, Gaumont; *Screenplay* Jean Aurenche and Pierre Bost, based on the novel by Marcel Aymé; *Photography* Jacques Natteau and Gilbert Chain; *Music* René Cloërec; *Set* Max Douy; *Sound* René Forget; *Editing* Madeleine Gug. Running time: 82 minutes.

Cast: Jean Gabin, Bourvil, Louis de Funès, Jeannette Batti, Robert Arnoux, Myno Burney, Monette Dinay, Georgette Anys, Jean Dunot, Anouk Ferjac, Albert Michel, Bernard Lajarrige, Harald Wolf, Laurence Badie, Jacques Marin, Claude Vernier, Germaine Delbat, Hans Werner, Hubert Noël, Hubert de Lapparent, Clément Harari, Maryse Paillet, Paul Barge, René Hell, Jean Vinci, Hugues Wanner, Georges Bever, Béatrice Arnac, Albert-Michel, Hubert Noël, Louis Viret, Clément Harrari, Harald Wolf, Hans Werner, René Brun, Yvonne Claudic, Anne Carrère, Martine Alexis, Yvette Cuvelier, Michèle Nadal

Martin (Bourvil), an unemployed taxi driver, works in the black market in Paris during the Occupation. A butcher hires him to transport a pig stuffed in four suitcases across the city. He hires a helper, Grandgil (Gabin), whom he mistakes for an unemployed house painter. They get arrested by a German patrol. Grandgil, who

La Traversée de Paris (Pig Across Paris), 1956; directed by Claude Autant-Lara.

is actually a wealthy artist, is set free, while Martin is deported. They meet on the platform of a train station years later, and Martin is still transporting, this time somebody else's luggage.

One of the best films ever made about the Occupation, this certainly ranks as one of Autant-Lara's finest. With a haunting grace and chilling confidence, he captures the night-time dealings of Occupied Paris. In dark corners and whispered tones, he creates the war-time world of the rulers and the ruled, the exploiters and the exploited, and yet it is not that simple. People are not what they seem. They are victims of circumstance and blessed by fate. Autant-Lara himself called Bourvil, Gabin and De Funès "an unbeatable trio." But he wished that he had changed the ending and had had Martin shot by Grandgil.

Even François Truffaut, who once complained that literary Autant-Lara was like a butcher who insisted on trying to make lace, loved *Pig Across Paris*. It was the co-winner of the French Critics' Prix Méliès and was nominated for the Oscar for Best Foreign Film in 1957.

367 *37.2 degrés le matin (Betty Blue)*   1986 Color   *Director* Jean-Jacques Beineix; *Producer* Beinex, Constellation, Cargo Film; *Screenplay* Jean-Jacques Beinex, based on the novel by Philippe Djian; *Photography* Jean-François Robin; *Music* Gabriel Yared; *Set* Carlos Conti; *Sound* Pierre Befve; *Editing* Monique Prim. Running time: 115 minutes.

Cast: Béatrice Dalle, Jean-Hughes Anglade, Consuelo de Haviland, Gérard Darmon, Clémintine Célarié, Claude Confortès, Philippe Laudenbach, Vincent Lindon, Raoul Billerey, Claude Aufaure, André Julien, Nathalie Dalyan, Louis Bellanti, Bernard Robin, Nicolas Jalowyj, Dominique Besnehard.

A tragic love story about Zorg (Anglade) and Betty (Dalle), who from the moment they meet are passionately in love. When she discovers the manuscripts that he has written, she becomes obsessed not only with him, but with his dream to be a writer. Her obsessions lead to madness, and eventually Zorg does have his novel published, but Betty ends up locked away in a mental home.

This love story is of an absolutely modern sensibility, but with the tragic proportions of centuries-old dramas. The aesthetic is the same the "super-cool" style Beineix mastered in his hit movie *Diva*. Betty and Zorg have been called examples of the lost youth of the 1980s: intensely passionate with no focus, they end up self-destructing. Or they can be seen as victims of the wild vicissitudes of art. Even for those who find the love story too melodramatic, Beineix's film is a visual and musical pleasure, making the tragic end that much harder to bear.

Some critics claimed that it is all style and no substance. Andrew Sarris believed it was "the most explicitly erotic" movie ever nominated for an Oscar for Best Foreign Film and "not for every taste."

368 *36 fillette*   1988 Color   *Director* Catherine Breillat; *Producer* CB Films, CFC Films; *Screenplay* Catherine Breillat; *Photography* Laurent Dailland; *Music* Maxime Schmitt; *Set* Olivier Paultre; *Sound* Jean Minondo; *Editing* Yann Dedet. Running time: 92 minutes.

Cast: Delphine Zentout, Etienne Chicot, Jean-Pierre Léaud, Jean-François Stévenin, Olivier Parnière, Berta Dominguez D., Diane Bellego, Adrienne Bonnet.

The story of an adolescent girl exploring the boundaries of her new-found sexuality. On vacation with her parents she meets an older man (Chicot), who takes her up to his hotel room. She teases him, but refuses to sleep with him. A hostile passion grows between them.

A shocking film that explores how teenage anguish can be turned into sexual politics. This is a modern Lolita film that plumbs the teenage psyche and finds adolescent confusion can lead to angst and odd behavior. Breillat wrote the novel and then its screenplay adaptation. She wanted to take an unromantic look at sexual initiation, and she does. There is little passion and lots of fumbling, which when it occurs between an awkward heavy teenager and a middle-aged man can be difficult to watch.

Some critics found the film offensive, others compared it to the art of *Last Tango in Paris*. *The Wall Street Journal* called it "an artful heavy breather about ... a rude little Lolita."

The Trial of Joan of Arc *see* **Le Procès de Jeanne d'Arc**

369 *Les Tricheurs (The Cheaters)*   1958 B&W   *Director* Marcel Carné; *Producer* Silver Films, Cinétel, Corona; *Screenplay* Marcel Carné and Jacques Sigurd; *Photography* Claude Renoir; *Music* Classic Jazz; *Set* Paul Bertrand; *Sound* Antoine Archimbaud; *Costumes* Mayo, Christian Dior, Virginie, Jacques Heim; *Editing* Albert Jurgenson. Running time: 120 minutes.

Cast: Jacques Charrier, Laurent Terzieff, Pascale Petit, Andréa Parisy, Dany Saval, Roland Lesaffre, Roland Armontel, Jean-Paul Belmondo, Denise Vernac, Jacques Portet, Gabrielle Fontan, Pierre Brice, Alfonso Mathis, Claire Olivier, Claude Giraud, Gérard Darrieu, Jacques Marin, Dominique Page, Michel Nastorg, Sandrine, Jean-François Poron, Suzanne Courtal, Jacques Chabassol, France Asselin, Francis Nani, Michèle Bardollet, Guy Bedos, Françoise Vatel, Jacques Berger, Nicole Dubois, Joël Schmidt, Monique Barbilla, René Sartoris, Anne-Marie Coffinet, Pierre Flourens, Gisèle Gallois, Jean Sylvère, Ariele Coignet, Maurice Derville, Andrée Servilange, Gérard Bayle, Sophie Poncin, Christian Azzopardi, Françoise Delpick, Jacques Perrin, Jocelyne Darche, Alan Scott, Brigitte Barbier, Alain Saury, Françoise Belin, Sergio Gobbi, Alain Janet.

A well brought up bourgeois young man, Bob (Charrier), meets Alain (Terzieff), a charming non-conformist. Through Alain and his friends, Bob meets Mic (Petit) and falls in love. The two try to deny their love, because, after all, love is merely a bourgeois custom. Mic even becomes the lover of Alain. Their game of indifference gets out of control and leads to a tragic end.

From the director of *Children of Paradise*, this is a sweet, sad movie that may not be as epic as Carné's masterpiece, but is very interesting, nonetheless. Carné returned to the themes of love and destiny, but as they plagued the youth of the 1950s on the Left Bank of Paris. He captured a postwar spirit of defiance very well, and he took it to its most extreme and destructive conclusion. As usual, the film is beautifully constructed and photographed, even if the dialogue is a bit stiff. Jean-Paul Belmondo had his very first small role in this film.

The Cheaters was an enormous success. *The New Yorker* called it "an impressionist's view of a crowd of wild young Parisians, this side and that side of twenty, who are apparently trying to lead an American existence." The film won the Grand Prix du Cinéma Français in 1958.

370 *Tristana*   1970 Color   *Director* Luis Buñuel; *Producer* Italia Film, Epoca Film, Selenia Cinematografica, Les Films Corona; *Screenplay* Luis Buñuel, Julio Alejandro, based on the novel by Benito Perez Galdos; *Photography* José Aguayo; *Set* Enrique Alarcon; *Sound* José Nogueira, Dino Fronzetti; *Costumes* Rosa Garcia; *Editing* Pedro del Rey. Running time: 100 minutes.

Cast: Catherine Deneuve, Fernando Rey, Franco Nero, Lola Gaos, Jesus Fernandez, Antoinio Casas, Sergio Mendizabal, José Caval, Mary Paz Pondal, Candida Losada, Vicente Soler, Fernando Cabrian, Juan José Menendez, Antonio Ferrandis, José Maria Caffarel, Joaquim Pamplona, José Blanch, Alfredo Santa Cruz, Luis Aller, Luis Rico, Saturno Cerra, Jesus Combarro, Vincente Roca, Ximenez Carrillo, Adriano Dominguez, José Riesgo, Rosa Gorostegui, Antonio Cintado, Pilar Vela, Lorenzo Rodriguez.

The story of a beautiful young woman, Tristana (Deneuve), who is left in the kind care of nobleman Don Lope (Rey). Though Don Lope vows to protect her, he ends up seducing her. When she falls in love with the artist Horacio (Nero), Tristana leaves Don Lope, only to return and accept his marriage proposal after she loses a leg to cancer.

The avant-garde master made this film at age 70 and showed the world that age can bring with it an even better twisted sense of humor. Buñuel's seemingly simple story is really a much larger political comment on compromise and hypocrisy in general, and the sad state of Spain in the 1970s in particular. He traces the transformation of Tristana from innocent schoolgirl to full-figured femme fatale. Deneuve and Rey get to use their talents to the broadest possible range.

Tristana was hailed by critics as one of Buñuel's finest moments. *Time* called it "a coda of inexhaustible power and sophistication."

371 *Trois Chambres à Manhattan (Three Rooms in Manhattan)* 1965 B&W *Director* Marcel Carné; *Producer* Montaigne; *Screenplay* Marcel Carné and Jacques Sigurd, based on the novel by Georges Simenon; *Photography* Eugen Schüfftan; *Music* Mal Waldrow; *Set* Léon Barsacq; *Sound* Jacques Lebreton; *Editing* Henri Rust. Running time: 112 minutes.

Cast: Annie Giradot, Maurice Ronet, Gabriele Ferzetti, Roland Lesaffre, Geneviève Page, Otto-Edouard Hasse, Margaret Nolan, Virginaa Vec, Robert Hoffman, June Elliott, Agnès Petit, Art Simmons, Leroy Haynes, Jean-François Rémi.

François (Ronet) meets Kay (Giradot) in a bar one night. She is depressed and has been drinking. She agrees to go home with him to a hotel room in Manhattan, where he takes pity on her and she professes her undying love. When she has to travel to Mexico, François gets involved with June (Nolan). Upon her return, François confesses everything to Kay, who is devastated and vows to leave him. He swears his undying love and a new chapter begins for them.

This offbeat love story about two lost souls in the modern metropolis who finally manage to connect was not entirely new terrain for Carné. His old-fashioned sensibility brings an interesting touch. Annie Giradot is superb as the desperate divorcée. In many ways, this film evoked a spirit of lonely hearts lost in the big city that is timeless.

Three Rooms in Manhattan did well in France, but was never released in the United States. The film won the Volpi Cup at the Venice Biennal, and Annie Giradot won the Grand Prize for Best Actress.

372 *Les Trois font la paire (Three Makes a Pair)* 1957 B&W *Director* Sacha Guitry; *Producer* CLM, Gaumont; *Screenplay* Sacha Guitry; *Photography* Philippe Agostini; *Music* Hubert Rostaing; *Set* Raymond Gabutti; *Sound* Jean Bertrand; *Editing* Paulette Robert. Running time: 85 minutes.

Cast: Michel Simon, Darry Cowl, Philippe Nicaud, Sophie Desmarets, Clément Duhour, Jean Rigaux, Robert Dalban, Julien Carette, Christian Méry, Jane Marken, Pauline Carton, André Chanu, Gilbert Boka, Jacques Ary.

Jojo (Nicaud) wants to join a gang, but in order to do so he must murder someone. He kills an actor and the murder is filmed. The police arrest a pair of twins (Nicaud), both of whom confess to the murder to protect the other twin. Jojo, who looks exactly like them, meanwhile goes free. The gangsters decide to take care of Jojo themselves and stage his suicide.

This is the last film by Guitry, the master of filmed theater. He once again takes on crime and the law, which seemed the obsession of his later years. This is a great example of the way in which Guitry could look at crime and justice in a cynical fashion. Simon is fantastic as the commissioner. As always, Guitry's wit and eloquence make for great dialogue and scenes.

Most critics applauded the film and reveled in the humor Guitry managed to bring to the crime genre. A few, however, said it proved that he had used up all of his talents.

373 *Trois Hommes et un couffin (Three Men and a Cradle)* 1985 Color   *Director* Coline Serreau; *Producer* Flash Films, Soprofilms, TF1 Films Productions; *Screenplay* Coline Serreau; *Photography* Jean-Yves Escoffier; *Set* Yvan Maussion; *Sound* Daniele Ollivier; *Editing* Catherine Renault. Running time: 100 minutes.

Cast: André Dussollier, Roland Giraud, Michel Boujenah, Philippine Leroy-Beaulieu, Dominique Lavanant, Marthe Villalonga, Annick Alane, Josine Comellas, Gabriel Jabour, Xavier Maly, Christian Bouillette, Jacques Poitrenaud, François Domange, Cécile Vassort, Gwendoline Mourlet, Jennifer Moret, Herma Vos, Valentine Monnier.

Three bachelors, Pierre (Giraud), Jacques (Dussollier) and Michel (Boujenah), happily share an apartment, until the day that a baby arrives from one of Jacques' old girlfriends. The men have to care for her until the mother returns in six months. The baby turns their lives and their home upside down with diapers and bottles, but she also gives them a needed new perspective on life.

With this remarkably successful film, Serreau discovered her magic recipe for filmmaking. Serreau was a stage actress and feminist author before she turned her talents to filmmaking. What she managed to combine in *Three Men and a Cradle* was a funny scenario and a socially aware perspective; the two made for popular appeal and influential art. In this, her first hit, she played on gender stereotypes and role reversal. Her bachelors were bumbling and charming men a decade before Mr. Mom became a talk-show regular. She brought a post–1968 awareness into the mainstream with warmth and wit that few others have been able to achieve, despite many poor imitations.

Three Men and a Cradle was not only France's biggest box-office hit of the year, but of the entire decade. American critics did not like it at all and were baffled by its supposed charm. It seemed further proof of the old Jerry Lewis enigma. It won the César for Best Picture, Best Screenplay and Best Supporting Actor in 1985. In 1987, a very popular, less interesting remake, *Three Men and a Baby*, was made in the United States.

374 *Trop belle pour toi (Too Beautiful for You)* 1989 Color   *Director* Bertrand Blier; *Producer* Ciné Valse, DD Productions, Orly Films, Sédif, TF1 Films Productions; *Screenplay* Bertrand Blier; *Photography* Philippe Rousselot; *Music* Franz Schubert; *Set* Théobald Meurisse; *Sound* Louis Gimel, Paul Bertault; *Editing* Claudine Merlin. Running time: 91 minutes.

Cast: Gérard Depardieu, Carole Bouquet, Josiane Balasko, Roland Blanche, François Cluzet, Didier Bénureau, Philippe Loffredo, Sylvie Orcier, Myriam Boyer, Flavien Lebarbe, Juana Marquès, Denise Chalem, Jean-Louis Cordina, Stéphane Auberghen, Philippe Faure, Jean-Paul Farré, Richard Martin, Sylvie Simon.

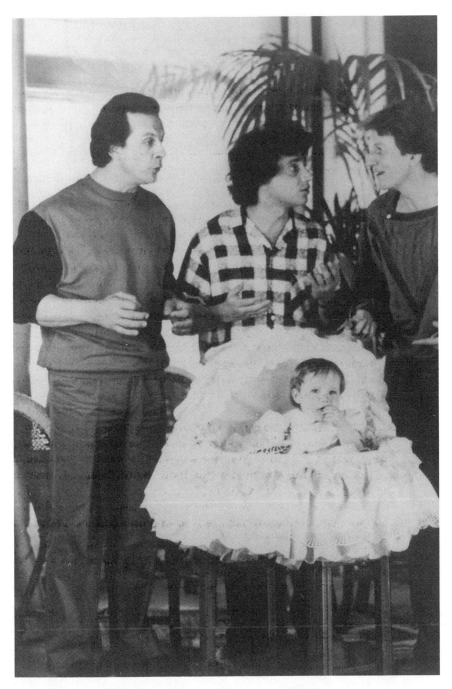

Trois Hommes et un couffin (Three Men and a Cradle), **1985; directed by Coline Serreau.**

The story of a businessman (Depardieu), who is married to an unusually beautiful woman (Bouquet), but falls passionately in love with his very plain secretary (Balasko). Despite his wife's efforts to save their marriage, he leaves her for his secretary, but then returns to her. Four years after his affair, he bumps into his secretary again, who is now married, and his wife decides to leave him.

In his inimitably subversive style, Blier has taken the stereotypical adultery tale and flipped it around to make a wonderful comedy-cum–social satire. Rather than having the husband run off with the pretty young thing, he falls for the dumpy frump with personality. Bouquet and Depardieu are wonderful as the picture perfect couple without passion. The editing and photography keeps the intrigue high.

The film was a big success in France and did quite well in the United States. *Variety* said: "This witty, cleverly structured film should have audiences chuckling wherever quality films are screened." The film won the Special Jury Prize at Cannes and the César for Best Film in 1989. It was also chosen to open the 27th New York Film Festival.

375 *Le Trou (The Night Watch* or *The Hole)* 1960 B&W *Director* Jacques Becker; *Producer* Play Art, Filmsonor, Titanus; *Screenplay* Jacques Becker, José Giovanni and Jean Aurel, based on the novel by José Giovanni; *Photography* Ghislain Cloquet; *Music* Jean Wiener; *Set* Rino Mondellini; *Sound* Pierre Calvet; *Editing* Marguerite Renoir and Geneviève Vaury. Running time: 83 minutes.

Cast: Marc Michel, Michel Constantin, Raymond Meunier, Philippe Leroy, Jean Kéraudy, Eddy Rasimi, Jean-Paul Coquelin, Catherine Spaak, André Bervil, Philippe Bancel, Dominique Zardi, Paul Préboist, Marcel Rouzé, Duriue, Paul Pavel, Philippe Dumat, Raymond Bour, Lucien Camiret.

Jo (Constantin), Roland (Kéraudy), Manu (Leroy) and Monseigneur (Meunier) are about to escape from prison when their cell gets a new prisoner. Claude Gaspard (Michel) is accused of trying to kill his wife. He threatens to jeopardize their escape, so they let him in on the jail break. Elaborate preparations are completed and the day that their hole to the sewers is finished, Claude is informed his wife has dropped the charges against him, an occurrence that has consequences for everyone.

Many believe this superb film was Becker's best. It feels remarkably like a documentary, with non-professional actors and a detailed account of the escape preparations. Becker set out to make a film about suspicion. He described it as "*The Three Musketeers* with mistrust." His characters' suspicions about each other turn out to be the wonderful source of suspense that drives the movie. *Night Watch* was Becker's last film; in fact, he died while finishing the dubbing. It stands as a great testament to France's "most reflective" filmmaker.

Night Watch came out in France the same week as *Breathless* and has since been hailed as the bridge between the quality films of the postwar era and the New Wave of the 1960s. It was the co-winner of the French Critics' Prix Méliès in 1960.

The Truck *see* **Le Camion**

The Truth *see* **La Vérité**

The Truth About Bébé Donge *see* La Vérité sur Bébé Donge

The Umbrellas of Cherbourg *see* Les Parapluies de Cherbourg

Under Satan's Sun *see* Sous le soleil de satan

Une si jolie petite plage *see under* Si

Une vie *see under* Vie

The Unfaithful Wife *see* La Femme infidèle

376 *Uranus* 1990 Color *Director* Claude Berri; *Producer* Renn Productions, Films A2, DD Productions; *Screenplay* Claude Berri and Arlette Langmann, based on the novel by Marcel Aymé; *Photography* Renato Berta; *Music* Jean-Claude Petit and W.A. Mozart; *Set* Bernard Vezat; *Sound* Louis Gimel; *Costumes* Caroline de Vivaise; *Editing* Heré de Luze. Running time: 100 minutes
   Cast: Philippe Noiret, Gérard Depardieu, Michel Blanc, Jean-Pierre Marielle, Michel Galabru, Gérard Desarthe, Fabrice Luchini, Daniel Prévost, Florence Darel, Danièle Lebrun, Myriam Boyer, Josiane Lévèque, Dominique Bluzet, Yves Afonso, Ticky Holgado, Hervé Rey, Vincent Grass, Alain Stern, André Chaumeau, Bernard Ballet, Paul Doumer, Gérard Bole de Chaumont, Partice Melennec.
   A few weeks after the end of World War II, a fugitive who helped the Nazis is hiding out from the authorities. Some of the villagers would turn him in if they knew where he was. Others help him hide. Their motivations have just as much to do with revenge and guilt as moral fortitude.
   This political drama is a fascinating look at a very real historical dilemma, as well as being one of Berri's characteristically beautiful films. Berri said he was thinking more about the political turmoil that followed the fall of Communism in Eastern Europe than of postwar France. In either case, he was concerned with people's behavior during extreme times. The cast is superb.
   The film was a great success in France, where the subject of French citizens' behavior during the war is a subject of eternal interest. American critics were less impressed. Though they found the film beautiful, Berri's moral message did not wash with them. *The Village Voice* said, "Witch-hunting is a fascinating subject, but that does not save *Uranus* from being static and histrionic."

377 *Les Vacances de Monsieur Hulot (Mr. Hulot's Holiday)* 1953 B&W *Director* Jacques Tati; *Producer* Fred Orain, Cady Films, Discinia; *Screenplay* Jacques Tati and Henri Marquet with Pierre Aubert and Jacques Lagrange; *Photography* Jean Mousselle and Jacques Mercanton; *Music* Alain Romans; *Set* Henri Schmitt, Briancourt; *Editing* Jacques Grassi, Suzanne Baron, Charles Bretoneiche. Running time: 86 minutes.
   Cast: Jacques Tati, Louis Perrault, Nathalie Pascaud, Michèle Rolla, Lucien Frégis, Raymond Carl, Valentine Camax, Marguerite Gérard, René Lacourt, André Dubois, Suzy Willy, Michèle Brabo, Georges Adlin, Francomme, Jean-Pierre Zola.

Les Vacances de Monsieur Hulot (Mr. Hulot's Holiday), **1953; directed by Jacques Tati.**

The bumbling Monsieur Hulot (Tati) sets off for a seaside holiday in his dilapidated car and a series of hilarious mishaps follow. To the horror of most of the other vacationers at the hotel and to the great amusement of the audience, Hulot cannot take a step without causing a small disaster.

This portrait of France in the 1950s is one of Tati (France's Chaplin) best and most adored works. The summer resort world of the era was rife with ancient customs and rigid social hierarchies. While Hulot tries to become part of this closed little world, he is hysterically funny. Tati was France's first great comic talent to emerge after World War II; he has been called this century's "everyman," who tries to fit into the modern world and its routines, but cannot. In the vacation mentality of a resort town, where everyone works to have a good time, Hulot is the only spontaneous creature in this very carefully planned film. Tati spent over a year at the tiny resort town of St.-Marc-sur Mer filming the movie. His wide-angle shots allow the audience to choose what to look at, which makes multiple viewings of his films all the more fun, as more and more details are noticed. Most of the cast were residents and visitors to the town. As with all of Tati's film, the strength of this, his second feature, is in its gags. The film is in fact so physical, the dialogue is almost unnecessary, which may be one reason the movie was an even bigger success in America than in France. The year it was released, it was the biggest grossing French film in the United States. The sound effects are wonderful. When the film was finished, some of the its backers doubted the movie would be a success, but as with *Jour de fête*, the audience's response at the preview allayed their fears. The movie really took off when there was a national strike (no train service) in France the summer of its release, so that Parisians who could not go on holiday went to the movies.

Janet Flanner reported in *The New Yorker* that Tati was "the man who during the strikes generously showed French vacations as something Parisians should be glad they had to miss." André Bazin called Hulot "a scatterbrained angel." In 1953 the film won the International Critics' Prize at Cannes and the Prix Louis Delluc. It might have won the Oscar for Best Foreign Film if the prize had existed then.

Vagabond *see* **Sans toit ni loi**

378 *Les Valseuses (Going Places)* 1974 Color *Director* Bertrand Blier; *Producer* Paul Claudon; *Screenplay* Bertrand Blier and Philippe Dumarçay, based on the novel by Bertrand Blier; *Photography* Bruno Nuytten; *Music* Stéphane Grappelli; *Set* Jean-Jacques Caziot; *Sound* Dominique Damasso; *Editing* Kenout Peltier. Running time: 117 minutes.

Cast: Jeanne Moreau, Gérard Depardieu, Patrick Dewaere, Miou-Miou, Isabelle Huppert, Brigitte Fossey, Michel Peyrelon, Jacques Chailleux, Christine Muller, Christian Alers, Dominique Davray, Jacques Rispal, Marco Perrin, Gérard Boucaron, Michel Pilorge.

The adventures of two thugs, Jean-Claude (Depardieu) and Pierrot (Dewaere), who first meet up with a sweet young woman, Marie-Ange (Miou-Miou), and later with an older woman, Jeanne (Moreau), who has just been released from prison. After the four spend a night of passion together, Jeanne kills herself. Jean-Claude and Pierrot have to run not only from the police, but from Jeanne's son, who also thinks that they killed Jeanne.

An erotic farce that sent a shocking jolt through the serenity of the French film world and was compared to Henry Miller's *Tropic of Cancer* for the passionate feelings it incited. Not only did it dare to celebrate the adventures of two grotesque, vulgar bums, but it portrayed them sympathetically. Jeanne Moreau's performance is glorious as usual, but more importantly, this film was the launching pad for three great new French actors: Depardieu, Dewaere and Miou-Miou, whom Blier discovered in a café theater.

Critics either thought it was great and funny or they found it infuriating. Likewise the public either laughed or took offense. The film raised cries of horror in the United States, because some women found the brutish behavior of Depardieu and Dewaere revolting and insulting.

379 *Van Gogh* 1991 Color *Director* Maurice Pialat; *Producer Screenplay* Maurice Pialat; *Photography* Emmanuel Machuel, Gilles Henri, Jacques Loiseleux; *Set* Philippe Pallut, Katia Vischkof; *Sound* Jean-Pierre Duret; *Costumes* Edith Vesperini; *Editing* Yann Dedet, Nathalie Hubert. Running time: 155 minutes.

Cast: Jacques Dutronc, Alexandra London, Gérard Sety, Bernard Le Coq, Corinne Bourdon, Elsa Zylberstein, Leslie Azzoulai, Jacques Vidal, Lisa Lametrie, Chantal Barbarit, Claudine Ducret.

The last 67 days of the great artist's life. Van Gogh (Dutronc) meets a collector, Doctor Gachet (Sety), and becomes the lover of his daughter, Marguerite (London). He argues with his brother, Théo (Le Coq), and his relationship with Marguerite has problems, including those posed by her father's objections. Van Gogh shoots himself in the stomach, and Théo and he are reconciled on his deathbed.

Pialat, who was a painter before he became a filmmaker, has done a great deal to challenge the established image of Van Gogh as the mad, one-eared artist. Pialat prefers to focus on the work and relationships of Van Gogh rather than on his most colorful moments of hysteria, which now seem to signify the behavior of a manic depressive. Van Gogh has been the subject of many movies, including Vincente Minelli's celebrated *Lust for Life* and Robert Altman's *Vincent and Theo*. Jacques Dutronc, a.k.a. "the Bob Dylan of Paris," plays Vincent very well.

French critics applauded Pialat's successful attempt to demystify the great artist. Others vociferously criticized him for making up an affair between Van Gogh and Marguerite, which never occured, just to flesh out his personality. *The New York Times* raved, "Maurice Pialat's dryly witty, revisionist film that liberates the artist from his ear-slashing, mad-genius image."

The Vanishing Corporal *see* **Le Caporal épinglé**

Le Vent souffle où il veut *see* **Un Condamné à mort s'est échappé**

380 *La Vérité (The Truth)* 1960 B&W   *Director* Henri-Georges Clouzot; *Producer* Han Productions; *Screenplay* Henri-Georges Clouzot, Jérôme Geronimi, Simone Drieu, Vera Clouzot and Michèle Perrein; *Photography* Armand Thirard; *Music* Jean André; *Set* Jean André; *Sound* William-Robert Sivel; *Editing* Albert Jurgenson. Running time: 124 minutes.

Cast: Brigitte Bardot, Samy Frey, Marie-José Nat, Charles Vanel, Jacqueline Porel, Paul Meurisse, Louis Seigner, Fernand Ledoux, André Oumansky, Suzy Willy, Barbara Sohmer, Jacques Perrin, Jean-Lou Reynald, Claude Berri, Louis Arbessier, René Blancard, Jacques Hilling, Paul Bonifas, Colette Castel, Marcel Cuvelier, Arlette Gleize, Christain Lude, Guy Tréjan, Hubert de Lapparent, Marcel Delaître, Charles Bouillard, Albert-Michel, Jean Houbé, Simone Berthier, Germaine Delbat, Jackie Rollin, Marcle Loche, Colette Régis, Betty Beckers, Francis Lemonnier, Claudine Berg, Jenny Doria, Jean Roucher, Yvonne Dany, Louis Saintève, Georgette Peyron.

Dominique Marceau (Bardot), a beautiful young woman, is accused of killing her lover, Gilbert (Frey). Gilbert had been her sister's boyfriend when Dominique seduced him for fun. But when he goes back to her sweet, more stable sister Annie (Nat) and asks her to marry him, Dominique realizes that she has fallen in love with him. Desperate without him, Dominique kills Gilbert, but as her trial grows nastier and nastier, with the opposing lawyers making her out to be a monster or a victim, the truth slips further away. Dominique slits her wrists in prison.

This is one of Clouzot's masterpieces. He explored the new amorality of youth that intrigued other filmmakers of the time as well, but Clouzot brought his own cold, objective angle to it. He reveals Dominique with all her flaws and yet seems to forgive her crime, because it was one of passion. Brigitte Bardot found one of her finest roles in this film; she is defiant and sexy. It was also the film that launched Samy Frey.

Critics hailed Bardot's performance as her best and Clouzot's editing as beyond compare. *The New York Post* raved: "This film is one of the rarities, a serious one which is also entertaining and sensational." The film won the Grand Prix du Cinéma Français and was nominated for the Oscar for Best Foreign Film in 1960.

381 *La Vérité sur Bébé Donge (The Truth About Bébé Donge)* 1952
B&W *Director* Henri Decoin; *Producer* UGC; *Screenplay* Maurice Aubergé, based
on the novel by Georges Simenon; *Photography* Léonce-Henri Burel; *Music* Jean-
Jacques Grunenwald; *Set* Jean Douarinou; *Sound* Constantin Evangélou;
Costumes Pierre Balmain; *Editing* Annick Millet. Running time: 104 minutes.

Cast: Danielle Darrieux, Jean Gabin, Daniel Lecourtois, Gabrielle Dorziat,
Claude Génia, Jacques Castelot, Marcel André, Jean-Marc Tennberg, Maurice
Bénard, Juliette Faber, Meg Lemonnier, Paul Bonifas, Madeleine Lambert, Noël
Darzal, Gaby Bruyère, Henri Houry, Alinda Kristensen, André Darnay, Yvonne
Claudie, Jacqueline Porel, Blanche Denège, Emma Lyonnel.

Elisabeth d'Onnenville (Darrieux), nicknamed Bébé (Baby), is married to
François Donge (Gabin), a wealthy businessman. Disappointed in her marriage,
Bébé poisons her husband. As François lies dying, he apologizes to Bébé for his
past cruelties, reminisces with her about their good times and forgives her for killing him. She gives herself up to the police.

This is Decoin's postwar masterpiece and one of the best French film noirs.
Decoin was interested in the rebellion of the moment. Bébé killed her husband
because she had stopped loving him and was trapped by the world in which they
lived. Gabin and Darrieux are both wonderful. The dialogue is very well-written.

French critics admired Decoin's intelligent analysis of a marriage gone awry.
The film was never distributed in the United States.

A Very Curious Girl *see* **La Fiancée du pirate**

382 *La Veuve Couderc (The Widow Couderc or The Widow)* 1971
Color *Director* Pierre Granier-Deferre; *Producer* Lira Films, Cinétel; *Screenplay*
Pierre Granier-Deferre and Pascal Jardin, based on the novel by Georges Simenon;
Photography Walter Wottitz; *Music* Philippe Sarde; *Set* Jacques Saulnier; *Sound*
Jean Babussière; *Editing* Jean Ravel. Running time: 90 minutes.

Cast: Simone Signoret, Alain Delon, Jean Tissier, Ottavia Piccolo, Bobby Lapointe, Monique Chaumette and the inhabitants of Cheuge.

Jean (Delon) is a convict, hiding out in the French countryside during the
1930s. He stays at the farm of the widow Couderc (Signoret) and becomes her
lover. He also becomes involved with the 16-year-old girl from the neighboring
farm. The widow's family hates Jean and tells his whereabout to the police. When
the house is surrounded, Jean and the widow are killed as he tries to escape.

Granier-Deferre is a master at adapting Simenon novels for big stars and this
is one of his greatest successes. Interested in exploring how people will react when
they are cornered by circumstances, Granier-Deferre created a beautiful film on
human claustrophobia. Set before World War II in a rural world, with the rumblings of fascism not totally absent, the atmosphere and photography give great
depth to this psychological drama. Delon and Signoret are superb.

A great success in France, *The Widow Couderc* did fairly well in the United
States. Critics either loved it or hated it. *The Daily News* said that "the plot could
not be more shoddy." *After Dark* declared it a "pastoral poem of the inevitabilities
of people." The film won the Grand Prix du Cinéma Français in 1971.

383 *La Victoire en chantant (Black and White in Color or Black Victory)* 1976 Color *Director* Jean-Jacques Annaud; *Producer* Reggane Films, SFP,

F.R.#, Smart Film Productions, SIC; *Screenplay* Jean-Jacques Annaud and Georges Conchon; *Photography* Claude Agostini; *Music* Pierre Bachelet; *Set* Max Douy and Henri Sonois; *Editing* Françoise Bonnot. Running time: 90 minutes.

Cast: Jean Carmet, Jacques Dufilho, Catherine Rouvel, Jacques Spiesser, Dora Doll, Maurice Barrier, Claude Legros, Jacques Monnet, Peter Berling, Marius Beugre Boignan, Baye Macoumba Diop, Aboutbaker Taoure, Dieter Schidor, Marc Zuber, Klaus Huebel, Mamadou Coulibaly, Memel Atchori, Jean-Françoise Eyou N'Guessan, Natou Koly, Tanoh Kouao.

At the beginning of World War I, two remote trading posts on the west coast of Africa, one French and one German, are carried away by their chauvinistic sentiments and after years of living together peacefully, they wage war when they finally learn their home countries are fighting. The French camp launches a pathetic attack on the German troops and a German, a former geographer (Spiesser), then assumes leadership of the French settlement, a position that transforms him from a peaceful idealist into a violent militarist.

Jean-Jacques Annaud's first feature film is a wonderful black comedy that condemns racism, colonialism, imperialism, militarism and blind jingoism. "I wanted to make a more or less comic film on a rather serious subject, a film which would be in part an anthology of stupidity and also a derisory and ironical comment on war," said Annaud. The characters are hilarious in their exaggeration. The film was not a success when it first opened in France, but when it won the Oscar, it was rereleased at home under the French translation of the American title and it did extremely well.

Critics on both sides of the Atlantic found the promise of great talent in this film. They were, of course, proven right. Upon its release, *Variety* called it "a return to a classical, probing, irreverent comedy of man's ways." It won the Oscar for Best Foreign Film in 1976.

384 *Une Vie (The End of Desire* or *One Life)* 1957 Color *Director* Alexandre Astruc; *Producer* Agnès Delahaie, Corona; *Screenplay* Alexandre Astruc, based on the novel by Guy de Maupassant; *Dialogue* Roland Laudenbach; *Photography* Claude Renoir; *Music* Roman Vlad; *Set* Paul Bertrand; *Sound* Antoine Archimbaud; *Costumes* Lucilla, Mayo; *Editing* Claudine Bouché. Running time: 86 minutes.

Cast: Maria Schell, Christian Marquand, Ivan Desny, Pascale Petit, Marie-Hélène Dasté, Louis Arbessier, Antonella Lualdi, Andrée Tainsy, Michel de Slubicki, Gérard Darrieu, Alain Astruc.

Set at the end of the nineteenth century in Normandy. A young woman, Jeanne Dandieu (Schell), meets and marries a handsome man from Paris, Julien de Lamare (Marquand). She is happy until she discovers that Julien married her for her money and is having an affair with her family servant, Rosalie (Petit). Rosalie leaves the family after having a baby. Years later, Julien falls in love with Gilberte de Fourcheville (Lualdi), an affair Jeanne is willing to tolerate, but M. de Fourcheville is not.

This beautiful film is not a strict adapatation of de Maupassant's novel, but rather Astruc's amazing, personal interpretation/invention. He was fascinated with the idea of realizing a trap of love, and he did so with wonderful costumes and color photography by Claude Renoir. Maria Schell is stunning and stirring in her role as the abused wife.

Some French critics found the film cold, others loved Astruc's distance. The film was not released in the United States until 1962. American critics found it for the most part old-fashioned and irritating. *The New York Journal* summed up their sentiments when it called it "a poor soap opera."

385 *La Vie à l'envers (Life Upside Down* or *Inside Out)* 1964 B&W *Director* Alain Jessua; *Producer* A.J. Films; *Screenplay* Alain Jessua; *Photography* Jacques Robin; *Music* Jacques Loussier; *Set* Olivier Girard; *Sound* Jean-Claude Marchetti; *Editing* Nicole Marko. Running time: 93 minutes.

Cast: Charles Denner, Anna Gaylor, Guy Saint-Jean, Nicole Guéden, Jean Yanne, Yvonne Clech, Jean Dewewer, Françosie Moncey, Robert Bousquet, Gilbert Meunier, Jenny Orléans, André Thorent, Nane Germon, Bernard Sury.

Jacques Valin (Denner) is a real-estate agent who lives with his girlfriend Viviane (Gaylor), who is a model. Vivane worries that Jacques has a problem when he begins to meditate frequently. He is in such a deep trance that he misses their wedding and loses his job. Eventually, he finds happiness in an asylum where he is able to meditate uninterrupted.

Jessua's first film is a strange and funny comment on modern anxieties. He was interested in blurring the lines between insanity and wisdom. In the tradition of Buñuel, he loved exploring the notion of madness in individuals and society, and he used his direction brilliantly to emphasize his character's situation. Denner gives a great performance as a split personality.

A great hit in France, this movie was well received by American critics. *The New York Times* called it "a snug, little movie that holds real freshness and terror." *The New York Post* said: "Thus the picture becomes an extraordinarily concentrated and intense experience, again demonstrating the power of the cinematic medium when it is in the hands of an artist capable of expanding the work of this great medium."

386 *La Vie de chateau (A Matter of Resistance)* 1965 B&W *Director* Jean-Paul Rappeneau; *Producer* La Guéville, Ancinex, Cobela; *Screenplay* Jean-Paul Rappeneau, Alain Cavalier, Claude Sautet and Daniel Boulanger; *Photography* Pierre Lhomme; *Music* Michel Legrand; *Set* Jacques Saulnier; *Sound* Jacques Maumont; *Editing* Pierre Gillette. Running time: 92 minutes.

Cast: Catherine Deneuve, Philippe Noiret, Pierre Brasseur, Mary Marquet, Henri Garcin, Carlos Thompson, Marc Dudicourt, Robert Moor, Donald O'Brien, Marie Marc, Niksa Stafanini, Christian Barbier, Jean-Pierre Moulin, Paul Le Person, Alexis Micha, Annie Guégan, Pierre Rousseau, Katia Christine, Valérie Camille.

A comedy about Marie (Deneuve), a young wife who lives with her husband (Noiret) in a chateau in Normandy during the Occupation. She falls in love with a young Resistance fighter, Julien (Garcin), whom she catches stealing apples from their orchard. He runs off with Marie, but she becomes lost, and to find her Julien joins up with the German major who is occupying her chateau. But on the day of the Allied landing, it is Marie's husband Jérôme (Noiret) who proves himself to be the real hero and wins back his wife.

Rappeneau's first film charmed France by presenting a novelty, a light, romantic, sweet film about World War II. Few before him had found anything to laugh about in the war, but Rappeneau, who helped write the screenplays for *Zazie* and *That*

Man from Rio, managed to make it a perfect setting for a laughing matter. His elegant style made for a wonderful Gallic farce. Deneuve and Noiret are delightful.

The critics and the public adored *A Matter of Resistance*. *The Daily News* exclaimed, "It is warm and downright funny." The film won the Prix Louis Delluc in 1966.

387 *La Vie devant soi (Madame Rosa)* 1977 Color   *Director* Moshe Mizrahi; *Producer* Lira Films; *Screenplay* Moshe Mizrahi, based on Emile Ajar's novel *Momo*; *Photography* Nestor Almendros; *Music* Philippe Sarde and Dabket Loubna; *Set* Bernard Evein; *Sound* Jean-Pierre Ruh, Georges Prat; *Editing* Sophie Coussein. Running time: 105 minutes.

Cast: Simone Signoret, Samy Ben Youb, Michel Bat Adam, Gabriel Jabbour, Bernard La Jarrige, Claude Dauphin, Mohammed Zineth, Geneviève Fontanel, Costa-Gavraz, Stella Anicette, Elio Bencoil, Vincent Hua, Bernard Eliazord, Stella Anicette, Math Samba, El Kébir, Ibrahim Seck, Théo Legitimus.

Madame Rosa (Signoret) is an elderly woman and former prostitute who survived a Nazi concentration camp. She now cares for the children of prostitutes in a poor Arab/Jewish section of Paris. Despite her age and failing health, she dutifully cares for the children as if they were her own. When she starts hallucinating and believes that the Gestapo are coming after her, she asks her favorite child, Momo (Youb), to hide her. When a doctor comes to check on her, Momo makes a fatal error by keeping his promise to her.

Complicated racial and cultural material is handled beautifully in this film. The director is an Israeli from Morocco, who lived in Paris for ten years, and he drew on all of his cultural influences for the movie. The film was based on Emile Ajar's best-selling book, *Momo*, which won France's most prestigious literary award, the Prix Goncourt, in 1975. Costa-Gavras, the famous director, stars in the movie. Signoret, who accepted the role against the advice of her husband Yves Montand, delivers a spectacular performance, symbolizing there is great life after sex.

Critics and the public loved the sweet, sad film. A Broadway version of the film called *Roza* and staged by Harold Prince came out a few years after the film's success. The film won the Oscar for the Best Foreign Film in 1977. Simone Signoret won the César for Best Actress.

388 *La Vie est un long fleuve tranquille (Life Is a Long Quiet River)* 1988 Color   *Director* Etienne Chatiliez; *Producer* Charles Gassot; *Screenplay* Etienne Chatiliez, Florence Quentin; *Photography* Pascal Lebègue; *Music* Gérard Kawczynski; *Set* Geoffroy Larcher; *Sound* Harrick Maury and Dominique Dalmasso; *Editing* Chantal Delattre. Running time: 90 minutes.

Cast: Hélène Vincent, André Wilms, Christine Pignet, Maurice Mons, Daniel Gélin, Catherine Jacob, Patrick Bouchitey, Benoit Magimel, Benoît Magimel, Valerie Lalande, Claire Prévost, Tara Romer, Jerôme Flock, Sylvie Cubertafon, Emmanuel Cendrier, Guillaume Hacquebart, Catherine Hiégel, Axel Vicart.

Two babies from very different social and economic backgrounds are switched at birth. Twelve years later, the truth comes out. The upper-class Catholic family buys back its child, Momo (Magimel), and the street child, who purse-snatches in his spare time, turns their very proper life into chaos. He corrupts his siblings and steals the silver, while his "original" parents extort more and more money.

Lā Vie est un long fleuve tranquille (Life Is a Long Quiet River), 1988; directed by Etienne Chatiliez.

Chatiliez' first film was quite a shocker. Full of bad language, vulgar behavior and class satire, it announced a new film talent with a touch that was not for all tastes. He found his inspiration in old comedies from the 1950s and from a career dreaming up witty one-liners at an advertising firm. Chatiliez satirizes families from both sides of the fence with glee.

The film was an enormous success in France, where lines from the movie entered popular culture. Critics either applauded it as a lewd liberation or dismissed it as vulgar vérité. *The New York Post* exclaimed, "Eccentric and hilarious, *Life Is a Long Quiet River* delivers its untidy lives with great charm."

389 *La Vie est un roman (Life Is a Bed of Roses)* 1983 Color *Director* Alain Resnais; *Producer* Soprofilms, A2, Fideline Films, Ariane Filmedis; *Screenplay* Jean Gruault; *Photography* Bruno Nuytten; *Music* Philippe Gérard; *Set* Jacques Saulnier, Enki Bilal; *Sound* Pierre Lenoir; *Costumes* Catherine Letterrier; *Editing* Albert Jurgenson, Jean-Paul Besnard. Running time: 111 minutes.

Cast: Vittorio Gassman, Géraldine Chaplin, Ruggero Raimondi, Fanny Ardant, Pierre Arditi, Sabine Azéma, Robert Manuel, Samson Fainsilber, Véronique Silver, André Dussolier, Sabine Thomas, Guillaume Boisseau, Rodolphe Schacher, Jean-Claude Arnaud, Jean-Louis Richard, Lucienne Hamon, Michel Muller, Hélène Patarot, Philippe Laudenbach, Flavie Ducorps, Jean-Michel Dupuis, Jean-Claude Corbel, Fabienne Guyon, Cathy Berberian, Francine Bergé,

Bernard-Pierre Donnadieu, Janine Magnan, Fabienne Mai, Noëlle Leiris, Yann Dedet, Pierre Londiche.

A comedy that takes place in three separate time periods in the same chateau. One period concerns Count Michel Forbek (Raimondi) and his "temple of happiness," where he uses a magic potion, blindfolds, enormous cribs and an assault of sweet sensations to lull his friends back to the peaceful pleasures of infancy. In the modern period, the chateau has been transformed into a progressive school, and intellectuals dissect the Count's theories. Finally, the third intercut time period is a fairy tale about the Middle Ages when a knight must battle an evil king, which is acted out by children staying at the chateau.

This is a complex film, but it is more fun than Resnais' usual fare. He said of the film: "The important thing for us is that we wanted to make a comedy." He paid tribute to three periods of French filmmaking. One section represents Méliès, another L'Herbier, and another Rohmer. In all the periods, the characters are on a quest for happiness and fulfillment. In many ways, this film is the literary equivalent to the scientific exploration of *Mon Oncle d'Amérique*. It remains an important part of Resnais' evolution as an artist.

Some critics complained that the narrative structure was laborious. Others felt Resnais had merely indulged his personal obsessions. *Time* magazine's critic said: "Imagine Fabergé making a lopsided Easter egg from old rusty iron, and you have some idea of the surprising clumsiness of Alain Resnais' *Life Is a Bed of Roses*." The film won the Grand Prix du Cinéma Français in 1983.

390 *La Vie et rien d'autre (Life and Nothing But)* 1989 Color *Director* Bertrand Tavernier; *Producer* Hachette Première, Groupe Europe 1 Communication, AB Films, Little Bear, Films A2; *Screenplay* Jean Cosmos and Bertrand Tavernier; *Dialogue* Jean Cosmos; *Photography* Bruno de Keyer; *Music* Oswald d'Andréa; *Set* Guy-Claude François; *Sound* Michel Desrois; *Costumes* Jacqueline Moreau; *Editing* Armand Psenny. Running time: 134 minutes.

Cast: Philippe Noiret, Sabine Azéma, Pascale Vignal, Maurice Barrier, François Perrot, Jean-Pol Dubois, Daniel Russo, Michel Duchaussoy, Arlette Gilbert, Louis Lyonnet, Charlotte Maury, François Caron, Thierry Gimenez, Frédérique Meninger, Pierre Trabaud, Jean-Roger Milo, Gabriel Cattand, Daniel Langlet, Georges Staquet, Marcel Zanini, Oswald d'Andrea, François Dyrek, Jean-Paul Comart, Alain Frérot, Jean Champion.

Just after World War I, three people are searching the French countryside for soldiers' remains. Major Dellaplane (Noiret) has been assigned 350,000 missing in action cases and the task of choosing one lost soldier to be the Unknown Soldier placed under the Arc de Triomphe. A young teacher, Alice (Vignal), is looking for her fiancé, and a wealthy Parisian, Irène (Azéma), hopes to locate her husband. Ultimately, all three must face death and the end of the war and decide how to go on with life.

This is one of Tavernier's best films and was seen as representative of the humanistic epics made in the Mitterrand era. It is an unusually beautiful film about the horrors of war. The moment when the nineteenth century was just coming to a real end and the twentieth century was truly beginning is captured perfectly, with beasts of burden, both human and animal, being exchanged for cars and railways. Tavernier explained that he wanted the chemistry between Azéma and Noiret to be similar to the patrician appeal of Katherine Hepburn causing sparks of tension against Cary Grant's down-home charm. The result from Azéma and Noiret brings out much deeper emotional ranges because the background for their passion is not *Bringing Up Baby* fare, but more of a massive grave digging.

Critics hailed this as an epic masterpiece. Jay Carr of The *Boston Globe* exclaimed: "Here's a masterwork, the most deeply felt and thoroughly satisfying wartime romantic film since Krysztof Zanussi's *Year of the Quiet Sun.*" Philippe Noiret won César for Best Actor.

391 *Les Vierges (The Virgins)* 1963 B&W *Director* Jean-Pierre Mocky; *Producer* Balzac Films, Boréal Films, Stella Films; *Screenplay* Jean-Pierre Mocky; *Adaptation and Dialogue* Alain Moury, Catherine Claude, Geneviève Dormann, Monique Lange; *Photography* Eugen Shuftan; *Music* Paul Mauriat and Raymond Lefebvre; *Sound* Jean Labussière; *Set* Pierre Tyberghein; *Editing* Marguerite Renoir. Running time: 92 minutes.

Cast: Charles Aznavour, Gérard Blain, Jean Poiret, Johnny Monteilhet, Francis Blanche, Charles Belmont, Stefania Sandrelli, Catherine Derlac, Catherine Diamant, Josiane Rivarolla, Anne-Marie Sauty, Jean-Pierre Honoré, Patrice Laffont, Paul Mercey, Jean Galland, David Gerson, Nathalie Pascoe, Paola Falchi, Paula Dehelly, Pierre Palau, Jean Tissier, Michel Serrault, Catherine Tchakotine, Maria-Luisa Bavastro.

Portraits of five young women right at the moment at which they lose their virginity. Worldly wise Marie Claude (Sandrelli) takes the whole event lightly and sleeps with a stranger. Her friend, Genevieve (Diamant), "saves herself" until her wedding night. Christine (Sauty) has to choose between sacrificing herself for love or for advancement. Two young lovers looking the perfect site for their love. Nora (Derlac) struggles with her love for a married man.

Mocky said of this innovative film: "It's a profoundly moral film, an advertisement full of sadness," and he believed it was romantic, despite its characters' disappointments, because it was about true love. Their reactions and situations range from the serious and sacred on the wedding night to the casual and sensual one-night stand, with one girl representing the sentimental, another the sensual, another the thinker, and so on.

Some critics accused Mocky of patronizing women by attempting to portray something that he had no way of understanding, though he did have three female screenwriters work on the film. Others loved the premise and the humor.

Vincent, Francois, Paul and the Others *see* **Vincent, François, Paul et les autres**

392 *Vincent, François, Paul et les autres (Vincent, Francois, Paul and the Others)* 1974 Color *Director* Claude Sautet; *Producer* Lira Films, Président Produzioni, Danon; *Screenplay* Jean-Loup Dabadie, Claude Neeron, and Claude Sautet, based on Claude Néron's novel *La Grande Marrade*; *Photography* Jean Boffety; *Music* Philippe Sarde; *Set* Théo Meurisse; *Sound* Jean-Pierre Ruh; *Editing* Jacqueline Thiédot. Running time: 118 minutes.

Cast: Yves Montand, Michel Piccoli, Serge Reggiani, Gérard Depardieu, Stéphane Audran, Ludmilla Mikaël, Marie Dubois, Antonella Lualdi, Catherine Allegret, Umberto Orsini, Jean-Denis Robert, Nicolas Vogel, Betty Beckers, Yves Gabrielli, Jean Capel, Mohamed Galoul, Jacques Richard, David Tonelli, Myriam

Viva Maria, **1965; directed by Louis Malle.**

Boyer, Maurice Auzel, Daniel Lecourtois, Pierre Maguelon, Marcel Portier, Robert Le Beal, Jacqueline Dufranne, Maurice Travail, Jean Lagache, Henri Coutet, Ermano Casanova, Carlo Nell, Pippo Merisi, André Cassan, Lucienne Legrand, Jacques Théry, Léo Peltier.

The friendship of four men: a doctor, François (Piccoli); an industrialist, Vincent (Montand); a boxer, Jean (Depardieu); and a writer, Paul (Reggiani). Every Sunday, they get together at each other's houses and talk about their work and personal problems. Vincent is ill. François' wife leaves him. Paul cannot finish his novel.

This is a very perceptive and moving portrait of the social upheaval of the 1960s, and the toll that it took on people's lives. Sautet, who is best known for drawing deep social critiques out of simple relationship movies, manages to do just that here. His characters wrestle with financial, professional and domestic worries that reflect the concerns of the society in which they live. The famous foursome of actors live up to their super reputations.

French, French, French—that was how Truffaut described Claude Sautet and *Vincent, François, Paul and the Others.* Some critics complained that despite the film's beauty, it was too depressing. It is about life, others lauded. Sautet himself said, "Life is hard in the details, but beautiful overall."

The Virgins *see* **Les Vierges**

393 *Viva Maria* 1965 Color   *Director* Louis Malle; *Producer* NEF, Dancigers, Vidès Productions; *Screenplay* Louis Malle and Jean-Claude Carrière; *Photography* Henri Decaë; *Music* Georges Delerue; *Set* Bernard Evein; *Sound*

José B. Carlès; *Costumes* Ghislain Uhry; *Editing* Kenout Peltier, Suzanne Baron. Running time: 120 minutes.

Cast: Jeanne Moreau, Brigitte Bardot, George Hamilton, Grégor von Rezzori, Paulette Dubost, Claudio Brook, Carlos Lopez Moctezuma, Francisco Reiguera, Poldo Bendandi, Jonathan Eden, José Angel Espinoza, Fernando Wagner, Adriana Roël, José-Luis Campa, Roberto Campa, Eduardo Murillo, José Esqueda, Ramon Bugarini, José Baviera, Alberto Pedret, Luis Rizo.

A comedy about the daughter of an Irish terrorist (Bardot), who joins a troupe of nightclub singers when she finds herself on the run in South America. Maria I (Moreau) and her new friend, Maria II (Bardot), invent a strip show, and when the revolution erupts the two join the rebels and help to overthrow the country's dictator.

The silver screen sizzles with two of France's greatest sex symbols sharing the set. After *The Fire Within*, Louis Malle wanted to make an action film with laughs, so he decided to parody revolution. He succeeded beautifully in making a burlesque full of gags, great color and light entertainment. France's two greatest sex kittens of the era, who shared the screen for the first time, pooled their sex appeal to great effect.

French critics did not receive *Viva Maria* too warmly when it came out. But many American critics loved it. *The Daily News* raved: "With Gallic humor and Hollywood know-how, obtained from keen observation, Louis Malle has made le western fou—meaning a mad, zany crazy western." The film won the Grand Prix du Cinéma Français in 1965.

394 *Vive la sociale* 1983 Color *Director* Gérard Mordillat; *Producer* Eric Lambert; *Screenplay* Gérard Mordillat, Jacques Audiard, Louis-Charles Sirjacq, based on the novel by Gérard Mordillat; *Photography* François Catonne; *Music* Jean-Claude Petit; *Set* Théo Meurisse; *Sound* Michel Vionnet; *Editing* Michèle Catonné. Running time: 95 minutes.

Cast: François Cluzet, Robin Renucci, Elisabeth Bourgine, Yves Robert, Judith Magre, Jean-Pierre Cassel, Alain Bombard, Maurice Baquet, Emmanuelle Debever, Claude Duneton, Henri Genès, Camille Grandville, Jean-Pierre Malignon, Christophe Odent, Nicolas Philibert, Pascal Pistacio, Jacques Rispal, Micheline Luccioni, Bernadette Le Saché, Michel Berto, Jean-Pierre Le Pavec, Ariane Ascaride.

A story about growing up in the twentieth arrondissement and the thick of Parisian socialism. Maurice (Cluzet) is the child of a communist and an anarchist. He lives in a working-class neighborhood and grows up to start a catering business and marry a Catholic Hungarian violinist. He forges his own way through, dealing with the Algerian war and the 1968 riots.

Mordillat adapted his first film from his own semi-autobiographical novel, and, despite its intimate portrait of an unusual life, what makes it so important is that it speaks to a part of French society that is rarely acknowledged. He depicts a working-class neighborhood in all its quirkiness and yet it represents a large segment of France. The acting, photography and balance between humor and poignancy are wonderful. It was a very promising debut.

French critics admired this film. *Cinéma* would not go so far as to call it a masterpiece, but felt it approached one. The film was never distributed in the United States. It won the Prix Jean Vigo in 1983.

395 *Vivement dimanche (Confidentially Yours* or *Finally, Sunday)*
1983 B&W   *Director* François Truffaut; *Producer* Films du Carrosse, Films A2,
Soprofilms; *Screenplay* François Truffaut and Suzanne Schiffman, based on
Charles Williams' novel *The Long Saturday Night*; *Photography* Nestor Almen-
dros; *Music* Georges Delerue; *Set* Hilton McConnico; *Sound* Pierre Gamet;
Costumes Michèle Cerf; *Editing* Martine Barraqué. Running time: 111 minutes.
   Cast: Fanny Ardant, Jean-Louis Trintignant, Philippe Laudenbach, Caroline
Sihol, Jean-Pierre Kalfon, Philippe Morier-Genoud, Xavier Saint-Macary, Anik
Belaubre, Jean-Louis Richard, Yann Dedet, Nicole Félix, Georges Koulouris,
Roland Thénot, Pierre Gare, Jean-Pierre Kohut-Svelko, Pascale Pellegrin, Hilton
McConnico, Castel Casti, Michel Aubossu, Paulina Aubret, Isabelle Binet, Dany
Castaing, Alain Gambin, Michel Grisoni, Marie-Noëlle Guillot, Pierrette Mon-
ticelli, Adrien Silvio.
   A thriller about a businessman (Trintignant) who hides from the police after
he is wrongly accused of murder. His lovely secretary (Ardant), meanwhile, hunts
for the real killer to save her boss's skin. Her detective skills may not be too
sophisticated, but the real killers are unmasked and the secretary and boss live happily ever after.
   Truffaut's last film is not one of his best, but it is a very capable thriller and
one final ode to films on film. Truffaut paid tribute to the old murder mysteries that
he grew up on during the 1930s and 1940s, as he did more than twenty years earlier
in *Shoot the Piano Player*. He delights in the old stereotypes while poking fun at
them. The film was a wonderful showcase for the lovely and talented Ardant.
   Of course, critics who expected Truffaut to outdo himself with one masterpiece after another were disappointed. But most critics admired and enjoyed the
film. *The Christian Science Monitor* raved, "A charmer all the way, it blends
elements of whodunit, romance, comedy, and melodrama into an unpredictable
package that's easily the best Truffaut movie in years."

396 *Vivre pour vivre (Live for Life)* 1967 Color   *Director* Claude
Lelouch; *Producer* Les Films Ariane–Les Productions Artistes Associés–Vides
Films; *Screenplay* Claude Lelouch and Pierre Uytterhoeven; *Photography* Patrice
Pouget; *Music* Francis Laï; *Set* Outdoors; *Sound* Antoine Petitjean; *Costumes*
Yves Saint-Laurent; *Editing* Claude Barrois. Running time: 140 minutes.
   Cast: Yves Montand, Annie Giradot, Candice Bergen, Anouk Ferjac, Jacques
Portet, Uta Taeger, Irène Tunc, Michel Parbot, Amidou, Yves Gabrielli, Florence
Schoeller, Jean Collomb, Anouk Aimée, Pierre Barouh, Léon Zitrone, Maurice
Séveno, Louis Lyonnet.
   Robert Collombs (Montand) is a television journalist, who starts an affair with
an American model, Candice (Bergen), while in Africa. When his wife, Catherine
(Giradot), learns of his affair, she leaves him. Life with Candice does not satisfy
him, though, and after six months, he leaves her to go work in Vietnam. He is
taken captive when reporting in Vietnam, and when he returns to Paris, Catherine
takes him back.
   Part Vietnam documentary and part messy marriage, this movie is a daring
balancing act. The fact that Lelouch included actual footage from the Vietnam
war in what many viewed as a soap-opera melodrama offended many people.
The photography is beautifully used to convey characters' emotional states. The
soundtrack to the film, like that of *A Man and a Woman*, was written by Francis

Vivre pour vivre (Live for Life), 1967; directed by Claude Lelouch.

Laï and became a bestselling record. And Annie Giradot delivers a fabulous performance as Catherine.

Any picture Lelouch made after his hit *A Man and a Woman* was bound to disappoint people. Many critics complained that this film was jumbled, sentimental and pretentious. *Cue*'s critic, however, exclaimed: "By the time the film has unraveled, the point has been indelibly made: life is so fleeting that the individual must make the most of his short presence amidst the turbulence. It has been said before, but the movie states it beautifully, with relevance for today." It was nominated for an Oscar for Best Foreign Film in 1967, and won the Grand Prix du Cinéma Français in 1967.

397 *Vivre sa vie (My Life to Live* **or** *It's My Life)* 1962 B&W *Director* Jean-Luc Godard; *Producer* Films de la Pléiade; *Screenplay* Jean-Luc Godard; *Photography* Raoul Coutard; *Music* Michel Legrand and Jean Ferrat; *Sound* Guy Villette; *Editing* Agnès Guillemot. Running time: 85 minutes.

Cast: Anna Karina, Sady Rebbot, André S. Labarthe, Guylaine Schlumberger, Gérard Hoffman, Monique Messine, Peter Kassowitz, Brice Parain, Gisèle Hauchecorne, Gilles Quéant, Mario Botti, Dimitri Dineff, Odile Geoffroy, Marcel Charton, Paul Pavel, Henri Attal, Jean Ferrat, Jean-Paul Savignac, Jacques Florency, Eric Schlumberger.

A documentary-like film that follows the career of a Parisian prostitute, Nana (Karina). She starts out working in a record store and for a while dreams of being an actress, but when she is thrown out of her house she prostitutes herself.

Vivre sa vie (My Life to Live), **1962; directed by Jean-Luc Godard.**

She meets a pimp, Raoul (Rebbot), and a philosopher, Brice Parain (Parain). But when Raoul sells her to another pimp, she is killed during a payment dispute.

Another Godard masterpiece. *My Life to Live* was Godard's fourth feature and starred his wife at the time, Anna Karina, in her finest screen role. Godard includes facts and figures about Parisian prostitutes, which makes the story more chilling for its reality. Split into 12 titled sections, the film was technically very innovative and successful. Godard's aim was "to film a working thought, the interior of someone as seen from outside." He created a sad and shocking portrait of a woman "who sells her body, but keeps her soul."

Some critics felt Godard's unscripted way of working created uneven quality, with some scenes working beautifully and others falling flat. The French critic Jean Douchet said *My Life to Live* was "a pure masterpiece, the first absolutely flawless film by Godard." Critic Georges Sadoul called it "a film of great purity." It won the Special Jury Prize at Cannes in 1962.

398 *Le Voleur (The Voleur* or *The Thief of Paris)*   1966 Color   *Director* Louis Malle; *Producer* Nouvelles Editions de Films, Artistes Associés; *Screenplay* Louis Malle, Jean-Claude Carrière, and Daniel Boulanger, based on the novel by Georges Darien; *Photography* Henri Decaë; *Music* Henri Lanoë; *Set* Jacques Saulnier; *Sound* André Hervée; *Costumes* Ghislain Uhry; *Editing* Henri Lanoë. Running time: 120 minutes.

Cast: Jean-Paul Belmondo, Geneviève Bujold, Marie Dubois, Françoise Fabian, Paul Le Person, Martine Sercey, Marlène Jobert, Bernadette Lafont, Christian Lude, Charles Denner, Madeleine Damien, Fernand Guiot, Marc Dudicourt,

Jacqueline Staup, Roger Crouzet, Jacques Debary, Irène Daix, Monique Mélinand, Julien Guiomar, Christian de Tilière, Nane Germon, Paul Vally, Nicole Chollet, Jacques David, Odette Piquet, Jean Champion, Isis Lally, Gabriel Gobin, Jacques Gheusi, Fernand Guiot, Duncan Elliott, Jean-Luc Bideau, Pierre Etaix, Gilbert Servien, Gaston Meunier, Dario Mescho, Maurice Auzel, Julien Loysel.

Set at the turn of the century, Georges Randal (Belmondo) comes from a good family, but he discovers a passion for crime when he steals from his uncle, who has cut him out of the family fortune. Georges becomes a professional thief and meets other thieves who teach him their tricks. Charlotte (Bujold), the cousin whom he has always loved, eventually joins him in his profession and he grows old and very rich through his desire to get back at the world.

This film is a wonderful psychological portrait of how a man enters a life of crime and then becomes trapped by it. The wealthy background is familiar terrain for Malle, who grew up in an upper-class family. Malle was interested in connecting the criminals and the victims and showing how social hypocrisy works at all moral and economic levels. The costumes were done by the artist Ghislain Urhy. Belmondo is fantastic.

Critics declared this further proof of Malle's talent as a young director. In the face of the years of great works that have followed, it has often been neglected, but it is an entertaining and interesting film.

The Voleur *see* **Le Voleur**

Voyage of Silence *see* **Le Saut**

The Wages of Fear *see* **La Salaire de la peur**

The Walls of Malapaga *see* **Au-delà des grilles**

The War Is Over *see* **La Guerre est finie**

War of the Buttons *see* **La Guerre des boutons**

We Are All Murderers *see* **Nous sommes tous des assassins**

We Will Not Grow Old Together *see* **Nous ne vieillirons pas ensemble**

399 *Weekend* 1967 Color   *Director* Jean-Luc Godard; *Producer* Copernic, Ascot Cinéraid; *Screenplay* Jean-Luc Godard; *Photography* Raoul Coutard; *Music* Antoine Duhamel; *Set* Outdoors; *Sound* René Levert; *Editing* Agnès Guillemot. Running time: 105 minutes.

Cast: Jean Yanne, Mireille Darc, Jean-Pierre Kalfon, Jean-Pierre Léaud, Blandine Jeanson, Yves Alfonso, Virginie Vignon, Daniel Pommereulle, Ernest Menzer, Laszlo Szabo, Valérie Lagrange, Juliet Berto, Paul Gégauff, Anne Wiazemsky, J.-C. Guilbert, Michel Cournot, Blandine Jeanson, Helen Scott, Corinne Gosset, Jean-Pierre Kalfon, Georges Staquet, Yves Beneyton, Louis Jojot, Isabelle Pons.

A social satire about a married couple, Roland (Yanne) and Corinne (Darc). They leave the city for a weekend visit to Corinne's mother, whom they intend to

Weekend, 1967; directed by Jean-Luc Godard.

murder for her estate. To avoid a traffic jam caused by an accident, they turn down a country road. Their trip leads them from one brutal and bloody scene to the next and eventually they end up meeting Mao terrorists who kill and eat Roland.

Godard manages to move from total gore and gruesomeness to great humor in this film, which many believe is his last great one. The traffic accident scenes are particularly haunting considering Godard's mother died in a car accident. Despite some didactic moments, Godard managed to make quite an engaging, albeit grueling, political critique of consumer culture.

French critics found Godard's apocalyptic vision an eerie omen foretelling the political upheaval that hit France in May 1968. *Cahiers du Cinéma* called it "a bloody and joyous poem."

The Well Made Marriage *see* **Le Beau Mariage**

Why Not! *see* **Pourquoi pas!**

The Widow *see* **La Veuve Couderc**

The Widow Couderc *see* **La Veuve Couderc**

The Wild Child *see* **L'Enfant sauvage**

The Woman Next Door *see* **La Femme d'à côté**

Woman of Antwerp *see* **Dédée d'Anvers**

The Wonderful Age *see* **Le Bel Âge**

World Without Sun *see* **Le Monde sans soleil**

400 *Yo Yo* 1967 B&W   *Director* Pierre Etaix; *Producer* Paul Claudon; *Screenplay* Pierre Etaix, Jean-Claude Carrière; *Photography* Jean Boffety; *Music* Jean Paillaud; *Set* Raymond Gabutti, Raymond Tournon; *Costumes* Jacqueline Guyot; *Editing* Henri Lanoë. Running time: 92 minutes.

Cast: Pierre Etaix, Philippe Dionnet, Luce Klein, Claudine Auger, Siam, Pipo, Dario, Mimile.

Yo Yo (Etaix) is a millionaire with everything in the world that a man could want, except for the love of a long lost circus performer. When Yo Yo loses his fortune, he joins her circus act and the two have a son. The son grows up to be a movie star and with his fortune he returns his parents to Yo Yo's long-lost castle. But they have found their happiness in the travelling circus life, and after a lonely time trying to relive a lost dream in the castle, their son returns to the show as well.

This film is widely regarded as Pierre Etaix's best. He wrote, directed and starred in the film as both father and son; so like his mentor, Tati, Etaix left little to chance. The influence of Tati, with whom Etaix worked on *My Uncle*, is clear, as is that of Buster Keaton and early silent film comedies. Etaix, in all his various roles, really does make this movie what it is, a charming comedy of the old school with gags worthy of Chaplin, which few filmmakers even bother attempting anymore.

Critics on both sides of the Atlantic praised this as the work of a great comedian. *The Sunday Times* described *Yo Yo* as a "comedy of elegance, the film that courts the chuckle rather than the guffaw."

The Young Girls of Rochefort *see* **Les Demoiselles de Rochefort**

401 *Z (The Anatomy of a Political Assassination)* 1969 Color   *Director* Constantine Costa Gavras; *Producer* Reggane, ONCIC; *Screenplay* Constantine Costa Gavras and Jorge Semprun, based on the novel by Vassilis Vassilikos; *Photography* Raoul Coutard; *Music* Mikis Théodorakis; *Set* Jacques d'Ovidio; *Sound* Michèle Boëhm, Sidi Boumedienne Dahmane, Jean Nemy, Alex Pront; *Editing* Françoise Bonnot. Running time: 125 minutes.

Cast: Yves Montand, Irène Papas, Jean-Louis Trintignant, François Périer, Jacques Perrin, Charles Denner, Pierre Dux, Julien Guiomar, Bernard Fresson, Renato Salvatori, Marcel Bozzufi, Jean Bouise, Georges Géret, Clotilde Joano, Jean Dasté, Magali Noël, Maurice Baquet, R. Van Doude, Jean-Pierre Miquel, Guy Mairesse, Gérard Darrieu, José Arthur, Steve Gadler, Hassan Hassani, Eva Simonet, Bob de Bragelone, Gabriel Jabbour, Andrée Tainsy, Jean-François Gobbi, Allel El Mouhib, Habid Reda, Agoumi, Georges Rouquier.

A political film about the assassination of "Z" (Montand), the head of a national peace movement. The chief of police tries to cover up the murder, making it look like an accident, but an honest judge (Trintignant) sees through him. With the help of a journalist, the two uncover the truth—that far-right extremists were behind the assassination and the police chief was involved. Their evidence vanishes before they can indict the guilty, and a dictator takes over the government.

The film was based on the real-life assassination of Gregoris Lambrakis, a left-wing Greek political figure, whose murder was covered up by the government. Costa-Gavras worked very closely from trial transcripts and real events taking place in Greece in the early 1960s. This was the first of Costa-Gavras' great political films, and he had a very hard time getting money to make the film because of the sensitive subject matter, but the thriller was a great success.

Despite producers' fears that a political film would not find a large following, Z became the year's most popular movie when it came out in 1969. It also marked the beginning of a new film genre: the political thriller. Z won the Special Jury Prize at Cannes, the New York Film Critics' award for Best Picture, the Oscar for Best Foreign Film and Best Editing. It was also nominated for Oscars for Best Picture, Best Director and Best Adapted Screenplay. Trintignant won Best Actor at Cannes.

Zazie *see* **Zazie dans le métro**

402 *Zazie dans le métro (Zazie* or *Zazie in the Underground* or *Zazie in the Subway)* 1960 Color   *Director* Louis Malle; *Producer* Nouvelles Editions de Films; *Screenplay* Louis Malle and Jean-Paul Rappeneau, based on the novel by Raymond Queneau; *Photography* Henri Raichi; *Music* Fiorenzo Carpi; *Set* Bernard Evein; *Costumes* Marc Doelnitz; *Editing* Kenout Peltier. Running time: 95 minutes.

Cast: Catherine Demongeot, Philippe Noiret, Hubert Deschamps, Carla Marlier, Vittorio Caprioli, Anni Fratellini, Yvonne Clech, Jacques Dufilho, Antoine Roblot, Odette Picquet, Nicolas Bataille, Marc Doelnitz, Little Bara, Georges Faye de Lannoye, Paul Vally, J.-P. Posier, Jean-Yves Bouvier, Jane Allard, Arlette Balkios, Jacqueline Doyen, Virginie Merlin, Irène Chabier, Allegrina, Christine Howard.

A very precocious 11-year-old girl, Zazie (Demongeot), who is from the provinces, is on vacation in Paris with her uncle (Noiret), who is a drag queen. All Zazie wants to do is ride on the Métro, but because of a strike it is closed. She has no interest in the landmarks and appalls everyone she meets with her foul language. When the strike finally ends, Zazie is so pooped from all of her high-jinx that she falls asleep on her Métro ride.

Adapted from the Queneau classic that played on France's love of playing games with language, Malle wanted to make Zazie a sort of *Alice in Wonderland*. Malle creates a jumbled Paris using different film styles and speeds. He plays with visual tricks, parodies New Wave films, and uses Queneau's wild argot to create a surrealistic Paris. He said of one of his aims: "Some of the more insane aspects of our civilization are magnified to nightmaresque dimensions."

Zazie was an extraordinary success in France in the 1960s and continues to be shown every week in Paris at one of the revival theaters. It was not so well received in the United States. The Queneau/Malle humor seemed either to appeal to only a Gallic sense of humor or to get lost in translation. Bosley Crowther wrote in the *New York Times*: "There is something not quite innocent or healthy about this film."

Zazie in the Subway *see* **Zazie dans le métro**

Zazie in the Underground *see* **Zazie dans le métro**

403 *Zéro de conduite (Zero for Conduct)* 1945 B&W *Director* Jean Vigo; *Producer* Nounex, Gaumont; *Screenplay* Jean Vigo; *Photography* Boris Kaufman; *Music* Maurice Jaubert; *Set* Jean Vigo and Henri Storck; *Sound* Maurice Royne, Bocquel; *Editing* Jean Vigo. Running time: 47 minutes.

Cast: Jean Dasté, Louis Lefèvre, Gérard de Bédarieux, Gilbert Pruchon, Constantin Goldstein, Robert Le Flon, Du Verron, Delphin, Léon Larive, Blanchar, Louis de Gonzague Frick, Georges Berger, Michèle Fayard, Henri Storck, Mme. Emile, Raphaël Diligent, Georges Parin, Félix Labisse, Georges Vakalo, Albert Riéra, Pierre Merle, Charles Goldbatt, Constantin Kelber, Georges Belmer, Emile Boulez, Maurice Cariel, Jean-Pierre Dumesnil, Igor Goldfarb, Lucien Lincks, Charles Michiels, Roger Porte, Jacques Poulin, Pierre Regnoux, Ali Ronchy, Georges Rougette, André Thille, Pierre Tridon, Paul Vilhem.

Set at a repressive boarding school, where, for the smallest insubordination boys are given "zero for conduct," which results in Sunday detention. Anger gradually builds up among the students until a full-fledged revolt is staged and an adolescent insurrection comes complete with a parade and a wonderful king-of-the-castle like victory as the rebel leaders celebrate their victory on the school's roof.

This is one of only two commercial films by Jean Vigo. *Zero for Conduct* was finished in 1933, but banned by the French censors for 12 years and not released until 1945, over a decade after Vigo's death. This very autobiographical film was, in many ways, a granddaddy of Truffaut and Malle's work in that it brilliantly showed the world through the eyes of children. Vigo's father was a militant anarchist who was killed in prison in 1917, and his fight against authority was carried on by his son in his art. The choppy editing style influenced New Wave directors, though it was more an accident than an artistic decision by Vigo when it occurred in the editing room.

Not released in United States until 1947. "The first thirty meters of *Zero for Conduct* establish Jean Vigo's reputation as a great director," wrote François Truffaut in his book, *The Films of My Life*.

Zero for Conduct *see* **Zéro de conduite**

Index

References are to entry numbers.
Boldface denotes pages with photographs.